Theatre for Youth II

Book Forty-One
Louann Atkins Temple Women & Culture Series

Mother Hicks,
Department of Theatre, University of Northern Iowa

THEATRE FOR YOUTH II
More Plays with Mature Themes

Edited by
Coleman A. Jennings
and
Gretta Berghammer

University of Texas Press, Austin

Printed in the United States of America
First edition, 1986; second edition, 2016
First paperback reprint, 2022

Requests for permission to reproduce material from this work should be sent to:
Permissions
University of Texas Press
P.O. Box 7819
Austin, TX 78713-7819
utpress.utexas.edu/rp-form
The paper used in this book meets the minimum requirements
of ANSI/NISO Z39.48-1992 (R1997) (Permanence of Paper).

Library of Congress Cataloging-in-Publication Data

Names: Jennings, Coleman A., 1933– editor. | Berghammer, Gretta, 1956– editor.
Title: Theatre for youth II : more plays with mature themes /
edited by Coleman A. Jennings and Gretta Berghammer. | Other titles:
Louann Atkins Temple women & culture series ; bk. 41.
Description: Second edition. | Austin : University of Texas Press, 2016. |
Series: Louann Atkins Temple women & culture series ; book forty-one
Identifiers: LCCN 2016004610
ISBN 978-1-4773-1101-1 (cloth : alk. paper)
ISBN 978-1-4773-1004-5 (pbk. : alk. paper)
Subjects: LCSH: Young adult drama, American. | Children's plays, American.
Classification: LCC PS625.5 .T463 2016 | DDC 812/.540809282 — dc23
LC record available at *http://lccn.loc.gov/2016004610*

For Jed H. Davis and his tireless dedication to the
field of Theatre for Young Audiences

Jed H. Davis
1922–2015

Theatre Professor Emeritus Jed Davis was on the faculty at the University of Kansas from 1960–1986. He was the first president of the American Theatre Association (successor to the American Educational Theatre Association and forerunner to American Theatre in Higher Education), a cofounder of the International Association of Theatre for Children and Young People (ASSITEJ), a fellow of the Mid-America Theatre Conference, and a member of the College of Fellows of the American Theatre of the Kennedy Center. He was a founder of the Lawrence Arts Center in 1975 and recipient of the UK Chancellor's Club Teaching Award in 1985. In 1987 he received the Campton Bell Award from the Children's Theatre Foundation of America for lifetime achievement.

Professor Davis established the University of Kansas as a national center for artistic and scholarly excellence in theatre for young audiences. Along with Mary Jane Evans he wrote *Theatre, Children, and Youth*, a textbook for the profession. As a progressive scholar he argued for cross-disciplinary research in psychology by crafting developmental age profiles and encouraging empirical research with child audiences. He published many works that challenged the field's theorized practices and affirmed the integral inclusion of TYA as a necessary component of all university theatre programs.

Contents

Appendices

Foreword

Sarah Rinner

Young people have the power to change the world. As caregivers, as teachers, as mentors, as *adults*, part of our job is to ensure that every child has the opportunity to do just that. Sometimes they need our gentle encouragement. Sometimes they need our sage advice. Sometimes they just need us to get out of their way.

As a youth theatre artist and educator with more than fifteen years of experience, I worry that we are not providing our young people the opportunities they need to discover and exercise that power of change. I frequently find myself looking for ways to give them the skills, context, and experiences they need to shape our world into one that is more understanding.

I was fortunate to sit in on the selection process for this second edition. While I can only imagine what the conversation must have been like choosing the scripts to be included in the first anthology, I'm sure what I heard and experienced on this particular afternoon was much the same—careful attention to the style, genre, and mood of each play and to the voices and themes they represent. The plays in this volume are uniquely qualified to help challenge, inspire, and entertain young audiences while developing empathy, introspection, and insight that will guide and empower young people to care about themselves and each other.

This anthology of plays represents a broad and diverse repertoire. Magical realism and fantasy, futuristic societies and science fiction, a stroke of history, a splash of literature—there is something for everyone. A well-written script lays the launchpad that can transport its audience to an alternate reality while still reflecting the audience's actual reality. Each play in this anthology offers an opportunity for our young people to connect to important universal ideas and think critically about how those ideas are meaningful. The dialogue and characters are powerful enough that, even though each of us may care about them differently, we connect to them universally. These plays ask our young audiences to empathize with diverse characters and to expand their worlds just a little bit. These plays give them the freedom to consider what they have seen on stage and what it means to them. And these plays may just inspire them to walk out of the theatre and be more thoughtful friends or siblings or students tomorrow. I think of my contribution to this anthology not as a foreword, but as a *forward*. It is an invitation for producers and artists, educators and students, to consider their roles in supporting our young people's journey in this world. We are all a part of supporting their futures and helping them move forward. And what better way for us to teach this than to model it, to keep moving forward, embracing change and broadening our perspectives to keep up with a world that is rich with diversity and desperate for compassion. If these are the stories that our young people see on the stage or read for a literature class, will they feel inspired as well as informed? Will they feel challenged as well as championed? Will they feel empowered as well as entertained? I think the answer is yes. Let's look forward to the third edition of *Theatre for Youth*, which will keep inspiring our future writers, designers, actors, and world changers.

Acknowledgments

Dramatic Publishing for permission to reprint
*Afternoon of the Elves, The Arkansaw Bear, Broken Hearts,
In the Garden of the Selfish Giant, Mother Hicks, la ofrenda,
Super Cowgirl and Mighty Miracle, Tomato Plant Girl,
The Transition of Doodle Pequeño, With Two Wings*

Pickwick Press, Midland Community Theatre
for permission to reprint *Courage!*

Sarah Yake, Literary Agent, Frances Collin Literary Agency
for permission to reprint *Johnny Tremain*

Jed H. Davis, author of the Foreword to the first edition of
Theatre For Youth: Twelve Plays with Mature Themes, 1986

Corey Atkins, associate producer at Cleveland Play House

Production Photographs: *Johnny Tremain*, Department of
Theatre & Dance, University of Texas at Austin; *Mother Hicks*,
Department of Theatre, University of Northern Iowa

The Houston Endowment for support from the
Jessie H. Jones Regents Professor in Fine Arts,
Department of Theatre & Dance, Emeritus

Theatre for Youth II

Introduction

We live in a time of incredible social, political, and technological change. From the Internet and the "digital revolution" to increased racial and ethnic diversity, from evolutions in media and popular culture to shifts in areas of social equality, the world has changed radically in the thirty years since the first volume of *Theatre for Youth: Twelve Plays with Mature Themes* was published. As we approached the task of revising this anthology we wondered: Has young people's need for plays like those in this anthology changed, as well?

Technology has become etched into the daily lives of millions of people, including youth, not just in the US but across the globe. The internet has created an amazing communication playground of information and access: Wikipedia has replaced the encyclopedia; Facebook and Twitter have literally become tools of revolution; and we have Google for everything else! Nearly two-thirds of all Americans have "smartphones," which support instant accessibility and connection through texting, email, and social media; whatever it is, "there's an app for that." Technology and electronic media have even become a necessity in education, with laptops and tablets seeming set to replace chalkboards and notebooks in classrooms populated by "digital natives."

In addition, ethnic diversity is far more prominent than it was thirty years ago. The US elected its first African American president. Numerous countries have been renamed and redefined as walls, states, boundaries, and governments were dissolved or redrawn—but "globalization" is, arguably, here to stay. Other global tensions have resulted in terrorist activity. The September 11 attacks on the US are the most deeply etched memory of most "millennial" Americans.

Popular culture and social norms, too, have experienced a seismic shift. Music has expanded, and once-new genres such as rap, hip-hop, indie, alternative, and electronica are shifting, too. Reality TV has grown into one of the most popular forms of mass entertainment. Both pop culture and political activism have helped LGBT issues take their place as the most prominent civil rights question so far this century; LGBT organizations now exist comfortably in many middle and high schools, providing support for students who identify as lesbian, gay, bisexual, or transgender, and same-sex marriage is perhaps the most present sociopolitical issue of the day. "Nontraditional families" are now, for many, traditional—as are organic and gluten-free eating, yoga and pilates studios, extreme workout gyms, and alternative medicine. Climate change, once denied by most, is now a scientifically proven fact whose deniers are the minority.

Literary works such as the *Harry Potter* and *Hunger Games* novels have sparked an interest among young readers (and many adults) in imaginative and futuristic worlds. Comic books have been elevated to the status of literary art; graphic novels are regular reading among growing numbers of readers of all ages.

Yet even with all of these changes, youth theatre, like all of the arts, continues to reflect society, as was the case thirty years ago.

The twelve plays chosen for inclusion in this edition reflect an artistic response to the changes outlined above. Back in 1986 the plays included in the anthology reflected themes that were considered on the forefront for young people: aging, death and dying, friendship, courage, conformity, maturation, sexuality, and struggles with moral judgment. The twelve scripts included in this volume, and the twenty-four titles listed at the end of the text, confront some of these same topics, but also include gender identity, poverty, diversity, and discrimination. Yet even as these plays explore some of the most difficult themes and challenges for today's youth, they share messages fundamental to us all: open your imagination and dare to dream; embrace life; honor your personal passion, beliefs, and creativity; take a risk; and love with all your heart.

Like the first edition, our second edition of maturely themed plays does not include any traditional fairy tales. What it does include are plays rich in original story (*Tomato Plant Girl, The Arkansaw Bear, Super Cowgirl and Mighty Miracle*), compelling adaptations (*Afternoon of the Elves, Broken Hearts, Courage!*), historical drama (*Mother Hicks, Johnny Tremain*), diverse themes (*la ofrenda, The Transition of Doodle Pequeño*), friendship (*In the Garden of the Selfish Giant*), and future societies (*With Two Wings*).

We hope you enjoy reading all of the titles included as much as we have enjoyed selecting them.

The Plays

Johnny Tremain,
Department of Theatre & Dance, University of Texas at Austin

Original Stories

The Arkansaw Bear

Drama by Aurand Harris

Tish's mother and aunt have excluded her as they cope with the impending death of her grandfather, to whom Tish is very close. In reaction she turns to an imaginary world to understand why her grandfather must die. Just after Star Bright, a talking star, agrees to grant Tish's wish for understanding, she encounters a fleeing bear, the World's Greatest Dancing Bear, who is being chased by the Great Ringmaster. Knowing his life is nearly over and fearful of death, the old bear realizes that passing on his dances to a Little Bear will extend his life into the next generation. Seeing the old bear teach the young-ster, Tish understands that she, too, can continue her grandfather's legacy. All people and animals are part of a great circle of life; each generation teaches the next. In the final scene, it is Tish, rather than the bereft mother and aunt, who understands the riddle of life.

Characters

TISH
STAR BRIGHT
WORLD'S GREATEST DANCING BEAR
RINGMASTER
LITTLE BEAR
MIME

Voices

MOTHER
AUNT ELLEN
ANNOUNCER

Scene: The present. Somewhere in Arkansas.

(As the house lights dim, there is a glow of light on the front curtain. Over a loud speaker a man's whistling of "O Susannah" is heard. The curtains open. TISH walks into a large spot of warm light at L. The whistling dims out. TISH is a little girl and carries some hand-picked flowers. She listens to the voices, heard over a loud speaker, and reacts to them as if MOTHER and AUNT ELLEN were on each side of her, downstage.)

TISH: I've come to see Grandpa.

MOTHER'S VOICE: No, dear. No. You can't go in.

TISH: But Mother—

MOTHER'S VOICE: No, Tish! You can't see Grandpa now.

TISH: I picked him some flowers. These are Grandpa's favorites.

AUNT ELLEN'S VOICE: *(TISH's great aunt, elderly, gentle and emotional)* Quiet, child.

TISH: But Aunt Ellen—

AUNT ELLEN'S VOICE: The doctor is here.

TISH: The doctor?

MOTHER'S VOICE: Tish, dear.

TISH: Yes, mother?

MOTHER'S VOICE: Grandpa had a turn for the worse. His heart—

AUNT ELLEN'S VOICE: Oh, it's the end. (*Cries quietly*)

TISH: The end?

AUNT ELLEN'S VOICE: The doctor said . . . no hope.

(*TISH reacts.*)

MOTHER'S VOICE: Don't cry, Aunt Ellen.

TISH: Is Grandpa going . . . to die?

AUNT ELLEN'S VOICE: Yes.

TISH: No! He can't.

MOTHER'S VOICE: We all have to die, dear.

TISH: I know. But not Grandpa. (*Starts to move*)

MOTHER'S VOICE: Stop. You can't go in.

TISH: Why can't he live forever!

AUNT ELLEN'S VOICE: You're too young to understand. Too full of life.

TISH: I have to tell him there's a circus coming. I saw a poster with a bear.

MOTHER'S VOICE: It doesn't matter now.

TISH: Yes, it does! Do something!

MOTHER'S VOICE: (*Firmly*) We've done all we can.

TISH: But not enough! I . . . I didn't do enough!

AUNT ELLEN'S VOICE: Quiet. Quiet.

TISH: (*Softly*) Yes, if I'd been quiet so he could sleep. And—Oh! Once when I was mad, I said . . . I wish he was dead. Oh, I didn't mean it, Grandpa. I didn't mean it.

MOTHER'S VOICE: Hush, dear. It's not your fault. Grandpa loved you.

TISH: Then why is he . . . leaving me? (*Pulls away as if being held*) Oh, let me go!

MOTHER'S VOICE: (*Sharply, becoming edgy with emotion*) Yes. Go put the flowers in some water.

TISH: He liked the pink ones. Now . . . he'll never see them. Oh, why . . . why does Grandpa have to die?

MOTHER'S VOICE: (*Sternly, trying to control and cover her grief*) Run along, dear. Run along.

AUNT ELLEN'S VOICE: Keep away. Away from his door. Away . . . away.

(*The voices of MOTHER and AUNT ELLEN overlap and mix together, as they keep repeating, "Run along," "Away," "Run . . . run," "Away . . . away," "Run," "Away," "Run . . . away; run . . . away." They build to a climax in a choral chant, "Run . . . away."*)

TISH: I will. I'll run away. Up the hill . . . to my tree . . . my tree.

(*TISH runs, circling to the tree which is at R, and on which the lights come up. The circle of light on the first scene dims out, and the chanting of the voices stop. TISH stands alone by her tree in the soft light of evening. She brushes back a tear, shakes her head, and throws the flowers on the ground. She sinks to the ground by the tree, hugs her knees, and looks up. She sees the first star, which is out of sight. Quickly she gets up, points to the star and chants.*)

TISH: (*Cont'd*) Star light, star bright, first star I see tonight, I wish I may, I wish I might, Have the wish I wish tonight. I wish . . . I wish . . . Oh, Grandpa . . . why? (*Goes back to tree*) Why do you have to die?

(*There is star music, tinkling with bells. From above, a small swing starts descending. Magic star light spots on it. STAR BRIGHT stands on the swing, which stops in mid-air. Music dims out.*)

STAR BRIGHT: Repeat, please.

TISH: I wish . . . I wish . . .

STAR BRIGHT: I know you are wishing. That's why I'm here. But WHAT? Repeat, please.

TISH: (*Sees and goes near him*) Who are you?

STAR BRIGHT: (*Slowly and proudly*) I am the first star out tonight! (*Happily*) I did it! I did it! I did it again! (*Excitedly*) First star . . . first star . . . first star out tonight! (*To TISH*) It's the early star, you know, who gets the wish. What is yours? Repeat, please.

TISH: Can you make a wish come true?

STAR BRIGHT: I've been making wishes come true for a thousand years.

TISH: A thousand years! You're older than Grandpa.

STAR BRIGHT: (*Sits on swing*) Old? Oh, no. I'll twinkle for another thousand years.

TISH: And then?

STAR BRIGHT: (*Cheerfully*) Then my light will go out.

TISH: Like Grandpa.

STAR BRIGHT: But there will be a new star. It's the great pattern . . .

TISH: I'll never have another Grandpa.

STAR BRIGHT: . . . the great circle of life. In every ending there is a new beginning.

TISH: (*Fully realizing it*) I'll never see Grandpa again. I'll never hear him whistle. (*Begins to whistle "O Susannah"*)

STAR BRIGHT: Your wish? What is your wish?

TISH: I wish . . . I wish Grandpa could live a thousand years!

STAR BRIGHT: (*Startled*) What? Repeat, please!

TISH: (*Excited*) I wish he'd never die. Nobody would ever die! Everyone live forever!

STAR BRIGHT: Oh, no, no, no! Think what a mixed up world it would be!

TISH: (*Speaks intently*) I wish . . . I wish I knew why . . . why Grandpa has to die.

STAR BRIGHT: That is not a quick one-two-buckle-my-shoe wish. No. That is a think-and-show-it, then-you-know-it, come-true wish.

TISH: Please.

STAR BRIGHT: (*With anticipated excitement*) Close your eyes. Whisper the words again. Open your eyes. And your wish will begin.

(*TISH closes her eyes. STAR BRIGHT claps his hands, then motions. There is music and beautiful lights. STAR BRIGHT is delighted with the effect.*)

STAR BRIGHT: (*Cont'd*) Very good! Repeat, please. (*Claps and waves his hand. Again there is music and beautiful lights.*) Excellent! Thank you!

(*The swing with STAR BRIGHT is pulled up and out of sight. The full stage is seen, lighted brightly and in soft colors. [Never is the stage dark, eerie, or frightening.] It is TISH's fantasy. The large tree is at R, and open space with beautiful sky. MIME appears at R. He is a showman, a magician and an accomplished mime who never speaks. He wears a long coat with many colorful patch pockets. He is NOT in white face, but his face is natural, friendly and expressive. He enters cautiously, carrying a traveling box, which he sets down at C. On the side the audience sees, is painted the word, "BEAR." On the other side is painted the word, "DANCING." He beckons off R. THE WORLD'S GREATEST DANCING BEAR enters R. He is a star performer, amusing, vain and lovable like a teddy bear. He does NOT wear an animal mask, nor is the actor's face painted, frightening or grotesque, with animal makeup. He wears his traveling hat. He hurries in, worried and out of breath.*)

BEAR: I must stop and get my breath. (*Pants heavily*) My heart is pounding. (*Looks about*) Are we safe? (*Frightened*) I don't see him. I don't hear him. Yes, we have out run him.

(*BEAR motions and MIME places box for BEAR to sit.*)

BEAR: (*Cont'd*) Where . . . where in this wide whirling wonderful world . . . do you think we are? Switzerland?

(*MIME makes pointed mountain with his wrist, runs his fingers up and down the "mountain," then shakes his head.*)

BEAR: (*Cont'd*) You are right. No mountains. England?

(MIME opens and holds up imaginary umbrella, holds hand out to feel the rain, shakes his head.)

BEAR: *(Cont'd)* You are right. No rain. India?

(MIME leans over, swings one arm for a trunk, then other for his tail and walks.)

BEAR: *(Cont'd)* No elephants.

TISH: Excuse me.

(They freeze. TISH comes to them.)

TISH: *(Cont'd)* I can tell you where you are. You are in Arkansas.

BEAR: Quick! Disguise. Hide.

(BEAR and MIME hurry to R. MIME quickly takes from one of his pockets a pair of dark glasses and gives them to BEAR who puts them on; then stands beside BEAR to hide him.)

TISH: *(Recites with pride)* Arkansas was the 25th state to be admitted to the union. It is the 27th in size, and the state flower is apple blossom.

BEAR: Who is it?

(MIME pantomimes a girl.)

BEAR: *(Cont'd)* A girl?

(MIME pantomimes a small girl.)

BEAR: *(Cont'd)* A little girl? Tell her to go away. To run away.

(MIME pantomimes to TISH. BEAR hides behind tree.)

TISH: I have. I have run away. Have you run away, too?

(MIME nods.)

TISH: *(Cont'd)* Why?

(MIME looks frightened off R, then puts finger to lips.)

TISH: *(Cont'd)* Who are you?

(MIME takes a card from a pocket and presents it to her. She reads.)

TISH: *(Cont'd)* "A Mime." You never speak.

(MIME shakes his head, and "walks" in one spot and tips his hat.)

TISH: *(Cont'd)* "A Magician." You do tricks!

(MIME pulls handkerchief from sleeve.)

TISH: *(Cont'd)* "Friend." You give help.

(MIME touches handkerchief under her eyes.)

TISH: *(Cont'd)* Thank you. I was crying because my Grandpa ... he's going to ...

(BEAR, without glasses steps out from behind the tree, does a loud tap dance step and

poses. *MIME turns the traveling box around and with a flourish points to the word painted on that side of the box. TISH reads it with amazement.*)

TISH: (*Cont'd*) Dancing.

(*MIME turns box around again. TISH reads.*)

TISH: (*Cont'd*) Bear.

(*MIME motions to BEAR who steps forward.*)

TISH: (*Cont'd*) I've never met a bear. I've never seen a DANCING bear.

BEAR: (*To MIME*) Should I?

(*MIME nods*)

BEAR: (*Cont'd*) Shall I?

(*MIME nods*)

BEAR: (*Cont'd*) I will! My Spanish hat.

(*MIME jumps with joy and gets hat from box. BEAR motions to TISH who sits on the ground.*)

BEAR: (*Cont'd*) Be seated, please.

(*MIME holds up a hand mirror, which he takes from a pocket, holds it up for BEAR to look at himself, and fixes the hat.*)

BEAR: (*Cont'd*) To the right . . . to the right . . . Ah, just right!

(*MIME motions and a spot light comes on. ANNOUNCER'S VOICE is heard over a loud speaker.*)

ANNOUNCER'S VOICE: Ladies and Gentlemen: Presenting in his spectacular, special, Spanish dance, the World's famous, the World's favorite, the World's Greatest Dancing Bear!

(*MIME motions and Spanish music is heard. BEAR steps into the spotlight. He dances with professional perfection a Spanish dance, but he does not finish. At a climactic moment, he stops, holds his hand against his heart and speaks with short breaths.*)

BEAR: Stop the music.

(*MIME motions. Music stops.*)

BEAR: (*Cont'd*) Dim the light.

(*MIME motions. Spot dims out.*)

TISH: What is it?

BEAR: (*Breathing heavily*) He is near. He is coming.

TISH: Who?

BEAR: He is almost here. Hide. I must hide. He must not find me.

(*MIME points to tree.*)

BEAR: (Cont'd) Yes, the tree. Hurry!

(MIME helps BEAR to tree.)

TISH: Who? Who is coming?

BEAR: The box. Cover the box.

(BEAR disappears behind the tree. MIME sits on traveling box. BEAR's head appears.)

BEAR: (Cont'd) Talk.

(MIME mime-talks with hands and face.)

BEAR: (Cont'd) Louder!

(BEAR's head disappears. MIME motions for TISH to talk.)

TISH: Talk? What about?

BEAR: (Head appears.) Arkansas. (Head disappears.)

TISH: (Recites nervously) Arkansas has mineral springs, natural caves, and . . . and . . . diamond mines. (Looks off R and whispers, frightened) I don't hear anyone. I don't see anyone.

(MIME motions for her to talk.)

TISH: (Cont'd) Arkansas was first known as the state of many bears. (Looks and whispers, mysteriously) There isn't anyone. Nothing. Just quiet, nothing. Who is he running away from?

(MIME motions "shh," then runs L to R and looks, then motions for BEAR to come out.)

BEAR: (Comes from behind tree) He didn't find me. I escaped . . . this time. (Pleased, but short of breath) My traveling hat. We must go on.

(MIME takes Spanish hat and gives BEAR traveling hat.)

TISH: Where? Where will you go?

BEAR: (Looks off R, afraid) I must keep ahead of him.

TISH: Ahead of who? Who!

BEAR: (Cautiously) Never speak his name aloud. (Looks around) He may be listening, and come at once.

(MIME gives BEAR the hat.)

BEAR: (Cont'd) Oh, my poor hat. You and I have traveled together for many a mile and many a year. We are both beginning to look a little weary. (Puts hat on)

TISH: Grandpa has an old hat.

BEAR: Perhaps, if it had a new feather. Yes! A bright new feather!

TISH: I think your hat is very stylish.

BEAR: (Pleased) You do?

TISH: And very becoming.

BEAR: (*Flattered*) Thank you. You are a very charming little girl. What is your name?

TISH: Tish.

BEAR: Tish-sh-sh! That is not a name. That is a whistle. Ti-sh-sh-sh-sh!

TISH: It's short for Leticia. It was my grandmother's name.

BEAR: Leticia. Ah, that is a name with beauty.

TISH: Grandpa calls me "Little Leticia."

BEAR: I shall call you . . . (*Rolling the "R"*) Princess Leticia.

TISH: Princess?

BEAR: All my friends are important people. Kings and Queens . . . Command performances for Ambassadors and Presidents . . . (*To MIME*) The velvet box, please.

(*MIME takes from a pocket a small box.*)

BEAR: (*Cont'd*) I will show you my medals, my honors.

TISH: My grandpa won a medal.

BEAR: Ah?

TISH: He was the best turkey caller in Arkansas.

BEAR: Turkey caller?

TISH: He won first prize!

BEAR: (*To MIME*) Pin them on me so she can see. And so that I can remember . . . once again . . . all my glories.

(*Royal music begins and continues during the scene. MIME puts ribbons and jeweled medals on BEAR as ANNOUNCER'S VOICE recognizes each decoration. Two are pinned on. One is on a ribbon which is fastened around BEAR's neck.*)

ANNOUNCER'S VOICE: The Queen's highest honor, the Royal Medallion.

BEAR: I danced in the Great Hall. It was the Queen's birthday party.

ANNOUNCER'S VOICE: The Diamond Crescent of the East.

BEAR: Fifteen encores. Fifteen encores and they still applauded.

ANNOUNCER'S VOICE: The Royal Ribbon of Honor for Distinguished Service.

BEAR: It was during the war. I danced for the soldiers.

ANNOUNCER'S VOICE: And today, a new decoration. Her Royal Highness, Princess Leticia presents, in honor of her Grandfather, the highest award in the State of Arkansas—the Turkey Feather.

(MIME takes a bright feather from a pocket and gives it to TISH. BEAR parades to her, with a few dance steps, and she puts the feather in his hat. Royal music stops.)

BEAR: Thank you. A party! We will celebrate my new honor! *(To MIME)* Food and festivities! Honey bread!

(MIME nods.)

BEAR: *(Cont'd)* Thick with honey spread!

(MIME nods twice, then makes magic motions toward BEAR. Suddenly MIME turns and points to TISH. She puts out her hand which, magically, holds a honey bun.)

TISH: *(Delighted)* O-o-oh! It looks delicious.

(MIME turns and points to BEAR who puts out his hand which, also magically, holds a colorful honey bun.)

BEAR: A-a-ah! It IS delicious.

(BEAR puts finger in it, then licks finger. MIME raises his hand.)

BEAR: *(Cont'd)* Yes, give us a toast.

(BEAR and TISH hold honey buns up. MIME pantomimes "A toast . . ." holds up his hand; "to the winner . . ." clasps his hands and shakes them high in the air; "of the turkey feather," walks like a turkey, bobbing his head, then MIME pulls out an imaginary feather from his hip.)

BEAR: *(Cont'd)* Thank you.

TISH: What did he say?

BEAR: You didn't listen.

TISH: How can I hear when he doesn't speak?

BEAR: You listen with your eyes, and then YOU say the words. Listen. He will repeat the toast.

(MIME pantomimes the toast again. She watches and speaks aloud.)

TISH: "A toast . . . to the winner . . . of the turkey feather!"

BEAR: Thank you. Now, entertainment! *(To MIME)* You, tell us a story. *(To TISH)* You, listen and say the words.

TISH: Me?

BEAR: And I will eat! *(Wiggles with excitement and sits on box)*

(MIME pantomimes a story which TISH, watching him, repeats in words.)

TISH: "Once there was . . . a princess . . . a beautiful princess!"

BEAR: Named *(Sings it)* Leticia. *(Takes a bite)*

TISH: "One day . . . in the woods . . . she met . . . *(Doubtful)* . . . a cat?"

(MIME shakes his head. Mimes again)

TISH: (*Cont'd*) A . . . goosey-gander?

(*MIME shakes his head. Mimes again*)

TISH: (*Cont'd*) A . . . bear!

BEAR: The World's Greatest Dancing Bear! (*Seated, makes his own vocal music and dances with his feet*)

TISH: "Under a spreading tree . . . they had a party . . . with honey bread, thick with honey spread."

BEAR: (*Licks his five fingers, one on each word*) Turn . . . yum . . . TO . . . the . . . last . . . crumb. (*Licks his hand and picks and eats crumbs from his lap*)

TISH: "Now honey bread, thick with honey spread . . . made the bear . . . very . . . sleepy. He yawned."

(*BEAR follows action of the story and goes to sleep.*)

TISH: (*Cont'd*) ". . . gave a little sigh . . . and took a little nap."

(*BEAR snores.*)

TISH: (*Cont'd*) He's asleep. Who . . . who is he running away from?

(*MIME goes to sleeping BEAR, puts his finger to his lips then mimes.*)

TISH: (*Cont'd*) "The World's Greatest Dancing Bear . . . is old and tired . . . and his heart . . . is tired." (*To herself*) Like Grandpa. (*Speaking for MIME*) "He is running away from . . ." Who? "Someone is coming to take him away . . . forever." Does that mean if he's caught, he will die?

(*MIME nods.*)

TISH: (*Cont'd*) Is he running away . . . from death?

(*MIME nods.*)

TISH: (*Cont'd*) Oh! I'll help him. Yes, I'll help him.

(*Faint music of a calliope is heard, BEAR stirs.*)

TISH: (*Cont'd*) He's waking up.

BEAR: (*Slowly wakes up*) Music . . . the calliope . . . circus music . . . of the Great Center ring! (*Rises*) The Ringmaster is coming!

TISH: (*To MIME*) Death?

(*MIME nods.*)

BEAR: He is near. I hear the music.

TISH: I don't hear it. (*To MIME*) Do you?

(*MIME shakes his head.*)

BEAR: Only I can hear him. Only I can see him. He is coming for me. Quick! We must go.

TISH: Yes, I'll help you.

BEAR: This way. Hurry!

(*MIME carries box. Led by BEAR they start L, but stop when the music becomes louder.*)

BEAR: (*Cont'd*) No! No! The music is here. Quick! Turn! Run the other way.

(*They rush to R and are stopped by music becoming louder.*)

BEAR: (*Cont'd*) No! The music is coming from here. It is all around us! Here! There! Look! (*Points off R*)

TISH: What?

BEAR: The Great Ringmaster. He is there! He is coming . . . for me!

(*RINGMASTER enters slowly from R. He wears an ornate ringmaster's jacket, boots and a tall hat. He has a friendly face, a pleasant voice, but walks and speaks with authority. He stops. Music stops.*)

BEAR: (*Cont'd*) Quick! Hide me! Hide me!

(*BEAR runs to L. TISH and MIME follow. He quickly hides behind them when they stop. BEAR peeks over TISH's shoulder.*)

BEAR: (*Cont'd*) Tell him to go away.

TISH: I can't see him. Where is he?

BEAR: There. (*Hides*)

TISH: (*Bravely speaks, facing front talking into space*) Excuse me . . . sir. This is my secret place . . . by the big tree. You must leave at once. Go away. Now. (*Whispers to BEAR*) Did he go?

BEAR: (*Peeks*) No. (*Hides*)

RINGMASTER: (*Distinctly and with authority*) I have come for the Dancing Bear. I have come to take him to the Great Center Ring.

BEAR: Tell him he has made a mistake.

TISH: Excuse me . . . sir. You have made a mistake.

RINGMASTER: (*Opens book*) No. It is written plainly in the book. The date is today. The name is . . . the Dancing Bear.

BEAR: (*Who was hidden by MIME at the side, now steps into view, wearing boxing gloves and a sport cap.*) You HAVE made a mistake. I am a BOXING bear.

(*MIME blows a whistle and continues to blow it, as BEAR shadow boxes, comically, with a few dance steps and kicks thrown in. He ends in a heroic pose.*)

BEAR: (*Cont'd*) Goodbye.

RINGMASTER: A boxing bear? (*Looks in book*) There has never been a mistake.

TISH: (*Whispers*) Have you tricked him? Outwitted him?

BEAR: (*Nods, then calls loudly*) Yes. Training time. On your mark; get set; ready— talleyho! (*Starts jogging off R*)

RINGMASTER: (*Reads*) The book says: His father, born in Russia, a dancing bear.

BEAR: (*Stops, indignant*) Correct that. He was Russia's most honored dancing bear.

RINGMASTER: His mother, born in Spain, also a dancing bear.

BEAR: She was the prima ballerina bear of all Spain!

RINGMASTER: He, only son—

BEAR: Is the World's Greatest Dancing Bear!

RINGMASTER: Then you are the one I have come for!

BEAR: Yes!

RINGMASTER: Then we will have no more tricks or games.

(*BEAR realizes he has revealed himself.*)

RINGMASTER: (*Cont'd*) Come. Take my hand.

(*BEAR always reacts with fear to the RINGMASTER's white gloved hand.*)

RINGMASTER: (*Cont'd*) I will show you the way to the Great Center Ring.

BEAR: No! No!

TISH: What is he saying?

BEAR: He is going to take me away.

RINGMASTER: Come. You must. And it is easier if you go quietly.

BEAR: No! I will not go with you. I will fight! (*Holds up boxing gloves*)

TISH: Fight him! I'll help you!

BEAR: I have fought all my life. Battled my way to the top. Look at my medals. I will fight to the end.

RINGMASTER: This, my friend, is the end.

BEAR: No! No! Not for me. Not yet! Stay away! I have new dances to do.

RINGMASTER: Today you will take you last bow.

BEAR: No! No. (*Savagely*) I will claw! I will eat! I will crush! I will kill! Kill to live! (*Violently throws boxing gloves away*) To live! To live!

RINGMASTER: Everyone shouts when he is frightened of the dark.

BEAR: I WILL NOT DIE!

RINGMASTER: You have no choice.

BEAR: But . . . why? Why me? ME!

RINGMASTER: You are like all the others. Everyone thinks HE will live forever. Come.

BEAR: No! What did I do wrong? What can I do now? To stop it!

RINGMASTER: Death comes to all. It has never been IF you will die. The only question has been WHEN you will die. Now you know.

BEAR: (*Runs*) I will run. I will hide.

RINGMASTER: (*With authority*) You cannot escape from death.

BEAR: (*Bargaining desperately*) More time. Give me more time. I have so much to do.

RINGMASTER: (*Slightly annoyed*) There is always that which is left undone.

BEAR: I don't know how . . . to die. I need to rehearse.

RINGMASTER: No one has to rehearse. It is very simple . . . very easy. (*Holds out hand*) Come. It is growing late.

BEAR: No! (*Desperate for any excuse*) I must write my memories! Tell the world the glories of my life. My life . . .

(*Pause. TISH and MIME rush to him as he falters, place box and help him sit.*)

BEAR: . . . it is almost over. And what was it? A few medals that will be lost. No. There must be more to life. Give me time. Time to find the answer.

TISH: (*Kneeling by him, pleads into space*) Please . . . let him live.

RINGMASTER: Your life is over. Today is the day.

BEAR: But my day is not over. (*To TISH*) The day is not ended, is it?

TISH: Give him to the END of the day!

BEAR: Yes! To the end. Oh, you are a very smart little girl!

RINGMASTER: Well . . . (*Looks in his book*)

TISH: What did he say?

BEAR: He's looking in his book.

RINGMASTER: The day you are to die is written plainly. But not the hour.

BEAR: Then give me the full day.

TISH: Please.

RINGMASTER: (*Pause*) I will give you until midnight. Until the last hour of your last day.

BEAR: YES!

TISH: Can you live?

BEAR: YES! Oh, let me shout to the world! I AM ALIVE! (*To MIME*) Give me my brightest, my happiest hat! (*To RINGMASTER, who has gone*) Oh, thank you ... thank you ... He is gone ... for a while. (*To TISH*) Oh, let me touch you. Let me feel the warmth ... the life in you. There is so much yet to do! And so little time. My life ... it went too fast. I didn't stop to listen ... I didn't stop to see.

(*MIME waves clown hat in front of BEAR.*)

BEAR: Oh, yes! I will be the clown! (*Puts hat on. To TISH*) Come. Dance with me! And we will make the world spin round and round with joy!

TISH: Grandpa taught me how to whistle and how to dance a jig. (*Quickly, she whistles "O Susannah," and does a little jig, looking at her feet*)

BEAR: No, no, no. To dance is a great honor. Hold your head high. (*Follows his own instructions*) And first you smile to the right ... then you smile to the left ... and you bow to the center ... and then ... begin.

(*MIME motions. A spotlight comes on BEAR. Music is heard. BEAR does a short, charming soft-shoe dance. Spotlight and music dim out. TISH applauds. BEAR sits on box which MIME places for him. BEAR is happy, but breathless.*)

TISH: Oh, how wonderful!

BEAR: Thank you.

TISH: You're better than Grandpa! He can only do a little jig.

BEAR: But he taught you?

TISH: Yes.

BEAR: And he taught you how to whistle?

TISH: Yes.

BEAR: (*Rises*) If I could teach my dances to someone ... if someone could carry on the fame of my family ... All my hats ... there will be no one to wear my hats. They, too, will be put in a box and forgotten. Tell me, are you like your grandfather?

TISH: Daddy says I'm a chip off the old block.

BEAR: You are a part of him. And you will carry on for him in life. (*Excited*) Yes! Yes, that is the answer to the riddle.

TISH: What riddle?

BEAR: The riddle of life. I must leave my dances! They will be a part of me that will live on! But who? Where! How!

TISH: Make a wish!

BEAR: A wish?

TISH: On the first star you see. And it will come true. It will. It will!

BEAR: (*Wanting to believe*) You are sure it will?

(TISH nods. BEAR turns to MIME.)

BEAR: Do you believe it will?

(MIME nods.)

BEAR: I could try.

TISH: Quick!

BEAR: Of course I don't believe in superstitions. But I did get up on the right side of the bed.

(MIME nods.)

BEAR: I did find a four leaf clover.

(MIME nods.)

BEAR: And I haven't sneezed once.

(MIME shakes his head.)

BEAR: Yes, luck is with me today! So . . . let me knock on wood—three times— and I will do it!

(MIME takes off hat. BEAR knocks on MIME's head three times, with sound effects.)

BEAR: What do I say?

TISH: Point to the first star you see.

BEAR: *(Looks about, then points)* There! I see a bright twinkling one.

TISH: Say, "Star light, star bright . . ."

BEAR: *(To MIME)* The rabbit's foot! This wish must come true. *(Looks up)* "Star light, star bright."

TISH: "First star I see tonight."

BEAR: "First star I see tonight." *(Takes rabbit's foot from MIME and rubs it vigorously)* Oh, bring me luck. Make my wish come true.

TISH: "I wish I may, I wish I might . . ."

BEAR: "I wish I may, I wish I might." Oh, it won't work. It's nothing but a nursery rhyme.

TISH: "Have the wish I wish tonight." Say it. Say it!

BEAR: "Have the wish I wish tonight." *(Pause)* Nothing. Nothing. I told you so.

TISH: Look. Look! It's beginning to happen.

(Star music and lights begin as STAR BRIGHT enters on swing. He is joyously happy.)

STAR BRIGHT: Tonight I'm blinking. Tonight I'm winking. Wishes are flying past. Wishes are coming quick and fast! I'm twinkling bright and RIGHT tonight! *(Laughs)* Your wish, please.

BEAR: (*Lost in happy memories*) Look. It is like the circus. The trapeze high in a tent of blue . . . the music of the band . . .

(*MIME motions. Soft band music of the circus is heard. Colorful lights play on the backdrop.*)

BEAR: . . . the acrobats; the jugglers tossing, catching bouncing balls . . .

(*MIME pantomimes juggling.*)

BEAR: . . . the delicious smell of popcorn . . . the dance on the high wire . . .

(*TISH holds up an imaginary umbrella and walks on an imaginary tight rope.*)

BEAR: . . . the sweet taste of pink lemonade . . . Oh, the beauty, the wonder of life. Let me look at it. The happiness of living . . . Oh, let me feel it. The joy of being alive! Let me keep it. Let me hold it forever. (*Holds out his arms to embrace it all*)

STAR BRIGHT: (*Claps his hands. Music and circus scene stop.*) Your wish. Your wish. Repeat, please.

BEAR: (*Confused, he is led by MIME to STAR BRIGHT.*) I wish to leave a footprint.

STAR BRIGHT: (*Puzzled*) Repeat, please.

TISH: The answer to the riddle.

BEAR: (*Intently*) I wish to leave with someone my dances so that I . . . so that they . . . will be remembered.

STAR BRIGHT: That is a wish I hear every night . . . every night. A wish to shine on Earth . . . and leave behind a trace . . . to learn, to earn the grace . . . of immortality. Of your wish, half I can do. The other half is left for you. But quick! You must start. Because all wishes on a star must be done before the star is over shadowed by the sun. (*Claps his hands. Magic music and lights begin.*) One, two; Sunset red; Midnight blue; The wish you wish I give to you.

(*Magic lights and music end as STAR BRIGHT exits up and out of sight. From off L, LITTLE BEAR is heard singing. All look to L. LITTLE BEAR enters finishing his song to the tune of "Turkey in the Straw." He is a small cub, wearing country overalls and a little turned-up straw hat. Over his shoulder he carries a small fishing pole.*)

LITTLE BEAR: (*Sings*) Turkey in the straw, haw, haw, haw; Turkey in the hay, hay, hay, hay; Bait the hook, give the line a swish; Jumpin' jiggers, I caught a fish.

TISH: A little bear.

(*LITTLE BEAR does a few dance steps of joy, and continues walking and singing.*)

BEAR: A little dancing bear. (*To MIME*) Meet him. Greet him. Make him welcome. (*To TISH*) Quick, the hand mirror.

(*TISH holds mirror which MIME gives her and BEAR preens. MIME hurries to LITTLE BEAR and pantomimes a big and friendly greeting. LITTLE BEAR, as if it were a game, happily imitates every movement of the MIME. It ends with both shaking hands. Then LITTLE BEAR gives a friendly goodbye wave and starts off R, singing.*)

BEAR: Stop him!

(*MIME rushes in front of LITTLE BEAR and turns him around.*)

BEAR: I am ready to be presented.

(*MIME, with a flourish, presents BEAR.*)

BEAR: How do you do.

LITTLE BEAR: Howdy-do to you.

BEAR: You have come from my WISHING on a star.

LITTLE BEAR: Huh-uh. I've come from my FISHING in the river.

BEAR: Oh, my little one, I am going to give you the treasure of my life. Bestow on you all my gifts.

LITTLE BEAR: I could use a new fishing pole.

BEAR: I am going to teach you all my dances. You will wear all my hats. Oh-ho! I have never felt so alive in my life!

(*BEAR gives a joyous whoop and jumps and clicks his heels. LITTLE BEAR is bewildered. BEAR, with the eyes of a dancing master, looks LITTLE BEAR over.*)

BEAR: Yes, you have a good build. Good stance. Relaxed torso.

(*BEAR taps LITTLE BEAR's waist. LITTLE BEAR wiggles and giggles from the tickling.*)

BEAR: Legs sturdy. Up! Leg up. Up!

(*LITTLE BEAR cautiously lifts leg.*)

BEAR: Up! Up! (*Raises LITTLE BEAR's leg high*)

LITTLE BEAR: Whoa!

BEAR: Point. Point!

LITTLE BEAR: (*Points with finger*) Point where?

BEAR: (*Holding LITTLE BEAR's foot high*) Point your foot. Ah, feet too stiff . . . too stiff.

(*BEAR lets leg down. LITTLE BEAR stands in profile, stomach pushed out.*)

BEAR: Stomach flat!

(*BEAR taps LITTLE BEAR's stomach. LITTLE BEAR pulls stomach in, but pushes hips out.*)

BEAR: Rear push in!

(*BEAR smacks LITTLE BEAR on the bottom. LITTLE BEAR pulls hips in, and turns facing audience.*)

BEAR: Stretch . . . up . . . up!

(*BEAR pulls LITTLE BEAR up who tries to stretch. His face is tense.*)

BEAR: Relax.

(*BEAR pats LITTLE BEAR on forehead. LITTLE BEAR slowly sinks to the ground. BEAR lifts him up.*)

BEAR: Smile.

(*LITTLE BEAR forces a tortured smile.*)

BEAR: Walk! Walk!

(*LITTLE BEAR starts walking stiffly.*)

TISH: Will he be a good dancer?

BEAR: He will be magnificent! (*Puts arm out and stops LITTLE BEAR's escape*) He will be—ME! My rehearsal hat. My father's Russian dancing hat! (*Dances a few steps of a Russian dance and shouts a few Russian words*) To the dressing room.

(*BEAR continues the dance steps and shouting as he exits R. MIME, with traveling box follows him, imitating the dance steps.*)

LITTLE BEAR: Who . . . who is he?

TISH: He is the greatest dancing bear in the world.

LITTLE BEAR: Oh!

TISH: And . . . he's going to die.

LITTLE BEAR: Oh.

TISH: My grandpa is going to die and I don't know what to do.

LITTLE BEAR: Up in the hills, I've seen a lot of them die.

TISH: You have?

LITTLE BEAR: Old ones, little ones, and big ones, too. And there ain't nothing you can do about it. 'Cause as sure as you're born, you're as sure of dying.

TISH: It's sad.

LITTLE BEAR: Course it's sad.

TISH: It's frightening.

LITTLE BEAR: (*Thinking it out*) No. It ain't dyin' that you're afraid of. It's the not knowin' what comes AFTER you die. That's what scares you.

TISH: (*Tearful*) I'll never see Grandpa again.

LITTLE BEAR: (*With gentle understanding*) You go on. You have yourself a good cry. It'll help you to give him up. And you got to. (*With emphasis*) You got to let him go.

TISH: No.

LITTLE BEAR: You have to! 'Cause he's gone . . . forever.

TISH: You don't know what it's like to have your grandpa die.

LITTLE BEAR: Yes, I do. My grandpa died last winter. And my papa . . . I saw a hunter shoot my papa.

TISH: (*Shocked*) Shoot your Papa! Oh, what did you do?

LITTLE BEAR: First, I cried. Yes, I cried, and then I started hatin' and I kicked and I clawed 'cause I felt all alone.

TISH: (*Nods*) All by yourself.

LITTLE BEAR: Then my mama said, "You have to go on living, so . . . do your best. Give yourself to the livin'. 'Cause that's the best way to say goodbye to your pa." So I made my peace.

TISH: Your peace?

LITTLE BEAR: Inside myself. Oh, it don't mean I understand about dyin'. I don't. But you do go on living. The next day. The next year. So if you love your grandpa like I loved my papa . . .

TISH: Oh, I do.

LITTLE BEAR: Then show him you do.

TISH: How?

LITTLE BEAR: Tell him goodbye . . . by giving your most to the living. I'm wanting to do something . . . something big . . . just for Papa.

BEAR: (*Off*) All is ready!

TISH: Please, dance with him. He needs you.

LITTLE BEAR: Well, I like to help folks.

TISH: You said, "Give to the living."

LITTLE BEAR: And I do like the dance!

TISH: (*Excited with a new idea*) This is the big thing you can do for your papa.

LITTLE BEAR: For Papa?

TISH: (*Points with her hand as she visualizes it*) Your name will be in lights. You will be the NEW World's Greatest Dancing Bear!

(*BEAR and MIME enter, BEAR wearing his Russian Cossack hat.*)

BEAR: Let the flags fly! Let the band play! (*To LITTLE BEAR*) We will start with a simple waltz. My mother's famous skating waltz. One, two, three; one, two, three . . . (*Dances, continuing during the next speeches*)

LITTLE BEAR: (*Tries to do the step, then stops*) No. I'm just a country bear, with no schoolin'.

TISH: You will be the famous . . . "Arkansas Bear!" (*Urges him on*)

LITTLE BEAR: Arkansas. I ain't right sure how to spell Arkansas. (*Moves in one spot to the beat of the music, wanting to dance, but afraid*)

TISH: Like it sounds. A-R-K-A-N-

LITTLE BEAR: (*Shouts, eager to dance*) S-A-W! (*With a burst of energy he follows BEAR and dances with joy, counting loudly and happily.*) One! Two! Three! One! Two! Three! I'm doing it!

(*The first chime of midnight is heard, loud and distinct. The other chimes follow slowly. MIME runs to BEAR, motions for him to listen.*)

TISH: What is it?

BEAR: The chimes are striking 12.

LITTLE BEAR: It's the end of the day. Midnight.

BEAR: No! No! Not yet! I have not taught you my dances. Stop the clock!

TISH: Run! Hide! Before he comes back!

BEAR: Where?

LITTLE BEAR: In the caves! In the hills!

TISH: Hurry!

(*TISH and LITTLE BEAR help BEAR. MIME carries box. All start toward back. Soft calliope music is heard. RINGMASTER enters R.*)

RINGMASTER: Twelve.

(*They stop.*)

RINGMASTER: Your day is ended. Your time is up. Come. I will take you to the Great Center Ring.

BEAR: No. No!

TISH: Is he here?

BEAR: Yes, he has come for me. (*Comes downstage. Backs off towards L*) Stop him.

RINGMASTER: There is no way to stop death.

TISH: I know a way. (*Grabs MIME and points up toward star*) You! Make a wish on the first star you see. Say, (*Shouts*) Star light, star bright, first star I see tonight . . .

(*MIME quickly points and looks up, rapidly miming the words of the rhyme.*)

STAR BRIGHT: (*Off*) Louder, please.

RINGMASTER: Come. (*Holds out his hand and slowly crosses toward BEAR at far L*)

(*MIME pantomimes, repeating with larger gestures, while TISH says the words.*)

TISH: I wish I may, I wish I might, Have the wish I wish tonight.

STAR BRIGHT: (*Quickly descends into view*) Wish quickly chanted. Wish quickly granted.

(*MIME pantomimes TISH's words.*)

TISH: Stop death!

(*With a sound effect of a roll on a cymbal, STAR BRIGHT points at RINGMASTER, who has advanced almost to BEAR. RINGMASTER stops in a walking position.*)

TISH: Make him go away!

(*A roll on a cymbal is heard, as STAR BRIGHT makes a circle with his hand. RINGMASTER slowly turns around.*)

TISH: LOCK HIM UP IN THE TREE!

(*Another roll on the cymbal*)

STAR BRIGHT: Walk to the tree.

(*RINGMASTER slowly walks to a tree.*)

STAR BRIGHT: Your home it will be . . . for a time.

(*RINGMASTER stops. STAR BRIGHT points to tree again. There is a roll on a cymbal as the trunk slowly opens.*)

STAR BRIGHT: It is open wide . . . to welcome you. Step inside.

(*RINGMASTER faces tree and slowly steps inside the tree trunk, and turns and faces audience.*)

STAR BRIGHT: Let it enfold and hold you . . . for a time.

(*STAR BRIGHT waves his hand. There is a last roll on a cymbal. The tree trunk slowly closes shut.*)

STAR BRIGHT: Locked, blocked, and enclosed! (*Laughs*)

BEAR: (*To TISH*) You did it! You stopped death!

(*TISH and BEAR shout together, while MIME jumps with joy and blows whistle.*)

TISH & BEAR: We did it!

STAR BRIGHT: (*Claps his hands*) Remember . . . soon will come the morning sun, and then . . . Remember that is when . . . all wishes become . . . undone.

(*Star music and light begin as he ascends out of sight, and then stops.*)

BEAR: (*Their joy changes to concern*) It is true! Time is short! Quick. I must teach the little one—

(BEAR *looks about.* LITTLE BEAR *has, unnoticed, slipped away when* RINGMASTER *appeared.*)

BEAR: Where is he?

TISH: Little Bear!

(*Pause. There is no answer.*)

BEAR: Little Bear, come back!

(TISH *and* MIME *run looking for him.*)

TISH: Little Bear?

BEAR: He was frightened . . . (*Looks at tree*) of death. He is gone. And with him all my hopes are gone. (*Slumps, wearily*)

TISH: (*Concerned, rushes to him*) You must rest, like Grandpa.

BEAR: Your Grandfather has you. (*Amused*) A chip off the old block, eh?

(TISH *nods.*)

BEAR: You gave him happiness in life . . . peace in death.

TISH: Are you all right?

BEAR: I am old, and weary and tired. And I am going to die.

TISH: No. We stopped death.

BEAR: But only for a brief time. Death, they say is a clock. Every minute our lives are ticking away. Now . . . soon . . . my clock will stop.

TISH: No.

BEAR: When I was young like you, I wondered, "Where did I come from?" And now, when I am old, I wonder, "Where am I going?"

(MIME *looks and listens off R, then runs to them and excitedly mimes that* LITTLE BEAR *is coming.*)

BEAR: What is it?

(MIME *pantomimes more.*)

BEAR: Who? Where?

(MIME *points to R. All watch as* LITTLE BEAR *enters.*)

BEAR: You have come back.

LITTLE BEAR: I left my fishing pole.

BEAR: Have no fear. Death is locked in the tree.

(LITTLE BEAR *reacts with fright at tree.*)

TISH: You have come back to help.

LITTLE BEAR: I come back to learn all your fancy dancin'.

TISH: (*Runs to LITTLE BEAR and hugs him*) Oh, you are the best, the sweetest, the most wonderful little bear in the world!

(*LITTLE BEAR is embarrassed.*)

BEAR: Yes! Quick! We must begin the lesson. There is so little time and so much to learn. (*Looks frightened off R. To MIME*) Stand watch. Yes, watch for the first rays of the sun!

(*MIME stands R, anxiously looking off. TISH sits on box. BEAR motions to LITTLE BEAR.*)

BEAR: Come! Come! Attention! I will teach you all I know. (*Takes position.*) First, you smile to the right.

(*BEAR does the action with the words. LITTLE BEAR watches and tries to do the action.*)

BEAR: You smile to the left. You bow to the center. And then . . . begin . . . to dance. We will start with my father's famous Russian dance. Master this and all else will be easy. (*To MIME*) How many more minutes?

(*MIME holds up 10 fingers.*)

BEAR: Ten! Position. Position!

(*LITTLE BEAR imitates him.*)

BEAR: Listen to the beat . . . the beat . . . (*Taps foot*)

LITTLE BEAR: Beat what?

BEAR: Your feet! Your feet! The beat . . . the beat . . .

(*BEAR taps foot. LITTLE BEAR slowly and timidly taps beat.*)

BEAR: Too slow. Too slow.

(*LITTLE BEAR pivots in a circle, weight on one foot while tapping fast with the other foot.*)

BEAR: Too fast. Too fast.

(*LITTLE BEAR does it right.*)

BEAR: Ah! Ah! Ah! Good! Good!

LITTLE BEAR: I'm doing it right!

BEAR: (*Shows him next Russian step*) The first step. Hop, hop, hop, switch, hop.

(*LITTLE BEAR tries, awkward at first, then better.*)

BEAR: Hop, hop, hop, switch, hop. Yes, hop, hop, hop, switch, hop. Yes! Yes! (*Shows him next step*) Deep knee, hop.

(*LITTLE BEAR shakes his head.*)

BEAR: Try. Try.

(*LITTLE BEAR tries deep knee bend with a hop.*)

BEAR: Deep knee, hop. Lower. Lower.

(*LITTLE BEAR puts hands on floor in front of him and does step. He smiles at the audience at the easiness of it.*)

BEAR: No, no, no! No hands!

(*Lifts LITTLE BEAR up. LITTLE BEAR continues to kick his feet.*)

BEAR: The next step. The finale. (*Shows step*) Turn, two, up, two. Turn, two, up, two.

LITTLE BEAR: Oh, my!

BEAR: Turn, two, up, two.

(*LITTLE BEAR tries.*)

BEAR: Turn, two, up, two. Faster. Faster.

LITTLE BEAR: (*Falls*) I can't do it. I can't do it.

BEAR: You will. You must do it. I must leave my dances with you.

TISH: Try, please, Please, try.

LITTLE BEAR: Well . . . (*Gets up*)

BEAR: Again. Again. Ready. Turn, two, up, two.

(*BEAR keeps repeating the count, and LITTLE BEAR does the step better and better, until he is perfect—and happy.*)

BEAR: He did it! He did it!

TISH: He did it!

LITTLE BEAR: I did it!

BEAR: (*To MIME*) How many minutes are left?

(*MIME holds up eight fingers.*)

BEAR: Eight minutes. Time is running out. Quick. The polka. The dance of the people. Music!

(*MIME motions. Music is heard. BEAR dances a few steps. LITTLE BEAR quickly follows him and masters them. Music stops. BEAR breathes heavily.*)

BEAR: How many more minutes?

(*MIME holds up seven fingers.*)

BEAR: Only seven minutes left! Hurry. My famous tarantella.

(*MIME motions and music is heard. BEAR does a few steps. LITTLE BEAR again quickly does them and they dance together. Music stops. BEAR pants for breath. MIME runs to him and holds up six fingers.*)

BEAR: Six minutes. And at the end take your bow. The first bow. (*Bows, short of* breath) The second bow. (*Bows, pauses, then with trembling voice he speaks with emotion, knowing it is his last bow.*) And the last and final bow.

TISH: More, more! Encore! Encore!

(*BEAR slumps to the floor. TISH rushes to him.*)

TISH: He's fallen.

(*TISH and MIME cradle BEAR on either side.*)

TISH: Are you all right?

BEAR: (*Stirs, weakly*) How . . . many more minutes . . . do I have left?

(*MIME holds up five fingers.*)

BEAR: My little one, you will do my dances, you will carry on for me?

LITTLE BEAR: Yes. Yes.

BEAR: Take my father's hat . . . and it was HIS father's hat . . .

LITTLE BEAR: No, you must wear it.

BEAR: I will not need it where I am going. I have taken my last bow.

TISH: No. (*Buries her head on his shoulder*)

BEAR: Ah, tears can be beautiful. But there is no need to cry. I am content. I was a part of what went before and I will be a part of what is yet to come. That is the answer to the riddle of life. (*Weakly*) How many more minutes?

(*MIME holds up two fingers.*)

BEAR: Two. Bring me my traveling hat. I will wear it on my last journey.

(*LITTLE BEAR gets traveling hat from box, as MIME and TISH help BEAR to stand.*)

BEAR: I must look my best when I enter the Great Center Ring.

(*MIME puts hat on BEAR, who smiles at TISH.*)

BEAR: Does it look stylish?

TISH: Yes.

BEAR: Is it becoming?

(*TISH nods.*)

BEAR: Then I am ready. (*Gently pushes TISH and MIME away*) No. This journey I must go alone. (*Extends hand to MIME*) Goodbye, good friend. Thank you for everything. And sometimes when the band plays . . . think of an old bear.

(*MIME motions for BEAR to wait. MIME quickly gets a pink balloon on a string from the side and holds it out to BEAR.*)

BEAR: Yes, I remember when once we said, "Life is like a bright balloon." Hold it tight. Hold it tight. Because . . . once you let it go . . . it floats away forever. (*Breathless*) How many more minutes?

(*MIME holds up one finger. BEAR turns to TISH.*)

BEAR: I have one last request. When the end comes . . . when I enter the Great Center Ring . . . I want music. I want you to whistle the tune your grandfather taught you.

TISH: "O Susannah."

BEAR: (*Nods and smiles*) You will find that when you whistle you cannot cry at the same time.

(*A rooster is heard crowing.*)

BEAR: Listen.

LITTLE BEAR: It's a rooster crowin'. It's almost mornin'.

TISH: The sun is up. The stars are fading away.

(*Star music is heard as STAR BRIGHT descends into view. He speaks softly.*)

STAR BRIGHT: Announcing: the first ray of sun is peeping out. Warning: all wishes end as the sun begins. The new day is starting, the old departing. That is the great pattern . . . the circle of life. Tomorrow is today.

(*STAR BRIGHT points at the tree, and claps his hands. The tree trunk slowly opens.*)

STAR BRIGHT: And the night and the stars fade away . . . fade away.

(*There is star music as STAR BRIGHT disappears. Soft calliope music is heard which continues during the scene.*)

RINGMASTER: (*Steps out from tree trunk. He speaks with authority.*) There is no more time. The book is closed.

BEAR: Poets tell us death is but a sleep, but who can tell me what I will dream?

RINGMASTER: (*Walks slowly to BEAR*) Take my hand.

BEAR: Tell me, tell me what is death?

RINGMASTER: When there is no answer, you do not ask the question. Come.

BEAR: Yes, I am ready. (*To LITTLE BEAR*) My little one . . . I give you my feather . . . and you . . . give joy . . . to the world. (*Gives turkey feather to LITTLE BEAR. Whispers*) Let the balloon go.

(*RINGMASTER holds out his hand, which BEAR takes. Together they walk off L slowly. MIME lets the balloon go. MIME, TISH and LITTLE BEAR watch as it floats up and out of sight. At the same time the calliope music builds in volume. There is a second of silence. Then ANNOUNCER'S VOICE is heard, loud and distinctly.*)

ANNOUNCER'S VOICE: Ladies and gentlemen: presenting for your pleasure and entertainment, the new dancing bear, the world's famous, the world's favorite, the world's greatest — The Arkansaw Bear!

(*During the announcement. MIME points to LITTLE BEAR. LITTLE BEAR looks frightened, amazed and pleased. MIME holds up mirror and LITTLE BEAR puts feather in his hat. MIME motions for LITTLE BEAR to step forward, then motions a circle of light on the floor. Spotlight comes on and LITTLE BEAR steps into the light. Over the loud speaker, BEAR's voice is heard. He speaks softly and with emotion. LITTLE BEAR follows his instructions.)*

BEAR'S VOICE: You smile to the right . . . smile to the left . . . bow to the center . . . and then begin to dance!

(Music begins, lively "Turkey in the Straw." LITTLE BEAR begins his dance.)

BEAR'S VOICE: My dances . . . your dances . . . and make the world spin 'round and 'round with joy.

(LITTLE BEAR dances with fun, excitement and joy, a wonderful short dance. During this TISH exits, and MIME exits with box. At the end of the dance, LITTLE BEAR bows as the audience applauds, and exits L, peeks out and waves again. Spotlight goes out. Fantasy music is heard and a soft night light illuminates the tree. TISH is leaning against it. She looks up, sighs, picks up the flowers and slowly circles back to the downstage area of the first scene, which becomes light as the tree area dims out. Fantasy music also fades out. The voices of MOTHER and AUNT ELLEN are heard, and TISH answers as if they were standing on each side of her downstage.)

MOTHER'S VOICE: *(Worried)* Tish? Tish, is that you?

TISH: Yes, Mother.

MOTHER'S VOICE: Where have you been?

TISH: I went up the hill to my tree. I want to see Grandpa.

AUNT ELLEN'S VOICE: He's dead . . . dead. *(Cries)*

TISH: *(Trying to be brave)* Dead. Tears can be beautiful, Aunt Ellen. But you have to give him up. Let the balloon go.

AUNT ELLEN'S VOICE: What?

TISH: *(Trying to keep back her tears)* I know everyone . . . everything has a time to die . . . and it's sad. But Grandpa knew the answer to the riddle.

AUNT ELLEN'S VOICE: The riddle?

TISH: He left his footprint. He left a chip off the old block.

MOTHER'S VOICE: What, dear? What did he leave?

TISH: Me! And I want to do something . . . something big for Grandpa. Because that's the best way to say goodbye. *(Softly)* Let me give him his flowers . . . the pink ones.

MOTHER'S VOICE: *(Positive, and with a mother's love and authority)* All right, dear. Come along. We'll go together and see Grandpa.

(TISH starts L, and begins to whistle.)

MOTHER'S VOICE: What are you doing?

TISH: Whistling ... for the bear ... and for Grandpa. Because it helps ... when you are afraid and in the dark. And . . . when you whistle, you can't cry. (*Whispers*) Goodbye, Grandpa, I . . . I love you.

(*TISH exits L, bravely trying to control her crying. At the same time, lights slowly come up so the full stage is seen. The light on TISH's area dims out. The stage is bright with soft beautiful colors. The lone whistling of "O Susannah," the same as at the beginning of the play, is heard. There is a moment of a final picture—the living tree standing, as it has through the years, against a beautiful endless sky. The whistling continues as the curtains close.)*

CURTAIN

Production credits from the premiere of *The Arkansaw Bear* and details concerning performance rights are included in the acting edition of the play as published by Dramatic Publishing.

Super Cowgirl and Mighty Miracle

Drama by José Cruz González

First grader Cory's *papi*, a struggling single father, must leave Cory with her estranged grandmother, Autumn, in order to take a new job. And no one is happy about it. Caring for Cory is just one more problem for Grandmother, who can't get a job, despite her college degree, and who has a terrible toothache (but no insurance) and a home close to foreclosure. Cory doesn't like following all of Grandmother's rules, being forbidden to wear her cowboy hat at church, or having no one to play with. When Dog, a neighborhood stray, appears and becomes Cory's new best friend, things begin to get better—until a game between the new friends accidentally destroys Grandmother's prized possession, her beautiful church hat. When *Papi* calls to check in, both Grandmother and Cory are surprised that he tells Cory she must try harder to behave and get along. Grandmother and granddaughter begin to listen and learn from each other, and new opportunities start to emerge. *Papi* is even making enough money to send some back home. With a little help—and bravery—from Dog, a new family bond forms as Cory and Grandmother Autumn learn to understand and respect each other. And Cory realizes she has the perfect name to give the newest four-legged family member: Mighty Miracle.

Characters

CORY: a 6-year-old girl of mixed heritage, Latina/African American. Bright, curious, wild imagination, loves to read and invent games.

GRANDMOTHER AUTUMN: a middle-aged African American woman with a toothache. College educated and unemployed. On the verge of losing her home. A church lady who loves to wear her hat to church. Regal, stern, independent and set in her ways. Widowed.

DOG/MIRACLE: a homeless dog with an unstoppable life force. Playful, happy, loving, nurturing, loves to run, chase things, chew stuff, eat and sleep on his back.

Time and Place

2011. A neighborhood where wild dandelions grow and foreclosure signs flourish.

(*GRANDMOTHER AUTUMN and CORY stand onstage. CORY wears a jacket, cowboy boots and a cowboy hat. She carries a backpack and holds onto a toy dog named Bandit.*)

GRANDMOTHER AUTUMN: (*To CORY's unseen father*) You want to leave your daughter with me?

CORY: (*To her unseen father*) *Papi*, I don't want to stay with her!

GRANDMOTHER AUTUMN: After everything we've gone through?

CORY: I don't care if she's my mommy's mommy!

GRANDMOTHER AUTUMN: You took my Sara away and now she's gone.

CORY: Her house is scary!

GRANDMOTHER AUTUMN: Don't make any promises you can't keep.

CORY: I'll stay in the truck and I won't whine!

GRANDMOTHER AUTUMN: I don't want her.

CORY: I want you!

GRANDMOTHER AUTUMN: What job?

CORY: Why can't I go?

GRANDMOTHER AUTUMN: I'm looking for work, too.

CORY: What city?

GRANDMOTHER AUTUMN: I burned through my savings.

CORY: Please take me with you!

GRANDMOTHER AUTUMN: I don't even have health insurance.

CORY: Please, *Papi!*

GRANDMOTHER AUTUMN: You're sleeping in a truck?

CORY: I won't be a crybaby!

GRANDMOTHER AUTUMN: What kind of father are you?

CORY: I'll be a good girl!

GRANDMOTHER AUTUMN: Fine, she can stay, but it's only temporary.

CORY: No!

GRANDMOTHER AUTUMN: There's the front gate.

CORY: Don't go!

GRANDMOTHER AUTUMN: Go!

CORY: *¡PAPI!*

(*A truck is heard driving away.*)

GRANDMOTHER AUTUMN: Lord, what now? (*To CORY*) There's no need for tears. It's cold. Let's go inside.

(*CORY doesn't move.*)

GRANDMOTHER AUTUMN: You can't stay out here by yourself. That's my first rule. There're vicious dogs running around the neighborhood. They're wild and hungry. I'll make supper.

(*In the kitchen. They sit. GRANDMOTHER AUTUMN serves CORY a bowl of soup. CORY smells it and makes a face.*)

GRANDMOTHER AUTUMN: Baby, you gotta eat your soup.

CORY: I'm no baby. My name is Cory. Cory *Angelica Torres.*

GRANDMOTHER AUTUMN: Torres?

CORY: *Torres.*

GRANDMOTHER AUTUMN: OK, Cory *Angelicaaa Torres!* You gotta eat your soup.

CORY: No.

GRANDMOTHER AUTUMN: I made it fresh for you.

CORY: It came out of a can I saw.

GRANDMOTHER AUTUMN: OK, you're right. You wanna grow up to be big and strong, don't you? That's why you gotta eat your chicken soup.

CORY: I don't like chicken soup. Chicken soup comes from chicken poop.

GRANDMOTHER AUTUMN: What?

CORY: They poop in everything especially soup.

GRANDMOTHER AUTUMN: That's nonsense.

CORY: (*Pointing into the bowl*) What's that?

GRANDMOTHER AUTUMN: That's chicken meat.

CORY: Poop.

GRANDMOTHER AUTUMN: No.

CORY: What's that?

GRANDMOTHER AUTUMN: Noodles.

CORY: Big poop.

GRANDMOTHER AUTUMN: Child, where did you learn this?

CORY: Madeleine Perry-Chang told me.

GRANDMOTHER AUTUMN: Who's she?

CORY: My study buddy.

GRANDMOTHER AUTUMN: You believe her?

CORY: Yup, ah huh, she's the smartest kid in first grade.

GRANDMOTHER AUTUMN: Well, she's wrong.

CORY: How do you know?

GRANDMOTHER AUTUMN: 'Cause I went to college. So who's smarter now? Eat your soup.

(*CORY refuses. She crosses her arms.*)

GRANDMOTHER AUTUMN: Food costs money. I count every penny. Second rule. "What Grandma Autumn serves, you'll eat or you'll sit there all night."

(*GRANDMOTHER AUTUMN crosses her arms.*)

CORY: Poop.

GRANDMOTHER AUTUMN: Soup.

CORY. Poop.

GRANDMOTHER AUTUMN: Soup.

CORY: Poop.

GRANDMOTHER AUTUMN: OK, time for bed!

CORY: But I'm not sleepy.

GRANDMOTHER AUTUMN: Well, I am. I'm older than you.

(*They prepare a place for CORY to sleep.*)

GRANDMOTHER AUTUMN: Now lie down.

CORY: My daddy reads to me before I sleep.

GRANDMOTHER AUTUMN: I can't picture that.

CORY: He's a real good reader. The best.

GRANDMOTHER AUTUMN: Fine.

(CORY hands GRANDMOTHER AUTUMN a book.)

GRANDMOTHER AUTUMN: *Forever Poppy.* "When—"

CORY: —Forever *Flor* Keyshawn *Isla*-Baptiste-Poppy was born—

GRANDMOTHER AUTUMN: "—her parents believed in honoring their ancestors—"

CORY: —by giving her a very long and complicated name.

GRANDMOTHER AUTUMN: "So Forever *Flor* Keyshawn *Isla*-Baptiste-Poppy—"

CORY: —was just known as Forever Poppy.

GRANDMOTHER AUTUMN: Why am I reading to you if you already memorized the book?

CORY: 'Cause it's my favorite in the whole world.

GRANDMOTHER AUTUMN: Maybe I should read you something else.

CORY: That's all I got. *Papi* had to sell everything. All my things fit in here. (*She holds up her backpack.*)

GRANDMOTHER AUTUMN: Well, this is all I got: four walls, a bedroom, kitchen and bathroom.

CORY: It's more than I got.

GRANDMOTHER AUTUMN: Well, then we agree on something.

CORY: (*Points*) What's that?

GRANDMOTHER AUTUMN: It's my church hat. You're not allowed to touch it. That's rule number three. Now, lie down and close your eyes.

CORY: I can't.

GRANDMOTHER AUTUMN: Why not?

CORY: The sofa bed creaks.

GRANDMOTHER AUTUMN: Well, that's 'cause it's old.

CORY: Something's outside my window.

GRANDMOTHER AUTUMN: It's a tree's shadow caused by the moonlight.

CORY: You got monsters under here?

GRANDMOTHER AUTUMN: Monsters? There's no such thing as monsters.

CORY: Yes, there is.

GRANDMOTHER AUTUMN: Well, they don't come near this house.

CORY: Why not?

GRANDMOTHER AUTUMN: 'Cause they're scared of me.

CORY: Why?

GRANDMOTHER AUTUMN: I deep fry them in oil and eat them with Tabasco sauce!

CORY: ¡PAPI!

GRANDMOTHER AUTUMN: It's a joke! I'm kidding! If there were monsters, they wouldn't come to my house 'cause I eat chicken soup. That's what really keeps them away.

CORY: Can I sleep in your bed?

GRANDMOTHER AUTUMN: You're a big girl. You've got your own space. I'll leave the light on.

CORY: Please don't close the door.

GRANDMOTHER AUTUMN: OK. Good night.

CORY: Night.

(GRANDMOTHER AUTUMN exits. CORY sits up. She peeks over the edge of the sofa bed.)

CORY: (Timidly) Is anybody there?

GRANDMOTHER AUTUMN: (Offstage) Go to sleep!

(CORY throws the blanket over her. The next morning. Music. GRANDMOTHER AUTUMN enters gently brushing her teeth. She stands before an imaginary sink and mirror. CORY gets up and brushes her teeth before an imaginary sink and mirror. They go through their morning ritual unaware what the other is doing. GRANDMOTHER AUTUMN puts on her church hat. CORY puts on her cowboy hat.)

CORY: Yeehaw, Super Cowgirl!

GRANDMOTHER AUTUMN: You can't wear that in church.

CORY: Why not?

GRANDMOTHER AUTUMN: 'Cause the Lord's house isn't the "Wild West."

CORY: The Lord should let cowgirls into church.

GRANDMOTHER AUTUMN: Well, you'll just have to take that up with him.

(GRANDMOTHER AUTUMN takes the cowboy hat off CORY.)

GRANDMOTHER AUTUMN: We're going to church, then the food bank, and come home.

CORY: Why do we got to go to church?

GRANDMOTHER AUTUMN: Your parents never took you to church?

CORY: Nope. We went for waffles, instead!

GRANDMOTHER AUTUMN: Oh, Lord!

(A church bell is heard. GRANDMOTHER AUTUMN carries an umbrella.)

CORY: Is it gonna rain?

GRANDMOTHER AUTUMN: No. It's to protect us from those wild dogs.

CORY: Why are they wild?

GRANDMOTHER AUTUMN: 'Cause the neighbors left them behind when they moved out.

CORY: There's nobody to love them?

GRANDMOTHER AUTUMN: There's nothing to love about them. They're nasty and they'll bite your head off. Now stay close. (A car passes by, sending out a friendly honk.) Good morning, Mr. Johnson!

CORY: Look at all those pretty flowers!

GRANDMOTHER AUTUMN: They're dandelions, unwanted weeds.

CORY: Can I pick some?

GRANDMOTHER AUTUMN: No, you can't.

CORY: But there's so many of them.

GRANDMOTHER AUTUMN: You see all them for sale signs? Most of my neighbors moved out 'cause they've been robbed of their homes.

CORY: How'd their homes get robbed?

GRANDMOTHER AUTUMN: By those no-good-for-nothing thieves in fancy suits and ties wearing expensive shoes and cologne on Wall Street. They're the ones that caused this mess. You borrow money from them and they'll choke the life out of you.

CORY: Their mommies or daddies should talk to them about being bad.

GRANDMOTHER AUTUMN: Take their privileges away!

CORY: Put them in time out!

GRANDMOTHER AUTUMN: Put them in jail!

CORY: No TV!

GRANDMOTHER AUTUMN: No parole!

(DOG enters. He carries an old belt with a shiny buckle in his mouth. He looks lost.)

CORY: Look, it's a doggy!

GRANDMOTHER AUTUMN: Don't go near him.

CORY: He looks friendly.

GRANDMOTHER AUTUMN: He might bite you.

CORY: He's got a belt in his mouth.

GRANDMOTHER AUTUMN: That's 'cause he's crazy. Shoo!

CORY: Poor doggy.

(CORY crosses to DOG. He drops the belt in front of her. He looks at her, then the belt, back to her, then the belt. He nudges her. She picks it up and pets him.)

CORY: Can we keep him?

GRANDMOTHER AUTUMN: What? No!

CORY: I promise I'll feed him!

GRANDMOTHER AUTUMN: I can't afford to raise you and a dog!

CORY: I'll play with him everyday!

GRANDMOTHER AUTUMN: He's dirty and carries diseases!

CORY: Please!

GRANDMOTHER AUTUMN: I said, "No!" (To DOG) GO AWAY! (Lifting her umbrella as if to strike him. He yelps and runs away. To CORY) Hurry now! Let's go before he follows us!

(Church music.)

GRANDMOTHER AUTUMN: (To the unseen church ladies) Good morning, Sister Edwina! What a beautiful new hat you have. My, they charged you that much? Sister Hattie, so very nice to see you! What an elegant hat you're wearing! Oh, it's from Atlanta? Sister Esther, I love the plumage! You look like a peacock! Praise the Lord.

CORY: Their hats are bigger than yours.

GRANDMOTHER AUTUMN: (To CORY) Shhh! (To the unseen church ladies) Who's this? It's my granddaughter.

CORY: Say hello to the nice ladies, Cory.

CORY: Hello.

GRANDMOTHER AUTUMN: They don't get to visit me much. I always have to go to them.

CORY: Huh?

GRANDMOTHER AUTUMN: Close your mouth, dear. It's not polite. (To the unseen church ladies) Kids, today! (Music is heard.) Ladies. (To CORY) Sit down.

CORY: You lied.

GRANDMOTHER AUTUMN: No, I didn't.

CORY: Broke the truth.

GRANDMOTHER AUTUMN: No, I bent it a little that's all.

CORY: I don't remember you ever coming to visit us.

GRANDMOTHER AUTUMN: That's 'cause you were a baby in diapers. All you could do is eat and sleep.

CORY: Can we go now?

GRANDMOTHER AUTUMN: No, service just started.

CORY: But I can't see anything.

GRANDMOTHER AUTUMN: Don't embarrass me in front of these ladies.

CORY: Can I have some gum?

GRANDMOTHER AUTUMN: No!

(*Church music begins. GRANDMOTHER AUTUMN stands and pulls CORY up, too. DOG walks in carrying a large feather in his mouth. He crosses to CORY dropping it in front of her.*)

CORY: Hey, is this for me? How did you find me? Have you come to pray? Don't let Grandma see you!

(*CORY pets him. DOG stands behind GRANDMOTHER AUTUMN and CORY. A woman's voice is heard screaming, "Lord, almighty!"*)

GRANDMOTHER AUTUMN: (*To DOG*) You! (*To congregation*) He's not my dog! I've never seen him before!

(*DOG yelps and runs off. Chaos ensues in church.*)

GRANDMOTHER AUTUMN: (*Taking CORY by the hand*) Let's go!

(*At the church food bank.*)

CORY: I'm hungry.

GRANDMOTHER AUTUMN: So am I.

CORY: We've been waiting in line forever.

GRANDMOTHER AUTUMN: Look, the food bank is open now. (*Beat. To the unseen church ladies*) Sister Edwina, Esther and Hattie? What a surprise to see you. No, I didn't come to volunteer today.

CORY: SpaghettiOs!

GRANDMOTHER AUTUMN: Don't be rude, Cory. We'll take whatever the good ladies give us. I'm here for her.

(*A bus is heard. GRANDMOTHER AUTUMN and CORY ride a bus. GRANDMOTHER AUTUMN carries a bag filled with groceries.*)

CORY: Are we there yet?

GRANDMOTHER AUTUMN: We're not far.

CORY: I'm tired.

GRANDMOTHER AUTUMN: I'll make us lunch when we get home.

CORY: I hope it's not chicken soup.

GRANDMOTHER AUTUMN: They gave us baloney, bread, milk, bananas and, yes, more chicken soup. You should be grateful for what we've been given.

CORY: Why do you always do that?

GRANDMOTHER AUTUMN: Do what?

CORY: Look like you're mad.

GRANDMOTHER AUTUMN: I've got a toothache.

CORY: Why can't you fix it?

GRANDMOTHER AUTUMN: When I get a job I will. Until then I'm just going to look mad.

(The bus stops. They get off. The bus drives away.)

CORY: We're home.

GRANDMOTHER AUTUMN: Stay in the yard. I'm getting yesterday's mail.

CORY: Yes, ma'am.

GRANDMOTHER AUTUMN: Remember now, keep that gate closed.

(GRANDMOTHER AUTUMN goes to get her mail. Dogs are heard.)

CORY: Grandma!

GRANDMOTHER AUTUMN: Shoo! Shoo!

(Dogs charge after the grocery bag.)

CORY: Grandma!

GRANDMOTHER AUTUMN: Stay in the yard! (She beats the dogs with her umbrella. Catching her breath) I'm fine. I'm fine.

CORY: Is it a letter from my *papi*?

GRANDMOTHER AUTUMN: I don't think—

CORY: He likes to draw pictures. Let's open it!

GRANDMOTHER AUTUMN: Child, it's not from your daddy, it's from the bank.

(DOG enters carrying a colorful piece of ribbon in his mouth.)

CORY: Hey— (DOG drops the ribbon in front of CORY.) Hello, boy! (DOG barks.)

GRANDMOTHER AUTUMN: No!

(GRANDMOTHER AUTUMN hits him with her umbrella. DOG yelps running off. CORY starts to cry.)

CORY: You hurt him! *Papi* said you were nice, but you're not! You're mean!

GRANDMOTHER AUTUMN: Watch your mouth, child!

CORY: I want my *papi*!

GRANDMOTHER AUTUMN: He's not here! It's just me!

CORY: I hate you!

GRANDMOTHER AUTUMN: I hate my life!

CORY: *Papi*!!!

(*CORY runs off.*)

GRANDMOTHER AUTUMN: Cory, come back here! Cory!

(*GRANDMOTHER AUTUMN chases after her. CORY re-enters. She realizes she's lost.*)

CORY: Grandma?

(*DOG enters carrying rhinestone trim in his mouth. He crosses to CORY dropping it in front of her.*)

CORY: It's you again! (*She hugs DOG.*) Why do you keep bringing me things?

(*GRANDMOTHER AUTUMN enters catching her breath.*)

CORY: I'm sorry Grandma scared you. She scares me. She don't like us.

(*DOG senses GRANDMOTHER AUTUMN. They turn to her.*)

GRANDMOTHER AUTUMN: (*To CORY*) Please don't do that again.

CORY: Grandma?

GRANDMOTHER AUTUMN: Now, let's go home.

CORY: No. You hit him. That was so mean.

GRANDMOTHER AUTUMN: Well, I'm sorry. Come on.

CORY: No, there's nobody to play with, and why can't I play outside?

GRANDMOTHER AUTUMN: OK, you can play in the front yard as long as you keep the gate closed.

CORY: Can he come, too?

GRANDMOTHER AUTUMN: Do you promise not to run away?

(*CORY nods her head "yes."*)

CORY: Does that mean I get to keep him?

GRANDMOTHER AUTUMN: I make no promises. We'll take it one day at a time.

CORY: (*To DOG*) Where's your family, boy? Are you hungry? I think he's hungry. I'm hungry.

GRANDMOTHER AUTUMN: Me, too.

(She holds out her hand to CORY. CORY takes it. They exit. DOG follows. The front yard. DOG enters and circles the yard. He pauses momentarily and resumes his play. GRANDMOTHER AUTUMN and CORY soon follow.)

GRANDMOTHER AUTUMN: That dog sleeps outside.

CORY: Can't he sleep with me?

GRANDMOTHER AUTUMN: No.

CORY: He's going to be scared at night.

GRANDMOTHER AUTUMN: He's a dog, not a human.

CORY: He's got feelings.

GRANDMOTHER AUTUMN: No, he doesn't.

CORY: Madeleine Perry-Chang says—

GRANDMOTHER AUTUMN: Who went to college?

CORY: You did.

GRANDMOTHER AUTUMN: *(Sniffing)* What's that awful smell?

CORY: Poop. You stepped in it.

(GRANDMOTHER AUTUMN groans and scrapes her foot on the ground next to the rose bush.)

GRANDMOTHER AUTUMN: Make sure that mutt stays away from my rose plant.

CORY: What rose plant?

GRANDMOTHER AUTUMN: *(Pointing to a plastic garbage bag)* This one.

CORY: Why do you got plastic on it?

GRANDMOTHER AUTUMN: To keep the cold out and the warmth in.

(GRANDMOTHER AUTUMN removes the plastic bag revealing a shoot in a flower pot.)

CORY: It looks like a stick.

GRANDMOTHER AUTUMN: It's a rose branch. It's going to grow back one day.

CORY: Is it sick?

GRANDMOTHER AUTUMN: Yes, it's been sick for a very long time.

CORY: Does it have a cold?

GRANDMOTHER AUTUMN: No.

CORY: Does it have a tummy ache?

GRANDMOTHER AUTUMN: No.

CORY: Does it have a toothache?

GRANDMOTHER AUTUMN: It's a plant. Plants don't get colds, tummy aches or toothaches.

CORY: Does it have a fever?

GRANDMOTHER AUTUMN: No.

CORY: Does it have a booboo?

GRANDMOTHER AUTUMN: No.

CORY: Maybe's it's sad.

GRANDMOTHER AUTUMN: Sad?

CORY: Sometimes when I get sick it's 'cause I'm sad.

GRANDMOTHER AUTUMN: My late husband planted it when your mommy was born. It bloomed beautiful roses for many, many years. I'd wear them in my hat to church. I miss those days.

CORY: I remember my mommy singing to me, combing my hair and giving me butterfly kisses before she went to heaven.

GRANDMOTHER AUTUMN: We lost your mommy to a sickness the doctors couldn't cure.

CORY: My *papi* taught mommy to be a cowgirl. They met at a rodeo. *Papi* was a bronc rider.

GRANDMOTHER AUTUMN: I never understood that attraction.

CORY: Huh?

GRANDMOTHER AUTUMN: Never mind.

(DOG comes up between them. GRANDMOTHER AUTUMN looks at him disdainfully. He backs away.)

GRANDMOTHER AUTUMN: (To CORY) Remember what I told you. (To DOG) Stay away from my rose plant.

(GRANDMOTHER AUTUMN exits.)

CORY: Boy, let's have some fun. We'll play "Tea and Biscuits!" It'll be you, Bandit and me. OK, you sit here. And I'll sit there. No, you sit here. And I'll sit there. No, you sit here. And I'll sit there. OK, you sit there and I'll sit here. No, you sit here and I'll sit there. Make up your mind, doggy! (DOG grabs her toy dog, Bandit, and runs around with it. CORY chases after him.) Hey, you can't do that! Give him back to me! (DOG drops the toy dog and bites an itch. She picks up her toy with two fingers.) Eew! Let's play "Jumping Bean," OK? Watch me!

Jump, jump, jumping bean, Jump!

(CORY jumps.)

Jump, jump, jumping bean, Jump!

(CORY jumps.)

Jump, jump, jumping bean, Jump!

(*CORY jumps.*)

Jump, jump, jumping bean,

(*DOG barks.*)

Jump, jump, jumping bean,

(*DOG barks.*)

Jump, jump, jumping bean,

(*DOG barks.*)

Jump, jump, jumping bean . . .

(*DOG spins.*)

Spin!

Jump, jump, jumping bean

Spin!

(*DOG spins and barks.*)

Jump, jump, jumping bean

Spin!

(*DOG spins and barks.*)

Jump, jump, jumping bean

Spin!

(*CORY and DOG spin. He barks.*)

Jump, jump, jumping bean, fall!

(*They fall to the ground.*)

You did it, boy! I'm a mess! Look at the clouds! That one looks like Deshana Puglese with pigtails. That one looks like a crocodile with spiky hair. Peace! That one . . . hmm . . . that one looks like a big booger! Do you know that d-o-g spelled backwards is g-o-d? Weird, huh?

GRANDMOTHER AUTUMN: (*Offstage*) Cory, dinner's ready! Come wash your hands!

CORY: OK! (*To DOG*) Stay.

(*DOG runs off. GRANDMOTHER AUTUMN enters with a small plate and bowl. CORY sits down.*)

CORY: (*Points*) What's that?

GRANDMOTHER AUTUMN: Don't point. It's not polite. It's spinach.

CORY: Yuck!

GRANDMOTHER AUTUMN: And chicken soup.

CORY: Again?

GRANDMOTHER AUTUMN: That's all that's left. So eat. Try the spinach. You'll like it. Superheroes eat it.

CORY: They do?

GRANDMOTHER AUTUMN: You ever heard of Popeye the Sailor Man?

CORY: Nope.

GRANDMOTHER AUTUMN: He could open a can with his bare hands.

CORY: For reals?

GRANDMOTHER AUTUMN: For real.

CORY: I'm not very hungry.

GRANDMOTHER AUTUMN: You'll eat every bite. That's my rule.

(DOG pops his head in to look. CORY notices him, but GRANDMOTHER AUTUMN does not.)

CORY: May I have a glass of water please?

GRANDMOTHER AUTUMN: OK.

(CORY signals to him and DOG enters. CORY tries to spoon-feed him soup.)

CORY: Go!

(DOG exits as GRANDMOTHER AUTUMN enters with a glass of water.)

GRANDMOTHER AUTUMN: Oh, I see you're eating your chicken soup! I was right, wasn't I?

(CORY smiles and looks in the direction of DOG. GRANDMOTHER AUTUMN sits down.)

CORY: May I have a napkin please?

GRANDMOTHER AUTUMN: I could have sworn I put one down. Never mind.

CORY: Thank you.

(GRANDMOTHER AUTUMN gets up and exits. CORY signals DOG back in. She holds the bowl out as DOG laps up the soup.)

CORY: Go!

(DOG exits. GRANDMOTHER AUTUMN enters with a napkin.)

GRANDMOTHER AUTUMN: My you're a messy eater. Here.

CORY: Thank you.

(GRANDMOTHER AUTUMN sits down again.)

CORY: May I have some Tabasco sauce?

GRANDMOTHER AUTUMN: Tabasco sauce? (Suspicious) Fine. I'll get you Tabasco sauce.

(GRANDMOTHER AUTUMN gets up and exits as DOG runs in lapping up the soup.)

CORY: Go!

(DOG runs out but charges right back in for one more taste. He exits as GRANDMOTHER AUTUMN enters.)

GRANDMOTHER AUTUMN: Tabasco sauce.

CORY: No, I changed my mind. I'm all done! Bye!

(CORY walks out. GRANDMOTHER AUTUMN picks up the soup bowl and finds a dog hair.)

GRANDMOTHER AUTUMN: You again! How did you get in my house?

(DOG pops his head in and slurps. He is unseen by GRANDMOTHER AUTUMN. She exits. The phone rings.)

GRANDMOTHER AUTUMN: Hello? Oh, it's you. I didn't expect you'd call. Cory's fine. It hasn't been easy. No thanks to you. What job? Construction? I can't imagine it. I received a letter from the bank. No, I haven't opened it. No, I'm not worried. Don't make any promises. I don't want to talk about it anymore. I'll get Cory. Cory!

CORY: (Entering) Yes?

GRANDMOTHER AUTUMN: It's your daddy. He's on the phone. He wants to speak to you.

(CORY takes the phone.)

CORY: *Papi!?! Te estraño mucho.* [*I miss you a lot.*] When are you coming home? A month? It's a long time. (Whispering) She's not very nice. She makes me eat chicken soup. She makes me go to church. I can't see a thing 'cause of those big hats. It's so boring! I found a dog. He likes to bring me things. He doesn't have a name yet. Can we keep him?

(GRANDMOTHER AUTUMN clears her throat.)

CORY: OK, bye, *Papi*! I love you! *¡Adios!*

GRANDMOTHER AUTUMN: Where are you sleeping? Is that safe? Who's worried? I'm not worried. Goodbye.

(GRANDMOTHER AUTUMN exits. Night. DOG enters whimpering. CORY follows. DOG carries a bow tie in his mouth.)

CORY: (Whispering) Shhh, we have to be quiet, boy! We don't want Grandma to know. You can sleep here tonight. You're safe with me. What'd you bring me this time? (He drops the bow tie.) It's pretty. I'll keep that, too.

(CORY picks up GRANDMOTHER AUTUMN's church hat and puts it on.)

CORY: Oooh, look at me! I'm Esther the peacock! Oooh, I like to wear fancy church hats! Oooh, praise the Lord! (She laughs. Imitating GRANDMOTHER

AUTUMN) Good morning, Sister Edwina! This is my granddaughter Cory. I won't let her wear a cowboy hat in church 'cause the Lord hates cowgirls!

GRANDMOTHER AUTUMN: (*Offstage*) Cory?

CORY: Sorry, Grandma! (*She puts the hat away and jumps onto the sofa bed. To DOG*) OK, you lie there and I'll lie here. No, you lie there and I'll lie here. No, you lie there and I'll lie here. OK, you lie there and I'll lie here. Make up your mind, doggy! (*DOG crosses to GRANDMOTHER AUTUMN's hat.*) What are you doing? You're supposed to be in bed. (*DOG starts sniffing a hat. He sneezes all over CORY and the hat.*) Hey! (*DOG barks and bites into the hat.*) Oh, no! Give me that!

GRANDMOTHER AUTUMN: (*Offstage*) What's going on?

(*CORY grabs the hat, and DOG thinks it's a game.*)

CORY: Let go!

GRANDMOTHER AUTUMN: Cory!

(*CORY jumps into her sofa bed and DOG follows. She puts the blanket over him as GRANDMOTHER AUTUMN enters wearing a robe.*)

GRANDMOTHER AUTUMN: What are you doing?

CORY: Nothing.

GRANDMOTHER AUTUMN: Go to bed!

CORY: OK!

(*CORY throws the blanket over her head. GRANDMOTHER AUTUMN exits. Under the covers they struggle for the hat.*)

CORY: Give it back! Let go!

GRANDMOTHER AUTUMN: Don't make me come in there!

CORY: You're gonna get us in trouble!

GRANDMOTHER AUTUMN: That's it!

CORY: Uh-oh!

(*GRANDMOTHER AUTUMN enters. CORY sticks her head out of the blanket.*)

GRANDMOTHER AUTUMN: Child, what is going on with you?

CORY: I can't sleep.

GRANDMOTHER AUTUMN Why?

CORY: 'Cause ... um ...

GRANDMOTHER AUTUMN: I'm waiting.

CORY: 'Cause there's a monster under my bed.

GRANDMOTHER AUTUMN: I told you there are no monsters.

CORY: Something's down there. I don't know.

GRANDMOTHER AUTUMN: I am not going to look.

CORY: Can I sleep in your bed?

GRANDMOTHER AUTUMN: Fine, I'll look.

(*GRANDMOTHER AUTUMN bends down and begins to crawl under the sofa bed. It's a tight space for her.*)

GRANDMOTHER AUTUMN: (*Struggling*) I see no monsters!

(*CORY lifts up the blanket and tries to pull the hat away from DOG.*)

CORY: Let go!

GRANDMOTHER AUTUMN: Hey, what's my letter doing under here? Was it that dog!?!

(*CORY and DOG pull at GRANDMOTHER AUTUMN's hat.*)

CORY: Give it here! (*DOG growls.*) Let go! Aaggghhh!

(*The hat is destroyed. GRANDMOTHER AUTUMN crawls out from under the sofa bed.*)

GRANDMOTHER AUTUMN: That's my hat!

(*DOG shakes the hat playfully in his mouth.*)

CORY: I'm sorry!

GRANDMOTHER AUTUMN: It's ruined!

CORY: I can fix it!

GRANDMOTHER AUTUMN: (*To DOG*) Get out of here!

CORY: No!

GRANDMOTHER AUTUMN: GET!

(*DOG exits. CORY runs out. GRANDMOTHER AUTUMN holds out the letter.*)

GRANDMOTHER AUTUMN: Oh, Lord. They're going to take my house.

(*She exits. DOG re-enters, retrieves the hat and exits. The phone rings. CORY and GRANDMOTHER AUTUMN enter answering the phone call.*)

CORY: (*Crying*) Papi, she sent him away.

GRANDMOTHER AUTUMN: I'm doing everything I can.

CORY: He's my only friend.

GRANDMOTHER AUTUMN: I've got till the end of the month to pay or I lose my home.

CORY: Make it up to her? How?

GRANDMOTHER AUTUMN: I'm at my wits end.

CORY: I'm being a good girl.

GRANDMOTHER AUTUMN: Please don't make any promises. You live in a truck.

CORY: OK, *sí*, OK. I'll try harder, *sí*!

(*They hang up.*)

CORY: I promise to eat your chicken soup and like it.

GRANDMOTHER AUTUMN: What?

CORY: I know that you hate *Papi* and me.

GRANDMOTHER AUTUMN: How can you think that?

CORY: You never talk nice to us and you're always in a bad way.

GRANDMOTHER AUTUMN: Well, I'm sorry. I have a lot on my mind and my tooth hurts.

CORY: Did you love my mommy?

GRANDMOTHER AUTUMN: Yes, I did. Very much. I don't hate you, OK?

CORY: OK.

GRANDMOTHER AUTUMN: You were right, you know?

CORY: About what?

GRANDMOTHER AUTUMN: At church when I bent the truth about visiting you. I never did. I wasn't very understanding of your mommy and daddy's love for one another. I didn't talk to her until it was too late when she was sick, and I'm truly sorry for that. Truly sorry.

CORY: My mommy told me that the butterfly kisses she liked to give me she learned from you.

GRANDMOTHER AUTUMN: She did?

CORY: Yup. You taught her that?

GRANDMOTHER AUTUMN: Ah huh.

(*They exit. Time has passed. CORY enters wearing a cape, goggles and cowboy hat.*)

CORY: Hey, boy, you're back! I missed you! (*DOG enters carrying a plastic rose flower. He drops it in front of Cory.*) You brought me a plastic flower. You wanna play superheroes? (*He barks.*) My *papi* helped me make my own cape! See! Now, you need one! Where can I—I know! (*CORY crosses to the covered rose bush and removes the plastic.*) This will do! Don't move! (*She places the plastic bag on him.*) Yeehaw, it's Super Cowgirl and Mighty Dog! We can fly fast, jump high and we're super strong! (*CORY runs around the yard as if she is flying. DOG follows. She stops and points.*) Oh, look, Mighty Dog, there's a little old lady who needs our help! Those wild dogs are gonna tear her to pieces! Let's use our super x-ray vision to stop them! (*She makes "buzzing" sound. DOG* barks.) It's no good! They got deflectors! It's time for super kung-fu! Let's kick butt! (*Kicking and karate chopping. DOG runs around barking.*) Hiya! Hiya! Hiya! We did it Mighty Dog! We saved the little old lady! (*DOG chews on the plastic.*) Hey, stop chewing your cape! You'll lose your super powers! (*DOG runs around barking and exits. To imaginary little old lady*) Don't cry, ma'am. No need for tears. Yes, I would love an ice cream cone with sprinkles! *Muchas gracias.* (*DOG enters carrying GRANDMOTHER AUTUMN's hat. He drops it in front of Cory.*) Hey, that's Grandma's hat. (*She picks up the hat and places it with the flower, side by side.*) That looks real pretty together. Hey, I bet if we add the other stuff you brought me Grandma would really like it! (*To DOG*) You did it, Mighty Dog!

GRANDMOTHER AUTUMN: (*Offstage*) Cory?

CORY: You gotta go! (*DOG sits.*) Why don't you ever do what I say?

GRANDMOTHER AUTUMN: (*Offstage*) Where are you?

(*DOG exits as GRANDMOTHER AUTUMN enters.*)

CORY: I'm out here all alone, Grandma.

GRANDMOTHER AUTUMN: You're supposed to keep the front gate closed. That's my rule remember?

CORY: Oh, yeah, I forgot. (*Holding out the church hat*) Look!

GRANDMOTHER AUTUMN: Is that my church hat?

CORY: Yup!

GRANDMOTHER AUTUMN: It looks different.

CORY: I think it's real pretty.

GRANDMOTHER AUTUMN: You did this?

CORY: The Lord works in mysterious ways.

(*GRANDMOTHER AUTUMN takes the hat from CORY.*)

GRANDMOTHER AUTUMN: I'll say. With a little cleaning, sewing and rearranging—

CORY: (*Holding up a feather*) And a big feather! It'll look like new!

GRANDMOTHER AUTUMN: We'll see about that.

(*GRANDMOTHER AUTUMN and CORY exit. DOG enters, takes the rose shoot and exits. The phone rings. GRANDMOTHER AUTUMN and CORY pick up.*)

GRANDMOTHER AUTUMN: Hello?

CORY: *Papi!*

GRANDMOTHER AUTUMN: She's fine.

CORY: I can't wait to see you.

GRANDMOTHER AUTUMN: What?

CORY: What time will you be here?

GRANDMOTHER AUTUMN: Overtime?

CORY: You're coming later?

GRANDMOTHER AUTUMN: You know that child has been expecting you all month.

CORY: You're not coming?

GRANDMOTHER AUTUMN: I'll think of something.

CORY: OK, OK, *sí, sí*.

GRANDMOTHER AUTUMN: Your *papi* is working real hard. I know it saddens him to be away from you, but it's only for a little while. He doesn't want you to live in a shelter or sleep in a truck anymore. He promised he'd write.

CORY: For reals?

GRANDMOTHER AUTUMN: For real.

(*Time passes. Music. GRANDMOTHER AUTUMN enters gently brushing her teeth. She stands before an imaginary sink and mirror. CORY gets up and brushes her teeth before an imaginary sink and mirror. They go through their morning ritual unaware of what the other is doing. GRANDMOTHER AUTUMN puts on her church hat. It is now smaller but more beautiful. CORY puts on her cowboy hat.*)

CORY: Yeehaw, Super Cowgirl!

GRANDMOTHER AUTUMN. You can't wear that in church.

CORY: But I spoke to the Lord and he said it was "OK."

GRANDMOTHER AUTUMN: The Lord didn't speak to me about it. (*She takes the cowboy hat off Cory. GRANDMOTHER AUTUMN carries her umbrella.*) Let's hurry!

(*Church music. GRANDMOTHER AUTUMN and CORY sit.*)

GRANDMOTHER AUTUMN: (*To the unseen church ladies*) Sister Edwina, Hattie, Esther. Oh, this? I made it myself . . . Saw it in a magazine from . . . Atlanta!

CORY: Huh?

GRANDMOTHER AUTUMN: (*To CORY*) Close your mouth! (*To the unseen church ladies*) It's what's called "vintage." It's the new thing these days. Ladies.

CORY: (*Whispering*) You lied again.

GRANDMOTHER AUTUMN. (*Whispering*) You're right. (*To the unseen church ladies*) Truthfully, Ladies, I didn't see it in a magazine. It's my old hat that I—We recycled into something new. Well, it does look new, doesn't it?

(*Church music is heard. GRANDMOTHER AUTUMN joins in with the congregation. DOG enters. In his mouth is the rose shoot. He drops it in front of GRANDMOTHER AUTUMN and CORY.*)

GRANDMOTHER AUTUMN: My rose plant! I'm going to kill that dog!

(*DOG yelps and exits.*)

CORY: No!

(*GRANDMOTHER AUTUMN chases after DOG. CORY follows. GRANDMOTHER AUTUMN enters with DOG on a leash. She secures it so he can't escape.*)

GRANDMOTHER AUTUMN: This dog is going to the pound!

CORY: What's that mean?

GRANDMOTHER AUTUMN: That's where bad dogs go.

CORY: If he goes, I go, too! Woof! Woof!

GRANDMOTHER AUTUMN: Stop it!

CORY: Woof! Woof!

GRANDMOTHER AUTUMN: Bad dogs go to the pound and they never come back!

CORY: No, you can't do that!

GRANDMOTHER AUTUMN: Now close that gate!

(*GRANDMOTHER AUTUMN exits.*)

CORY: I won't let her take you to the pound. You're my best friend. We're gonna have to go far away, OK? (*She unties the leash. DOG becomes alert.*) What is it, boy? (*DOG growls as a pack of wild dogs approach.*) Oh, no! Grandma! (*DOG steps in front of CORY, confronting the wild dogs.*) GRANDMA!

(*Fierce barking is heard as DOG fights them while CORY pulls his leash back. GRANDMOTHER AUTUMN enters with a broom, beating them back.*)

GRANDMOTHER AUTUMN: Get! Get! GET!

(*DOG is lying on the ground.*)

CORY: He's hurt real bad!

GRANDMOTHER AUTUMN: Don't touch him!

CORY: Grandma, do something!

GRANDMOTHER AUTUMN: We're taking Mr. Johnson's car!

CORY: You saved me, boy. He saved me.

GRANDMOTHER AUTUMN: Get in!

(*Sound of car starting up.*)

CORY: (*To DOG*) It's gonna be OK, boy!

GRANDMOTHER AUTUMN: Put your seatbelt on!

CORY: You're my best friend.

GRANDMOTHER AUTUMN: Where's the clutch?

CORY: Grandma, do you know how to drive?

GRANDMOTHER AUTUMN: Here goes nothing!

(GRANDMOTHER AUTUMN floors the gas pedal.)

CORY: Look out for Sister Esther!

GRANDMOTHER AUTUMN: Get out of the way! Sorry!

CORY: I should've kept the gate closed!

GRANDMOTHER AUTUMN: It's not your fault.

CORY: I should've remembered your rule!

GRANDMOTHER AUTUMN: You're not to blame.

CORY: Stupid girl!

GRANDMOTHER AUTUMN: No, you're not a stupid girl! (Car screeches to a stop. Speaking to the unseen veterinarian) Can you save him, Doctor?

CORY: He's gonna fix you up, boy!

GRANDMOTHER AUTUMN: What two options?

CORY: Good as new!

GRANDMOTHER AUTUMN: How much?

CORY: We'll play together again!

GRANDMOTHER AUTUMN: No, I don't want him put down!

CORY: Grandma!

GRANDMOTHER AUTUMN: I don't care how much it costs! Take my wedding ring!

CORY: He's not breathing!

GRANDMOTHER AUTUMN: He saved my grandbaby!

CORY: He's not breathing!

GRANDMOTHER AUTUMN: Please we need a miracle!

(They exit. A few days later. CORY re-enters. She wears her cowboy hat. GRANDMOTHER AUTUMN wears her church hat.)

GRANDMOTHER AUTUMN: Shall we begin?

CORY: OK. (She digs a hole in the ground.)

GRANDMOTHER AUTUMN: Bow your head. We return this mighty gift back from whence it came. Thank you for its many blessings—

(CORY *holds up the rose shoot.*)

GRANDMOTHER AUTUMN: —and for giving us a second chance. (*She buries it.*)

CORY: Amen.

GRANDMOTHER AUTUMN: I've been angry and feeling sorry for myself and I blamed everyone. You're the best thing in my life, a real Super Cowgirl.

CORY: Me?

GRANDMOTHER AUTUMN: You never gave up on us. (*Beat*) You remind me of your mommy.

CORY: I do?

GRANDMOTHER AUTUMN: She had a beautiful smile like you, such an imagination, and she always wanted a dog. That's why I gave her Bandit.

(*GRANDMOTHER AUTUMN hands CORY her toy dog.*)

CORY: You gave him to her?

GRANDMOTHER AUTUMN: Yes.

CORY: And now he's mine.

(CORY *hugs her toy dog. DOG enters wearing a sling on his arm.*)

CORY: Hey, boy!

(CORY *places her toy dog away and crosses to DOG.*)

GRANDMOTHER AUTUMN: You pick a name for him yet?

CORY: Nope.

GRANDMOTHER AUTUMN: I think you should name him "Wimpy." (*She imitates DOG.*) Oh, I forgot! I've got something for you.

CORY: Is it a monkey?

GRANDMOTHER AUTUMN: What? No.

CORY: Is it a rhino on a skateboard?

GRANDMOTHER AUTUMN: No, but I see what you're doing.

CORY: Is it a duck with glasses?

GRANDMOTHER AUTUMN: No.

CORY: Is it a—

GRANDMOTHER AUTUMN: Here!

(*GRANDMOTHER AUTUMN gives CORY an envelope.*)

CORY: It's from *Papi*!

GRANDMOTHER AUTUMN: What's he say?

(*CORY rips opens the envelope, removing the letter. DOG discovers the envelope on the ground.*)

CORY: He drew me a picture with words. *Papi's* wearing cowboy boots, hat and riding in a rodeo! I'm there too! Look, that's you.

GRANDMOTHER AUTUMN: He drew me into the picture?

CORY: That's 'cause you're family.

GRANDMOTHER AUTUMN: He told you that?

CORY: Yup. He said that you brought Mommy into the world and that was pretty special 'cause he would have never met Mommy and I'd never been born. (*Taking the envelope from DOG*) Look!

GRANDMOTHER AUTUMN: What is it?

CORY: Money.

(*CORY hands it to GRANDMOTHER AUTUMN.*)

GRANDMOTHER AUTUMN: I didn't expect this . . .

CORY: Are you crying?

GRANDMOTHER AUTUMN: I'm not crying.

CORY: Are we going to have to live in a truck again?

GRANDMOTHER AUTUMN: Don't you worry none. We're going to manage. With what your *papi* sent and with what the church ladies are willing to pay me—

CORY: Pay you for what?

GRANDMOTHER AUTUMN: Child, they liked my vintage hat so much that they're going to pay me to redo all of theirs. Our church has a lot of old ladies with a lot of old hats! We're gonna be busy. Super Cowgirls!

CORY: Yeehaw!

(*DOG runs up to GRANDMOTHER AUTUMN.*)

GRANDMOTHER AUTUMN: Dog, you need a bath.

CORY: I know what to name him now!

GRANDMOTHER AUTUMN: What?

CORY: Miracle!

GRANDMOTHER AUTUMN: Miracle?

GRANDMOTHER AUTUMN & CORY: (*Proudly*) Mighty Miracle!

(*MIRACLE barks.*)

CURTAIN

Production credits from the premiere of *Super Cowgirl and Mighty Miracle* and details concerning performance rights are included in the acting edition of the play as published by Dramatic Publishing.

Tomato Plant Girl

Wesley Middleton

New to Heretown, Little Girl adjusts by playing with Bossy Best Friend, even though Bossy has rules for everything—from playing with Barbie dolls and gardening to not acting "like a foreigner." When Bossy goes on a shopping trip, leaving behind her jealously guarded tomato plant, Little Girl decides to disobey the order never to touch Bossy's garden. Intending to transplant the ailing plant into her own garden where she can care for it, Little Girl pulls it out of the ground only to see Tomato Plant Girl climb out of the earth after it. Little Girl's self-confidence increases as she teaches a few words of English to the messy, unassuming, and curious Tomato Plant Girl. In return, the cheerful Tomato Plant Girl teaches Little Girl ways of communicating through gesture. When Bossy returns more imperious than ever, Little Girl must decide what a real friend is and how to stay true to herself in this contemporary tale of peer pressure and manipulation.

Characters

LITTLE GIRL: A small girl, about 10 years old. Recently moved to Heretown from Thereville. Loves books and tomatoes.

BOSSY BEST FRIEND: Older, richer and girlier than Little Girl. Has always lived in Heretown. Loves Barbies and clothes.

TOMATO PLANT GIRL: A tomato spirit who appears in Heretown in the shape of a girl. Does not understand Heretown's rules.

VOICE OF BOSSY BEST FRIEND'S MOTHER

(may be expanded with "stagehand" roles)

SETTING: Heretown, a small American town where foreigners are suspicious and rules are important.

TIME: Summertime.

Scene 1

SETTING: *The action takes place in a makeshift garden. The garden is a fenced vacant lot on a small-town residential street. It belongs to LITTLE GIRL and BOSSY BEST FRIEND. Mostly BOSSY BEST FRIEND. There are two tomato plants in the garden. One is dry and wilted. A sign beside it says: "DO NOT TOUCH!" The other is healthy and green, with a single young tomato.*

AT RISE: *We hear the sound of quick, rhythmic ticking. BOSSY BEST FRIEND enters. Everything matches on BOSSY BEST FRIEND: her cute summer dress, the big bow in her hair, her bag. She carries a parasol to shade her from the sun. BOSSY BEST FRIEND looks around the garden. Takes a deep breath. Smiles. Consults her big plastic watch.*

BOSSY BEST FRIEND: Four fifty-eight and thirty seconds.

(*She straightens her bow. Looks back at her watch.*)

BOSSY BEST FRIEND: Four fifty-eight and forty-eight seconds. Four fifty-eight and forty-nine seconds.

(*She looks off, then back at her watch.*)

BOSSY BEST FRIEND: Four fifty-eight and fifty-two seconds. Fifty-three. Fifty-four. Fifty—

(*LITTLE GIRL runs in, excited and anxious. She wears overall shorts, a T-shirt and a hat. She carries a big book,* Tales of Tomatoes, *with a tomato on the cover.*)

LITTLE GIRL: Five? Is it five o'clock?

(*BOSSY BEST FRIEND holds out her watch, points at it, then hides it, fast. She's lying.*)

BOSSY BEST FRIEND: And 10 seconds. You're late!

LITTLE GIRL: I was reading!

BOSSY BEST FRIEND: You're *late*.

LITTLE GIRL: About tomatoes! (*Holding out the book*) Grandma gave it to me. When she was alive.

BOSSY BEST FRIEND: Poor dear. Put it out of your mind.

(*BOSSY BEST FRIEND tries to take the book. LITTLE GIRL holds on.*)

LITTLE GIRL: We could read to the plants!

BOSSY BEST FRIEND: It is *not* time to read! Give me the book *now*, Book-nose. *Please.*

(*LITTLE GIRL lets BOSSY BEST FRIEND take the book. BOSSY BEST FRIEND puts it with her things.*)

LITTLE GIRL: Grandma used to read to me.

BOSSY BEST FRIEND: Well, maybe you'll meet *my* grandma someday.

LITTLE GIRL: Really?

BOSSY BEST FRIEND: If you're a *very* good friend. We'll see. Now hurry. We're late for your favorite game!

(*BOSSY BEST FRIEND smiles and claps twice.*)

BOSSY BEST FRIEND: Mother May I!

(*LITTLE GIRL, who does like this game, walks several paces away from BOSSY BEST FRIEND and turns to face her.*)

BOSSY BEST FRIEND: Ready? Good. Two queenly curtsies.

LITTLE GIRL: Mother may I?

BOSSY BEST FRIEND: Yes you may.

(*LITTLE GIRL curtsies twice.*)

BOSSY BEST FRIEND: Lovely! Three ballerina twirls.

LITTLE GIRL: Mother may I?

BOSSY BEST FRIEND: Yes you may.

(*LITTLE GIRL does three twirls.*)

BOSSY BEST FRIEND: Gorgeous! Five giant steps.

LITTLE GIRL: Mother may I?

BOSSY BEST FRIEND: Yes you may.

(*LITTLE GIRL starts giant-stepping toward BOSSY BEST FRIEND.*)

BOSSY BEST FRIEND: *Backward.*

(*LITTLE GIRL freezes mid-step, then steps backward with the same foot, almost losing her balance. She does the five steps.*)

BOSSY BEST FRIEND: Now hop eight times on your left-hand foot. Forward. Hurry up!

LITTLE GIRL: Mother may I?

BOSSY BEST FRIEND: Yes you may.

(*LITTLE GIRL starts to hop. BOSSY BEST FRIEND interrupts.*)

BOSSY BEST FRIEND: Now stand on your tippy tiptoes and eat dirt!

(*LITTLE GIRL quickly picks up some dirt, stands on tiptoe, and starts to bring the dirt to her lips.*)

BOSSY BEST FRIEND: Ha! Quit, silly girl! We don't eat dirt!

LITTLE GIRL: (*Freezes*) I forgot.

BOSSY BEST FRIEND: Poor Booknose. Still—you did *very* well. You get a gold star!

(*BOSSY BEST FRIEND takes a big gold star from her pocket and sticks it on LITTLE GIRL's forehead.*)

BOSSY BEST FRIEND: Ta-da!

(*They do a very proper "buddy" handshake.*)

BOSSY BEST FRIEND, LITTLE GIRL: Best friends forever—Number One!

(*LITTLE GIRL smiles proudly and curtsies, removing her hat. As she does, she feels the sun on her face and hair.*)

LITTLE GIRL: Mmmm.

(*She closes her eyes, stretches upward, breathes.*)

LITTLE GIRL: The sun!

BOSSY BEST FRIEND: Booknose! *Careful!* The ultraviolent rays!

LITTLE GIRL: But—

BOSSY BEST FRIEND: Sunburn is *wrong*! Put on your hat!

(*LITTLE GIRL puts on her hat.*)

BOSSY BEST FRIEND: Now. What time is it?

LITTLE GIRL: Book time!

BOSSY BEST FRIEND: *No*—

LITTLE GIRL: Tomato plant time!

BOSSY BEST FRIEND: *No.* Not five-fifteen. What time is it?

LITTLE GIRL: Barbie.

(*BOSSY BEST FRIEND smiles, snaps her fingers once. LITTLE GIRL gets in place for the game. BOSSY BEST FRIEND takes out two Barbies. One wears a fancy dress. The other wears a plain dress and has bad hair. BOSSY BEST FRIEND hands the latter Barbie to LITTLE GIRL.*)

BOSSY BEST FRIEND: You're this one.

LITTLE GIRL: I know.

(*BOSSY BEST FRIEND and LITTLE GIRL place their Barbies in stiff standing positions.*)

BOSSY BEST FRIEND: One-two-three!

(*Both speak, in quick rhythm, as their Barbies.*)

BOSSY BEST FRIEND: Dena!

LITTLE GIRL: Lena!

(*The Barbies cheek-kiss loudly, three times. Rhythm: "Dena! Lena! Kiss kiss kiss!"*)

LITTLE GIRL: How are you?

BOSSY BEST FRIEND: Just grand!

LITTLE GIRL: And your job?

BOSSY BEST FRIEND: Unsurpassed!

LITTLE GIRL: And your boyfriends?

BOSSY BEST FRIEND: Ooh la!

LITTLE GIRL: You look lovely.

BOSSY BEST FRIEND: Can't hear you!

LITTLE GIRL: Just *lovely.*

BOSSY BEST FRIEND: Why thanks. Are you wearing that dress to my party tonight?

LITTLE GIRL: Of course.

BOSSY BEST FRIEND: But it's ugly!

LITTLE GIRL: Oh. Then I'll wear—a satin ball gown with rose petticoats!

BOSSY BEST FRIEND: You can't have a new dress!

LITTLE GIRL: (*As herself*) But I've got a gold star!

BOSSY BEST FRIEND: (*As her Barbie*) Guess all the young beaus will be looking at me!

LITTLE GIRL: Beaus?

BOSSY BEST FRIEND: Young *beaus.* At the party! The *boys!*

LITTLE GIRL: Oh.

BOSSY BEST FRIEND: You're jealous!

LITTLE GIRL: (*Matter of fact*) I'm not.

BOSSY BEST FRIEND: Yes you are.

LITTLE GIRL: (*As before*) No. You can go. I'll read.

(*LITTLE GIRL reaches for her book. BOSSY BEST FRIEND stops her, snatches her Barbie.*)

BOSSY BEST FRIEND: (*As herself*) Your Barbie loves parties and would *die* for a beau. Your Barbie wants what *my* Barbie wants but *my* Barbie can have it and your Barbie can't. That's the game! Now what do you say?

LITTLE GIRL: I'm sorry.

BOSSY BEST FRIEND: What time is it?

LITTLE GIRL: Tomato plant—

BOSSY BEST FRIEND: NO!! (*BOSSY BEST FRIEND composes herself to lecture.*) Booknose: who were you three months ago?

(*LITTLE GIRL starts to speak.*)

BOSSY BEST FRIEND: You were no one. You were the new girl, just moved here from Thereville. Always alone—reading, walking, talking to plants . . . till I found you and told you: you need a friend. I taught you not to act like a (*lowers her voice*) *foreigner.*

(*LITTLE GIRL gasps at the word. BOSSY BEST FRIEND points to LITTLE GIRL; LITTLE GIRL recites the definition with military precision.*)

LITTLE GIRL: Foreigner: Anyone who looks acts speaks appears seems or suggests themselves to be in any way different from the glorious ways of the virtuous people of Heretown!

BOSSY BEST FRIEND: You're lucky I've taught you. Don't forget to play right. You're this one.

(*She holds out LITTLE GIRL's Barbie. LITTLE GIRL looks at her, doesn't take it.*)

BOSSY BEST FRIEND: What?

LITTLE GIRL: (*Matter of fact*) It's tomato plant time.

BOSSY BEST FRIEND: You're *this* one!

LITTLE GIRL: It's time! It's past five-fifteen!

(*Reluctantly, BOSSY BEST FRIEND checks her watch.*)

BOSSY BEST FRIEND: (*Annoyed*) All right. No Barbie.

(*BOSSY BEST FRIEND puts the Barbies in the bag.*)

BOSSY BEST FRIEND: You'll do better next time. Now—

LITTLE GIRL: Now for the glorious harvest! Hurrah!

(*LITTLE GIRL starts to run toward her planter.*)

BOSSY BEST FRIEND: Hold your little ponies.

(*LITTLE GIRL stops.*)

BOSSY BEST FRIEND: We go at the *same* time. Remember?

(*Slowly, the two turn together toward the garden plots and walk toward them. They stand in front of their respective garden plots. Both gasp.*)

BOSSY BEST FRIEND: Oh! This can't be right!

LITTLE GIRL: Wow. Velvet green leaves and flowers of gold! Look! Come look.

BOSSY BEST FRIEND: (*Approaches the plant*) Well, Little Girl. What a *beautiful* plant. Look at mine.

LITTLE GIRL: Oh! It's-um, it's—

BOSSY BEST FRIEND: Dead. It's *dead*. It's all your fault.

LITTLE GIRL: My fault?

BOSSY BEST FRIEND: (*Mocking her*) "Put it in the sun!"

LITTLE GIRL: Sun's good for them!

BOSSY BEST FRIEND: It's withered!

LITTLE GIRL: Did you water it?

BOSSY BEST FRIEND: What?

LITTLE GIRL: Plants need water!

BOSSY BEST FRIEND: Since when?

LITTLE GIRL: I told you!

BOSSY BEST FRIEND: You don't water yours.

LITTLE GIRL: I do.

(*BOSSY BEST FRIEND is shocked. LITTLE GIRL realizes she said the wrong thing.*)

BOSSY BEST FRIEND: You've been coming in *secret* to water your plant?

LITTLE GIRL: To make sure it lived.

BOSSY BEST FRIEND: And make sure mine died!

LITTLE GIRL: No!

BOSSY BEST FRIEND: You didn't water *my* plant.

LITTLE GIRL: You said never touch it! You said "DO NOT TOUCH!"

BOSSY BEST FRIEND: Give me your plant.

LITTLE GIRL: (*Shocked*) I couldn't!

BOSSY BEST FRIEND: If I had a gorgeous green plant, Little Girl, and yours was wilted and withered and dead, I'd give you my plant if you wanted it.

(*LITTLE GIRL says nothing.*)

BOSSY BEST FRIEND: Little Girl?

LITTLE GIRL: I wouldn't want that.

BOSSY BEST FRIEND: But I would do it—because I'm your *friend*. Just like you're mine. You *are* my friend. Aren't you?

LITTLE GIRL: Yes. I'm your friend.

BOSSY BEST FRIEND: So give me your plant!

(*LITTLE GIRL wrings her hands.*)

BOSSY BEST FRIEND: Little Girl—*please?*

LITTLE GIRL: The plant is precious.

BOSSY BEST FRIEND: The plant will be fine.

LITTLE GIRL: Will you water it?

BOSSY BEST FRIEND: Little Girl: I'm your friend! What's more important? Me or the plant?

(*LITTLE GIRL looks at the plant. BOSSY BEST FRIEND glares at her. LITTLE GIRL gives in.*)

LITTLE GIRL: When we move it, we have to be careful. OK?

BOSSY BEST FRIEND: Good, Little Girl! You did the right thing.

(*BOSSY BEST FRIEND pats LITTLE GIRL on the shoulder. Then smiles at the plant.*)

BOSSY BEST FRIEND: Now, tomato plant: this won't hurt a bit. We'll just move you to my pretty side of the garden. We'll do that right now. Together.

(*BOSSY BEST FRIEND looks at LITTLE GIRL. LITTLE GIRL helps, reluctantly. BOSSY BEST FRIEND points to LITTLE GIRL's plant. LITTLE GIRL carefully uproots it. BOSSY BEST FRIEND plucks up the dead plant from her own planter and pitches it over her shoulder, out of the garden—preferably offstage. It must be offstage by the start of Scene 2. Then she takes LITTLE GIRL's plant from her, and crudely replants it in her own planter.*)

LITTLE GIRL: Careful!

BOSSY BEST FRIEND: All done!

(*LITTLE GIRL hovers, worried, over the plant. BOSSY BEST FRIEND stands in front of it, moving her out of the way. She smiles at LITTLE GIRL.*)

BOSSY BEST FRIEND: Thank you for your beautiful gift.

LITTLE GIRL: Gift?

BOSSY BEST FRIEND: Of course. You gave it to me.

LITTLE GIRL: (*Confused*) But you made me—

BOSSY BEST FRIEND: (*Gives LITTLE GIRL her book*) Okay, Booknose. That's all for today. (*Sweetly*) Here's your book. Time to go read!

(*LITTLE GIRL takes the book, looks back at the plant. BOSSY BEST FRIEND moves her off.*)

BOSSY BEST FRIEND: Toodle-oo! See you tomorrow! Bye-bye!

(*LITTLE GIRL goes, looking back at the plant. BOSSY BEST FRIEND preens and admires the plant.*)

BOSSY BEST FRIEND: Mm-hm. Mm-hm. Mm-hm. Ooh, lovely plant! Now you're all *mine!*

(*BOSSY BEST FRIEND blows her plant a kiss, then exits.*)

Scene 2

(*The next day. LITTLE GIRL runs onstage with a watering can. She checks to make sure BOSSY BEST FRIEND isn't there, then rushes to the plant.*)

LITTLE GIRL: Oh, poor plant! You're thirsty!

(*LITTLE GIRL raises the watering can, about to water the plant. The sound of quick, rhythmic ticking. LITTLE GIRL freezes. BOSSY BEST FRIEND enters, carrying her bag.*)

BOSSY BEST FRIEND: You're early! It's four fifty-nine.

(*BOSSY BEST FRIEND puts her hand out for the watering can, clears her throat. LITTLE GIRL hands it over.*)

BOSSY BEST FRIEND: Thank you.

LITTLE GIRL: The plant—

BOSSY BEST FRIEND: The plant is fine.

LITTLE GIRL: It's unhappy!

BOSSY BEST FRIEND: I watered it.

LITTLE GIRL: When?

BOSSY BEST FRIEND: Last night.

LITTLE GIRL: Are you sure?

BOSSY BEST FRIEND: (*Points at her watch*) Oh my. Look at the time! Come on, Little Girl: your favorite game!

(*BOSSY BEST FRIEND claps twice. LITTLE GIRL steps into position for the start of Mother May I. She does not stop looking at the plant.*)

BOSSY BEST FRIEND: Ready? Good. Five helicopter twirls.

LITTLE GIRL: Mother may I?

BOSSY BEST FRIEND: Yes you may. (*LITTLE GIRL starts doing big twirls toward the plant.*) *This* way! Stop! Start over!

(*LITTLE GIRL stops. BOSSY BEST FRIEND glares, then claps twice.*)

BOSSY BEST FRIEND: Now. Three teeny-tiny baby steps.

LITTLE GIRL: Mother may I?

BOSSY BEST FRIEND: Yes you may.

(*LITTLE GIRL does the steps, bigger than usual, moving toward the plant.*)

BOSSY BEST FRIEND: *Booknose!*

(*BOSSY BEST FRIEND stands between LITTLE GIRL and the plant.*)

BOSSY BEST FRIEND: No more game. Barbie time.

(*BOSSY BEST FRIEND snaps her fingers once. She takes the Barbies from the bag and holds out the one with bad hair.*)

BOSSY BEST FRIEND: You're this one.

LITTLE GIRL: I know.

BOSSY BEST FRIEND: One—two—three!

(*As Barbies.*)

BOSSY BEST FRIEND: Dena!

LITTLE GIRL: Lena! (*Kiss-kiss-kiss*) How are you?

BOSSY BEST FRIEND: (*As an adjective*) Ladeda!

LITTLE GIRL: And your job?

BOSSY BEST FRIEND: Tip-top.

LITTLE GIRL: And your plant?

BOSSY BEST FRIEND: My *what?*

LITTLE GIRL: Your tomato plant!

(*BOSSY BEST FRIEND grabs LITTLE GIRL's Barbie.*)

BOSSY BEST FRIEND: (*As herself*) NO! That's not it! That is not how we play! Dumb tomato plant girl. Dumb like a plant!

(*Tears start down LITTLE GIRL's cheeks. She turns away to hide them.*)

BOSSY BEST FRIEND: Are you crying?

LITTLE GIRL: No.

BOSSY BEST FRIEND: (*Wipes a tear off LITTLE GIRL's cheek*) Yes you are. Only foreigners cry!

(*She hands LITTLE GIRL a hanky.*)

BOSSY BEST FRIEND: Here. Hurry up. Don't let anyone see!

(*LITTLE GIRL dries her tears. BOSSY BEST FRIEND grabs the hanky back.*)

BOSSY BEST FRIEND: And don't be a worry wart. My plant will be fine. Of course, it will miss me when I go away—

LITTLE GIRL: You're going away?

BOSSY BEST FRIEND: To my grandma's.

LITTLE GIRL: (*Wistful*) Oh.

BOSSY BEST FRIEND: (*Gloating*) Back-to-school shopping! It could take a week.

LITTLE GIRL: But the plant—

BOSSY BEST FRIEND: Will miss me. But it will be *fine.*

LITTLE GIRL: I'll take care of it.

BOSSY BEST FRIEND: No.

LITTLE GIRL: But you can't—

BOSSY BEST FRIEND: Little Girl: I can do what I like! I can water the plant or leave it be. I can pick the fruit, I can preen the vine, I can perfume the flowers—I can pluck off a leaf!

(*BOSSY BEST FRIEND plucks off a leaf, crumples it, and tosses it into the air.*)

BOSSY BEST FRIEND: It's my plant! It lives for me!

(*LITTLE GIRL gasps, in shock, and covers her mouth with her hands.*)

BOSSY BEST FRIEND: What climbed up *your* nostril?

(*LITTLE GIRL, mouth still covered, makes a noise of distress.*)

BOSSY BEST FRIEND: *Girl*—

(*Sound of quick, rhythmic ticking. BOSSY BEST FRIEND's MOTHER calls from offstage. BOSSY BEST FRIEND jumps and freezes.*)

BOSSY BEST FRIEND'S MOTHER: (*Recorded; snooty, agitated*) *Dar*—ling!

LITTLE GIRL: Your mother.

BOSSY BEST FRIEND: Shut up! (*To MOTHER, nervous*) Yes ma'am!

BOSSY BEST FRIEND'S MOTHER: (*Off*) Grandma's waiting!

BOSSY BEST FRIEND: (*Gathers her things*) Yes ma'am! (*To LITTLE GIRL*) I'll be back.

BOSSY BEST FRIEND'S MOTHER: (*Off*) *Darling!*

BOSSY BEST FRIEND: (*To MOTHER*) Yes ma'am! (*To LITTLE GIRL*) And don't you forget—

BOSSY BEST FRIEND'S MOTHER: (*Off*) You're *late!*

BOSSY BEST FRIEND: If you *touch* my new plant—

BOSSY BEST FRIEND'S MOTHER: (*Off*) If you're late for Grandma—

BOSSY BEST FRIEND: I'll rip up your book and feed it to my poodle!

BOSSY BEST FRIEND'S MOTHER: (*Off*) I'll melt down those Barbies and serve them for dinner.

BOSSY BEST FRIEND & MOTHER: We wouldn't want *that* to happen.

BOSSY BEST FRIEND: (*To MOTHER*) I'm coming!

BOSSY BEST FRIEND'S MOTHER: (*Off*) Hurry up!

BOSSY BEST FRIEND: (*To LITTLE GIRL*) Be good!

BOSSY BEST FRIEND & MOTHER: Now do as I say, dearie. Or else!

(*BOSSY BEST FRIEND runs off. LITTLE GIRL watches her go, then explodes.*)

LITTLE GIRL: *Oooh* wicked badness meanmeanmean tomato-hating leaf-killing evil rudeness jerk!

(*LITTLE GIRL claps her hand over her mouth. She can't believe what she just said. Then she kneels near the tomato plant.*)

LITTLE GIRL: Oh plant—I won't let you suffer. I'll replant you on my good side of the garden.

(*LITTLE GIRL closes her eyes.*)

LITTLE GIRL: Okay.

(*LITTLE GIRL puts her hands around the stem.*)

LITTLE GIRL: (*To the plant*) Ready? (*To herself*) Ready. One— two— three.

(*LITTLE GIRL begins to pull up the plant. But the root system has grown. It is yards and yards long. Endless.*)

LITTLE GIRL: All these *roots*!

(*LITTLE GIRL keeps pulling up roots. A low, vibrating sound—the Earthsoil Hum— fills the garden. LITTLE GIRL looks around, a bit scared.*)

LITTLE GIRL: What's that noise?

(*The roots start coming more slowly. Something heavy is attached to the roots, moving upward with them, through the soil.*)

LITTLE GIRL: What's *that*?

(*LITTLE GIRL pulls harder. The ends of the roots emerge, clutched in two small hands. Arms and shoulders follow—*)

LITTLE GIRL: Ohh—

(*Then a face: the face of TOMATO PLANT GIRL. She is messy, dirt-covered. Her eyes are closed. She is totally new to her body.*)

LITTLE GIRL: *WHOA!*

(Stunned, LITTLE GIRL lets go of the roots, reeling backward. TOMATO PLANT GIRL opens her eyes, lets go of the roots, and opens her mouth; she spits out dirt and a burst of sound. [The words should not sound like words.])

TOMATO PLANT GIRL: Ooohtomatomeanmeanmeansufferleafplantready onetworoot!

(TOMATO PLANT GIRL and LITTLE GIRL are both startled by the sound. LITTLE GIRL gasps. TOMATO PLANT GIRL slowly moves her head till she sees LITTLE GIRL. TOMATO PLANT GIRL looks at her and bursts into laughter. After some hesitation, LITTLE GIRL, still nervous, starts laughing too. TOMATO PLANT GIRL laughs so hard that she cries. Then she actually starts to cry. She looks at the strange world around her and big red tears roll down her cheeks.)

LITTLE GIRL: Don't cry. Only foreigners cry! Stop! Stop! Don't let anyone see!

(TOMATO PLANT GIRL doesn't stop. Anxious, LITTLE GIRL hesitates, then gathers resolve. LITTLE GIRL wipes a tear from TOMATO PLANT GIRL's cheek. She steps back and looks at the tear.)

LITTLE GIRL: Red!

(LITTLE GIRL looks at TOMATO PLANT GIRL. Very cautiously, she tastes the tear.)

LITTLE GIRL: *(With wonder)* Tomato.

(TOMATO PLANT GIRL picks up a handful of dirt, then hums and lets it fall through her fingers. She is calling the Earthsoil Hum. The Earthsoil Hum returns. TOMATO PLANT GIRL welcomes the hum with a gesture, closes her eyes and hums with it.)

LITTLE GIRL: What is it? What's that sound?

(TOMATO PLANT GIRL keeps humming, eyes closed. LITTLE GIRL covers her ears, steps away from TOMATO PLANT GIRL.)

LITTLE GIRL: I'm sure you're very nice and from a very nice place, and I'd like to welcome you and show you around, but I can't. *(TOMATO PLANT GIRL keeps humming, eyes closed.)* So—I'm sure you have to go, and when I get back, you'll be gone. And I'll replant the plant, and everything will be fine.

(The Earthsoil Hum fades. TOMATO PLANT GIRL opens her eyes. Looks at LITTLE GIRL.)

LITTLE GIRL: I have to go now. It's dinner time. Mom-Dad-table-TV! Nice to meet you. Have a good trip! Goodbye!

(LITTLE GIRL rushes off. TOMATO PLANT GIRL emerges fully from the earth. She moves and makes sounds as she discovers her new body. She tastes some of the garden dirt: it's too dry. As she spits it out, she discovers her tongue. She realizes she is thirsty. TOMATO PLANT GIRL looks at the sky. Then, with purposeful gestures, she calls on the rain [It does not come.] TOMATO PLANT GIRL continues this movement until LITTLE GIRL approaches.)

Scene 3

(*The same night. About an hour later. The uprooted tomato plant from Scene 2 and its long roots are in a pile on the ground. LITTLE GIRL approaches the garden. She carries a watering can and flowerpot. She's nervous.*)

LITTLE GIRL: (*Continuous, as she enters*) Is she here is she here is she here is she here is she here is she here?

(*At the sound of the voice, TOMATO PLANT GIRL hides. LITTLE GIRL looks, quickly, for TOMATO PLANT GIRL. Doesn't see her.*)

LITTLE GIRL: Ha! She's not here!

(*LITTLE GIRL approaches the dead plant.*)

LITTLE GIRL: She's not here and now I can help my poor plant! Look, plant— look what I've got! It's Mom's best topsoil! With minerals! Yum!

(*LITTLE GIRL attempts to replant the dead plant. She reaches into the flowerpot for topsoil, sprinkling it on the roots. TOMATO PLANT GIRL emerges from hiding and begins to eat topsoil from the pot, unseen by LITTLE GIRL.*)

LITTLE GIRL: See? It'll put you in tip-top shape. My best friend will come back, and she'll be so happy—

(*LITTLE GIRL reaches back into the flowerpot and accidentally touches TOMATO PLANT GIRL's hand. She shrieks. She doesn't look at TOMATO PLANT GIRL.*)

LITTLE GIRL: Go away. You're not here!

(*TOMATO PLANT GIRL eats another handful of dirt, looks intently at LITTLE GIRL. Slowly, LITTLE GIRL turns to look at TOMATO PLANT GIRL.*)

LITTLE GIRL: Hey! Hey! *No!* We don't eat *dirt!*

TOMATO PLANT GIRL: Dirrrrrrtt.

(*TOMATO PLANT GIRL eats noisily and happily. LITTLE GIRL grabs the flowerpot.*)

LITTLE GIRL: Don't do that! Dumb tomato plant girl!

(*LITTLE GIRL stops, hearing herself.*)

LITTLE GIRL: (*To herself*) Tomato Plant Girl.

(*TOMATO PLANT GIRL looks at LITTLE GIRL, confused. LITTLE GIRL picks up the flowerpot, starts to pace.*)

LITTLE GIRL: I need to line things up in my brain.

(*TOMATO PLANT GIRL follows her, tugs on the flowerpot.*)

TOMATO PLANT GIRL: *Mm.*

LITTLE GIRL: What?

TOMATO PLANT GIRL: *Mmm.* Dirrt.

LITTLE GIRL: (*Showing her it's empty*) No. No more. You ate it!

(*TOMATO PLANT GIRL moans.*)

LITTLE GIRL: Sorry.

TOMATO PLANT GIRL: "Sorry."

LITTLE GIRL: (*Pointing to herself*) "I'm sorry."

(*TOMATO PLANT GIRL points at LITTLE GIRL, as if "Sorry" is her name.*)

TOMATO PLANT GIRL: Sorry.

LITTLE GIRL: No. Sorry. It means—I should have done something, but I didn't. Or I shouldn't have, but I did.

(*TOMATO PLANT GIRL looks puzzled.*)

LITTLE GIRL: It's important. (*Pointing to herself again*) "I'm sorry." It's *important. Big!*

(*LITTLE GIRL does a "big" movement. TOMATO PLANT GIRL mirrors it, laughs.*)

TOMATO PLANT GIRL: BIG! (*TOMATO PLANT GIRL points at LITTLE GIRL, makes the "big" movement.*) BIG SORR-RRY!

LITTLE GIRL: *Shhh!*

TOMATO PLANT GIRL: "SHHH!"

LITTLE GIRL: *Shhh.*

(*In "SHHH!" TOMATO PLANT GIRL hears the sound of water. She begins to do her rain-calling movement, now directed at LITTLE GIRL.*)

TOMATO PLANT GIRL: Shhhhhh.

LITTLE GIRL: What? What—you want a shower? Not at my house—*my* shower's clean! My parents work hard and our house is neat. You eat dirt and you dress upside-down!

(*TOMATO PLANT GIRL continues the motion, but opens her mouth and tilts her face to the sky.*)

LITTLE GIRL: What? What? Oh! (*Pointing to her mouth*) Drink!

TOMATO PLANT GIRL: Drrrink!

LITTLE GIRL: Drink.

(*LITTLE GIRL holds up the watering can and pours water into TOMATO PLANT GIRL's mouth.*)

LITTLE GIRL: You were thirsty.

(*LITTLE GIRL suddenly remembers the [dead] plant.*)

LITTLE GIRL: *Oh!* Thirsty!

(*LITTLE GIRL rushes to the plant, pours water on it.*)

LITTLE GIRL: Here, poor plant—

(*TOMATO PLANT GIRL follows, tugs on the watering can, points to herself.*)

TOMATO PLANT GIRL: Drink.

LITTLE GIRL: No! It's for the plant!

(*LITTLE GIRL pours the rest of the water on the plant. TOMATO PLANT GIRL moans and shakes her head, confused.*)

LITTLE GIRL: Lots of things went backwards and I need to fix them up.

(*LITTLE GIRL kneels next to the plant.*)

LITTLE GIRL: I need to replant these roots—all these roots—

(*LITTLE GIRL pushes the rest of the roots underground, covering them with soil. TOMATO PLANT GIRL grabs a root and looks at LITTLE GIRL.*)

TOMATO PLANT GIRL: *Root.*

LITTLE GIRL: (*Puts the root back*) Root. There. In place. Ready, plant? One, two, three!

(*LITTLE GIRL tries to stand the plant up. The plant flops over. LITTLE GIRL tries again.*)

LITTLE GIRL: (*To the plant*) Plant! PLANT! Come on. You're *not dead*. You're not dead.

(*TOMATO PLANT GIRL points to the plant. She is matter-of-fact.*)

TOMATO PLANT GIRL: Dead.

LITTLE GIRL: (*Knowing it's true*) Not dead.

TOMATO PLANT GIRL: (*As before*) Dead.

(*TOMATO PLANT GIRL holds a handful of dirt out to LITTLE GIRL. LITTLE GIRL looks at TOMATO PLANT GIRL. Then at the plant.*)

LITTLE GIRL: (*Slowly accepting it*) Dead.

(*LITTLE GIRL takes the dirt. She helps TOMATO PLANT GIRL bury the plant. They are silent for a moment. The Earthsoil Hum returns. TOMATO PLANT GIRL hears it. As before, she gestures to acknowledge its presence, then hums with it. LITTLE GIRL covers her ears.*)

LITTLE GIRL: That hum—

TOMATO PLANT GIRL: Humm.

(*LITTLE GIRL cautiously uncovers her ears for a moment, then covers them.*)

LITTLE GIRL: It's from down in the earth!

TOMATO PLANT GIRL: Errth.

LITTLE GIRL: Earth . . . hum.

(The Earthsoil Hum fades. LITTLE GIRL slowly uncovers her ears. She looks at the buried plant.)

LITTLE GIRL: My grandma said, when plants die, they go back to the earth and feed other plants. So they might go away, but they're not really gone.

(LITTLE GIRL looks at TOMATO PLANT GIRL. TOMATO PLANT GIRL looks at LITTLE GIRL.)

TOMATO PLANT GIRL: *(Agreeing)* Errth.

(LITTLE GIRL smiles. Then TOMATO PLANT GIRL motions to the watering can and flowerpot.)

TOMATO PLANT GIRL: Dirrrt . . . drrink.

LITTLE GIRL: You eat a lot!

TOMATO PLANT GIRL: *(A hungry noise)* Mmm.

LITTLE GIRL: You need to learn some things.

(TOMATO PLANT GIRL holds the flowerpot and watering can out to LITTLE GIRL.)

TOMATO PLANT GIRL: Dirt drink.

LITTLE GIRL: If you're going to stay here —

TOMATO PLANT GIRL: DIRT! DRINK!

LITTLE GIRL: Okay!

(LITTLE GIRL takes the flowerpot and watering can.)

LITTLE GIRL: But you have to learn how to play.

TOMATO PLANT GIRL: *(Confused)* Mmm?

LITTLE GIRL: Mother May I. I'll teach you tomorrow. Here. At tomato plant time! Five-fifteen.

(LITTLE GIRL goes.)

TOMATO PLANT GIRL: Sorry? *(Calling LITTLE GIRL's "name")* Sorrrry! Dirt . . . drink.

(TOMATO PLANT GIRL turns back to the garden. She stands and does her rain-calling gesture.)

Scene 4

(The next day. TOMATO PLANT GIRL sits, holding her belly. She moans. LITTLE GIRL enters with the flowerpot and watering can.)

LITTLE GIRL: Tomato Plant Girl? It's time for a game!

(TOMATO PLANT GIRL rushes to the flowerpot and watering can.)

LITTLE GIRL: Hey! Wait.

(*LITTLE GIRL holds the flowerpot and watering can in the air so TOMATO PLANT GIRL cannot reach them.*)

LITTLE GIRL: First you learn to play. Then: dirt and drink. Okay. Mother may I!

(*LITTLE GIRL claps twice.*)

LITTLE GIRL: Ready? Good. Three queenly curtsies! Watch. (*LITTLE GIRL begins to demonstrate.*) One — two —

(*TOMATO PLANT GIRL rushes to the flowerpot, grabs it, eats a handful of dirt.*)

LITTLE GIRL: No no wait! You have to play right!

(*LITTLE GIRL grabs the flowerpot back. TOMATO PLANT GIRL makes a frustrated noise.*)

LITTLE GIRL: You didn't say "Mother may I!" Start over. Say "Mother may I!"

TOMATO PLANT GIRL: Mmm — mthrrrr —

(*TOMATO PLANT GIRL spits out the word, laughs at the sound. LITTLE GIRL creates a hand gesture to represent the words.*)

LITTLE GIRL: Here. "*Mother may I!*"

(*LITTLE GIRL does the gesture. TOMATO PLANT GIRL repeats it.*)

LITTLE GIRL: Good! Now —

(*TOMATO PLANT GIRL, repeating the "Mother may I" gesture, moves toward the dirt and drink, with no curtsies.*)

TOMATO PLANT GIRL: Mthrr mthrr mthrr —

LITTLE GIRL: No! Curtsy curtsy curtsy!

(*TOMATO PLANT GIRL stops and does one slow curtsy to LITTLE GIRL.*)

TOMATO PLANT GIRL: Crrrtze.

LITTLE GIRL: (*Giving in*) You'll do better next time.

(*LITTLE GIRL gives TOMATO PLANT GIRL a handful of dirt. TOMATO PLANT GIRL eats avidly. LITTLE GIRL pours water into TOMATO PLANT GIRL's mouth. TOMATO PLANT GIRL, after drinking her fill, holds onto a big mouthful of water, so she can share a trick with LITTLE GIRL.*)

LITTLE GIRL: Next is ballerina twirl. It's difficult.

(*LITTLE GIRL gets into position for the twirl.*)

LITTLE GIRL: You start like this. Watch carefully.

(*Gleefully, TOMATO PLANT GIRL spits a spray of water in the air. It sprinkles down on her and on LITTLE GIRL.*)

LITTLE GIRL: Hey!

TOMATO PLANT GIRL: Mmmm. Currt-ze!

(*TOMATO PLANT GIRL does her own big curtsy of joy.*)

LITTLE GIRL: That's not the *game!*

(*On "game," LITTLE GIRL makes an emphatic gesture. TOMATO PLANT GIRL repeats the gesture.*)

TOMATO PLANT GIRL: (*Liking the sound*) Gaaame.

LITTLE GIRL: "Game." It has rules. It's very specific.

(*TOMATO PLANT GIRL begins to repeat the "game" gesture, transforming it each time, creating her own game, inviting LITTLE GIRL to join her.*)

TOMATO PLANT GIRL: (*Continuous*) Gamegamegame —

LITTLE GIRL: One person tells the other: do something. The other asks permission: "Mother may I." Then — What are you doing?

TOMATO PLANT GIRL: (*Shows LITTLE GIRL the gesture*) *Gaaaame.*

(*Warily, LITTLE GIRL watches TOMATO PLANT GIRL and mirrors her gesture. Note: While it should appear to be improvised, the following action is "very specific." It is important that the audience see LITTLE GIRL and TOMATO PLANT GIRL mirroring each other, paying attention to each other's movements, and transforming gestures together.*)

TOMATO PLANT GIRL, LITTLE GIRL: (*Together*) *Gaaame.*

LITTLE GIRL: Right. A game has rules.

(*TOMATO PLANT GIRL moves into a new gesture, an exaggeration of LITTLE GIRL's gesture from the line, "A game has rules."*)

TOMATO PLANT GIRL: Gaame . . . ruulz!

(*LITTLE GIRL is surprised to see herself in TOMATO PLANT GIRL's gesture. She laughs, then transforms the gesture into a new one.*)

LITTLE GIRL: Gameruulz!

(*Facing each other, they do LITTLE GIRL's gesture together.*)

LITTLE GIRL, TOMATO PLANT GIRL: Gameruulz! (*They transform LITTLE GIRL's gesture to create a new gesture together.*) Gaameruulz!

LITTLE GIRL: We made a new game!

(*TOMATO PLANT GIRL motions for LITTLE GIRL to stay put. Then she picks up the flowerpot and watering can and moves to where LITTLE GIRL stood during the Mother May I game. TOMATO PLANT GIRL begins to reward LITTLE GIRL. She holds out a handful of dirt.*)

TOMATO PLANT GIRL: Dirrrt!

(LITTLE GIRL politely refuses. TOMATO PLANT GIRL eats the dirt, then holds up the watering can.)

TOMATO PLANT GIRL: Drrink.

(Cautiously, LITTLE GIRL opens her mouth. TOMATO PLANT GIRL pours water in LITTLE GIRL's mouth. LITTLE GIRL gets a mouthful of water. She looks impishly at TOMATO PLANT GIRL. She spits the water up in the air—just for a second. LITTLE GIRL takes the watering can and starts to give TOMATO PLANT GIRL a drink. TOMATO PLANT GIRL leads LITTLE GIRL to LITTLE GIRL's side of the garden, where her plant once grew, and stands with her arms outstretched. LITTLE GIRL "waters" TOMATO PLANT GIRL. TOMATO PLANT GIRL starts to grow. The Earthsoil Hum returns. Again, TOMATO PLANT GIRL acknowledges it with a gesture.)

LITTLE GIRL: The Earth hum!

(As before, LITTLE GIRL covers her ears. TOMATO PLANT GIRL, still turning, begins to grow bigger, redder, greener.)

LITTLE GIRL: Tomato Plant Girl—you're growing!

(LITTLE GIRL removes her hands from her ears and watches the process, amazed.)

LITTLE GIRL: Wow!

(TOMATO PLANT GIRL makes one full turn, then yawns and settles to the ground, asleep. LITTLE GIRL sits watching her, intrigued. The sound of quick, rhythmic ticking. LITTLE GIRL looks around, nervous. A pink plastic postcard drops from the sky. LITTLE GIRL jumps, then catches the postcard and silently reads.)

VOICE OF BOSSY BEST FRIEND: *(Off)* Dear Booknose—Hope you're not too lonely. Don't worry, dear; I miss you too. I'll be back in two days, three hours, and forty-five minutes. In the meantime, be good and keep your hands off my plant!

(LITTLE GIRL looks at TOMATO PLANT GIRL, and at BOSSY BEST FRIEND's side of the garden.)

LITTLE GIRL: *(Panicked)* "Keep your hands off my plant—" Oh no!

(LITTLE GIRL paces, remembering.)

LITTLE GIRL: I should have, but I didn't . . . I shouldn't have, but I did . . . "Do as I say—or else!" Oh no!

(LITTLE GIRL takes a deep breath. Thinks for a moment. Looks at TOMATO PLANT GIRL. Makes a decision. Then picks up the postcard, flowerpot, and watering can. She turns back to the sleeping TOMATO PLANT GIRL.)

LITTLE GIRL: Don't go away! I'll be back! I'll be back.

(LITTLE GIRL exits, quickly.)

Scene 5

(The next day. TOMATO PLANT GIRL wakes, stretches slowly, then stands with her eyes closed, her arms reaching up and her face tilted into the sun. She touches her cheeks lightly with her fingertips, making light kissing sounds. She plays with new sounds to describe the feel of the sun.)

TOMATO PLANT GIRL: Firrre — kissss!

(LITTLE GIRL rushes in, carrying the flowerpot, the watering can, and her book, Tales of Tomatoes.)

LITTLE GIRL: Tomato Plant Girl — *(Seeing TOMATO PLANT GIRL in the sun)* Hey! Hey careful!

(LITTLE GIRL stands in front of TOMATO PLANT GIRL, blocking the sun. TOMATO PLANT GIRL tries to move around her. LITTLE GIRL doesn't let her.)

LITTLE GIRL: The ultraviolent rays! Sunburn is *wrong.*

TOMATO PLANT GIRL: *(Reaches for the flowerpot and watering can)* Drink. Dirt!

LITTLE GIRL: Okay!

(LITTLE GIRL gives TOMATO PLANT GIRL dirt and water. TOMATO PLANT GIRL eats and drinks quickly, avidly.)

LITTLE GIRL: Tomato Plant Girl: this is important!

TOMATO PLANT GIRL: *(Satisfied)* Ahhh.

(TOMATO PLANT GIRL tilts her head back to the sun.)

TOMATO PLANT GIRL: *(To herself)* Firrre —

LITTLE GIRL: Listen! You're going to be my best friend!

TOMATO PLANT GIRL: *(To herself)* kisss . . .

LITTLE GIRL: You're going to come home and live with me! We'll go to school and play games every day — and no one will know you're a *(Lowers her voice)* — *foreigner.* See?

(TOMATO PLANT GIRL looks down at herself, looks back at LITTLE GIRL.)

LITTLE GIRL: Come on! I'll show you my house! Let's go!

TOMATO PLANT GIRL: *(Not moving)* Root. I.

LITTLE GIRL: You can wash, and dress, and eat normal food — and borrow my books! I'll teach you to read!

(LITTLE GIRL holds out the book.)

LITTLE GIRL: I'll teach you to be like a real normal girl so you can be my best friend and be happy!

TOMATO PLANT GIRL: *(Looks at LITTLE GIRL, shakes her head)* Grow.

LITTLE GIRL: (*Tries not to cry*) My best friend's coming back, and she's going to be angry! If you're not my best friend, I'll be all alone!

(*TOMATO PLANT GIRL looks at LITTLE GIRL, picks up a handful of dirt, shows it to her.*)

TOMATO PLANT GIRL: *Grow I.*

LITTLE GIRL: (*Hurt*) Fine then! You grow!

(*Hurt, LITTLE GIRL turns away from TOMATO PLANT GIRL. She opens her book, tries to read. TOMATO PLANT GIRL knows something is wrong.*)

TOMATO PLANT GIRL: Sorry . . .

LITTLE GIRL: What?

TOMATO PLANT GIRL: Sor-ry!

(*TOMATO PLANT GIRL tugs on the book.*)

TOMATO PLANT GIRL: Mmm.

LITTLE GIRL: (*Still hurt*) It's just a book.

TOMATO PLANT GIRL: (*Points at the cover*) Red.

(*She makes the "BIG" gesture.*)

TOMATO PLANT GIRL: TOMATO!

(*LITTLE GIRL smiles in spite of herself.*)

TOMATO PLANT GIRL: TO-MA-TO!

(*TOMATO PLANT GIRL sweeps the book out of LITTLE GIRL's hands, dances with it.*)

TOMATO PLANT GIRL: TOMATO!

LITTLE GIRL: HEY! That's my book!

(*LITTLE GIRL takes the book back.*)

LITTLE GIRL: I'm glad you like it—but you can say "please."

TOMATO PLANT GIRL: Plse.

LITTLE GIRL: It means, "If it pleases you."

(*LITTLE GIRL holds out the book.*)

LITTLE GIRL: Say you want this book. But the book is mine; it's precious to me. So I need you to ask and say "please."

(*TOMATO PLANT GIRL points at the book, naming it "Please."*)

TOMATO PLANT GIRL: Please!

LITTLE GIRL: No . . .

(*LITTLE GIRL decides to demonstrate.*)

LITTLE GIRL: Here. Hold it. Just for a second.

(*Carefully, LITTLE GIRL hands TOMATO PLANT GIRL the book. TOMATO PLANT GIRL holds the book carefully, watching LITTLE GIRL. LITTLE GIRL points at the book.*)

LITTLE GIRL: Book.

(*LITTLE GIRL pretends to admire the book.*)

LITTLE GIRL: Mmm!

(*LITTLE GIRL gestures toward the book, asking permission.*)

LITTLE GIRL: Please?

(*TOMATO PLANT GIRL hands LITTLE GIRL the book.*)

LITTLE GIRL: Yes! That's right!

(*Excited, TOMATO PLANT GIRL does a sped-up, auto-version of the previous actions.*)

TOMATO PLANT GIRL: Book—Mmm! *Please?*

(*Skeptical, LITTLE GIRL holds the book out to TOMATO PLANT GIRL. TOMATO PLANT GIRL grabs onto it.*)

TOMATO PLANT GIRL: Yezatsright!

LITTLE GIRL: (*Takes the book back*) If you say "please" but you don't really mean it, then it's just like you're grabbing the book. But if you say "please" and you really *do* mean it, then I have a choice. I can give you the book.

(*TOMATO PLANT GIRL looks at LITTLE GIRL. Motions to the book.*)

TOMATO PLANT GIRL: Please?

LITTLE GIRL: Yes!

(*LITTLE GIRL hands TOMATO PLANT GIRL the book.*)

LITTLE GIRL: Thank you for asking!

(*TOMATO PLANT GIRL gently touches the page, then lifts and turns it. She sees something.*)

TOMATO PLANT GIRL: Ahh—firre!

(*TOMATO PLANT GIRL buries her head in the book. LITTLE GIRL reaches toward the book.*

LITTLE GIRL: Fire? Let me see!

(*TOMATO PLANT GIRL looks at LITTLE GIRL.*)

LITTLE GIRL: Please?

(*TOMATO PLANT GIRL shows LITTLE GIRL the picture.*)

LITTLE GIRL: Oh! That's the sun!

(*LITTLE GIRL points at the sky.*)

LITTLE GIRL: Remember, I told you—it's dangerous!

TOMATO PLANT GIRL: (*Points at the sky*) Firrrekisss!

(*TOMATO PLANT GIRL tilts her face to the sky. Then she remembers the book and carefully hands it back to LITTLE GIRL before stretching into the sun, as before.*)

TOMATO PLANT GIRL: *Mmm.*

(*Intrigued but still concerned, LITTLE GIRL moves between TOMATO PLANT GIRL and the sun.*)

LITTLE GIRL: The sun is *ultraviolent.*

TOMATO PLANT GIRL: (*Calling LITTLE GIRL by her name*) Sorry.

(*TOMATO PLANT GIRL moves around LITTLE GIRL, back into the sun. Then she has an idea. She turns back to LITTLE GIRL. She points to the spot next to her.*)

TOMATO PLANT GIRL: Root you. Please.

(*LITTLE GIRL, wary, moves toward TOMATO PLANT GIRL. TOMATO PLANT GIRL shares her "Firekiss" gestures with LITTLE GIRL: she stretches into the sun, then does the sun-kissing gesture and sound.*)

TOMATO PLANT GIRL: *Fiire kiss.*

LITTLE GIRL: (*Watching TOMATO PLANT GIRL*) Firekiss.

(*Slowly, LITTLE GIRL tilts her head into the sun.*)

LITTLE GIRL: Mmm.

(*LITTLE GIRL does the sun-kissing gesture and sound.*)

TOMATO PLANT GIRL: Mmm!

LITTLE GIRL: Firekiss!

(*LITTLE GIRL takes off her hat. They stand there for a moment, side by side. They speak separately, but at the same time.*)

LITTLE GIRL, TOMATO PLANT GIRL: Fiirre . . . kisss!

(*Sound of quick, rhythmic ticking. LITTLE GIRL jumps. BOSSY BEST FRIEND calls from offstage.*)

BOSSY BEST FRIEND: (*Offstage*) Hello-o! I'm back! Who missed me?

LITTLE GIRL: Oh no!

(*LITTLE GIRL looks around, panicked. TOMATO PLANT GIRL thinks it's a game, mirrors her.*)

TOMATO PLANT GIRL: Oh no!

LITTLE GIRL: Tomato Plant Girl! Over here!

(*LITTLE GIRL crouches down. TOMATO PLANT GIRL crouches down too. LITTLE GIRL hands the book to TOMATO PLANT GIRL, then stands in front of her, attempting to block her from view. BOSSY BEST FRIEND sails in like a queen. She wears fancy new clothes and carries her bag. She makes a big show of closing her eyes and breathing in the air of the garden.)*

BOSSY BEST FRIEND: Ahh. Lovely to be back.

(BOSSY BEST FRIEND opens her eyes. LITTLE GIRL waves with forced enthusiasm, still trying to hide TOMATO PLANT GIRL.)

LITTLE GIRL: Hello. Hi!

BOSSY BEST FRIEND: I'm early. I know. I was worried, poor dear. You've been here all alone —

(BOSSY BEST FRIEND sees her plant is gone.)

BOSSY BEST FRIEND: Where's my plant? Did you let it die?

LITTLE GIRL: You said not to touch it!

BOSSY BEST FRIEND: You should have known better!

(TOMATO PLANT GIRL, still hidden, points at a picture in the book.)

TOMATO PLANT GIRL: RED!

(BOSSY BEST FRIEND hears the sound; LITTLE GIRL tries to distract her and block TOMATO PLANT GIRL.)

LITTLE GIRL: (*Loudly*) Yes! You're right! I'm very sorry!

(BOSSY BEST FRIEND moves LITTLE GIRL aside. Shocked, she stares at TOMATO PLANT GIRL.)

BOSSY BEST FRIEND: Who's that thing.

LITTLE GIRL: She's new.

BOSSY BEST FRIEND: She's *repulsive*.

LITTLE GIRL: She's nice.

BOSSY BEST FRIEND: She's got that dumb book.

(TOMATO PLANT GIRL stares, fascinated, at BOSSY BEST FRIEND. LITTLE GIRL tries to take the book from TOMATO PLANT GIRL, who holds on.)

LITTLE GIRL: Tomato Plant Girl —

BOSSY BEST FRIEND: "Tomato Plant Girl"?

LITTLE GIRL: —please give me the book!

(TOMATO PLANT GIRL lets LITTLE GIRL have the book. Still watching TOMATO PLANT GIRL, BOSSY BEST FRIEND sweeps the book away from LITTLE GIRL.)

BOSSY BEST FRIEND: Thank you.

(BOSSY BEST FRIEND puts the book in her bag. LITTLE GIRL watches, upset, but says nothing. BOSSY BEST FRIEND clears her throat, suddenly very polite.)

BOSSY BEST FRIEND: Excuse me, you grimy strange girl. You're in my garden. I'd like to know who you are.

(*BOSSY BEST FRIEND summons TOMATO PLANT GIRL with a wave. TOMATO PLANT GIRL moves toward her, intrigued, imitating the wave.*)

LITTLE GIRL: There's nothing wrong with her. She's new.

(*BOSSY BEST FRIEND walks slowly around TOMATO PLANT GIRL, inspecting her at a slight distance.*)

BOSSY BEST FRIEND: Mmm-hmm — mmm-hmm — mmm-hmm.

(*TOMATO PLANT GIRL notices the bow on BOSSY BEST FRIEND's dress. She becomes entranced. She tugs at and unties it, makes a sound of delight. BOSSY BEST FRIEND gasps, whirls around. TOMATO PLANT GIRL looks at her, innocent. LITTLE GIRL starts to laugh. BOSSY BEST FRIEND turns back to LITTLE GIRL, furious.*)

BOSSY BEST FRIEND: *Booknose*— (*LITTLE GIRL stands at attention.*) Come here.

(*BOSSY BEST FRIEND motions for LITTLE GIRL to stand behind her and tie the bow. She does, but sneaks a look at TOMATO PLANT GIRL. TOMATO PLANT GIRL stands up close, facing BOSSY BEST FRIEND, and stares at her.*)

BOSSY BEST FRIEND: You're *dirty*.

TOMATO PLANT GIRL: (*Gleeful*) DIRRT!

(*BOSSY BEST FRIEND stamps her foot, turns to LITTLE GIRL, points at her watch.*)

BOSSY BEST FRIEND: It's five-o-five. Barbie time. Now.

(*BOSSY BEST FRIEND snaps her fingers once, then points for LITTLE GIRL to set up the game. She does. BOSSY BEST FRIEND holds out LITTLE GIRL's Barbie. TOMATO PLANT GIRL stands between them and watches, fascinated.*)

BOSSY BEST FRIEND: You're this one.

LITTLE GIRL: I know.

BOSSY BEST FRIEND: One—two— (*To TOMATO PLANT GIRL*) Move away, please!

TOMATO PLANT GIRL: (*Recognizing the word*) Please!

LITTLE GIRL: (*To BOSSY BEST FRIEND*) She can watch.

BOSSY BEST FRIEND: (*Glaring*) One. Two. Three.

(*LITTLE GIRL is quiet. During the next lines, TOMATO PLANT GIRL hovers over BOSSY BEST FRIEND's shoulder, moving her head with the rhythm of the words. LITTLE GIRL plays with one eye on TOMATO PLANT GIRL.*)

BOSSY BEST FRIEND: Dena!

LITTLE GIRL: Lena! (*Three loud, fakey kisses*) How are you?

BOSSY BEST FRIEND: Terrific.

LITTLE GIRL: And your job?

BOSSY BEST FRIEND: Perfecto.

LITTLE GIRL: And your boyfriends?

BOSSY BEST FRIEND: Too fine.

LITTLE GIRL: You look—

TOMATO PLANT GIRL: HA!

(TOMATO PLANT GIRL plucks the Barbie from BOSSY BEST FRIEND's hand. She shakes the Barbie around until its hair is big and messy. Then she puts the Barbie's feet in her mouth. BOSSY BEST FRIEND grabs the Barbie and points it at TOMATO PLANT GIRL.)

BOSSY BEST FRIEND: *You stop that and say sorry!*

TOMATO PLANT GIRL: (*To LITTLE GIRL*) Sorry?

LITTLE GIRL: Never mind. It's okay. (*LITTLE GIRL starts to show TOMATO PLANT GIRL how to hold Barbie.*) Here. Watch.

(*BOSSY BEST FRIEND takes LITTLE GIRL's Barbie from her hand and moves her aside.*)

BOSSY BEST FRIEND: Excuse me. Thank you. (*BOSSY BEST FRIEND stands next to TOMATO PLANT GIRL and smiles, holding up LITTLE GIRL's Barbie.*) *This* is how we play with Barbie. Like this. Feet. Head. (*Smoothing the hair*) Hair. In place. Then: arrange Barbie.

(*BOSSY BEST FRIEND puts the Barbie's arms in a proper position. She hands it to TOMATO PLANT GIRL. LITTLE GIRL watches. TOMATO PLANT GIRL holds the Barbie right side up, pats her hair, then starts to move her into an odd position.*)

LITTLE GIRL: (*Correcting her*) No, like this—

(*BOSSY BEST FRIEND glares at LITTLE GIRL.*)

BOSSY BEST FRIEND: (*To TOMATO PLANT GIRL*) You're such a fast learner. That's lovely.

(*BOSSY BEST FRIEND takes the Barbie and hands it back to TOMATO PLANT GIRL. LITTLE GIRL watches, frustrated.*)

BOSSY BEST FRIEND: Now. One-two-three. (*As her own Barbie*) Dena! (*Pointing at TOMATO PLANT GIRL's Barbie*) Lena!

TOMATO PLANT GIRL: LEEENA!

BOSSY BEST FRIEND: (*As herself*) Beautiful. Now—

TOMATO PLANT GIRL: LEENA LEENA—

LITTLE GIRL: (*Starting to join her*) LEENA—

BOSSY BEST FRIEND: (*To LITTLE GIRL*) *Stop!* (*To TOMATO PLANT GIRL*) Lena.
   That's right.

(*BOSSY BEST FRIEND takes the Barbie and keeps it away from TOMATO PLANT GIRL.*)

BOSSY BEST FRIEND: Now watch. One-two-three. (*BOSSY BEST FRIEND demonstrates with both Barbies.*)

   Dena!

   Lena!

(*Kiss-kiss-kiss.*)

   How are you?

   Just *terrific.*

   And your job?

   Perfecto.

   And your boyfriends?

   Too —

(*TOMATO PLANT GIRL picks up a stick from the ground and holds it up proudly between the Barbies, as if it is a doll. This is her way of playing.*)

TOMATO PLANT GIRL: *Stick!*

BOSSY BEST FRIEND: Stop it! (*Handing LITTLE GIRL her Barbie*) Tell her to
   stop.

TOMATO PLANT GIRL: (*As Stick, to the other Barbies*) *Stick* Bar-bieee! Stick I!

(*TOMATO PLANT GIRL kisses LITTLE GIRL's Barbie on the cheek.*)

LITTLE GIRL: (*As her Barbie*) Oh! Hello Stick!

(*TOMATO PLANT GIRL repeats "Stick" over and over, moving around BOSSY BEST FRIEND and LITTLE GIRL.*)

BOSSY BEST FRIEND: (*To LITTLE GIRL*) Stop playing like that! (*As her Barbie*)
   Now listen, Stick —

TOMATO PLANT GIRL: (*To LITTLE GIRL*) Terrrriffic! Stick I!

LITTLE GIRL: (*As her Barbie*) Perfecto! Too fine!

BOSSY BEST FRIEND: (*To LITTLE GIRL*) You're doing it wrong!

(*BOSSY BEST FRIEND takes LITTLE GIRL's Barbie and blocks TOMATO PLANT GIRL's way.*)

BOSSY BEST FRIEND: Stop playing with her! I'm your friend!

LITTLE GIRL: She's my friend too!

BOSSY BEST FRIEND: *I'm* your friend.

LITTLE GIRL: (*Matter-of-fact*) And she's my—

BOSSY BEST FRIEND: Dumb Booknose. Dumb *foreigner* girl!

(*LITTLE GIRL freezes.*)

TOMATO PLANT GIRL: (*In LITTLE GIRL's face*) Stick!!

LITTLE GIRL: (*To TOMATO PLANT GIRL*) STOP. Stop that now.

(*LITTLE GIRL grabs Stick Barbie out of TOMATO PLANT GIRL's hand. TOMATO PLANT GIRL makes an indignant noise.*)

LITTLE GIRL: This is *not* how we play. It's loud and dangerous. *Now sit over there and calm down. Right now.*

(*Cornered, TOMATO PLANT GIRL bites LITTLE GIRL's pointing finger in self-defense, then runs off.*)

LITTLE GIRL: (*Shocked*) Ow! Tomato Plant Girl—wait!

(*LITTLE GIRL starts to go after TOMATO PLANT GIRL. BOSSY BEST FRIEND blocks her way.*)

BOSSY BEST FRIEND: Don't.

LITTLE GIRL: But I—

BOSSY BEST FRIEND: You did the right thing. (*Holding up LITTLE GIRL's Barbie*) You're this one. (*LITTLE GIRL doesn't take it.*) You're *this* one.

(*LITTLE GIRL makes a decision. She takes her Barbie, looks at BOSSY BEST FRIEND.*)

LITTLE GIRL: I know.

BOSSY BEST FRIEND: One—two—three! (*BOSSY BEST FRIEND speaks as her Barbie.*) Dena!

(*LITTLE GIRL plays, ignoring BOSSY BEST FRIEND's game.*)

LITTLE GIRL: *Root!*

BOSSY BEST FRIEND: Don't I look *stunning?*

LITTLE GIRL: *Dirrrt.*

BOSSY BEST FRIEND: My job is divine!

LITTLE GIRL: Fiire—

BOSSY BEST FRIEND: (*Furious*) That's a horrible dress!

LITTLE GIRL: —kissssun!

(*BOSSY BEST FRIEND grabs LITTLE GIRL's Barbie.*)

BOSSY BEST FRIEND: Your Barbie wants what my Barbie wants but my Barbie can have it and your Barbie—

LITTLE GIRL: No!

BOSSY BEST FRIEND: That's the game.

LITTLE GIRL: *Your* game.

BOSSY BEST FRIEND: Our game!

LITTLE GIRL: *Your* game. I don't like it. (*BOSSY BEST FRIEND starts to speak. LITTLE GIRL steps forward.*) And I didn't like you taking my book or making me give you your plant!

BOSSY BEST FRIEND: *Making* you?

LITTLE GIRL: Yes!

BOSSY BEST FRIEND: I said "please"!

LITTLE GIRL: You didn't mean it!

BOSSY BEST FRIEND: Fine. Never mind. We'll play Mother May I.

(*BOSSY BEST FRIEND claps twice. LITTLE GIRL picks up the stick.*)

LITTLE GIRL: *Stick!*

(*LITTLE GIRL spins and plays with the stick.*)

BOSSY BEST FRIEND: Put it down.

LITTLE GIRL: (*Still playing*) No.

BOSSY BEST FRIEND: (*Grabs hold of the stick*) Little Girl: I'm your *friend!*

LITTLE GIRL: (*Matter-of-fact*) No.

(*LITTLE GIRL lets go of the stick.*)

BOSSY BEST FRIEND: You're not. Booknose: be careful. Your other friend's gone.

LITTLE GIRL: (*Uncertain*) Then—I'll play alone.

BOSSY BEST FRIEND: (*Scornful*) You'll play *alone?*

LITTLE GIRL: (*More confident*) I'll play alone.

(*BOSSY BEST FRIEND drops the stick on the ground. She picks up her Barbies and bag and turns to go.*)

LITTLE GIRL: Wait—

BOSSY BEST FRIEND: (*Turns back, expectant*) Yes?

LITTLE GIRL: My book. (*Respectfully*) Please.

(*Crushed, BOSSY BEST FRIEND glares at LITTLE GIRL. BOSSY BEST FRIEND takes the book from her bag and holds it high in the air.*)

BOSSY BEST FRIEND: Dumb boring foreigner book!

(*BOSSY BEST FRIEND drops the book. LITTLE GIRL catches it.*)

BOSSY BEST FRIEND: Have fun alone!

(*BOSSY BEST FRIEND turns on her heel and exits. LITTLE GIRL hugs the book.*)

LITTLE GIRL: (*To herself*) I'll play alone. (*Pause. LITTLE GIRL looks around her, uncertain.*) Alone. (*Calling*) Tomato Plant Girl?

(*LITTLE GIRL takes a deep breath and closes her eyes, gathering courage.*)

LITTLE GIRL: I'll play alone.

(*LITTLE GIRL breathes deep, eyes closed, hugging the book. TOMATO PLANT GIRL enters. She is fully grown: a red, round tomato. But she is still hurt and wary of LITTLE GIRL. She approaches LITTLE GIRL and gently taps her shoulder. LITTLE GIRL jumps, looks at TOMATO PLANT GIRL.*)

LITTLE GIRL: Tomato Plant Girl! Wow! Look at you!

TOMATO PLANT GIRL: Grow I.

(*Pause. They look at each other, then away. They start to speak at the same time.*)

LITTLE GIRL: (*An apology*) I'm sorry.

TOMATO PLANT GIRL: (*LITTLE GIRL's name*) Sorry—

(*They laugh for a moment.*)

LITTLE GIRL: I should have, but I didn't. I shouldn't have, but I did.

(*TOMATO PLANT GIRL points at LITTLE GIRL, imitating her reprimand.*)

TOMATO PLANT GIRL: Sitoverthere! SitoverthereNOW!

LITTLE GIRL: I didn't know what to do.

(*TOMATO PLANT GIRL imitates BOSSY BEST FRIEND yelling "Foreigner!" at LITTLE GIRL.*)

TOMATO PLANT GIRL: "Forrner!"

(*TOMATO PLANT GIRL imitates LITTLE GIRL gasping in shock.*)

LITTLE GIRL: I *like* being a foreigner! That's why I like you. That's why I'm your friend.

TOMATO PLANT GIRL: (*Unsure of the meaning*) Frrrend.

LITTLE GIRL: Someone who ... knows who you are. And likes you. All of you. (*Pause*) Are you still my friend?

(*TOMATO PLANT GIRL takes LITTLE GIRL's hand and kisses the finger she bit earlier.*)

TOMATO PLANT GIRL: Frrrend.

(*LITTLE GIRL starts to cry and laugh at the same time. TOMATO PLANT GIRL starts to cry/laugh too. TOMATO PLANT GIRL lifts her index finger and reaches out toward LITTLE GIRL's face. LITTLE GIRL slowly does the same. At the same moment, each wipes a tear from the other's cheek. LITTLE GIRL tastes TOMATO PLANT GIRL's tear.*)

LITTLE GIRL: Friend.

(*TOMATO PLANT GIRL tastes LITTLE GIRL's tear.*)

TOMATO PLANT GIRL: Friend.

(*They stand facing each other a moment.*)

LITTLE GIRL: Tomato Plant Girl—

TOMATO PLANT GIRL: Grow I.

LITTLE GIRL: I know.

TOMATO PLANT GIRL: Errth.

LITTLE GIRL: (*Remembering*) Plants go back to the earth . . . to feed other plants. (*To TOMATO PLANT GIRL*) You have to go back, don't you?

TOMATO PLANT GIRL: (*Affirming*) Errth.

LITTLE GIRL: (*Holds out her book to TOMATO PLANT GIRL*) Here. I want you to have it.

TOMATO PLANT GIRL: (*Takes the book*) Red!

LITTLE GIRL: It's a gift.

TOMATO PLANT GIRL: Gifft. (*Thanking her*) Tomato.

(*TOMATO PLANT GIRL hugs the book, accepting it. She motions to LITTLE GIRL.*)

TOMATO PLANT GIRL: Root you. Please.

(*TOMATO PLANT GIRL scoops up handfuls of dirt from LITTLE GIRL's side of the garden. She begins to hum as she sprinkles the dirt onto LITTLE GIRL.*)

TOMATO PLANT GIRL: Grow you. Gift.

(*LITTLE GIRL smiles, rubs the dirt on her hands and face.*)

LITTLE GIRL: Gift. (*The Earthsoil Hum returns.*) The Earth hum!

(*LITTLE GIRL acknowledges the Earthsoil Hum with TOMATO PLANT GIRL's gesture. TOMATO PLANT GIRL joins her in the gesture and the hum. They continue to hum, transforming the gesture, once, then twice. The second time, they join hands. They spin in a circle, facing each other.*)

LITTLE GIRL: Tomatosweetleafplantreadyonetwo!

(*LITTLE GIRL drops a hand. They hold on by one.*)

LITTLE GIRL: Velvet green and flower-sun gold! In root, in heart, in sun— alone!

(*LITTLE GIRL lets TOMATO PLANT GIRL go. TOMATO PLANT GIRL spins off and folds back into the earth at the same spot where she emerged. LITTLE GIRL stops spinning.*)

LITTLE GIRL: Alone. I'll play alone.

(*LITTLE GIRL looks at the place where TOMATO PLANT GIRL disappeared. She picks

up two handfuls of earth and sprinkles it over the spot. Then she stretches up and
spins, breathing out. She reaches up and lets the earth fall through her fingers.)

LITTLE GIRL: Gift I. Grow I. Grow I.

(In the place where TOMATO PLANT GIRL folded into the earth, a new tomato plant
springs up, healthy and green, with a single red tomato.)

CURTAIN

Production credits from the premiere of *Tomato Plant Girl* and details concerning performance rights are included in the acting edition of the play as published by Dramatic Publishing.

Dramatic Publishing, Inc.
311 Washington Street
P. O. Box 129
Woodstock, IL 60098

Compelling Adaptations

Afternoon of the Elves

Broken Hearts

Courage!

Afternoon of the Elves

A Play in Two Acts

For 1 Man, 2 Women, 4 Girls (one possible double)

Adapted by Y. York

Based on the book by Janet Taylor Lisle

This story is based on the 1990 Newbery Honor book by Janet Taylor Lisle. Ten-year-old Hillary wants to be accepted by her classmates, so she's very excited when two of the most popular girls in the fourth grade invite her to be their friend. But she is equally intrigued when her odd next-door neighbor, Sara Kate, tells her magical tales of elves who have built houses in her weed-filled backyard. Though Sara Kate's strange clothes and behavior have made her an outsider at their school, Hillary risks her social standing to help take care of the little village. As the girls form a unique friendship, Hillary learns that Sara Kate's fantasy village is an escape from the challenges of her real-life: for the past year she has been the sole caretaker for her invalid mother and their household. Sara Kate makes Hillary promise not to tell anyone because she fears that her mother will be taken away. With this secret weighing on her, Hillary understands the weight that Sara Kate must feel and tries to decide how to help Hillary find the same real-life safety of home that the girls created for their imaginary elves.

Characters

JANE and ALISON: stars of the fourth grade

HILLARY LENOX: has recently joined their ranks

SARA KATE CONNOLLY: an upperclassman, held back for a second try in the fifth grade

MR. and MRS. LENOX: Hillary's parents

MRS. CONNOLLY: Sara Kate's mother, unable to cope

ACT ONE

Scene 1

(AT RISE: Outside of school, Friday afternoon. A bright fall day. JANE WEBSTER and ALISON MANCINI, dressed alike with matching hairdos, leaving school with books, giggling, etc.)

HILLARY: *(Off)* Wait up!

ALISON: *(Playing)* Do you hear something, Jane?

JANE: *(Ibid.)* Not a thing, Alison.

HILLARY: *(Off)* It's me, Hillary, wait!

ALISON: Oh, it's *Hillary*, Jane. Do you think we should wait for *Hillary*?

JANE: Hillary-who-didn't-do-her-hair?

HILLARY: *(Off)* I didn't have time!

ALISON: *We* had time.

JANE: We *made* time.

(HILLARY enters. She is dressed as they, but with different hair. She carries a book bag.)

HILLARY: *(Out of breath, defensive)* My mother didn't have time.

JANE: You let your mother do your hair?

ALISON: I don't let my mother *touch* my hair. She pulls it, then when I scream and run she says, "Alison Mancini, get in this chair or I'm going to call your father at the office." *(Sarcastically)* "I tremble, Mother, I just tremble." I do my own hair.

JANE: I do, too.

ALISON: *(To JANE)* You *have* to do your own hair.

JANE: *(Defensive)* So what?

ALISON: So nothing.

HILLARY: How do you do it by yourself?

ALISON: With two mirrors and a chair.

JANE: (*To ALISON*) And a hairbrush.

HILLARY: I don't think I can do it.

ALISON: Well, you have to learn so we can be the Mighty Three.

HILLARY: Guess what? I heard Mr. Decker call us the Three Musketeers; I heard him say so to Mrs. Gray this morning. "Well, I see you've got the Three Musketeers in your class," he said.

JANE: Too-too good.

ALISON: Write it down, Hillary.

HILLARY: I already did. (*Hugs book bag*)

ALISON: We're getting famous. That's what happens when there's three of you; people start to notice you; you get famous.

JANE: And three's the right number.

ALISON: Yes, if you're four, people think you're a gang.

JANE: (*Rhyme rap*) The number four is very poor!

ALISON: Oh, stop it, already. We all know you can rhyme.

JANE: I have to keep in practice.

HILLARY: Practice for what?

ALISON: Jane's father only lets her watch TV if she rhymes.

HILLARY: Wow, that's crummy.

JANE: It won't last; his new girlfriend is a poet. (*Rhyming*) The number two is one too few.

ALISON: Yeah. Two is no good. If there's only two, it's the same as one; nobody notices.

HILLARY: We, the Mighty Three.

JANE: (*Singing*) Alison, Hillary and Me. Hey! Maybe we should be a band. We already match.

ALISON: (*To JANE*) You can write the songs. Let's start right away. Where should we go?

JANE: My house.

HILLARY: (*Same time*) My house.

JANE: Pididdle!

HILLARY: (*Almost the same time*) Pididdle!

JANE: I said it first.

HILLARY: (*At the same time*) I said it first.

JANE: Who said it first, Alison?

ALISON: Jane.

JANE: I win. Okay, okay. Name ten . . . stars.

(*HILLARY names current popular rock, movie, and/or TV stars, while JANE punches her in the arm and counts off each star.*)

JANE: One . . . two . . . three . . . four . . . five . . . six . . . seven . . . eight—

(*Enter SARA KATE CONNOLLY, as if she has been watching. She is unkempt in the way of the neglected and poor.*)

SARA KATE: Stop hitting her.

JANE: Gross, gross.

ALISON: Are you spying on us, Sara Kate Connolly?

JANE: You spy.

SARA KATE: I said, don't hit her.

HILLARY: Nobody's hitting me, I'm fine.

ALISON: See? She's fine. You can be on your way, before you cause trouble.

SARA KATE: I'm not causing trouble.

JANE: You cause trouble just by being around. You made me lose my whole lunch appetite when you sat down next to me.

SARA KATE: I mind my own business.

JANE: Alison, have you ever seen what she eats? Mush in a thermos.

ALISON: Really, I thought her whole family ate nothing but pesticide.

HILLARY: (*Uncomfortable*) If they ate pesticide, they'd be dead.

ALISON: Maybe they *are* dead. Nobody's ever seen them.

HILLARY: *I've* seen them.

ALISON: Where have you seen them?

HILLARY: I've seen Mrs. Connolly. They live behind my house.

JANE: Yuk.

ALISON: Maybe that's just a ghost; the ghost of Sara Kate's mother, oooo.

JANE: Or a magic trick. Sara Kate is a magician.

SARA KATE: I am not.

JANE: Sure you are. Whenever you're around, people's things *disappear.* Where's that bike you stole, Sara Kate?

SARA KATE: (*To HILLARY*) I need to talk to you.

ALISON: You need to talk to who?

SARA KATE: Not you. (*To HILLARY*) You.

HILLARY: Why do you need to talk to me?

SARA KATE: I need to talk to you *alone.*

ALISON: Oh, brother.

JANE: Well, you can't.

SARA KATE: It's actually very important. And private.

JANE: She'll tell us later.

SARA KATE: Maybe. Maybe not.

HILLARY: I don't have anything to say to you.

SARA KATE: Of course you don't have anything to say to me. I have something to say to you. But you will have to tear yourself away from these two chaperones.

HILLARY: (*Mad*) They're not chaperones! (*Beat*) What are chaperones?

SARA KATE: Body. Guards. For the young and frightened.

HILLARY: I'm not frightened.

SARA KATE: Then let's talk. You. And me. Over there.

ALISON: She doesn't want her stuff disappeared.

HILLARY: (*Whispers to JANE and ALISON*) Hey, it's all right. I better talk to her or she'll never go away.

ALISON: (*Whispers*) Do you want us to stay and listen?

HILLARY: No, it's okay. I'll see you tomorrow.

JANE: What about our song?

HILLARY: We can do it tomorrow. At my house.

ALISON: Okay. Bye-bye, Hillary. Abracadabra, Sara Kate Connolly.

(*ALISON and JANE exit. Brief pause*)

SARA KATE: Why did you let her hit you?

HILLARY: It was a pididdle.

SARA KATE: A *what?*

HILLARY: A pididdle. We said the same thing at the same time. Then Jane said pididdle so I had to name ten stars and let her punch me 'til I got done.

SARA KATE: That doesn't even make sense!

HILLARY: It's just a game.

SARA KATE: It's a stupid one!

HILLARY: (*Pause*) What do you want?

SARA KATE: (*Formally*) Are you Hillary Lenox?

HILLARY: You know who I am. Our backyards touch.

SARA KATE: I can't be sure who you are, you're dressed exactly like Alison Mancini and Jane Webster. Girls of a predatory and evil nature. You should hope they never commit a crime; you might get blamed.

HILLARY: Why?

SARA KATE: You dress like them; the witness might identify *you* by mistake.

HILLARY: Well, it's me, Hillary.

SARA KATE: If you're Hillary Lenox, I need to talk to you about a matter concerning our touching backyards. (*Beat*) Have you peeked through the vegetation into my backyard lately?

HILLARY: (*Annoyed*) I *never* have peeked into your backyard, through the vegetation *or* the bushes.

SARA KATE: Then, it's as I thought. (*Beat*) I am the only one who knows.

HILLARY: (*Annoyed*) What? The only one who knows what?

SARA KATE: About the elves.

HILLARY: What are you talking about?

SARA KATE: In my backyard that touches your backyard, even as we speak, there is a village of tiny houses built for and by elves.

HILLARY: That's crazy.

SARA KATE: You haven't seen it.

HILLARY: Is this some kind of trick?

SARA KATE: No, it's not a trick. I don't blame you for not believing; I wouldn't believe either if I hadn't seen it with my own eyes. Right in the yard, tiny little houses that nobody but a tiny elf could live in.

HILLARY: Well, let's go take a look.

SARA KATE: Not yet. Come after four.

HILLARY: I want to go now.

SARA KATE: Well, you don't get what you want. Come to my house after four.

HILLARY: Maybe I will; maybe I won't.

SARA KATE: (*Beat*) You will. Don't come to the front. Come to the backyard. After four.

Scene 2

(*Friday afternoon. The lights reveal the Lenox backyard, a stoop and a back door to the house, a shed, tools and catalogs onstage. This yard is manicured and sculpted. A new birdbath. MR. and MRS. LENOX and then HILLARY.*)

MR. L: (*About birdbath*) Do you think it's all right here?

MRS. L: Frank, it's fine, it's great. It's been great every place we've put it in the last hour. Let's leave it there.

MR. L: (*Looks at a catalog*) It looks bigger in the picture.

MRS. L: There's nothing around it to compare it to in the picture.

MR. L: I should have ordered the biggest one.

MRS. L: This one is fine.

MR. L: Do you really think it looks okay?

MRS. L: Yes, it looks okay!

MR. L: *Just* okay?

MRS. L: It looks . . . fabulous. Authentic.

MR. L: Yeah, I guess I think it does, too.

MRS. L: Can we address the mess behind the garage now?

MR. L: Now, honey, I'll get to that, after the yard. All things in good time.

(*He leaves the catalog on the stoop with the others. HILLARY enters skipping.*)

HILLARY: Wow, that is too-too good.

MR. L: Hillary, honey, don't skip on the grass, skip on the cement. You're tearing up the lawn.

HILLARY: Sorry, Dad. Looks good, really nice. A lot nicer than the picture.

MR. L: Thanks, honey. Do you think it looks good here?

HILLARY: Well . . .

MRS. L: Yes, you do, you do.

HILLARY: Yeah, looks good, Dad.

MRS. L: (*About book bag*) Did they give you homework over the weekend?

HILLARY: No. It's just my diary inside. (*Beat*) Can Alison and Jane come over tomorrow?

MRS. L: Sure. You can play in the yard.

MR. L: —I gotta move it.

MRS. L: No!

MR. L: No, I gotta. I can't have little girls poking it and knocking it.

HILLARY: We don't do that.

MRS. L: Never mind, honey. Your dad has temporarily lost his reason. (*Beat*) Were the girls mad we didn't do your hair?

HILLARY: . . . It was okay.

MRS. L: I'll do it tomorrow.

HILLARY: I can do it myself.

MRS. L: Was it fun to dress alike?

HILLARY: Too-too fun, Mom. Everybody noticed.

MR. L: And that's good?

HILLARY: Dad! Of course it's good. It's too-too good. Jane and Alison know all about it. They've been doing it for a long time, and everybody in school knows who they are.

MR. L: And that's too-too good?

HILLARY: Yeah, it's too-too good.

MRS. L: (*Beat*) Are they nice to you, honey?

HILLARY: They let me dress like them!

MRS. L: They've been friends for a long time. You're still the new kid.

HILLARY: Mom, they're nice to me, it's fine.

MRS. L: Okay. Do you want a snack?

HILLARY: No. I'm going to visit Sara Kate.

MRS. L: (*Surprised*) Sara Kate? Next-door Sara Kate?

MR. L: I thought you were friends with Alison and Jane.

HILLARY: I'm not *friends* with Sara Kate; I'm only visiting her.

MRS. L: Why don't you invite her over here instead?

HILLARY: Because she doesn't go places.

MRS. L: That house looks like it's going to fall down.

HILLARY: I'm not going in the house; we're going to play in her yard.

MR. L: (*Sarcastic*) The yard, great. You'll probably come home with some disease.

HILLARY: There's no disease over there.

MR. L: Or lice. Or poison ivy. We should call the health department.

HILLARY: Dad, you can't call the health department! You can't!

MR. L: Don't raise your voice to me, young lady.

HILLARY: Oh, I tremble, I just tremble!

MRS. L: Hillary!

HILLARY: Whaaat?!

MRS. L: . . . We're not going to call the health department. Your dad is just having an opinion. (*Beat*) How come Sara Kate invited you? What's the occasion?

HILLARY: No occasion. She invited me and I want to go. (*Beat*) You're always saying how we should be nice to the less fortunate.

MRS. L: (*Beat*) All right. But go get a snack. I think you're having low blood sugar. Eat some protein.

HILLARY: Yes, ma'am. (*Exits*)

MR. L: "I tremble, I just tremble"?

MRS. L: I don't know where she comes up with these things.

MR. L: Where do you come up with low blood sugar?

MRS. L: I don't know. (*Beat*) Do you think we should have had more kids?

MR. L: Ask me on a different day.

MRS. L: Not for *us*; for her.

MR. L: She's fine, honey, she's just fine. (*Beat*) Except we'll probably have to delouse her when she gets home from Sara Kate's.

MRS. L: Don't I recall some stories about you and head lice?

MR. L: (*Defensively*) We all had 'em.

MRS. L: And we all survived. She'll be okay.

MR. L: (*Beat*) What about that bike business?

MRS. L: Honey, we don't even know if that story is true; let's give Sara Kate the benefit of the doubt.

Scene 3

(*Sara Kate's yard. It's the antithesis of the Lenox yard. There are old appliances, car engines, tires, brambles. There, in the midst of the mess, is an orderly elf village. Little houses built with sticks, string, rocks, and leaves; separated by rows of rocks into an elf development. A well in the center of "town." SARA KATE is working on the elf village. HILLARY enters, with her book bag, through the hedge; without looking at HILLARY, SARA KATE speaks.*)

SARA KATE: I first saw it a couple of days ago; it just sort of appeared. They must work all through the night, but it isn't done. You can see where a couple of houses aren't finished, and there's places made ready for houses with no houses on them yet.

HILLARY: How did you know I was here?

SARA KATE: Do you want to see the village or not?

HILLARY: Okay. (*Impressed*) Wow. Too-too good. Look, they used sticks and leaves for roofs. And rocks to separate the little houses. It's a little neighborhood.

SARA KATE: Yeah, they took rocks from our driveway.

HILLARY: They stole them?

SARA KATE: Yeah, there's rocks gone from our driveway.

HILLARY: Should we put them back?

SARA KATE: No, the elves need them, and we don't even have a car anymore.

HILLARY: You don't have a car?

SARA KATE: No. So what?

HILLARY: Nothing. (*Beat*) Well, they shouldn't steal. Even rocks.

SARA KATE: The elves don't think so.

HILLARY: (*Shocked*) They don't think it's wrong to steal?

SARA KATE: Elves have different rules.

HILLARY: They steal?!

SARA KATE: Just stuff nobody is using. Or stuff from mean rich people.

HILLARY: How do they know who's mean?

SARA KATE: They just know.

HILLARY: It *all* looks real fragile. What happens when it rains?

SARA KATE: They rebuild and repair. Elves are at the complete mercy of earth forces.

HILLARY: (*Pause*) How do you know so much?

SARA KATE: . . . I think the elves sneak stuff into my brain.

HILLARY: What do you mean?

SARA KATE: I tried to haul up some water and all of a sudden I was thinking "the elves won't like this."

HILLARY: Sara Kate, are you sure elves built this? Maybe this was built by mice. Mice could live in these houses quite nicely.

SARA KATE: Mice! That is really—that is just—that is so stupid! When did you ever hear of mice building houses?!

HILLARY: Or even a person could have built these homes.

SARA KATE: Look, I didn't have to invite you here today, and I didn't have to show you this. I thought you might like to see an elf village for a change. If you don't believe elves built this, that's your problem. I know they did.

HILLARY: I haven't seen elves in *my* backyard.

SARA KATE: Well, of course not.

HILLARY: What do you mean?

SARA KATE: (*Sincere, kind*) Elves would never go in that backyard, no offense, Hillary, but your backyard would not offer any protection. See, elves need to hide, they hate it when people see them. In the olden days, it didn't matter so much, but now, there's too many people, and too many bad ones; elves can't risk being seen by a bad person.

HILLARY: (*Worried*) Why? What would happen?

SARA KATE: There's no telling, but it would be very terrible. They know they're safe here, there's a million places to hide in this yard.

HILLARY: (*Looks around, impressed*) Yeah. I see what you mean. (*She sneaks up on things and peeks behind them, looking for elves, as she begins to believe SARA KATE's elf information.*)

SARA KATE: Where, for example, would they find stones in your yard to make these little private lots?

HILLARY: (*Realization*) Right. Our driveway is all paved with cement. There's no rocks anywhere in our yard. And Dad rakes the leaves the second they fall; so there's nothing to make a roof out of! (*She begins to skip.*) Wow. Your yard is perfect for elves! Look at all the junk to hide in, and strings and wire to make the houses, and rocks, and leaves for roofs. (*She stops skipping abruptly.*) Oh, is it all right to skip?

SARA KATE: What are you talking about? (*SARA KATE skips and jumps and prances about.*) Of course it's all right to skip. It makes the elves really happy.

HILLARY: It does? (*She skips.*)

SARA KATE: Yes! And if you make them happy enough, they trust you and let you peek at them. (*Stops suddenly*) Listen! I hear them laughing now.

(*HILLARY stops skipping. They listen.*)

SARA KATE: Their language is like earth sounds. But if you listen real close, you can hear that it's really elves.

(*Both girls are affected by a felt presence. HILLARY is amazed.*)

HILLARY: (*Whispers*) Sara Kate? I think they're here.

SARA KATE: Yes, I feel it too. Don't talk about them or they'll go away. Act natural.

(*HILLARY tries to act natural. She hums and opens her book bag.*)

SARA KATE: (*Disdain*) Are you doing homework?!

HILLARY: (*Whispers*) I was going to write something down. In my diary.

SARA KATE: Don't whisper, whispering isn't natural. What are you going to write?

HILLARY: About the elves. I keep a record, a written record of everything. I document my life.

SARA KATE: Why do you want to do that?

HILLARY: In case we get famous—me and Alison and Jane. I'm keeping all our documentation in my diary.

SARA KATE: I don't want to be famous. (*Beat*) I'm going to straighten the rocks.

HILLARY: I can do that, too.

SARA KATE: I don't want to interrupt your documenting.

HILLARY: It's no interruption.

(*HILLARY puts diary in book bag. The girls start to straighten rocks at one of the "lots."*)

HILLARY: Oh, look.

SARA KATE: Little steps.

HILLARY: (*At the same time*) Little steps!

SARA KATE: Oh! Orion's belt, the big dipper, the little dipper, the Pleiades, Virgo, Gemini, Aquarius, Libra, Pisces, Capricorn. Ten! (*Beat*) How come you didn't punch me?

HILLARY: What are you talking about?!

SARA KATE: Ten stars. We said the same thing at the same time. You're supposed to punch me while I say ten stars.

HILLARY: (*Realizing*) Sara Kate, you're supposed to say "pididdle," and then make *me* say ten of something, and punch *me*. You don't have it right at all.

SARA KATE: (*Flares up*) Who cares?! It's *your* stupid game. I just did it because I thought you liked it, I don't like it, it's a stupid game. Who cares?!

HILLARY: (*Trying to end the argument*) I'm sorry. I didn't mean—you're right! It *is* a stupid game, you're right. Who cares?!

SARA KATE: Yeah, who cares.

(*Pause. HILLARY walks near the elf houses.*)

HILLARY: (*An idea*) The elves must think we're giants!

SARA KATE: (*Impressed*) What?!

HILLARY: Yes! They think we are kindly human giants! (*Stands on something to look around*) Kindly giant sisters who watch over elves.

SARA KATE: (*Pretending to keep watch, a giant voice*) The kindly giant sisters scan the horizon for signs of danger! All clear on the western bank!

HILLARY: (*Playing along*) All clear on the eastern bank.

(*HILLARY walks in a large fashion. A lumbering, giant walk. SARA KATE does, too.*)

HILLARY: The kindly giant sisters walk the land, keeping watch.

SARA KATE: The ground quakes with their steps.

HILLARY: But the elves have no fear.

(*A figure appears in a window. It is a thin woman wearing a nightgown; she is clearly very ill, with wild hair.*)

SARA KATE: No dangerous humans in sight.

HILLARY: Only the kindly giant sisters.

SARA KATE: (*At the same time*) Giant sisters. All elves may proceed to their homes.

(*HILLARY sees the figure in the window. She is frozen in fear.*)

SARA KATE: Elves may continue construction on the village. The kindly giant sisters will lift and carry objects of great size—(*Notices HILLARY and looks to the house where she sees the figure*) You have to go.

HILLARY: What is—who is—

SARA KATE: Just go. You have to.

HILLARY: But I—

SARA KATE: No buts. Get going.

HILLARY: But you shouldn't—

SARA KATE: Here! Here's your bag. Just take it and go. Go home, Hillary.

(*HILLARY leaves through the hedge. SARA KATE sighs and turns toward the house, where the figure has disappeared.*)

Scene 4

(*Immediately following. The Lenox backyard. HILLARY enters her backyard again, out of breath and confused. She is glad to see the familiar, friendly, neat garden. She sits under the back stoop light, removes diary from her book bag and records her confused, scattered thoughts.*)

HILLARY: There's a ghost in Sara Kate Connolly's yard. We were playing with the elves, I mean their village. I didn't think it would be real. Why would elves build in Sara Kate's yard? She is a human mess. She's bony and dirty and dresses bad. There's nothing magical about her. Elves should live in a yard of someone . . . beautiful or . . . soft. I don't know why they chose Sara Kate's brain to leave messages in or Sara Kate's yard to live in. Unless they like haunted houses. Alison said Mrs. Connolly is dead and maybe she is because I just saw a ghost in the window—It looked more like a ghost than a person. A skinny, creepy, sickly—

MR. L: (*At the door*) Hillary?

HILLARY: Oh!!

(*HILLARY gasps and jumps away in fright, dropping her diary to the ground. MR. LENOX enters.*)

MR. L: Boo.

HILLARY: (*Relieved*) I thought you were a ghost.

MR. L: Not yet. You better get on in, honey; *somebody* hasn't set the table yet!

HILLARY: Oh, man, the table!

(*HILLARY leaves the diary where it fell. MR. LENOX picks up his catalogs, absently snatches the diary, puts everything in a small shed that is attached to the side of the house. He enters the house. Lights fade. A person carrying a candle is seen in the Connolly window.*)

Scene 5

(*Saturday morning, the next day. The Lenox backyard. MR. and MRS. LENOX are working in the yard. They are happy.*)

MR. L: I'm going to become a gardener.

MRS. L: You mean more than weekends?

MR. L: Yeah, a for-real gardener. On somebody's gigantic estate. The gardener, taking care of the big boss's flowers and shrubs.

MRS. L: And what will I be doing?

MR. L: You'll be a corporate lawyer. That way I can afford to be somebody's gardener.

MRS. L: Why don't you become a cook?

MR. L: A cook? Not a gardener?

MRS. L: Yeah, rustle us up some pancakes.

(*HILLARY runs into the garden in her nightgown. MR. LENOX grabs her.*)

MR. L: Whoa.

HILLARY: Mom, Dad, I was having the best dream, it was the best dream, all about elves. It was so real. There was an elf mayor, and elf villagers, and an elf ballerina. I want to go see.

MR. L: Honey, it was a dream.

HILLARY: Yeah, but there are elves. Over there. (*Points*)

MRS. L: Maybe you should get dressed first.

HILLARY: (*Looking at her nightgown, surprised*) Oh, man. I was going next door in my nightgown. I need to get dressed. I need to wake up.

MRS. L: What time are Alison and Jane coming?

HILLARY: Alison and Jane are coming! I forgot. I completely forgot. I got to do my hair. (*Runs toward the house*)

MRS. L: Don't forget to get dressed.

HILLARY: Oh, Mother! (*Exits*)

MRS. L: I recognize that tone of voice. I think I used it on *my* mother.

MR. L: (*Joking*) Was your mother as unreasonable as you?

MRS. L: Probably.

MR. L: (*Beat*) I don't remember elves in my youth.

MRS. L: Your youth is too far away to remember.

MR. L: I wish they'd play in our backyard. Where it's neat, and clean, and safe.

MRS. L: Neat and clean and safe is no fun.

(*ALISON and JANE come into the yard; they are wearing matching jackets. ALISON carries a department store bag. The girls are overtly polite to parents; the parents are tolerant, but not fooled.*)

JANE: Good morning, Mrs. Lenox; good morning, Mr. Lenox.

ALISON: We hope we're not disturbing you.

JANE: Hillary invited us.

MRS. L: We know. We're getting the yard ready.

JANE: Oh, we don't need anything special.

MR. L: It isn't for you, it's for the yard.

MRS. L: Frank. Nice jackets.

ALISON: Oh, Mrs. Lenox, I'm so glad you like them. We just got them, just now, this morning.

JANE: My dad dropped me off early at Alison's.

ALISON: Too early to come here. So Mom took us to Mildred's.

JANE: These were on sale.

ALISON: Really inexpensive.

JANE: Mrs. Mancini paid for them. She said they were on her because they were so cheap. We got one for Hillary.

ALISON: I hope it's okay.

MR. L: How do you know she'll like it?

ALISON: She'll like it; *we* like it.

(*The parents exchange a look.*)

MR. L: It's okay, but next time, ask in advance.

ALISON: Oh, we will. This was an emergency.

MR. L: Now, girls, this is new sod. No running and jumping and carrying-on that's going to rip it up. And be careful of the birdbath, it isn't cemented in yet. And watch where you walk, there's new ground cover planted.

MRS. L: (*High irony*) Yes, girls, Mr. Lenox is working hard on the yard so Hillary has a nice place to play.

MR. L: (*To MRS. L*) Now, honey, it isn't ready for play yet, when it's ready for play, then they can play as hard as they want. In the meantime, they have to be careful. Now, here, right here, you can play, do whatever you want, right here.

JANE: Where, Mr. Lenox?

MR. L: Right here, between here and here.

(*The girls walk to the safe patch. It's very small.*)

ALISON: Here?

MR. L: Yeah.

MRS. L: We were just discussing pancakes. Have you girls eaten?

JANE: Yes.

ALISON: Uh huh.

MRS. L: Okay.

MR. L: Have fun.

ALISON: Thank you.

MR. L: (*Points*) Right here, have fun right here . . .

MRS. L: Come on, honey.

(*ALISON and JANE smile until the LENOXES go inside, then they start jumping on the safe patch.*)

JANE: You can play right here.

ALISON: Play where it's safe!

JANE: Don't knock over the birdbath!

ALISON: Don't tear up the sod!

JANE: Don't rip up the ground cover.

ALISON: What *is* ground cover?

JANE: What's *ground cover*? What's *sod*?

(*They are laughing when HILLARY comes out. Her hair matches theirs. She has her book bag.*)

HILLARY: Hi.

JANE: We got you a jacket.

HILLARY: (*Opens box and puts on jacket*) Wow.

ALISON: Just like ours. Your mother says it's okay.

HILLARY: Too-too good.

ALISON: Your hair looks good.

HILLARY: I did it myself.

JANE: See.

HILLARY: Two mirrors, like you said. Look, it fits. (*Beat*) What do you want to do?

JANE: Let's knock over the birdbath.

(*JANE and ALISON laugh.*)

HILLARY: (*Worried that they might*) It's probably too heavy.

JANE: He said we could stand right here, between here and here. Come on, let's see if we even all fit.

(*They try.*)

JANE: Closer, closer!

ALISON: Inhale and we'll all fit.

(*They don't fit, they giggle.*)

ALISON: Your father is mental, Hillary.

JANE: Not mental, demented.

HILLARY: All fathers are demented.

ALISON: My father's never *been* in our yard. The only yard he goes on is the golf course. He goes every weekend.

JANE: My father hires somebody.

HILLARY: He just likes the yard, is all.

JANE: He's demented. Hey! I forgot. What happened with Sara Kate yesterday?

ALISON: Oh, yeah. What was her big secret?

HILLARY: Just something in her yard.

ALISON: What?

HILLARY: It's this little town. She says elves built it.

ALISON: Elves?! Is she nuts or what?

JANE: There's no such thing as elves.

ALISON: Did you go over there? (*HILLARY nods.*) By yourself?

HILLARY: Just for a minute.

ALISON: Yuk.

JANE: Next time, wait for us. (*Rhymes*) The Migh-tee Three visit Sara Kate Con-no-lly. Hey! Does anybody want to hear my song?

ALISON: Oh! It's too-too- good, Hillary.

HILLARY: Sing it.

(*JANE sings, ALISON sings along for some.*)

> We are the Mighty Three,
> Alison, Hillary and Me.
> We dress alike and we never fight,
> Don't listen to you 'cause we know we're right.
> We are three friends for sure.
> And we don't want any more.
> We are the Mighty Three,
> Alison, Hillary and Me.

HILLARY: That is too-too good.

ALISON: We can sing it at the next assembly.

HILLARY: Then we'll really be famous.

ALISON: Did you write down the words?

JANE: No, they're in my head.

ALISON: You should document them, Hillary.

HILLARY: Yeah. (*She looks in her book bag.*) My diary's gone.

ALISON: Oh, brother.

HILLARY: Maybe it's in my room.

JANE: Forget it; you can write the words later.

HILLARY: (*Worried*) I wonder what I did with it.

ALISON: It doesn't matter.

HILLARY: Yes, it does. I had it yesterday. I wrote what Mr. Decker said about us. I always put it in here.

ALISON: Did you take it next door?

HILLARY: I take it everywhere.

ALISON: Well, that's where your diary went, Hillary.

JANE: Oh, yeah. Sara Kate Connolly made it disappear.

HILLARY: No, she didn't.

ALISON: Sure she did. You're going to have to buy a new diary, Hillary. That's all there is to it.

(SARA KATE enters through the hedge.)

ALISON: Don't look now, Hillary, but your new best friend has arrived.

HILLARY: What do you want?

JANE: Were you spying behind the bushes?

SARA KATE: I need to talk to Hillary.

JANE: (Snide) Did you bring her diary?

SARA KATE: What?

HILLARY: Where's my diary?

(Pause. SARA KATE walks around the yard. She is amazed by what is to her great opulence.)

SARA KATE: I need to talk to Hillary.

HILLARY: What? What do you want?

ALISON: We don't have any secrets. Talk.

HILLARY: It's true, we don't have secrets; talk, or get out.

SARA KATE: There's been a surprising development in the elf village.

HILLARY: (Excited, in spite of herself) What is it? Did you see elves?

JANE: Or the Easter Bunny?

ALISON: Or Santa?

SARA KATE: I didn't see them, but they've been there.

HILLARY: (Torn) Well . . . how do you know?

ALISON: Oh, brother.

SARA KATE: They've *been* there! They built something. Something . . . impressive.

JANE: Let's go see.

SARA KATE: No. Only Hillary is invited.

ALISON: Well, Hillary won't go.

JANE: Not unless you invite us, too.

SARA KATE: Hillary? Do you want to come see what the elves built?

HILLARY: Yes . . . but only if Alison and Jane can come, too.

SARA KATE: Suit yourself. (*Walks in front of each, counting and pointing*) One, one, one.

(*SARA KATE exits through the hedge. The girls are momentarily stunned. Pause, then.*)

JANE: Weird, she's *weird*. One, one, one, what? Is that as high as she can count?

ALISON: She's mental. She's too-too mental for me.

JANE: You don't believe in elves, Hillary.

HILLARY: (*Hesitating*) No. But there is something in Sara Kate's yard. A little town. Somebody had to build it.

JANE: Yeah, somebody. Somebody Sara Kate Connolly.

ALISON: We have a song to practice, Hillary. We don't have any time for elves. Okay?

HILLARY: Yeah. I know.

(*JANE and ALISON begin the song. HILLARY hesitates, then joins in.*)

Scene 6

(*The Connolly backyard. SARA KATE. An elf-sized Ferris wheel made from bicycle tire rims. Quite amazing. There are other changes as well. HILLARY, carrying her old jacket and book bag, comes quietly through the hedge. SARA KATE couldn't possibly hear.*)

SARA KATE: Isn't it beautiful?

HILLARY: I didn't make a sound; how did you know I was here?

SARA KATE: I don't know; I just . . . know. What do you think?

HILLARY: (*Drops her jacket and book bag and admires the Ferris wheel*) It's really something. Tiny little seats.

SARA KATE: Elf-size.

HILLARY: How did they carry the tires?

SARA KATE: Many many of them working together.

HILLARY: How do you know?

SARA KATE: Information gets into my brain.

HILLARY: Is it a voice gets in your brain?

SARA KATE: Yes.

HILLARY: What's it sound like?

SARA KATE: It sounds . . . like *me*. (*Beat*) The tires are from that old bike. See? The bike tires are gone. These are those tires.

HILLARY: How are you going to ride it?

SARA KATE: It's an old piece of junk; nobody could ride it. See this?

(*Something that might be a tiny swimming pool.*)

HILLARY: A swimming pool. Oh my goodness! They made a little swimming pool.

SARA KATE: Or something.

HILLARY: You know what? I bet they're going to make a whole amusement park. Right in your backyard. Merry-go-round, roller coaster. It's perfect. The elves will ride the rides until they get hot, and then they'll go for a swim.

SARA KATE: (*Unconvinced*) Maybe.

HILLARY: What do you mean "maybe"?

SARA KATE: Elves are not tiny human beings. They're elves, completely different from humans. It's possible to jump to wrong conclusions.

HILLARY: (*Considers the pool; an idea*) It's a power source.

SARA KATE: (*Impressed*) Aaaah, yessss; combination hydro and photovoltaics.

HILLARY: Yeah, a power source.

SARA KATE: (*Playing*) The power streams down from the sun —

HILLARY: (*Playing*) And the stars, too. It never stops coming down, a never-ending source of power.

SARA KATE: If you're feeling a little energy drain, stop at the power pool —

HILLARY: For a fill-up. (*Sticks her finger in the pool; she expands.*) I'm filling up with energy. Pow, pow.

SARA KATE: Don't explode!

HILLARY: Now I'm full of energy. Energy to heat the houses.

SARA KATE: Except elves don't get cold.

HILLARY: No way!

SARA KATE: Well, they dooooo, but not until it's freezing. When they finally get so cold they can't stand it, they move into empty human houses. (*Neatening up the village*) Come on; the kindly giant sisters must help the elves again.

HILLARY: The Hillary giant lines up the scattered stones around the elf houses.

SARA KATE: The Sara Kate giant gathers berries for the elves' dinner.

HILLARY: And the Hillary giant helps her.

(SARA KATE eats berries. HILLARY sees and tries some; they're terrible.)

HILLARY: Yuk. These are terrible, yuk. Poison I bet.

SARA KATE: (Playing) Not to an elf. (Pops a berry in her mouth)

HILLARY: (Serious) Don't eat that, Sara Kate. (Beat) Are you hungry?

SARA KATE: (Serious) I'm not hungry.

HILLARY: You can eat dinner at my house.

SARA KATE: (Subdued) No. I eat with my mom. (The game again) Here. Put leaves and little sticks in this box, Hillary giant.

(SARA KATE suddenly turns, as if to see something. HILLARY looks, too, but the elves are gone.)

SARA KATE: Gone.

HILLARY: I wish I could see an elf.

SARA KATE: You have to sort of see them out of the corner of your eye.

(HILLARY looks forward, trying to see sideways.)

SARA KATE: Don't worry if you don't see one right away. It might take them a long time to trust us. Move your bag.

HILLARY: (Picks up her book bag, remembers her diary. Starts looking around.) If the elves took the tires and all, but they need them to cool off and stuff, I think that's all right.

SARA KATE: (Not really paying attention, walking in the giant way) Of course, it's all right.

HILLARY: But it would probably be wrong if they took somebody's personal stuff.

SARA KATE: Human rules don't work for elves. What are you doing way over there?

HILLARY: If there was something that a human being owned and needed and loved, and an elf didn't need it or love it or anything. It would be wrong for that elf to take it.

SARA KATE: What are you doing? There's no building materials over there.

HILLARY: I'm looking for something.

SARA KATE: What?

HILLARY: My diary. I'm looking for my diary.

SARA KATE: Your diary isn't over there.

HILLARY: (*Hopeful*) Where is it?

SARA KATE: How should I know? Is that what this is about? Your diary? (*Beat*) You *do* think I stole your diary.

HILLARY: (*Too fast*) No. No. I . . . I lost it. I can't find it. And I had it here yesterday, so I thought, maybe . . .

SARA KATE: What?! You thought, what?!

HILLARY: I thought . . . maybe . . . I left it here. By mistake.

SARA KATE: You think I sneaked into your stupid book bag and stole your stupid diary. Boy, you *are* the same as Jane and Alison. Every time something happens, you blame it on me. You are sickening.

HILLARY: (*Getting mad*) What am I supposed to think? The last time I ever saw it, I was here—

SARA KATE: (*Shouting*) Who cares what you think? You're a stupid little girl with stupid little friends.

HILLARY: (*Shouting*) I am not stupid and my friends are not stupid. We have a song—

SARA KATE: A stupid song to show how stupid your brains are—

HILLARY: Don't you call us stupid. You got held back. You're the only one's stupid around here.

SARA KATE: Get out. Get out of my yard.

HILLARY: I was going to give you my jacket. I brought my jacket all the way over here to give it to you.

SARA KATE: Who wants your stupid jacket?! Get out.

(*The Ferris wheel spins by itself, whirs, dazzles. The girls are silent, amazed. HILLARY stops it.*)

SARA KATE: (*Gently*) Why did you stop it?

HILLARY: It scared me.

SARA KATE: (*Sympathizing*) Oh, don't be scared of elves. Elves can't hurt people. People can hurt elves is all.

(*The window shade on the house is pulled to one side.*)

HILLARY: Do you want my jacket? My mother said I could give it to you. I got this new one.

SARA KATE: So you could match your good friends.

HILLARY: . . . You never wear a coat.

SARA KATE: I don't . . . get cold.

HILLARY: Like an elf.

SARA KATE: (*Notices the window shade*) Oh, man. I gotta go before the bank closes. Do you want to go shop with me?

HILLARY: Do you go to the corner, to Mr. Neal's?

SARA KATE: No. I go to the supermarket. Things are cheaper, and it's . . . just better to go to the big stores.

HILLARY: My mother would kill me if I went all the way to the supermarket.

SARA KATE: So don't go, no skin off my nose.

HILLARY: No, okay, I'll go with you.

Scene 7

(*Immediately following. The girls walk into the big city. There is a bigness all around them, a large city with accompanying sounds. Tall buildings, traffic. A bigness in which a little girl can move anonymously. HILLARY stands back and watches and listens amazed at SARA KATE. SARA KATE talks to unseen functionaries. At the bank. SARA KATE downstage, front; HILLARY watches slightly upstage.*)

SARA KATE: (*Ultra sweet*) Hello, I need to cash my mother's check, ma'am. See? She signed it right on the back. Her signature is on file here and you can look it up. I cash the checks because she works and can't come here, and it's real convenient for me to do it because the bank is right near our house. (*Worried*) I always do it, ask anybody. (*Relieved*) . . . Twenties will be fine.

(*SARA KATE and HILLARY walk. Street sounds. Then they enter the pharmacy. HILLARY watches as SARA KATE talks.*)

SARA KATE: (*Worried*) I *know* the prescription has run out, but the person who was here yesterday promised to call the doctor to okay the refill. This is very terrible. You see, my mother needs her medicine and she's already gone a whole day without it, because that other man, he said he'd call the doctor. Could you just give me one refill for one month's supply? . . . Great, great.

(*At the grocery store. Walking with HILLARY.*)

SARA KATE: (*To HILLARY*) In the grocery store, you only buy *plain* boxes of stuff, no brands, because they cost more money. If you buy the stuff in the plain boxes, it costs a lot less. Cream of Wheat in the plain box lasts a long time and it really fills you up when you're hungry. That way you have enough to send some money to the electric company and the phone bill; you don't want them turned off because to get them turned back on, you gotta give them *more* money, for a deposit.

HILLARY: What's a deposit?

SARA KATE: It's a whole bunch of money that you don't get anything for. Only poor people have to pay one.

HILLARY: . . . That doesn't make sense.

SARA KATE: You're tellin' me.

(*HILLARY is amazed.*)

Scene 8

(*Lenox yard. Saturday dusk. MRS. LENOX is puttering. HILLARY enters from the hedge. HILLARY is nervous because she knows her mother would be furious if she knew she'd been shopping with SARA KATE.*)

MRS. L: It's about time you were home.

HILLARY: Why?

MRS. L: It's getting dark is why. It's time you were home.

HILLARY: Well, I *am* home.

MRS. L: And you should be.

HILLARY: Well, I am.

MRS. L: Hillary!

HILLARY: Whaaat?

MRS. L: (*Beat*) I think being with Sara Kate is making you cross.

HILLARY: (*Cross*) I'm not cross.

MRS. L: If Sara Kate is going to put you in a bad mood, we're not going to let you go over there.

HILLARY: Mom, you have to let me.

MRS. L: No, we don't have to.

(*MR. LENOX enters from house. He carries an envelope.*)

MR. L: (*To MRS. L*) Honey, did you pay the phone bill last month?

MRS. L: Sure I did.

MR. L: This says second notice.

MRS. L: (*Testy*) I guess I forgot, I don't know.

MR. L: Okay, I just don't want, you know, the old credit rating to slip.

MRS. L: (*Testy*) I'm sorry.

HILLARY: Don't worry. They don't turn off the phone unless you skip *two* months.

MR. L: I didn't know that.

HILLARY: Yeah, and if they *do* cut it off, there's a kind of phone service you can get for free.

MR. L: What kind is that?

HILLARY: It's a kind of phone service that you can only call out on.

MR. L: Why would I want that?

HILLARY: It's for emergencies; Sara Kate says the phone company *has* to let you have one. It's so you can call 911. But nobody can call you.

MR. L: What else does Sara Kate say?

HILLARY: She says you can get water from the hydrant for free.

MR. L: Oh?

HILLARY: Yeah, and the electric bill, if you just pay little bit, they won't turn it off, they're not allowed to if you're trying to pay.

MR. L: Oh, boy.

(*The parents exchange a look.*)

HILLARY: What?

MR. L: Hillary, what happens if everybody does that?

HILLARY: I don't know!

MR. L: Somebody has to pay for that electricity. The way it gets paid is everybody else's rates go up.

HILLARY: Poor people have to pay a deposit!

MR. L: (*Pause, gently*) Hillary, I think you shouldn't play with Sara Kate anymore.

HILLARY: But, Dad—

MR. L: No, I think it would be better if you don't see her anymore.

HILLARY: But you don't even know her.

MR. L: Honey, life is hard enough if people play by the rules; it's impossible if they don't.

HILLARY: But, Dad—

MR. L: Hillary. No. Everybody has to do their part. It's like a relay race—if somebody on the team doesn't run their part, the whole team loses.

HILLARY: We don't even have races like that at my school. (*Brief pause*)

MRS. L: Hillary, honey, go wash up for dinner.

(*HILLARY sighs, goes inside.*)

MR. L: Don't say it.

MRS. L: She's a little kid.

MR. L: She's not too little to learn.

Scene 9

(ALISON enters, mad, sits in a huff. JANE enters, then HILLARY, who is walking like a giant.)

ALISON: How could you, how *could* you, after we practiced all week? We practiced *all week.*

HILLARY: I looked into the audience and all of a sudden I couldn't remember the words or anything.

JANE: What are you *doing?*

HILLARY: *(Caught)* Oh! I was walking like a giant.

ALISON: Walking—?! Pay attention, Hillary. We worked so hard on the song to make it right. And it was stupid. What's the point of practicing if we're stupid?

JANE: What were you thinking about, Hillary?

HILLARY: I was wondering what to do when the toilet gets stopped up.

ALISON: The toilet! You are mental; you're mental!

JANE: You call your father, that's what you do.

ALISON: Kids don't have to fix toilets, Hillary.

HILLARY: Some kids do, I bet.

ALISON: Well, we don't.

HILLARY: We're pretty lucky. We're lucky.

ALISON: We're not lucky.

HILLARY: We are. Our parents can buy us stuff, and we have outfits. Everybody doesn't have outfits. Or dinners.

ALISON: Oh boy, wrap it up and send it to the starving children around the world, Hillary.

HILLARY: I'm just saying.

ALISON: Are we supposed to stand around and feel bad because we're not starving?

HILLARY: I don't know.

ALISON: Well I know. And it's stupid to feel bad because somebody else is starving.

HILLARY: Sara Kate doesn't have it so good.

ALISON: Is that what this is about? Sara Kate!?

JANE: *(Holds a pencil to her nose, prances around)* Hey, hey! Who am I? Who *am* I?

HILLARY: What are you doing?

JANE: I was being Sara Kate Connolly.

ALISON: (*To HILLARY*) Sara Kate took a math test with her pencil taped to her nose.

HILLARY: No!

ALISON: For sure. Right before she disappeared!

HILLARY: Maybe she had a . . . fit or something. Maybe that's why she hasn't been in school.

JANE: I never heard of a fit where you tape pencils to your nose.

HILLARY: There's all kinds of fits! Maybe she's really sick.

ALISON: She *is* really sick, Hillary. That's what we've been telling you.

JANE: She's mentally sick.

HILLARY: Sometimes I think *you're* mentally sick.

JANE: *What* did you say?

HILLARY: . . . I was joking.

ALISON: Ha, ha.

HILLARY: I mean, if somebody is really sick then somebody should visit her.

JANE: You better not.

HILLARY: I mean, who's taking care of the elf village?

ALISON: Oh, brother.

JANE: Your parents will get really mad if you go over there.

HILLARY: I can't. I have to go straight home. (*Beat*) I said I would.

JANE: (*To ALISON, exiting*) Come on, Alison, you and me can go practice.

ALISON: (*Exiting*) We don't need to practice; *we* didn't forget the words.

HILLARY: Bye. (*She watches until the girls are out of sight, then runs off.*)

Scene 10

(*Inside the Connolly house. It is very rundown. A knock at the door.*)

HILLARY: (*Off*) Hello? Is anybody home? Sara Kate? (*Pushes open the door and sticks her head in*) Hello, your door is open. (*Enters and gasps*) Wow, they're gone. They're all moved away! (*She enters, finds it a scary, uncomfortable place, starts to exit, hears something — the sound of a rocking chair on wood.*) Sara Kate? (*The sound continues. She looks toward the sound.*) Elves! It's the elves.

(*HILLARY crosses the stage in the semi-darkness, following the sound, which grows louder. Pushes open "a door," where in full window-light she sees SARA KATE in rocking chair with her mother. MRS. CONNOLLY is a thin, sick, frightened woman.*)

She and SARA KATE look toward HILLARY. HILLARY gasps. She is confused. She starts to babble.)

HILLARY: I thought no one was here. I thought the sound was elves. What's wrong with your mother?

(SARA KATE carefully gets up so as not to startle her mother, as HILLARY continues to babble.)

HILLARY: You weren't in school, I thought you were sick; I thought the elves needed help. The Ferris wheel is knocked over. I saw it in the yard. I'm not allowed to come here anymore. What's wrong with your mother?!

SARA KATE: (Whispers, practically hissing) Get out. Get out of my house. Don't ever come back. And don't you tell anybody.

HILLARY: I won't —

SARA KATE: Don't you *dare* tell anybody.

HILLARY: Sara Kate, it's me, Hillary.

SARA KATE: You get out and don't you come back. You forget you ever were in this house. You forget it, erase it from your mind, it didn't happen.

(HILLARY runs out. MRS. CONNOLLY covers her face with her hands; SARA KATE comforts her.)

END ACT ONE

ACT TWO

Scene 1

(AT RISE: A week later, the Lenox yard. Home from school, HILLARY reads the diary entry she just wrote.)

HILLARY: Dear Diary. (*Beat*) Dear Diary *Substitute*, or Journal, or whatever you are. I'm not mad at Sara Kate anymore about my real diary she stole, even though I know I ought to be. I can't be mad at her anymore. Once I almost told Alison and Jane what I saw, but I promised not to. Even if I did tell about it, I don't know what I would say; sometimes I think maybe it wasn't real. Maybe it was another elf dream. A bad one this time.

(MR. LENOX enters from the gate with a large trellis.)

MR. L: Hey, there's my girl.

HILLARY: Dad! What are you doing home?

MR. L: I took the afternoon off. Look what I got. I'm going to plant a trumpet vine next spring. Now it will have something to grow on.

HILLARY: Next spring is a long way away, Dad.

MR. L: Nah, it's right around the corner. Trumpet flowers are gorgeous.

HILLARY: I don't think I know what they look like.

MR. L: Gorgeous. Last night, I dreamt I *was* one. What do you think of that?

HILLARY: That's pretty weird. Did you come home early just to work in the garden, Dad?

MR. L: Just! Just to work in the garden?! Yeah, I did.

HILLARY: Wow. Too-too good.

MR. L: I'll say, too-too good. Plants don't talk back.

HILLARY: Plants don't talk at all.

MR. L: Even better. Where should we put the trellis?

HILLARY: I don't know.

MR. L: How about by the hedge?

HILLARY: Okay.

(*They put the trellis in front of the hedge. HILLARY stands back to look.*)

HILLARY: (*Sad*) Oh. Oh, Dad, can we put it somewhere else?

MR. L: What's wrong with here?

HILLARY: I just—I don't—It's like we're putting up bars between us and Sara Kate. (*She turns abruptly, gasps slightly.*)

MR. L: What?

HILLARY: Did you see something over there?

MR. L: No.

HILLARY: I thought I saw something. Right there.

MR. L: It was probably a bird.

HILLARY: Maybe.

(*HILLARY is silent. MR. LENOX moves the trellis away from the hedge.*)

MR. L: We'll put the trellis somewhere else.

HILLARY: Okay.

MR. L: I didn't know you were still thinking about Sara Kate.

HILLARY: Dad. I *want* to forget about her; I want to forget all about her, but she's always in my brain. I think I see her out of the corner of my eye, but then I turn to look, and she's not there.

MR. L: You weren't friends very long.

HILLARY: Dad. Dad. I know, I *know*. And sometimes it wasn't even very fun to be friends with her. But it was special. She's special.

MR. L: (*Beat*) I guess I didn't realize. (*Beat*) Hey, let's plant some bulbs. It'll clear our brains.

HILLARY: Now? In the cold?

MR. L: Yeah, plant them in the fall for flowers in the spring.

HILLARY: Okay.

MR. L: Get the bulb thing out of the shed.

(*HILLARY looks in the shed.*)

MR. L: There's a lot of gardening to be done in winter. Planting bulbs, pruning trees.

HILLARY: (*At shed*) I don't see the bulb thing.

MR. L: Look on the shelf. It's much less traumatic to the tree if its branches are cut in winter when the sap is slow.

(*HILLARY crosses back to MR. LENOX with her diary.*)

MR. L: Whatcha got there? That's not the bulb thing.

HILLARY: Dad, this is my diary. What's my diary doing in the shed?

MR. L: *That's* your diary? Oh. Oops. I put it there; I put it in the shed. I didn't think.

HILLARY: Oh, man, oh, no, oh, Dad. Oh, Dad. Sara Kate thinks I think she stole my diary.

MR. L: Why does she think that?

HILLARY: Because I *did* think it. Oh, man.

MR. L: Sorry, honey, really.

HILLARY: (*Miserable*) I'm an idiot.

MR. L: (*Beat*) Well, maybe you better get over there and apologize.

HILLARY: Really?

MR. L: Yeah, okay, go on.

Scene 2

(*The Connolly backyard, near dusk. HILLARY comes through the hedge. The elf village is in disarray; the Ferris wheel is on its side. She walks around for a moment. SARA KATE enters, she wears no coat in spite of the cold.*)

SARA KATE: Hello.

HILLARY: (*Startled*) Oh. Oh. Sara Kate, it's you. I didn't hear you. You're here!

SARA KATE: Of course I'm here.

HILLARY: I thought—I don't know, I haven't seen you. (*Beat*) How's your mother?

SARA KATE: She's fine. How should she be?

HILLARY: Sometimes she's sick.

SARA KATE: Sometimes everybody is sick.

HILLARY: When she gets sick, you take care of her.

SARA KATE: So what? When I get sick, she takes care of me.

HILLARY: But that's different—

SARA KATE: No, it's the same.

HILLARY: . . . How are the elves?

SARA KATE: They're okay.

(*They are quiet, not knowing what to say. SARA KATE rights the Ferris wheel.*)

HILLARY: Is it broken?

SARA KATE: No, it's fine.

HILLARY: What a mess.

SARA KATE: Yeah, I've been real busy. I'm trying to clean up.

HILLARY: Can I help?

SARA KATE: Here. (*Hands her a box*) Pick up the junk.

HILLARY: Okay. Your yard looks soooooo good.

SARA KATE: You just said it's a mess.

HILLARY: No, it's a great mess. An elf mess. There's nothing like this anywhere else.

SARA KATE: That's why the elves come.

HILLARY: I know. Some things only make sense here.

SARA KATE: Yes.

HILLARY: (*Beat*) Sara Kate? Did you tape a pencil to your nose?

SARA KATE: Yes. So what?

HILLARY: What for?

SARA KATE: So it wouldn't fall off when I took the math test.

HILLARY: Yeah, but, why did you *take* a math test with the pencil taped to your nose?

SARA KATE: I was practicing. You can do anything if you practice. You can learn anything. They read us that story about Pierre the Package. You know that story?

HILLARY: No, they didn't read us that story.

SARA KATE: Yeah, it's for older kids. Pierre doesn't have any arms or legs. Nothing. He's just a head and a body. So when he needs to write, somebody tapes a pencil to his nose so he can type.

HILLARY: Why don't they just type the letter for him?

SARA KATE: A million reasons why! Maybe it's a love letter; or maybe he wants to write it himself. If he wants to do it himself, he should be allowed.

HILLARY: It must be very hard.

SARA KATE: Lots of things are hard. You have to learn how to do them is all.

HILLARY: Like taking care of a house. (*Beat*) I found my diary.

SARA KATE: (*Sarcastic*) Congratulations.

HILLARY: Remember? I thought I left it here.

SARA KATE: You thought I stole it.

HILLARY: Yeah. I'm sorry.

SARA KATE: Who wants to read about the Mighty Three?

HILLARY: I don't write about that anymore.

SARA KATE: I don't see what's so great about being the same as them.

(*MRS. CONNOLLY appears in the window. SARA KATE sees her.*)

HILLARY: I'm not the same as them. They're not even the same as each other.

(*MRS. CONNOLLY disappears.*)

SARA KATE: (*Sighs*) I have to go in.

HILLARY: Is it your mother?

SARA KATE: Yes. She wants me to come in.

HILLARY: Do you want me to go home?

SARA KATE: (*Looks closely at HILLARY*) Listen —

HILLARY: Yes.

SARA KATE: Can you keep a secret?

HILLARY: I can. I can keep one forever.

SARA KATE: Okay. My mother has been worse lately and she likes to have me stay near. Do you have any money?

HILLARY: A little.

SARA KATE: We're out of stuff. Food. My mother likes coffee and milk. And sugar. We need bread and fruit. She likes fruit. And aspirin.

HILLARY: What else?

SARA KATE: Whatever you can get.

Scene 3

(*HILLARY is daunted by the enormity of the task, jams her hands in her pocket, takes a big breath, and begins to walk into the sounds of the city.*)

Scene 4

(*Later that day, inside the Connolly house. It is cold and barren. A knock. SARA KATE runs to the door, peeks out, and opens it for HILLARY, who enters completely out of breath carrying two large shopping bags.*)

SARA KATE: Look at all this stuff.

HILLARY: (*Out of breath*) Yeah, I got a real lot.

SARA KATE: I thought you said you only had a little money.

HILLARY: I broke up my bank. Forty bucks. I had to stop and rest a lot of times.

SARA KATE: You should have swiped a cart.

HILLARY: Oh. I didn't know.

SARA KATE: (*Pause*) You didn't tell, did you?

HILLARY: No, I didn't tell!

SARA KATE: (*Emptying a bag*) You got everything! Milk and cereal. You got the kind with raisins!

HILLARY: Yeah. Sorry. I couldn't find the plain white boxes, the cheap ones you said are better.

SARA KATE: Oh, no, don't apologize, this is fine, really great! Bread and bologna! You got bologna!

HILLARY: Yeah. Boy, stuff costs a lot.

SARA KATE: I know. (*Beat*) I got to take some stuff to my mother.

HILLARY: Okay.

(*SARA KATE puts some stuff in the empty grocery bag and exits. HILLARY takes the rest of the groceries out. She opens the refrigerator, finds the light doesn't go on and that it is not working.*)

HILLARY: Oh, man. Gross. This is gross.

(*Shuts refrigerator, sees a bug, jumps. Stands on a chair. SARA KATE returns.*)

SARA KATE: What are you standing there for?

HILLARY: I'm cold.

SARA KATE: Yeah, it gets cold. The furnace broke.

HILLARY: What do you do when the furnace breaks?

SARA KATE: First you call the oil company. Then they send a guy who says how much it costs. Then you tell them never mind because it's so much.

HILLARY: How do you keep warm?

SARA KATE: The stove. Upstairs I got three electric heaters and electric blankets.

HILLARY: Electric blankets give you cancer!

SARA KATE: Yeah, but if you don't keep warm you freeze to death.

HILLARY: How's your mother?

SARA KATE: She's okay. Let's have sandwiches, bologna sandwiches.

HILLARY: (Looks toward roaches) I'm not hungry.

SARA KATE: Suit yourself. I love white bread. (Finds mayonnaise) And mayonnaise! You need mayonnaise on bologna sandwiches.

HILLARY: Yeah, you do. I think I changed my mind.

SARA KATE: Two bologna sandwiches coming up!

HILLARY: I thought all you ate was berries off trees.

SARA KATE: Why eat berries off trees when you have bologneeee!?

HILLARY: (Happy) I don't know. I saw roaches.

SARA KATE: They don't hurt anybody. Roaches are misunderstood.

HILLARY: (Laughs) Somebody sprays our house.

SARA KATE: We used to get that. Now we try to get along with them.

HILLARY: Yuk.

SARA KATE: Roaches are very clean. I saw it on TV. Before they took the TV back. Here's a sandwich. Yippee, bologneee.

HILLARY: Who took the TV back?

SARA KATE: That's what happens when you don't have any money; people come and take your stuff away.

HILLARY: That's crummy.

SARA KATE: Yes, it's very terrible. I try to keep things paid. But sometimes, the money's just gone.

HILLARY: Man.

SARA KATE: But it helps when I send the bill people letters. I write and say I'll send them money next month.

HILLARY: (Slowly) You. You do everything.

SARA KATE: No. I mean. I *help* ... sometimes. I *help*.

HILLARY: No. You do everything. You pretend that your mother tells you what to do, like everybody else's mother. But that's not right. She doesn't tell you anything. She's took sick. You're the one taking care of her.

SARA KATE: So what! I learned how; I can do it.

HILLARY: Don't be mad. I was just trying to imagine it. What happens with the big stuff—I mean, the big stuff?

SARA KATE: I do it ... I do the big stuff, whatever happens, I do it. I sign it; I write it; I talk on the phone. I tell people what to do, and if they don't do it, I find some other way. My mother gets so upset when we run out of money.

HILLARY: Don't *you* get upset?!

SARA KATE: Sometimes my father can send money and sometimes he can't. When he can't, I just have to manage.

HILLARY: But how?

SARA KATE: People leave stuff. There was a whole cart full of food in the supermarket parking lot one time. At school, there's lost and found.

HILLARY: They give you lost and found?

SARA KATE: Sure, I say it's mine, and they give it to me.

HILLARY: You should tell. If people knew you were taking care of your mother by yourself, they'd do something about it.

SARA KATE: NO! They'd take my mother away.

HILLARY: You can't take care of her forever.

SARA KATE: I've been doing it for a year, and nobody even knows.

HILLARY: (*Quietly*) A year.

SARA KATE: People are stupid. They don't have a clue to what's going on right in their own backyards.

HILLARY: (*To herself*) I know.

SARA KATE: People don't like anybody who is sick. They put us where they can't see us.

HILLARY: Like the starving people around the world.

SARA KATE: Yeah, so if you're thinking of getting help for us, forget it.

HILLARY: My parents aren't like other people; we could ask my—

SARA KATE: No. No, Hillary. Somebody like you can ask for help; somebody like me has to steal it.

HILLARY: (*Beat*) Sara Kate? Are you an elf?

(*A loud knock at the door.*)

SARA KATE: Oh, no.

MRS. L: (*Off*) Hillary? Sara Kate? It's Mrs. Lenox. Mrs. Connolly, are you there?

SARA KATE: Get rid of her.

HILLARY: (*Peeks through the door*) Hi, Mom, I'm coming. Bye-bye, Sara Kate. (*Tries to exit*)

MRS. L: Just a minute, Hillary.

HILLARY: Let's go, Mom.

MRS. L: Where is Sara Kate?

HILLARY: Come on, Mom.

MRS. L: Hillary! Just a minute. (*Sees into the room*) What is . . . ? Sara Kate? What have you girls done to this room?

HILLARY: It's nothing; it's just Sara Kate.

MRS. L: What have you been doing? Where is your mother?

SARA KATE: (*With practiced courtesy*) Hello, Mrs. Lenox. I'm so glad to be seeing you again. It's been a long time, hasn't it. My mother is fine, but she's upstairs having a nap, now. I know this room looks terrible. We're having it fixed. That's why everything is moved. I'm sorry you had to come looking for Hillary.

MRS. L: (*Confused*) I tried to call . . .

SARA KATE: Yes, the phone's been turned off since this morning, which you probably found out. There must be a line down somewhere. There's a man coming to fix it.

MRS. L: Is the heat off, too?

SARA KATE: Yes. They had to turn off the heat. Just for an hour or so. They're working on pipes.

MRS. L: Pipes?

SARA KATE: Yes. So they had to turn off the heat. They always do that.

MRS. L: Who?

SARA KATE: Workmen. The workmen who fix pipes.

MRS. L: (*Pause*) I would like to see your mother.

SARA KATE: She can't be bothered. She'll call you when the phone is fixed.

MRS. L: Is she upstairs?

SARA KATE: Of course. She's taking a nap.

MRS. L: I'm going to go up.

SARA KATE: No! No. You can't go up.

MRS. L: Sara Kate, I need to speak with your mother.

SARA KATE: Would you please go away?! Just go away!

MRS. L: No, I'm not going to go away. I'm going to go talk to your mother. (*Exits*)

HILLARY: Do something. Can't you do something? She'll find out. She'll see your mother. Fix it.

SARA KATE: I don't know how to fix this. I should never—never—

HILLARY: Never what? Should never what?

SARA KATE: I should never have invited you.

HILLARY: To see the elves?

SARA KATE: People ruin everything.

HILLARY: I didn't. I didn't mean to.

SARA KATE: What you meant doesn't matter. It's all ruined. (*She puts her face in her hands.*)

HILLARY: It'll be okay. Mom's not like that. You'll see. Don't cry.

SARA KATE: (*Crying*) I . . . I'm so tired.

(*MRS. LENOX reenters greatly subdued.*)

HILLARY: Mom. What are you going to do?

MRS. L: Sara Kate. Sara Kate, stay with your mother. I'll be right back, do you understand? I'm going to take Hillary home, and then I'll be right back. Don't worry, Sara Kate. We're going to take care of your mother. Come on, Hillary.

(*MRS. LENOX leads HILLARY to the door. HILLARY turns back.*)

HILLARY: I'm sorry. I'm sorry, Sara Kate.

(*SARA KATE does not acknowledge HILLARY, but looks out blankly.*)

Scene 5

(*A week later, the Lenox garden. The bright sunny daylight contrasts strongly with the cold evening light of the previous scene. It's the comfort of daylight after a bad dream. HILLARY, with a pencil taped to her nose, writes the last word, then reads the diary entry.*)

HILLARY: Dear Diary. I stayed home again today. Mom and Dad act like I'm sick. If I don't eat enough dinner, they bring something special to my room, like soup with meatballs and crackers. Mom even made pie. But I hardly ate any. I guess I have to go back to school soon, but I don't want to. I don't want to see anybody. Nobody understands. They all have stuff and food and all.

(ALISON and JANE arrive at the gate. They are dressed alike. HILLARY puts down diary, and begins to rake leaves.)

ALISON: *(Pause)* Hi.

JANE: Can we come in?

HILLARY: It's a backyard, anybody can come in.

JANE: We brought your homework.

HILLARY: *(Sarcastic)* Great.

JANE: It's really hard. It's math and it's new.

ALISON: You should get your father to put in a swing set back here.

HILLARY: He says I'll outgrow it and then we'll still have the cement pilings.

ALISON: Your father is mental.

JANE: Too-too mental.

HILLARY: He isn't mental. He likes his yard.

JANE: When you coming back to school? We miss you.

ALISON: We thought you were sick.

HILLARY: You knew I wasn't sick.

JANE: But you haven't been at school. Not since they found out Sara Kate kept her mother a prisoner.

HILLARY: She did not keep her mother a prisoner.

ALISON: That's what it said in the paper. It said she kept her mother from getting medical attention.

HILLARY: Sure, medical attention in some asylum.

ALISON: What's the matter with you, Hillary?

JANE: Alison, be quiet. Want some help, Hillary?

HILLARY: I don't care.

JANE: *(Gets rake)* Hey! My dad's getting married, and guess what?

HILLARY: *(Not interested)* What?

JANE: I get to be in the wedding ceremony and you and Alison get to go as my guests.

ALISON: What should we wear, Hillary?

HILLARY: I don't know.

ALISON: Maybe we should dress like Jane in her flower-girl dress.

HILLARY: I don't know if I can go.

JANE: No, you can't dress like me; people won't know who is me. I have to be separate.

HILLARY: I might be sick that day.

JANE: Hillary, don't worry if you still feel a little bad about Sara Kate. She was even worse than we thought. And you're tied up in knots about it.

ALISON: You shouldn't feel stupid because you fell for all her lies, even though me and Jane never did.

JANE: Sara Kate was very terrible; she made up the whole thing about elves and how they live and what they eat and stuff.

ALISON: Don't worry. We don't blame you at all. It wasn't fair to pick on someone so much younger. We blame Sara Kate.

HILLARY: I don't blame Sara Kate. I blame you. You don't know anything about it; you don't know anything about elves.

JANE: If elves are so great, why did Sara Kate leave the village behind?

HILLARY: (*Surprised, then making it up*) She left it for me. She knows I'll take care of it.

ALISON: She didn't leave it for you; she didn't have time to take it with her when she ran away, is all.

HILLARY: (*Pause*) She ran away?

ALISON: She didn't want to go to a foster home. (*Beat*) It says so in the paper.

HILLARY: Do you believe everything it says in the stupid newspaper?!

ALISON: Newspapers never lie.

HILLARY: They do; all the time.

ALISON: Don't be stupid, Hillary. You're being an idiot over nothing.

HILLARY: Sara Kate is not nothing.

(MRS. LENOX appears at the back door.)

MRS. L: Hey! What's all this yelling?

ALISON: We didn't do anything; it's Hillary.

JANE: We didn't start it.

MRS. L: Start what? Jane, put down that rake.

JANE: I didn't do anything.

MRS. L: I think you girls better go home.

JANE: When is Hillary coming back to school?

MRS. L: Soon. She'll be back soon.

JANE: Bye, Hillary. Sorry. (*Exiting*)

ALISON: We don't have to apologize; we didn't do anything.

(*Girls exit. Brief pause.*)

MRS. L: What was that all about?

HILLARY: They said Sara Kate ran away. Because she didn't want to go to a foster home. She doesn't have to go to a foster home, does she?

MRS. L: Hillary, Sara Kate is on her way to Kansas. To her father.

HILLARY: Because if she didn't have any place to stay, well, she could stay with us.

MRS. L: Sara Kate is a very troubled little girl.

HILLARY: She's very smart. She took care of her whole house.

MRS. L: I know, Hillary. But what she did, the letters, the lying—

HILLARY: She was afraid, Mom. And she was right.

MRS. L: Hillary . . . Mrs. Connolly needs to be in a hospital.

HILLARY: Everything she was afraid would happen happened.

MRS. L: Her mother wasn't getting better; she was getting worse.

HILLARY: They took her mother, Mom. Just like Sara Kate said. Her mother.

MRS. L: Hillary, she was too little to take care of her mother herself. She was too little to take care of herself, herself. Now they both have a chance to get better.

HILLARY: Could I write to her?

MRS. L: We'll wait and see if she writes to you.

HILLARY: She'll probably ask about the elf village.

MRS. L: She probably will. Why don't you bring it over here? So you can keep an eye on it for her.

HILLARY: What? Are you nuts?

MRS. L: Hillary!

HILLARY: I'm sorry, I'm sorry. I didn't mean—Mom. Mom. Dad would, Dad would, he'd—

MRS. L: It's Dad's idea.

HILLARY: Dad's?

(*MR. LENOX at the door.*)

MR. L: Yeah, your *Dad's*.

HILLARY: Dad!

MR. L: People are coming to haul the junk out of the yard, thank goodness.

MRS. L: Then they're going to start showing it to people. To buy.

MR. L: I don't think anybody's going to want to have an elf village in his backyard.

HILLARY: (*Looks around, it's not possible*) Oh, man. Thanks, thanks really. But I don't think it'll work out. Our yard's too neat. The elves won't come here.

MRS. L: How about behind the garage? It's a mess back there.

HILLARY: Yeah. (*Beat*) Yeah! It's a disaster back there. It's perfect.

MR. L: I knew I had some reason for not cleaning it up.

HILLARY: That's great. That's great. Thanks, thanks a lot.

Scene 6

(*Immediately following, the Connolly yard. The village is in disarray. HILLARY starts to pack up the village.*)

HILLARY: (*Whispering*) You elves are very untidy. Oh! Don't whisper. Whispering is unnatural. (*Beat*) Maybe you aren't untidy, maybe it's earth forces messing up your village each time. (*She gasps and turns to see an elf, but it's gone.*) Someday you'll let me see you. I won't have to work at it at all; one day I'll see an elf. (*Beat*) How'd I know that? (*Realizes*) The elves are sneaking information into my brain! Hey, elves! Sneak information into Sara Kate's brain—a message from me. (*Remembers playing with SARA KATE*) Sara Kate? The elves are going to live in the mess behind my garage. There's plenty of places for them to hide back there. I'll take extra rocks to separate their little lots. They're starting to trust me a little. I almost saw one.

(*As lights fade and music cue sounds, SARA KATE appears on stage. HILLARY speaks to her as if she were really there. The girls walk in the giant way.*)

HILLARY: You don't have to worry at all; I remember everything you said. I will be one kindly giant sister, making sure no evil forces harm the elves or their village. I will climb the tallest hill and scan the horizon, waiting for your return.

(*The Ferris wheel turns, as lights fade.*)

CURTAIN

Production credits from the premiere of *Afternoon of the Elves* and details concerning performance rights are included in the acting edition of the play as published by Dramatic Publishing.

Broken Hearts

Dramatized by Gretta Berghammer and Rod Caspers

Based upon stories by Oscar Wilde: "The Birthday of the Infanta," "The Devoted Friend," and "The Happy Prince"

Three of Oscar Wilde's most poignant children's stories are woven together in *Broken Hearts*. In "The Birthday of the Infanta," a young princess's heartless disregard for the feelings of a "Fantastic" — an imperfect boy brought to entertain at her birthday party — causes his heart to break. "The Devoted Friend" finds three villagers gathered in a tavern relating the perils of a one-sided friendship. "The Happy Prince" reveals the magical tale of a selfish prince turned into a statue, and a selfless swallow who helps him right past wrongs. Told by an ensemble of actors and connected by moments of simple narration, Wilde's biting wit and social critique are made accessible to new generations of young people, who are left to consider how the stories' timeless morals echo in their own modern lives.

Prologue

The Birthday of the Infanta

The Devoted Friend

The Happy Prince

Epilogue

Characters

The Birthday of the Infanta

NARRATOR
THE INFANTA OF SPAIN
DON PEDRO, HER UNCLE
THE CHILDREN:
  MARIA
  SOPHIA
  ANDRES
  MULDANADO
  ROSA
  JUANITA
  THERESE
THE FANTASTIC

The Happy Prince

NARRATOR
THE HAPPY PRINCE
THE MAYOR
THE COUNCILOR
THE SWALLOW
THE MOTHER
THE SON
THE YOUNG MAN
THE FATHER
THE MATCH-GIRL
THE FIRST GIRL
THE SECOND GIRL
THE WATCHMAN

The Devoted Friend

NARRATOR
VILLAGER 1
VILLAGER 2
BARKEEP
TRAVELER 1
TRAVELER 2
HUGH, THE MILLER
HIS WIFE
HIS CHILD
LITTLE HANS
DOCTOR

Prologue

(*A musical overture begins as a pool of light reveals NARRATOR standing alone in the middle of the stage. Gradually, a second pool of light fades up, revealing a frozen tableau from THE BIRTHDAY OF THE INFANTA. The scene is the FANTASTIC, dancing for the INFANTA. As the tableau comes to life, NARRATOR crosses toward the scene and turns to face the audience.*)

NARRATOR: The innocence of a young boy who dances his heart out for a young princess who has no heart.

(*With NARRATOR's final words, the tableau freezes and a second pool of light fades up, revealing a frozen tableau from THE DEVOTED FRIEND. The scene is that of LITTLE HANS taking notes as the MILLER utters a statement about friendship. The tableau comes to life as NARRATOR crosses toward the scene.*)

NARRATOR: The irony of a miller who manipulates the good heart of his loyal companion—all in the name of friendship.

(*As before, with NARRATOR's final words, the tableau freezes and a third pool of light fades up, revealing a frozen tableau from THE HAPPY PRINCE. The scene is that of SWALLOW sitting at the foot of the HAPPY PRINCE. The tableau comes to life as NARRATOR crosses toward the scene.*)

NARRATOR: The beauty of a prince and a bird who are willing to sacrifice their hearts so that others will not suffer. (*Again, the tableau freezes with NARRATOR's final words. The NARRATOR crosses to center stage.*) "Broken Hearts." (*The lights and music fade.*)

The Birthday of the Infanta

NARRATOR: It was the birthday of the Infanta!

(*ENSEMBLE rushes on, laughing, talking, playing a game of Blind Man's Bluff. The INFANTA is blindfolded, and is attempting to win the game. The OTHERS are biding their time, either encouraging her on with the game, or mildly teasing and taunting her. The INFANTA's uncle, DON PEDRO, watches the festivities from one side. They freeze as NARRATOR continues.*)

NARRATOR: Although she was a real princess and the Infanta of Spain, she had only one birthday every year, just like children of quite ordinary people. Usually she was only allowed to play with children of her own rank, so she always had to play alone. But her birthday was an exception, and her father, the King of Spain, had given orders that she was to invite any of her young friends, rich and poor, to come and amuse themselves with her. (*ENSEMBLE Unfreezes and continues to play.*)

INFANTA: There Sophia, I can hear you giggling. I shall find you for sure. (*Darts to tag SOPHIA, who moves away at the last minute. The INFANTA misses. She regains her composure and begins again.*) This time I'll get you for sure. Watch me, Father! Watch me! (*The INFANTA waves to her FATHER, who is off-stage. This scene freezes.*)

NARRATOR: From the palace window, a very sad and melancholy king watched his daughter playing and laughing. Near her stood his brother, Don Pedro of Aragon, whom he hated. Sadder than ever was the King, for as he watched the Infanta delight in her party and wave to him, he could only think of the young queen, the Infanta's mother, who had died when the Infanta was only six months old. The queen had come from the gay country of France, and her spirit had gradually withered away in the somber splendor of the Spanish court. So great had been the king's love for the queen that he could not bear the thought of burying her beneath the ground. So instead, he had had her body embalmed, and for the past eleven-and-a-half years it lay on a tapestried bier in the chapel of the palace. It was here the king often went to be comforted by her memory, leaving the Infanta quite alone. (*Their teasing and taunting whispers increase, as do the INFANTA's failures to find them. As she lunges once again, she stumbles and falls to all fours. She rises before DON PEDRO can help her.*)

INFANTA: Now stop. I am the daughter of the King of Spain and a real princess, and I hereby order you to freeze where you are. Anyone who dares to disobey me shall have to appear before my father and his council, and shall risk being beheaded! (*The CHILDREN in turn approach the INFANTA and allow themselves to be caught easily. When the last child, MULDANADO, has been discovered the INFANTA removes blindfold proudly.)* There, Father, look! See! I've won! I've won! *(She notices her FATHER is gone from the window.)*

DON PEDRO: *(Rushing to her rescue)* Congratulations, sweet niece. How well you played the game.

INFANTA: Why has my father left the courtyard window? Doesn't he care about my party?

DON PEDRO: Of course he does, Your Highness. Why, he has issued a proclamation throughout the entire country ordering that you must have a really fine day on the occasion of your twelfth birthday.

INFANTA: Will my father be attending my celebration with me, or has he chosen to busy himself with other matters?

DON PEDRO: The king is indisposed this afternoon, Your Highness. Unfortunately, he must attend to State affairs, but he does send his love and best wishes to you.

INFANTA: Surely he might have stayed with me on my birthday. What do stupid State affairs matter today? Or could it be that you are lying and that in truth he has gone to that gloomy palace chapel, where the candles are always burning, and where I am not allowed to enter? *(The INFANTA turns as if to leave the celebration, but stops when DON PEDRO calls to her.)*

DON PEDRO: Your Highness!

INFANTA: How silly of him, when the sun is shining so brightly, and everyone is so happy . . . But come, Uncle, or we will be late for the festivities that are to be performed. *(An elaborate procession is assembled, and the INFANTA proudly marches to her throne. DON PEDRO stands at her side, and the CHILDREN group themselves at her feet.)*

MARIA: What if she doesn't like the presentation?

SOPHIA: Just do it.

ANDRES: And don't forget to curtsy.

MARIA: What if we don't perform well? Look how angry she got just now playing that stupid game, just because she couldn't win.

MULDANADO: Look at the Infanta. How could anyone so lovely looking ever be cruel to anyone? Take your places, and I will go and do the introductions. Your Highness, in honor of your birthday, a pantomime has been especially prepared for you. *(MULDANADO ad libs a short introduction for the "bullfight," introducing MARIA, SOPHIA, and ANDRES, who perform with him. MULDANADO, MARIA and SOPHIA perform as toreadors in an elaborate bullfight dance-pantomime, using hobby horses and toy swords. ANDRES plays the bull in this splendid and prolonged fight, during which one of the hobby horses is gored right through, and the rider is forced to dismount and battle on foot. Eventually, MULDANADO kills the bull with his sword and presents its piñata heart to the INFANTA: The heart is broken open, and out spills candy and other treats, which the CHILDREN, at the INFANTA's command, readily divide among themselves and begin to enjoy.)*

INFANTA: *(To MULDANADO)* It certainly was a marvelous bullfight . . . much nicer than the real bullfight I saw in Seville with the Duke of Parma. And who will perform for me next, Uncle?

DON PEDRO: Two magicians, Your Highness, with some fine new tricks. *(Next, JUANITA and THERESE come forth and perform a series of stunts and magic tricks. These may include juggling and sleight-of-hand tricks. Ends with thunderous applause.)*

INFANTA: That was fun, but surely there is something even more spectacular prepared. Uncle, where is my present from you?

DON PEDRO: And now for the grand finale of the afternoon. I have prepared a very special surprise entertainment that not even the Infanta knows of. Now, if you will all close your eyes, I will summon for the Infanta's present.

(ENSEMBLE freezes as DON PEDRO moves upstage. From the wings emerges the FANTASTIC, a young boy of grotesque appearance. His back is crooked and distorted, his hair long and unkempt, his face twisted, and his limbs somewhat contorted. He is dragging a decorated trunk, large enough to eventually conceal him.)

DON PEDRO: Now . . . you remember what I told you to do.

FANTASTIC: Oh yes! You said that I must smile and bow! You said that my smile was very funny and my bow was funnier. I never try to be funny.

DON PEDRO: Some boys are funny even when they don't try to be.

FANTASTIC: I don't feel funny. I just feel happy, and when I feel happy people laugh. I hope I can feel happy here. This place is so strange, and not at all like my home in the woods. When am I going home?

DON PEDRO: When you make the Infanta happy.

FANTASTIC: I always make people happy when they look at me. I hope the Infanta will be pleased. Am I really happy looking?

DON PEDRO: You are a Fantastic!

FANTASTIC: That sounds happy.

DON PEDRO: I hope it always will be. Now, into the chest so that your arrival will surprise and delight the Infanta. And remember, you must dance your best. Smile. Be brave. And do not speak until you are asked to. *(The FANTASTIC crawls into the trunk, and DON PEDRO freezes as he closes the lid.)*

NARRATOR: It was the custom at the Spanish court, always noted for its cultivated passion for the horrible, to present members of the nobility with humans who were inferior to them, in both birth and appearance. Don Pedro's present to the Infanta was no exception; he had gotten a horrible, fantastic monster. Such a sight had never been seen by this court before. He had been discovered only the day before by two court nobles, running wild through the forest. They had carried him off as a surprise for the Infanta. The little monster's father, a poor charcoal-burner, was all too pleased to get rid of so ugly and useless a child, and had sold him to the noblemen for three gold pieces. But what amused Don Pedro most was the little monster's complete unconsciousness of his own grotesque appearance. (*ENSEMBLE comes to life as DON PEDRO speaks.*)

DON PEDRO: You may all open your eyes now. The surprise has arrived. Happy birthday, Your Highness. Go and open the trunk. (*The INFANTA cautiously taps on the lid of the trunk as the CHILDREN encourage her. Suddenly, out pops the FANTASTIC, sporting a low respectful bow. He is the instant delight of the INFANTA and CHILDREN. The INFANTA claps her hands and laughs in sheer delight. The FANTASTIC looks fearfully over at DON PEDRO, who encourages him to begin.*) Bow again and then begin to dance. (*The FANTASTIC makes another low sweep and in his enthusiasm tumbles out of the trunk.*)

INFANTA: Oh please go on. Isn't he funny? (*The INFANTA seats herself on a small stool, and the FANTASTIC hides behind his trunk until the music begins. His dance is lovely and comic, full of acrobatics and leaps. The laughter of the CHILDREN makes him laugh and dance all the more, and he smiles and nods at them as though he were one of them. He is absolutely fascinated by the INFANTA, and can scarcely keep his eyes off her as he performs. At the end of his dance, the INFANTA is so charmed, she removes a single white rose from her hair and hands it to the FANTASTIC. The FANTASTIC takes the matter quite seriously. He presses the flower to his lips, puts his hand on his heart and sinks to one knee before her, grinning from ear to ear. To DON PEDRO.*) Oh, Uncle. He's absolutely delightful. He is so very ugly and very crooked, and very, very funny to look at. I should like him to dance for me again. The same dance.

DON PEDRO: Your Highness, the sun is too hot, and besides, you must prepare for your birthday feast. It would be better that Her Highness should return without delay to the palace, where a wonderful feast has been prepared for you. Your father and guests will be waiting, and you must see the huge birthday cake with your initials on it in painted sugar, and a lovely silver flag waving from the top.

INFANTA: Very well, then. He will dance for me after my hour of siesta, and when I return from my chambers, I shall stroke his hump for luck. (*The INFANTA and DON PEDRO exit. As INFANTA leaves, she looks once more at the FANTASTIC, and breaks into a laugh. The FANTASTIC is delighted, and stands looking after her. The OTHERS prepare to leave. They talk among themselves as the FANTASTIC remains enraptured by the INFANTA, and begins kissing the rose and making other gestures of delight.*)

ROSA: He is really far too ugly to be allowed to play in any place where we are.

JUANITA: He should drink much wine and go to sleep for a thousand years.

MULDANADO: He certainly should be kept indoors for the rest of his life. Look at his hunched back and crooked legs.

SOPHIA: He is a perfect horror. Why, he is twisted and stumpy and his head is completely out of proportion with his legs. Really, he makes me feel prickly all over, and if he comes near me I will hit him.

MARIA: I can't believe the Infanta gave him her best blossom. I gave it to the Infanta this morning myself, as a birthday present, and now she has given it away to this pathetic creature.

ANDRES: It is disgusting the way he jumps about merrily, as though he were no different than any of us. Why, I think he fancies himself one of the court.

THERESE: I think he fancies himself one of the Infanta's suitors.

MULDANADO: He doesn't know she admires him only because he is so horrible.

ANDRES: Still, he is a Fantastic. I suggest we all touch his hump for luck! (*All this time, the FANTASTIC has paid no attention to the taunts of the CHILDREN, who finish cleaning up. As a group, they converge on him, touch his hump, and run screaming and laughing from the room. The FANTASTIC is visibly shaken by this, and is frightened by being suddenly alone. He begins to calm himself with a daydream, a fantasy of always being with the INFANTA. As this daydream is played out in his mind, he begins to calm down.*)

(*As the FANTASTIC begins to speak, DON PEDRO appears upstage, secretly listening to the FANTASTIC's words.*)

FANTASTIC: The Infanta of Spain is the daughter of the king, and I have made her smile. And she has given me a beautiful white rose, and has asked me to dance a second time. Surely she must love me! Oh, how I wish I could be with her now. She would have taken me by the hand, and smiled at me, and never left my side. (*He mimes this action, and begins an imaginary walk through the woods with the INFANTA on his arm around and around the throne room.*) And I would show her where the pigeons build their nests and where the rabbits play in the ferns, and introduce her to the great wise tortoises. And I would give her my own little bed to sleep in, and all night long I would keep watch outside her window to see that the wolves did not harm her. And at dawn I would tap at the shutters and wake her, and we would go out and dance together all day long. (*DON PEDRO exits as the FANTASTIC looks about him.*) But where is she? Where could she have gone? The whole palace must be asleep. I want to find her alone, and tell her that I love her, too, and ask her to come away with me when I have finished my second dance. Perhaps she is in the room beyond. Perhaps she is hiding behind that . . .

(*MIRROR 1 appears. The FANTASTIC crosses to where the INFANTA made her exit, only to find himself blocked by a MIRROR, held by a member of the ensemble. The FANTASTIC, who has never seen his reflection, gasps in horror at the image, which he believes to be another person. The FANTASTIC plays before the MIRROR, unaware of its grim reality.*)

FANTASTIC: Who are you, you little beast . . . You are making me afraid . . . You are so very crooked looking . . . and you are so funny . . . Don Pedro says my smile is funny, and my bow is funnier still . . . (*He does these actions.*) But not as funny as yours! If you could see yourself, you'd laugh still more . . . (*The mockery is becoming too clever.*) . . . You mock me, you beast . . . Stop it . . . Why do you frown at me? Don't look at me that way, you are scaring me . . . Can't you talk? You only move your lips. (*He runs forward and puts out his hand. He rubs his hand over the face of the MIRROR, brushes his hair from his eyes, makes faces, etc. He begins to realize that everything about the room is repeated in the mirror. He darts to an area R and a second MIRROR played by a member of the ENSEMBLE appears, frightening the FANTASTIC and sending him scurrying back C; three more MIRRORS appear, and all FIVE close in a semi-circle around the FANTASTIC. Everywhere he looks, he sees his own reflection. He now realizes he is the horrid creature in the mirror. He kisses the rose, presses it to his heart, and with a painful cry sinks to the floor. The MIRRORS slowly begin to converge on him C, repeating the following lines in any pattern or order.*)

MIRRORS:
1. He is so very funny.
2. He is so very funny to look at.
3. He is so very crooked.
4. Some boys are funny without trying to be.
5. Stroke his hump for luck.
1. He is too ugly to be allowed to play.
2. Look at his hunched back.
3. Look at his crooked legs.

4. He is a perfect horror.

5. He is twisted.

1. He is stumpy.

2. He is ugly.

3. He doesn't know the Infanta admires him only because he is so horrible.

4. He doesn't know the Infanta admires him only because he is so horrible.

5. He doesn't now the Infanta admires him only because he is so horrible.

1. I think he fancies himself one of the Infanta's suitors!

FANTASTIC: See this! This is the rose the Infanta gave to me to thank me for my dancing. It is the only one like it in the whole world. She gave it to me—to me. (*The FANTASTIC tears the petals from the rose with his teeth, then he collapses DC on the INFANTA's stool. The MIRRORS, which have converged on him, exit slowly. Lights change.*)

(*Enter the INFANTA and DON PEDRO. At the sight of the FANTASTIC, the INFANTA stops and begins to laugh.*)

INFANTA: Look at him. His dancing was funny, but his acting is funnier still. Come now, enough of this. Dance for me. Yes, you must get up and dance, and then I shall play some more. My funny little Fantastic is sulking. You must wake him up and tell him to dance for me.

DON PEDRO: You must dance, my little monster. The Infanta of Spain has commanded to be amused.

INFANTA: A whipping master must be sent for. Make him dance, or I shall have him flogged. (*DON PEDRO goes to the FANTASTIC, kneels, feels his heart, and sees the crushed rose.*)

DON PEDRO: My little princess, your funny little Fantastic will never dance again.

INFANTA: (*Laughing*) Heavens! Why not?

DON PEDRO: Because his heart is broken. (*He hands the crushed rose to the INFANTA.*)

INFANTA: In the future then, let those who come to play for me have no hearts. (*She drops the rose and exits. DON PEDRO places the rose on the top of the FANTASTIC's lifeless body, picks him up, kisses his forehead and then cradles him in his arms. The lights fade.*)

END

The Devoted Friend

AUTHOR'S NOTE: When a character name appears in brackets before an underlined portion of text, the underlined words are to be spoken in unison by the indicated characters.

(SCENE: The lights reveal BARKEEP busy behind his imaginary bar as two VILLAGERS remain occupied with their mugs and their conversation. As NARRATOR stands C to introduce the scene, two TRAVELERS enter from U and join pub CROWD.)

NARRATOR: In a small town that was known for its hospitality and civilized society, a group of friends had gathered at Time's Pub to share in conversation and ale. (NARRATOR joins BARKEEP behind the bar, becoming a waitperson/ observer for the rest of the scene.)

TRAVELER 2: Love is all very well in its way, but friendship is much better.

TRAVELER 1: Indeed, I know of nothing in the world that is either nobler or rarer than a devoted friendship.

BARKEEP: And what, pray, is your idea of the duties of a devoted friend?

VILLAGER 1: Yes, that is just what I want to know.

VILLAGER 2: Me, too!

TRAVELER 1: I should expect my devoted friend to be devoted to me, of course.

BARKEEP: And what would you do in return?

TRAVELER 1: I don't understand you.

BARKEEP: Let me tell you a story on the subject. Once upon a time, there lived an honest little fellow named Hans.

(HANS enters DL in the area which becomes his cottage.)

BARKEEP: Hans had a great many friends. But his most *devoted* friend . . .

VILLAGER 2: (Interrupting) Only because Hugh told him so!

BARKEEP: . . . his most *devoted* friend was Hugh, the miller.

(The MILLER enters and approaches HANS.)

MILLER: Good morning.

HANS: Good morning.

MILLER: And how have you been all winter?

HANS: Well, really, it is very good of you to ask. I am afraid I had a rather hard time of it, but now that spring has come, I am quite happy. All of my flowers are doing well.

MILLER: My wife and I often talked of you during the winter, Hans, and wondered how you were getting on.

HANS: That was kind of you. I was half afraid you had forgotten me.

MILLER: Hans, I am surprised at you! [BARKEEP] *Friendship never forgets.* That is the wonderful thing about it. I am afraid you do not understand the poetry of life. How lovely your primroses are looking.

HANS: It is a most lucky thing for me that I have so many. I am going to take them into the market and sell them in order to buy back my wheelbarrow.

MILLER: Your wheelbarrow? You don't mean to say you have sold it? [TRAVELER 2] *What a very stupid thing to do.*

HANS: Well, the fact is that I was obliged to. You see, the winter was very hard for me and I really had no money at all to buy bread with. First I sold the silver buttons off my Sunday coat. Then I sold my silver chain, then my big pipe . . . But I am going to buy them all back again.

MILLER: Hans, I will give you my wheelbarrow. It is not in good repair, indeed one side is gone, and there is something wrong with the wheel spokes. But in spite of that, I will give it to you.

HANS: Why, thank you very much.

MILLER: I know it is very generous of me, and a great many people would think me extremely foolish for parting with it, but I'm not like the rest of the world. I think that [BARKEEP] *generosity is the essence of friendship.*

HANS: I see.

MILLER: Besides, I have got a new wheelbarrow for myself. Yes, you may set your mind at ease, I will give you my wheelbarrow.

HANS: Well, really, that is generous of you.

TRAVELER 2: I can't believe his stupidity.

HANS: I can easily put it in repair, as I have a plank of wood in the house.

MILLER: Why that is just what I need for the roof of my barn. There is a very large hole in it, and the corn will get damp if I don't stop it up. How lucky you mentioned it! It is remarkable how one good action always breeds another. I have given you my wheelbarrow, and now you are going to give me your plank. Of course, the wheelbarrow is worth far more than the plank, but [BARKEEP] *true friendship never notices things like that.* Pray, get it at once.

HANS: Certainly. (*HANS hands the MILLER an imaginary plank.*)

BARKEEP: And the rich miller took the plank clean away from his poor little friend.

TRAVELER 2: Just took it without paying anything in return?

HANS: Here we are!

MILLER: It is not a very big plank! I am afraid that after I have mended my barn roof, there won't be any left for you to mend the wheelbarrow; of course, that is not my fault. But now, as I have given you my wheelbarrow, I am sure you would like to give me some flowers in return. Here is the basket. Mind you, fill it quite full.

HANS: Quite full? But . . .

MILLER: Well, really, as I have given you my wheelbarrow, I don't think that it is much to ask you for a few flowers. I may be wrong, but I should have thought that friendship, [VILLAGER 2] *true friendship*, [VILLAGER 1] *was quite free from selfishness of any kind*. It will make you feel happy.

HANS: Dear friend, my best friend, you are welcome to all the flowers in my garden. I would much sooner have your good opinion than my silver buttons any day.

MILLER: Goodbye, little Hans.

HANS: Goodbye. (*The MILLER exits with his "plank" and "basket."*)

TRAVELER 1: Well, I know of nothing in the world that is either nobler or rarer than a devoted friendship, such as you describe.

TRAVELER 2: Sounds to me as if this little Hans was somewhat of a fool.

BARKEEP: Sometimes the neighbors thought it strange that the rich miller never gave little Hans anything in return. But Hans never troubled his head about such things. Nothing gave him greater pleasure than listening to all the wonderful things the miller used to say about the [HANS] *unselfishness of true friendship*. Hans wrote all such statements down in a notebook, and used to read them over during hard times, especially in the winter. He felt very proud to have a friend with such noble ideas.

(*The MILLER, with his WIFE and CHILD, is seen having supper in his cottage.*
CROWD in the pub freezes as the action onstage picks up the story they were telling.)

MILLER: There is no good in my going to see little Hans as long as the snow lasts, for when people are in trouble they should be left alone, and not be bothered by visitors. That at least is my idea about friendship, and [BARKEEP] *I am sure I am right*.

WIFE: You are certainly very thoughtful of others. It is quite a treat, husband, to hear you talk about friendship.

CHILD: But could we not ask little Hans here? If poor Hans is in trouble, I will give him half of my porridge, and show him my white rabbits.

MILLER: What a silly child you are! What is the use of sending you to school? Why, if little Hans came here and saw our warm fire, and our good supper, and our great cask of red wine, he might get envious. [WIFE, CHILD, and BARKEEP] *Envy is a most terrible thing, and would spoil anybody's nature.* I certainly will not allow Hans' nature to be spoiled. I am his best friend and I will always watch over him to see that he is not led into any temptations.

WIFE: Why, what a good heart you have! You are always thinking of others.

MILLER: Besides, if Hans came here, he might ask me to let him have flour on credit, and that I could not do.

CHILD: But Father, you have so much stored away that . . .

MILLER: Flour is one thing, and friendship is another, and they should not be confused. Everybody can see that.

TRAVELER 2: How well he talks! It is just like being in church. I feel drowsy.

MILLER: Lots of people act well, but very few people talk well, which shows that talking is much the more difficult and finer of the two.

(The MILLER enters and approaches HANS, carrying a heavy sack of imaginary flour on his back.)

MILLER: Hans. Hans. Hans!

HANS: Good morning!

MILLER: Hans, would you mind carrying this sack of flour for me to the market?

HANS: Oh, I am so sorry, but I am really very busy today. I have got all my creepers to nail up, and all my flowers to water, and all my grass to plant.

MILLER: Well, really, I think that considering that I am going to give you my wheelbarrow, it is rather unfriendly of you to refuse.

HANS: Oh, don't say that. I wouldn't be unfriendly for the whole world.

VILLAGER 2: Despite his plans, Hans took the flour to the market for the miller.

BARKEEP: Then, on the following day, the miller walked to Hans' cottage to get the money for his sack flour. When he arrived, Hans was still in bed, he was so exhausted from the day before.

MILLER: Upon my word, you are very lazy. I should think you might work harder, Hans. Idleness is a great sin, and I certainly don't like any of my friends to be idle or sluggish.

HANS: I am very sorry, but yesterday's trip . . .

MILLER: You must not mind my speaking quite plainly to you. Of course, I should not dream of doing so if I were not your friend. But what is the good of friendship if one cannot say exactly what one means? Anybody can say charming things and try to please and to flatter, [BARKEEP] *but a true friend* always says unpleasant things, and does not mind giving pain.

HANS: I am very sorry, but I was so tired that I thought I would lie in bed for a little time, and listen to the birds singing. Do you know that I always work better after hearing them?

MILLER: Well, I am glad of that, for I want you to come to the mill as soon as you are dressed, and mend my fence for me.

HANS: Do you think it would be unfriendly of me if I said I was busy?

MILLER: Well, really, I do not think it is much to ask of you, considering that I am going to give you my wheelbarrow; but of course, if you refuse, I will go and do it myself.

HANS: Oh! On no account!

TRAVELER 2: I don't believe his stupidity.

MILLER: Ah, there is no work so delightful [BARKEEP] *as the work one does for others.* (*HANS starts mending.*)

HANS: It is certainly a great privilege to hear you talk, a very great privilege. I am afraid I shall never have such beautiful ideas as you have.

MILLER: Oh, they will come to you, but you must take more pains. At present you have only the practice of friendship; someday, you will have the theory also.

HANS: Do you really think I shall?

MILLER: I have no doubt of it. But now that you have mended the fence, you had better go home and rest. Goodbye.

HANS: Goodbye.

MILLER: For I want you to drive my sheep to the mountain tomorrow. (*HANS goes to his cottage, the MILLER to his area.*)

TRAVELER 2: Friend?

VILLAGER 1: And besides, the miller was going to give him his wheelbarrow, and that is an act of pure generosity.

BARKEEP: Now it happened that one evening little Hans was sitting by his fireside when a loud rap came at the door.

VILLAGER 1: It was a very wild night, and the wind was blowing and roaring 'round the house. (*The MILLER rushes to HANS' cottage and bursts in the imaginary door.*)

MILLER: Dear little Hans, I am in great trouble. My child has fallen off a ladder and hurt herself, and I am going for the doctor.

HANS: I am so sorry to hear . . .

MILLER: But the doctor lives so far away, and it is such a bad night, that it just occurred to me that it would be much better if you went instead of me. You know I am going to give you my wheelbarrow, and so it is only fair [BARKEEP] *that you should do something for me in return.*

HANS: Certainly, I take it quite as a compliment your coming to me, and I will start off at once. But could you lend me your lantern? The night is so dark that I am afraid I might fall into the ditch.

MILLER: I am very sorry, but it is my new lantern, and it would be a great loss to me if anything happened to it. (*HANS crosses to the DOCTOR's house as the MILLER leaves for his own area.*)

BARKEEP: What a dreadful night it was. The night was so black that little Hans could hardly see, and the wind was so strong that he could scarcely stand.

DOCTOR: Who is there?

HANS: Little Hans, Doctor.

DOCTOR: What is the matter, little Hans?

HANS: The miller's daughter has fallen from a ladder and has hurt herself, and the miller wants you to come at once.

DOCTOR: All right! I'll be there in a minute. (*The DOCTOR crosses the stage and exits, leaving HANS to find his own way. He mimes the VILLAGERS' speeches, disappearing off one edge of the set as he "drowns."*)

BARKEEP: The storm grew worse and worse, and little Hans could not keep up with the doctor. At last he lost his way, and wandered off on the moor, which was a very dangerous place as it was full of deep holes, and there poor little Hans was drowned. His body was found the next day floating in a great pool of water, and was brought back to the cottage by some shepherds.

VILLAGER 2: Everybody went to little Hans' funeral, as he was so popular, and the miller was the chief mourner. (*The MILLER stands with his WIFE and CHILD, preparing for HANS' funeral.*)

MILLER: As I was his best friend, it is only fair that I should have the best place. So I will walk at the head of the procession in a long black cloak.

WIFE: Little Hans is certainly a great loss to everyone.

MILLER: A great loss to me at any rate. Why, I had as good as given him my wheelbarrow, and now I really don't know what to do with it. It is very much in my way at home, and it is in such bad repair that I could not get

anything for it if I sold it. I will certainly take care not to give away anything again. [BARKEEP] *One always suffers for being generous.* (*They exit.*)

TRAVELER 1: Well?

BARKEEP: Well, that is the end.

TRAVELER 1: But what became of the miller?

BARKEEP: Oh! I really don't know, and I am sure that I don't care.

TRAVELER 1: It is quite evident then that you have no sympathy in your
nature.

BARKEEP: I am afraid you don't quite see the moral of the story.

TRAVELER 1: The what?

TRAVELER 2: The moral.

TRAVELER 1: Do you mean to say that the story has a moral?

ALL: (*Except TRAVELER 1*) Certainly.

VILLAGER 2. There is nothing so noble as a devoted friend.

VILLAGER 1: One should always be thoughtful of others.

TRAVELER 2: Little Hans was a fool! (*ALL ad lib argument.*)

TRAVELER 1: (*To BARKEEP*) Well, really, I think you should have told me that
before you began. If you had done so, I certainly would not have listened to
you. (*TRAVELER 1 hands mug to BARKEEP and exits. The lights fade.*)

The Happy Prince

(*SCENE: NARRATOR dresses the HAPPY PRINCE with his cape and sword, and sets him on his pedestal.*)

NARRATOR: High above the city on a tall column stood the statue of the happy prince. He was gilded all over with thin leaves of fine gold. For eyes he had two bright sapphires and a large red ruby glowed on his sword hilt. Ah, he was very much admired indeed. One morning, the mayor and a town councilor were walking through the square, and as they passed the column they looked up at the statue.

MAYOR: Why, look at our prince! He is as beautiful as a weathercock, isn't he?

COUNCILOR: Yes, indeed. Only not quite so useful.

MAYOR: Yes, he is somewhat impractical. (*They exit.*)

NARRATOR: One night, there flew over the city a little swallow. All day long she had flown and at night she arrived in the city.

(*SWALLOW lights at the foot of the HAPPY PRINCE.*)

SWALLOW: I will put up here. It is a fine position with plenty of fresh air. Ah, I have a golden bedroom.

NARRATOR: But just as she was about to tuck her head under her wing, a large drop of water fell on her.

SWALLOW: What a curious thing. There is not a cloud in the sky and the stars are quite clear and bright, and yet it is raining. The climate here is really quite dreadful.

NARRATOR: Then another drop fell.

SWALLOW: What is a use of a statue if it cannot keep the rain off? I must look for a good chimney pot.

NARRATOR: But just as she was spreading her wings, a third drop fell on her.

SWALLOW: Who are you?

HAPPY PRINCE: I am the happy prince.

SWALLOW: Why are you weeping then? Your eyes are filled with tears, and they are running down your golden cheeks. You have quite drenched me.

HAPPY PRINCE: When I was alive and had a human heart, I did not know what tears were, for I lived in the Palace of Sans Souci, where sorrow was not allowed to enter. In the daytime I played with my sisters in the garden, and in the evening I led the dance in the Great Hall. 'Round the garden ran a very lofty wall, but I never cared to ask what lay beyond it. Everything about me was so beautiful.

SWALLOW: Well?

HAPPY PRINCE: My courtiers called me the happy prince, and happy indeed I was, if pleasure be happiness. So I lived and so I died. And now that I am dead, they have set me up here so high that I can see all the ugliness and all the misery of my city, and though my heart is made of lead yet I cannot choose but weep. (*SWALLOW turns away.*)

SWALLOW: What, he is not solid gold . . .

HAPPY PRINCE: Far across the city on a little street, I can see a small house. One of the windows was open, and through it I can see a woman seated at a table. Her face is thin and worn, and she has coarse red hands, all pricked by the needle, for she is a seamstress. In a bed in the corner of the room, her little boy is lying ill.

SON: Mother, I am so hot and thirsty.

MOTHER: Yes, my love. The fever continues.

SON: Could I please have but one orange?

MOTHER: I am sorry but we have none. All that I have is water from the river.

SON: But Mother, please . . .

MOTHER: Patience, my little one. Perhaps I can get some money from this embroidery. Yes, then I will buy some oranges. (*MOTHER and SON freeze in an appropriate stage picture.*)

HAPPY PRINCE: Swallow, will you take her the ruby from my sword hilt? My feet are fastened to this pedestal, and I cannot move.

SWALLOW: I am waited for in Egypt. My friends left weeks ago and by now are flying up and down the Nile talking to the large lotus flowers. Soon they will be asleep in the tomb of the great king. The king himself is there in his painted coffin. I must not delay any longer.

HAPPY PRINCE: Please stay with me for one night and be my messenger, will you? The boy is so sick and the mother so sad.

SWALLOW: I don't know if I like boys. Last summer when I was staying on the river, there were two rude boys, the miller's sons, who were always throwing stones at me. (*SWALLOW relives the moment through movement as she begins to boast.*) They never hit me of course. We swallows fly far too well for that, and besides, I come from a family famous for its agility. But still, it was a mark of . . . (*She turns to see the HAPPY PRINCE crying.*) It is very cold here. If you promise to stop crying, I will stay with you one night and be your messenger.

HAPPY PRINCE: Thank you, swallow.

NARRATOR: So the swallow plucked out the great ruby from the prince's sword, and flew away with it over the roofs of the town. She passed by the cathedral towers where the white marble angels were sculpted. And she passed by the river and saw the lanterns hanging by the masts of the ships. (*SWALLOW has been moving as if in flight throughout the narration. MOTHER and SON gradually become unfrozen.*) At last she came to the small house and looked in. The boy was tossing feverishly in his bed and the mother, so exhausted, had fallen asleep. The swallow placed the ruby next to the woman and then flew gently around the bed, fanning the boy's forehead with her wings.

SON: How cool I feel! I must be getting better.

MOTHER: Oh, I am hopeful you are. But now you must go back to sleep.

SON: Look, Mother! (*SON points to ruby on the floor. MOTHER picks the jewel up and studies it.*)

MOTHER: Can it be? A ruby! Oh my son, tomorrow I shall provide you with oranges and much more. (*MOTHER and SON embrace, then exit.*)

NARRATOR: Then the swallow returned to the prince and told him what she had done.

SWALLOW: It is curious. I feel quite warm now, though it is so cold.

HAPPY PRINCE: That is because you have done a good action.

(*At this point, there needs to be a light change and music break to indicate the passing of time.*)

NARRATOR: When day broke, the swallow was preparing for her journey. (*SWALLOW is stretching, looking off in the distance toward Egypt, testing the direction of the wind, etc.*)

(*A YOUNG MAN enters downstage and seats himself with his ledger and quill.*)

SWALLOW: Good morning! Have you commissions for Egypt? I am just starting.

HAPPY PRINCE: Swallow, will you not stay with me one night longer?

SWALLOW: I am waited for in Egypt! Tomorrow my friends will fly up to the Second Cataract.

HAPPY PRINCE: Far across the city, I see a young man in his garret. He is leaning over a desk covered with papers. His hair is brown and his lips are raw, and he has large, dreamy eyes. He is trying to finish a play for the director of the theatre, but he is too cold to write any more.

YOUNG MAN: (*As if talking to himself*) My fingers are so brittle, so cold. And I'm so hungry. I simply cannot go on . . . Oh, if only I had enough money to buy more firewood, I am sure I could finish the play. (*YOUNG MAN freezes in an appropriate stage picture.*)

HAPPY PRINCE: Swallow, little swallow, please? (*SWALLOW looks at the YOUNG MAN, considers, then returns to the HAPPY PRINCE.*)

SWALLOW: I will wait with you one night longer. Shall I take him another ruby?

HAPPY PRINCE: Alas, I have no ruby now. My eyes are all that I have left. They are made of rare sapphires, which were brought out of India a thousand years ago. Pluck one of them out and give it to him. He will sell it to a jeweler, and buy food and firewood, and finish his play.

SWALLOW: Dear Prince, I cannot do that. Your eyesight is one thing I will not take from you.

HAPPY PRINCE: Swallow, do as I command you.

NARRATOR: The swallow began to weep, but she plucked out the prince's eye, and flew away to the student's garret. (*Once again, SWALLOW pantomimes the journey as it is narrated.*) It was easy enough to get in, as there was a hole in the roof. Through this, she darted and came into the room. He did not hear the flutter of bird's wings.

YOUNG MAN: This is truly a blessing! (*He picks up the sapphire.*) Now I am certain to finish my writing for the fire will once again burn bright. Where did this come from? Maybe I am beginning to be appreciated. Perhaps this is from some great admirer.

(*Once again there needs to be a light change and music break indicating the passing of time. SWALLOW returns to the foot of the HAPPY PRINCE while the YOUNG MAN exits.*)

HAPPY PRINCE: Good morning!

SWALLOW: This day I must go to Egypt. I have come to say goodbye.

HAPPY PRINCE: Little swallow, will you please stay with me for one night longer?

SWALLOW: I cannot. It is winter, and the chill snow will soon be here. In Egypt, the sun is warm on the green palm trees, and the crocodiles lie in the mud and look lazily about them. Dear Prince, I must leave you, but I will never forget you, and next spring, when I return, I will bring back two beautiful jewels in place of those you have given away. The ruby shall be redder than a red rose, and the sapphire shall be as blue as the great sea.

HAPPY PRINCE: In the square below, I see a little match-girl and her angry father.

(*MATCH-GIRL and the FATHER enter. MATCH-GIRL falls and tries to gather her spilled matches.*)

HAPPY PRINCE: Her matches have fallen into the gutter, and they are all spoiled.

FATHER: You must not return this evening until you have something to show for your work! Yesterday, you brought no money!

MATCH-GIRL: But Father, all my matches are ruined.

FATHER: If you don't sell those matches, you will not eat!

MATCH-GIRL: Oh, but it is so cold outside, and I have no shoes and nothing to cover my head.

FATHER: Ah, be gone with you, child! (*MATCH-GIRL begins to cry.*)

HAPPY PRINCE: If she does not bring home some money, her father will beat her. Oh, and now she is crying. You must pluck out my other eye and give it to her.

SWALLOW: I will stay with you one night longer, but I cannot pluck out your other eye. You would be quite blind then.

HAPPY PRINCE: Do as I command you. Please. Do as I command . . .

NARRATOR: So the little swallow plucked out the prince's other eye and darted down with it. She swooped past the little match-girl, and slipped the jewel into the palm of her hand. (*As before, SWALLOW moves as if in flight while NARRATOR speaks.*)

MATCH-GIRL: (*Realizes there is something in her hand, and holds it up to observe it in the light*) What a lovely bit of glass! I can sell it, get more matches, and take some money home to my father. Oh, thank you, thank you!! (*MATCH-GIRL turns to go, then returns to kiss the SWALLOW on the forehead. MATCH-GIRL exits.*)

NARRATOR: Then the swallow returned to the prince.

SWALLOW: You are quite blind now; therefore, I cannot leave you.

HAPPY PRINCE: No, little swallow, you must go to Egypt.

SWALLOW: I will stay with you always.

NARRATOR: And the swallow slept at the prince's feet.

(*Once again, a light change and music break is needed to suggest a passing of time.*)

NARRATOR: All the next day, she sat close by the prince and told stories of what she had seen in strange lands. She spoke of the red ibises, who stand in long rows on the banks of the Nile . . .

SWALLOW: . . . and catch gold fish in their beaks.

NARRATOR: And the Sphinx . . .

SWALLOW: . . . who is as old as the world itself, and lives in the desert, and knows everything. And the merchants walk slowly by the sides of the camels and carry amber beads in their hands.

HAPPY PRINCE: Dear little swallow, you tell me of marvelous things, but more marvelous than anything is the suffering of men and women. There is no mystery so great as misery. Swallow, climb up on my pedestal and tell me what you see.

SWALLOW: I see the rich making merry in their beautiful houses, while the beggars are sitting at the gates. I see the white faces of starving children looking out listlessly at the black streets. Under the archway of a bridge, two little girls are lying in one another's arms to try to keep themselves warm.

(ENSEMBLE enters severally, acting as beggars.)

FIRST GIRL: My feet are so cold!

SECOND GIRL: And I am so hungry!

FIRST GIRL: Oh, if we could only find better shelter . . .

WATCHMAN: Better shelter you both must find!! Get away, both of you. You must not lie here.

HAPPY PRINCE: Friend, I am covered with fine gold. You must take it off, leaf by leaf, and give it to my poor. The living always think that gold can make them happy.

NARRATOR: So leaf after leaf of fine gold the swallow picked off, till the happy prince looked quite dull and gray. (The stripping of the gold leaf is pan-tomimed by SWALLOW as is the following flight.) Leaf after leaf of the fine gold the swallow gave to the poor, and the children's faces grew rosier, and they laughed and played games in the street. (FIRST GIRL and SECOND GIRL briefly pantomime a joyous dancing game.) But then the snow came, and after the snow came the frost. The streets looked as if they were made of silver, they were so bright and glistening. Long icicles like crystal daggers hung down from the eaves of the houses, everybody went about in furs, and the little boys wore scarlet caps and skated on the ice. (ENSEMBLE members assume the roles mentioned by NARRATOR. The stage is a whirl of motions. As it clears, we see SWALLOW huddled still, trying desperately to keep warm.) As the days passed, the poor little swallow grew colder and colder, and tried to keep herself warm by flapping her wings. She picked up crumbs outside the baker's door when the baker was not looking. (SWALLOW gathers crumbs, but her energy is beginning to visibly fade.) But at last the swallow knew that she was going to die. (*SWALLOW struggles up to the foot of the statue.*) Finally, she found the strength to fly up to the prince's side once more.

SWALLOW: Dear Prince, I have come to say good-bye. Will you let me kiss your hand?

HAPPY PRINCE: I am glad that you are going to Egypt at last, little swallow. You have stayed too long here. But you must kiss me on the lips, for I love you.

SWALLOW: It is not to Egypt that I am going. I am going to the House of Death. Death is the brother of Sleep, is he not? (*SWALLOW pantomimes this act — almost as if in slow motion, resulting in a frozen tableau. SWALLOW lies dead at the feet of the HAPPY PRINCE. As NARRATOR speaks, the lighting changes so that the tableau is lit in a single pool of light.*)

(*NARRATOR enters holding the cracked leaden heart.*)

NARRATOR: At that moment, a curious crack sounded inside the statue, as if something had broken. The fact is that the leaden heart had snapped right in two. As the statue was no longer beautiful, the mayor ordered that it be melted down and a new statue erected in his honor. The next day, the foreman at the foundry noticed the heart. It would not melt in the furnace. So he threw it on the dust heap, the same dust heap where the dead swallow was also lying.

Epilogue

NOTE: The action should continue here without any break.

(SCENE: Music is heard, perhaps the same music used at the beginning of the play. Two pools of light fade up to reveal frozen tableaus depicting the final moment from each of the earlier stories: the FANTASTIC cradled in DON PEDRO's arms and the MILLER at HANS' funeral. As NARRATOR speaks the closing lines of the play, he weaves his way through all three tableaus and gently touches the FANTASTIC, the HAPPY PRINCE, the SWALLOW and LITTLE HANS—bringing them with him to DC. They stand in a golden pool of light.)

NARRATOR: "Bring me the most precious things you can find," said God to one of His angels. And the angel brought to him the leaden heart, the miller's devoted friend, the dancing Fantastic and the dead bird. "You have chosen rightly," said God, "for in my garden of paradise, Hans shall be my friend, the Fantastic will dance, the swallow shall sing, and the happy prince shall praise me forevermore." (Music continues as the lights fade to black.)

CURTAIN

Production credits from the premiere of *Broken Hearts* and details concerning performance rights are included in the acting edition of the play as published by Dramatic Publishing.

Courage!

Ed Graczyk

Based on The Red Badge of Courage by Stephen Crane

When eighteen-year-old Henry Fleming hears that Lincoln has called for 300,000 men to join the Union in fighting the Civil War he knows he must be among their number, even against his mother's wishes. But it soon becomes clear that Henry's idea of war—clean blue uniforms, shiny medals and the thrill of the fight—was nothing but a boy's storybook fantasy. Weeks of exhausting marching, waiting, and fellow soldiers' tales make Henry anxious about how he'll react when actually confronted with the enemy. When his first battle finally comes, he is gripped with fear and runs from the fight. Overwhelmed with guilt he rejoins the regiment, but lies and says that a scrape on his head is a bullet wound received on the battlefield. The contrast of his own perceived cowardice with the experiences of his fellow soldiers, including a friend's death, make Henry wish for an actual battle scar—a "red badge of courage"—in hopes it might banish his shame. As the realties of war press in around him, Henry rises to the call of his conscience.

Cast

YOUNG MAN (HENRY FLEMING)
YOUNG BOY (HENRY FLEMING)
MOTHER
TALL SOLDIER
LOUD SOLDIER
TATTERED SOLDIER
LIEUTENANT
DECAYED SOLDIER
CHEERY SOLDIER
HARMONICA
TRUMPET
BANJO
DRUM
FLUTE
WOUNDED SOLDIER
FRIENDLY SOLDIER
SCARED SOLDIER
GLUM SOLDIER
SINGING SOLDIER
TOWNSPEOPLE

ACT 1

(*The set, revealed as the audience enters, is a stark unit center stage, composed of sweeping ramps and platforms elevated by tall wooden posts. These posts rise far above the top level of the platform, reaching high for the sky. The center platform in the unit is reached by two steep sweeping ramps on either side. A small set of stairs reaches from this platform to another smaller one, even higher, just downstage and to the right of it. Another smaller one to the left rear is also reached by a ramp in the back. The entire unit must be airy and spacious, not heavily burdened with bracing and supports, to allow easy movement in, around and about. The towering posts should suggest giant trees and the ramps and platforms, paths and hilltops. The wood they are constructed of is old and weathered and firmly embedded into the earth. On either side of the unit are hanging sections of gray scrim that will be used for the projection of slides. As the houselights dim, we hear the distant sound of drums* and bugles. The YOUNG MAN enters from up the rear ramp to the center platform. He carries a milk bucket and pauses to wipe his brow. He hears the sound and looks about for its source. The YOUNG BOY, dressed exactly the same as the YOUNG MAN, runs on from the right, also carrying a bucket. It is important that it be clear from the beginning that the YOUNG BOY and the YOUNG MAN are one and the same person, the YOUNG BOY being the child and conscience of the YOUNG MAN.)

BOY: Do ya hear? . . . Do ya hear the sound of the drums?

YOUNG MAN: It's comin' from town . . . hear tell there's a recruitin' rally this afternoon.

BOY: What are they recruitin'?

YOUNG MAN: Soldiers! . . . For the war . . . President Lincoln's called for 300,000 recruits.

BOY: Do ya think they'd let me join up?

YOUNG MAN: They need *men* for the war . . . Haven't you ever seen pictures in books? . . . Heroes are men, not boys.

BOY: Why ain't you down there joinin' up, 'stead of totin' milk buckets from the barn?

YOUNG MAN: I've been athinkin' about it . . . saw a poster nailed to the fence over yonder an' it sure looks excitin' . . . bright shiny uniforms, drums, bugles . . . (SLIDE: Recruiting poster, colorful and inviting to the imagination.) and it says my country needs *me*.

(SLIDES: Quick succession: Enlistment posters from many wars.)

BOY: Wish I was grow'd enough to join up and be a hero . . . you sure are lucky.

YOUNG MAN: A lotta the guys from town my age are goin' . . . hate to be left outta my share of the medals.

BOY: They may even write books about yeh like all those heroes I've read about.

(SLIDES: Quick succession: Knight poised over dragon; revolutionary war soldiers; storybook soldiers. All are brightly colored. The slides continue to flash as they speak.)

YOUNG MAN: An' when I got back from the war with my chest all loaded with medals and my head all bandaged up from the fightin' . . . the whole town would turn out to cheer and yell out my name.

BOY: They might even name the town after yeh.

YOUNG MAN: Never can tell. (Thinks) Sure would be swell to be a hero.

BOY: Yeh could get killed.

YOUNG MAN: Heroes don't get killed . . . only cowards get killed!

VOICE OF MOTHER: Son! . . . Are you out there dreamin' 'stead a doin' your chores?

YOUNG MAN and BOY: (Together) No, Ma . . . just thinkin'!

MOTHER: (Entering) Well, what are yeh thinkin' of?

BOY: (Crossing to MOTHER. YOUNG MAN remains, staring at them.) Thinkin'
   about volunteerin' for the war, Ma.

MOTHER: Nonsense, Son, you're too young.

YOUNG MAN: (From his spot) No I ain't, lots are joinin' up that are my age.

MOTHER: I need yeh here, Son . . . What with yer pa gone, I need yeh all the
   more than ever. Yer confusin' yer thinkin' with dreamin'. War's a dangerous
   thing, Son. You could get yourself serious hurt.

BOY: (Crossing to YOUNG MAN) She doesn't want me to be no hero.

YOUNG MAN: (Crossing down ramp toward MOTHER) It ain't so, Ma, the country needs me too. I hear tell we're losin' bad . . . Mr. Lincoln needs all the
   help he can get.

MOTHER: You're just a boy.

BOY: No I ain't, Ma . . .

MOTHER: Don't yeh be a fool now, Son . . . Carry that milk outta the sun before it spoils, and get yourself washed up for lunch.

YOUNG MAN: But, Ma!

MOTHER: (To BOY) I don't want to hear no more talkin' of war and joinin' up
   . . . You can do a great service to yer country right here on the farm by pro-
   vidin' food for everyone.

BOY: They don't make heroes outta farmers . . .

YOUNG MAN: Yeh need to be in the action, yeh need to be fightin' . . . fighters
   is what they're needin', not farmers.

MOTHER: Wash up . . .

(She exits.)

YOUNG MAN: She treats me like a boy . . . like I have no sense of my own . . .

BOY: She doesn't want me to be a hero.

(SOUND: A bright, rousing march, recorded: "The Battle Cry of Freedom." At first very
dim.)

YOUNG MAN: This is the opportunity of my life . . .

BOY: . . . Castles and crowns, slaying dragons by the dozens . . .

YOUNG MAN: . . . There may never ever be another war . . . I've got to join up
   before it's too late.

BOY: A' be a hero like in all the books! . . .

YOUNG MAN: They'll not leave me behind to be forgotten.

(SLIDES: A combination of the recruiting posters and the storybook heroes.)

(SOUND: The march builds slowly.)

YOUNG MAN: I'm comin', Father Abraham! . . .

MOTHER: (Off) Did yeh hear me, Son?

BOY: I'm comin' . . .

YOUNG MAN: I'm comin' to join yer war . . .

MOTHER: Hurry up now, it's getting' late.

YOUNG MAN: (To poster) That bright blue coat's gonna be on me . . .

BOY: I'll wear it all the time, for everyone to see.

YOUNG MAN: Drums and bugles callin' out . . . callin' out for me to join the fight.

BOY: I'll show yeh! . . . You'll be proud of me, all dressed up in bright blue and brass. I'll slay that gray dragon singlehanded.

YOUNG MAN: With drums and bugles blaring out my name.

(SOUND: The march builds to a crescendo as soldiers march on up the back ramp; townspeople enter waiving small flags and cheering. The YOUNG MAN and BOY move into the CROWD.)

(The CROWD ignores the YOUNG MAN and the BOY as they cheer the SOLDIERS. At the end of the song, the SOLDIERS stand at attention up and down the ramps. The CROWD gives one last cheer and freezes.)

BOY: (Pointing to TALL SOLDIER) Look, there's one of my friends from school . . .

YOUNG MAN: (To LOUD SOLDIER) . . . And there's another . . . they're already joined up.

BOY: They got a uniform before I did.

YOUNG MAN: Tell me what to do. How do I join up too?

BOY: I have a right to a gun and some cheers too.

WOMAN IN CROWD: (Breaks freeze) Let's give a cheer for the new recruits!

BOY: (To CROWD) I want one of them bright blue suits!

(Drum roll)

SOLDIERS: Give that boy a bright blue suit!

(Cheer and drum roll as the TOWNSPEOPLE put a coat, brighter than all the others, on him.)

YOUNG MAN: How about some shiny black boots?

(Drum roll)

SOLDIERS: Give that boy some shiny black boots!

(*Cheer and drum roll as the CROWD gathers around him removing his farm pants. His blue pants and boots are underdressed.*)

BOY: Can I have me a gun that shoots?

(*Drum roll*)

SOLDIERS: Give that boy a gun that shoots!

(*Sound of guns. The CROWD cheers and hands him a rifle.*)

BOY: What else do I need to be a hero?

(*No sound*)

TOWNSPEOPLE: What else does that boy need to be a hero?

(*Drum roll*)

SOLDIERS: Give that boy a sword!

(*CROWD cheers and gives him a toy wooden sword.*)

Give that boy a cap!

(*CROWD cheers and does.*)

YOUNG MAN: (*Entering dressed in blue like the other SOLDIERS*) Give that boy a word! . . .

(*Drum roll as they all turn to the YOUNG MAN.*)

SOLDIERS and CROWD: Courage!

(*SOUND: A reprise of "The Battle Cry of Freedom" from the crescendo as everyone crowds around the YOUNG MAN. The LOUD SOLDIER and the TALL SOLDIER slap him on the back congratulating him, etc. Two other SOLDIERS carry the BOY on their shoulders up the left ramp, leaving the YOUNG MAN below. As they reach the bottom on the other side where the YOUNG MAN is, the MOTHER ENTERS and the music stops.*)

YOUNG MAN: Ma, I've enlisted.

MOTHER: (*After short silence*) The Lord's will be done, Son.

(*She crosses stage right. The CROWD and SOLDIERS back off slowly, leaving the YOUNG MAN and BOY.*)

BOY: She's crying . . . she's not proud of what I've done.

YOUNG MAN: I'm sure she is . . . she has to be.

BOY: She never mentioned my bright new uniform.

MOTHER: (*As she sits quietly on the edge of the right ramp*) You watch out, Son, and take good care of yourself in this here fighting business—you watch out, an' take good care of yerself.

BOY: (*Crossing in to her*) But, Ma . . .

MOTHER: Don't go a-thinkin' you can lick the whole Army at the start, because yeh can't. Yer just one little feller amongst a whole lot of others, and yeh've got to keep quiet an' do what they tell yeh. I know how you are, Son.

(*The BOY crosses to a box under the platform and carries it away from them, left. As she continues to speak, he takes out dozens of toy soldiers — about one foot high — and places them in a small group, arranging them in a regiment.*)

I've knit ye eight pairs of socks, Son . . . to be used fer the winter . . . but I suppose yeh will be needin' 'em more now. I'll pack ye a bundle an' put in all yer best shirts. I want my boy to be jest as warm and comf'table as anybody in the Army.

(*During the above, she pantomimes packing a bundle.*)

Whenever they get holes in 'em, I want yeh to send 'em right away back to me so's I kin darn 'em.

(*Hands imaginary bundle to him and crosses slowly to the BOY, not talking to him, but is near to him*)

Ye be careful now, Son . . . there's lots of bad men in the Army. The Army makes 'em wild, and they like nothing better than the job of leading off a young feller like you, as ain't never been away from home much. I don't want yeh to ever do anything that yeh would be 'shamed to let me know about. Jest think as if I was a'watchin' yeh. If yeh keep that in mind allus, I guess yeh'll come out about right. I don't know what else to tell yeh, Son, excepting that yeh must never do no shirking, child, on my account. If so be a time comes when yeh have to be kilt or do a mean thing, why, Son, don't think of anything 'cept what's right 'cause there's many a woman has to bear up 'ginst sech things these times, and the Lord'll take keer of us all.

(*Turns to YOUNG MAN*)

Don't fergit to send yer socks to me the minute they git holes in 'em, and here's a little Bible I want yeh to take along with yeh.

(*Hands him an imaginary Bible*)

I don't presume yeh'll be a'sitting reading it all day long, child, ner nothin' like that. Many a time yeh'll fergit yeh got it, I don't doubt. But there'll be many a time too, Son, when yeh'll be wanting advice, and all like that. And there'll be nobody around, perhaps, to tell yeh things.

(*Crosses back to her spot*)

Don't fergit about the socks an' the shirts, child, and I've put a cup of blackberry jam with yer bundle because I knew yeh like it above all things . . .

Good-bye, Son . . . Yeh may think of yerself as a man, but yeh'hve still got a
lot of the boy within yeh.

(*The BOY rises and starts to run to the MOTHER.*)

BOY: Ma!

(*The YOUNG MAN stops him. Together, they turn, the YOUNG MAN's arm about
the BOY's shoulder, and walk back to the army of toy soldiers. They turn back to the
MOTHER who rises, and with her back to them, wipes her eyes with a corner of her
apron.*)

BOY: I'm scared . . .

YOUNG MAN: Too late now for any turnin' back . . .

TALL SOLDIER: (*Rushing in*) Come on, the regiment's formin' up in the square
to move out. Are yeh through sayin' yer farewells?

YOUNG MAN: Suppose so.

TALL SOLDIER: Then get a-movin' afore yeh get left behind . . . (*As he exits*) . . .
Don't want to be labeled a coward afore ye even begin, do yeh?

YOUNG MAN: I ain't no coward! . . . I'll fight 'long side the best of yeh . . .
you'll see.

(*SOUND: Recorded, "We Are Coming, Father Abraham," coming from the distance,
building to the foreground, then fading out. The YOUNG MAN exits, leaving the BOY
who sits among the toy soldiers arranging them into rows.*)

(*SLIDES: The toy soldiers marching in rows and various quick close-ups of the
uniform, cap, drum, etc. . . . as the music plays.*)

(*At the end of the song, lights come up on YOUNG MAN, LOUD SOLDIER and TALL
SOLDIER being served food by village ladies.*)

LOUD SOLDIER: Wow, this is the life, ain't it? . . .

TALL SOLDIER: Ever tasted such fancy cookin'?

YOUNG MAN: Sure treat us boys in blue like kings . . . cheer at us every town
an' village we pass through.

LOUD SOLDIER: Did yeh get a look at the girls in the last town? . . . Yahoo,
they sure took a lookin' at us.

TALL SOLDIER: One singled me out from all the others and gave me a wink.

LOUD SOLDIER: Ah, g'wan!

TALL SOLDIER: Ain't lyin' . . .

(*To YOUNG MAN*)

You saw her, didn't yeh?

YOUNG MAN: I thought she was winkin' at me.

(TALL SOLDIER and LOUD SOLDIER laugh hysterically as the lights fade. SOUND: Recorded, "Hold On, Abraham".)

(SLIDES: Toy soldiers marching, this time adding toy cannons and quick close-ups of the flag, buttons, buckles, etc.)

(After the song, the lights come up on the same group a bit wearier than before.)

LOUD SOLDIER: *(Rubbing his feet)* Sure wish they'd stop all this marchin' and settle down in one spot for a while ... my feet have nearly marched through the bottoms of my boots.

TALL SOLDIER: Aw, yeh ain't happy 'less yeh have somethin' tuh complain about.

LOUD SOLDIER: Sure saw yeh limpin' mighty heavy last day or so.

TALL SOLDIER: Had a stone in my boot.

LOUD SOLDIER: Musta' been that loose one's been rollin' aroun' in yer head. *(Laughs)*

YOUNG MAN: Is that all there is to war is marchin'? ... When's the fightin' start?

TALL SOLDIER: We'll be getting' there soon enough ... just keep yer pants on.

LOUD SOLDIER: What's yer big hurry ... Plan to lick the whole Rebel Army singlehanded in an afternoon so's yeh can be back home fer supper? *(Laughs)*

YOUNG MAN: Jest aim tuh do my part ...

LOUD SOLDIER: Jest make sure that's all yeh do. Save some for us. *(He laughs.)*

LIEUTENANT: *(From off)* All right, everyone fall in ... rest's over ... time to march on!

LOUD SOLDIER: *(Groaning)* Easy fer him tuh say; he gets to ride a horse.

LIEUTENANT: Quit all the moanin' and groanin' like a bunch of little boys.

TALL SOLDIER: ... Heard tell the Lieutenant's pushin' pretty hard for camp in two days.

LOUD SOLDIER: No rest, no sleep ... no nothin' till we get there.

LIEUTENANT: Sound the call! ... We're movin'!

(Bugle call and all the SOLDIERS begin to rise, groaning. Recorded music will only be used from here on for special sound effects. All singing will be done live to the occasional accompaniment of a HARMONICA, SNARE DRUM, BANJO, FLUTE and TRUMPET which are played by the SOLDIERS: The lights on the marching SOLDIERS are dim, the spot on the BOY and the toy soldiers a bit brighter. The DRUMMER

starts the beat of "John Brown's Body," the FLUTE follows in and the BOY sings the first line. The other SOLDIERS follow to the end. They will march in one spot, getting wearier as the song progresses.)

BOY: John Brown's body lies a-molderin' in the grave.

SOLDIERS:

> John Brown's body lies a-molderin' in the grave,
> John Brown's body lies a-molderin' in the grave,
> His soul is marchin' on . . .
> We'll hang Jed Davis to a sour apple tree,
> We'll hang Jed Davis to a sour apple tree,
> We'll hang Jed Davis to a sour apple tree,
> As we go marching on.

(SLIDES: Muddy boots, close-ups of mud-spotted blue uniforms, missing buttons, etc.)

(The DRUMMER slows his tempo and the BOY and YOUNG MAN sing slowly.)

BOY and YOUNG MAN:

> Mine eyes have seen the glory of the coming of the Lord;
> He is trampling out the vintage where the grapes of wrath are stored.
> He has loosed the fateful lightning of his terrible swift sword.
> His truth is marching on.

(The SOLDIERS sing slowly as they begin to set up camp below the platform.)

SOLDIERS:

> Glory! Glory Hallelujah! Glory! Glory Hallelujah!
> Glory! Glory Hallelujah! His truth is marching on.

(They repeat the chorus until only the BOY is left singing amid his toy soldiers. A sentry is on the small tall platform playing "Jeanie with the Light Brown Hair" on his harmonica while leaning back against a post. Several others lie back against posts, some writing letters, others sleeping, playing cards, etc.)

(SLIDE: A Union camp.)

LOUD SOLDIER: *(Entering from under the platform)* Anyone seen Conklin tonight?

SOLDIER: Over by the river doin' some washin'.

LOUD SOLDIER: *(To YOUNG MAN)* Well, yeh couldn't wait for us to get here . . . and here we are . . . two months now an' jest a-sittin' an' a-waitin'.

YOUNG MAN: What are we waitin for? . . . When are we gonna move in on 'em?

LOUD SOLDIER: Someone aroun' here's gotta have some answers.

(The TALL SOLDIER rushes in waving a shirt.)

TALL SOLDIER: We're goin' t' move to'morra—sure . . . We're goin' way up the river, cut across an' come around in behind 'em.

LOUD SOLDIER: It's a lie! . . . That's all it is—a thunderin' lie!

(Walks away with his hands in his pockets)

LOUD SOLDIER: I don't believe the derned old Army's ever gonna move. I've got ready to move eight times in the past two weeks, and we ain't moved yet.

TALL SOLDIER: Well, yeh kin believe me or not, jest as yeh like. I don't care a hang.

(He exits.)

YOUNG MAN: It could be true . . . t'morrow could be the day. (To BOY) Are yeh ready?

BOY: I don't know . . . I want it to come, but I'm kinda afraid of it too . . . afraid when the battle comes I'll run.

YOUNG MAN: (Crossing to BOY) What makes yeh think you'll run?

BOY: Dunno. Things ain't turnin' out like I imagined 'em to be.

YOUNG MAN: Sure ain't the kinda war I hoped for. I gotta admit I'm kinda at a loss here, like a stranger . . . sure glad I got you around.

(TALL SOLDIER enters, followed by the LOUD SOLDIER.)

TALL SOLDIER: That's all right, you can believe me or not, jest as you like. All you got to do is sit down and wait as quiet as you can, then pretty soon you'll find out I was right.

LOUD SOLDIER: Well, yeh don't know everything in the world, do yeh?

TALL SOLDIER: Didn't say I knew everything in the world.

YOUNG MAN: Goin' to be a battle sure, is there?

TALL SOLDIER: Of course there is, of course there is. You jest wait till tomorrow and you'll see one of the biggest battles ever was. You jest wait.

BOY: Thunder!

TALL SOLDIER: Oh, you'll see fightin' this time, what'll be regular out-and-out fightin'!

LOUD SOLDIER: Huh!

YOUNG MAN: Jim!

TALL SOLDIER: What?

YOUNG MAN: How do you think the regiment will do?

TALL SOLDIER: Oh, they'll fight all right, I guess, after they once get into it. There's been heaps of fun poked at us 'cause we're new and young and all that, but they'll fight all right, I guess.

YOUNG MAN: Think any of the boys'll run?

TALL SOLDIER: Oh, thre may be a few of 'em run, but there's them kind in every regiment, 'specially when they first goes under fire. Of course, it might happen that the hull kit and caboodle might start and run if some big fightin' came first off. And then again, they might stay and fight like fun. But you can't bet on nothin'. Of course, they ain't never been under fire yet and it ain't likely they'll lick the hull Rebel Army all-to-oncet the first time, but I think they'll fight better than some, if worse than others. That's the way I figger.

LOUD SOLDIER: Oh, you think you know!

TALL SOLDIER: Well, I sure know better'n you . . .

LOUD SOLDIER: You don't know nothin'!

YOUNG MAN: (*Interrupting*) Did you ever think you might run yourself, Jim?

(*Laughs suddenly, as if he meant it to be a joke*)

TALL SOLDIER: Well, I've thought it might get too hot for Jim Conklin in some of them scrimmages, and if a whole lot of boys started and run, why, I suppose I'd start and run. And if I once started to run, I'd run like the devil! But if everybody was a-standing and a-fighting, why, I'd stand and fight. By jiminey, I would . . . I'll bet on it.

LOUD SOLDIER: Huh!

YOUNG MAN: (*To BOY . . . his conscience*) See that there . . . they all got the same feelin' you do.

BOY: Still don't answer my question.

YOUNG MAN: What's that?

BOY: Will *I* run like a coward or fight like a hero an' maybe die?

YOUNG MAN: Guess only time will tell . . . Are yeh afraid of dyin'?

TALL SOLDIER: (*Answering*) Ain't thought much about it . . . all depends, I guess. If it happens quick-like so's I don't now about it, guess I won't mind . . . but if it's goin' tuh linger on tuh make me think about it, guess I'd prob'ly mind a lot.

YOUNG MAN: Don't yeh want tuh die a hero?

TALL SOLDIER: Jest want tuh do my best . . . If it turns out they make me a hero for doin' it . . . sure would make my ma proud . . . wouldn't make *me* no never mind . . . wouldn't be here to get the medal anyhow.

LOUD SOLDIER: Not likely you'll die anyhow . . . Yer too darned stubborn.

(*SOUND: "Taps," played by TRUMPET on the tall platform.*)

TALL SOLDIER: I'll outlast you, I'll bet . . . Come on, let's get us some shuteye . . . gotta be ready fer the fightin' t'morra.

(Starts to exit)

LOUD SOLDIER: Huh! I'll believe it when I see it.

(Exits)

BOY: (To YOUNG MAN) Do yeh think he's right? . . . About the fightin'?

YOUNG MAN: Hope so . . . (Picks up guitar and strums lightly) Sure would like tuh know what it's like.

BOY: Been thinkin' a lot about Ma . . . Wonder how she's getting' along without me.

YOUNG MAN: Not getting' homesick, are yeh?

BOY: Suppose I never see her again? . . . Suppose I die t'morra and never see her again.

YOUNG MAN: (Picking out the chords of "Just Before the Battle, Mother" on the guitar) Funny, ain't it, 'bout how she had it all figured out right?

BOY: (Singing softly to the accompaniment of the YOUNG MAN's playing. The HARMONICA also joins in.)
    Just before the battle, Mother,
    I am thinking most of you,
    While upon the field we're watching,
    With the enemy in view.

(YOUNG MAN joins in.)
    Comrades brave and round me lying,
    Filled with thoughts of home and God;
    For well they know that on the morrow,
    Some will sleep beneath the sod.

(The SOLDIERS join in softly.)
    Farewell, Mother, you may never
    Press me to your heart again;
    But, O, you'll not forget me, Mother,
    If I'm number'd with the slain.

(The HARMONICA plays another chorus and the SOLDIERS hum during the following.)

BOY: Maybe I'll get wounded and wear a white bandage to show off my bravery. What good's courage if yeh can't show it?

YOUNG MAN: What happens if it turns out you're a coward? What'll yeh wear then?

BOY: (*No answer*)

YOUNG MAN: I don't have an answer either.

(*The lights fade slowly with the singing, leaving only the SLIDES. Then abruptly the sound of a TRUMPET. The SLIDES change quickly to scenes of sunrise through trees and a spot comes up on the SOLDIER and his TRUMPET on the highest level. The other lights fade up, revealing the SOLDIERS walking and moving into line. The BOY is arranging his toy soldiers in the same formation.*)

LOUD SOLDIER: (*To TALL SOLDIER as they move into line*) Well, it's t'morra. Where's all that fightin' yeh was promisin' us?

TALL SOLDIER: They were supposed tah move in durin' the night.

LOUD SOLDIER: Told yeh it weren't nothin' but another of yer lies.

TALL SOLDIER: Weren't no lie! . . . I heard it!

LOUD SOLDIER: From Lincoln himself, I suppose!

YOUNG MAN: Yeh mean there ain't goin' to be any fightin'?

TALL SOLDIER: If this here loudmouth don't shut up, there will be.

LOUD SOLDIER: I'll show yeh a fight if yeh want one!

(*Starts after TALL SOLDIER. Several SOLDIERS pull him away.*)

Leave me be, he's long overdue for a good sluggin'!

LIEUTENANT: (*Off*) Prepare to move out!

LOUD SOLDIER: Move out?!

HARMONICA: More marchin'?!

LOUD SOLDIER: (*As the line breaks up to gather their belongings*) I can't stand this much longer. I don't see what good it does to make us wear out our legs for nothin'.

BANJO: I suppose we must go reconnoitering around the countryside jest to keep 'em from getting too close, or to develop our muscles, or something.

LOUD SOLDIER: Huh!

SINGING SOLDIER: I'd rather do anything 'most than go tramping 'round the country all day doing no good to nobody and jest tiring ourselves out.

LOUD SOLDIER: So would I. It ain't right. I tell you, if anybody with any sense was a-runnin' this Army, it . . .

TALL SOLDIER: Oh, shut up! . . . You little fool! You little damn cuss, you ain't had that there coat and them pants on for two months, and yet you talk as if . . .

LOUD SOLDIER: Well, I wanta do some fightin' anyway. I didn't come here to walk. I could've walked at home . . . 'round and 'round the barn if I jest wanted to walk.

(He crams things in his sac.)

GLUM SOLDIER: They say we're catchin' it over on the left. They say the enemy drove our line intuh a devil of a swamp an' took Hannises' Battery.

HARMONICA: No sech thing. Hannises' Battery was 'long here jest last night.

GLUM SOLDIER: I met one of the 148th Maine boys an' he says his brigade fought the hull Rebel Army fer four hours over on the turnpike road an' killed about five thousand of 'em. He sez one more sech fight as that an' the war'll be over.

LOUD SOLDIER: The war'll be nothin' but a memory before we see any action . . . durn it all anyhow!

LIEUTENANT: (Off) All right, men, let's move on out.

(The band begins the music to "Marching Through Georgia" as they again begin to march in their spots.)

(SLIDES: Roads, paths, forests from all over the world, interspersed with SLIDES of toy soldiers. The SLIDES should encompass several days . . . morning sunrise to noon to setting sun to night.)

SOLDIERS: (Sung)
> Bring the good old bugle boys,
> We'll sing another song.
> Sing it with the spirit
> That will start the world along.
> Sing it as we used to sing it,
> Fifty thousand strong,
> While we are marching through Georgia.
> Hurrah, hurrah, we bring the jubilee . . .
> Hurrah, hurrah, the flag that makes you free,
> So we sing the chorus from Atlanta to the sea
> While we are marching through Georgia.
>
> Yes, and there were Union men,
> Who wept with joyful tears
> When they saw the honored flag
> They had not seen for years.
> Hardly could they be restrained
> From breaking forth in cheers
> While we are marching through Georgia.
> Hurrah, hurrah, we bring the jubilee . . .

> Hurrah, hurrah, the flag that makes you free,
> So we sing the chorus from Atlanta to the sea
> While we are marching through Georgia.

(As they finish, it is night and they collapse, set up camp, etc. The YOUNG MAN settles near the BOY and his soldiers.)

BOY: It feels like I was home again makin' the rounds from the house to the barn . . .

YOUNG MAN: From the barn to the fields . . .

BOY: From the fields to the barn . . .

YOUNG MAN: And from the barn to the house.

BOY: I'd trade in my bright blue uniform and all its brass buttons if I could just go back home . . . I ain't like them. I ain't cut out to be their kind of soldier.

YOUNG MAN: The darkness seems to be sharin' my feelin's tonight.

(Laughter from the soldiers)

BOY: Listen to 'em laughin' . . . They ain't even like the heroes in my books.

YOUNG MAN: Ain't no way I could ever join in with 'em; they can't understand things like I do.

BOY: I understand yeh.

YOUNG MAN: You're different. You're so much a part of me by now, ain't no way I'd ever be able to shake yeh loose.

BOY: *(Excited)* We could run away . . . they'd never even miss us. They'd think we just got lost along the way.

YOUNG MAN: Couldn't run back home . . . folks would call us cowards. No, I could never face 'em.

(LOUD SOLDIER moves in.)

LOUD SOLDIER: What are ye doin' way over here by yourself?

YOUNG MAN: Oh, thinkin'.

LOUD SOLDIER: *(Sitting down)* You're actin' kinda blue . . . What the dickens is wrong with yeh?

YOUNG MAN: Oh, nothin'.

LOUD SOLDIER: *(Changing the subject and being very excited)* We've got 'em now. At last, by the eternal thunders, we'll lick 'em good.

YOUNG MAN: I thought you were objectin' to this march a little while back.

LOUD SOLDIER: Oh, it wasn't that. I don't mind marchin' if there's goin' to be fightin' at the end of it, and I got me a feelin' in my bones we're goin' to be seein' it right soon.

(*Rises and moves about, almost show-offy*)

Gee rod! How we'll thump 'em! Yes siree, we'll thump 'em real good!

YOUNG MAN: Oh, you're going to do great things, I suppose!

LOUD SOLDIER: Oh, I don't know . . . I don't know. I s'pose I'll do as well as the rest.

YOUNG MAN: How do you know you won't run when the time comes?

LOUD SOLDIER: Run? . . . Run? . . . Of course not!

(*Laughs*)

YOUNG MAN: Well, lots of good-a-nough men have thought they were going to do great things before the fight, but when the time came they skedaddled.

LOUD SOLDIER: O, that's all true, I s'pose. But *I'm* not going to skedaddle. The man that bets on my runnin' will lose his money, that's all.

YOUNG MAN: Oh, shucks! . . . You ain't the bravest man in the world, are yeh?

LOUD SOLDIER: No, I ain't . . . an' I didn't say I was the bravest man in the world neither. I said I was going to do my share of fighting . . . that's what I said. And I am too. Who are you anyhow? You talk as if you thought you was Napoleon Bonaparte!

(*Storms away*)

YOUNG MAN: Well, yeh needn't git mad about it.

(*To BOY*)

See what I mean? They ain't like me . . . we ain't alike in no way.

BOY: He don't seem to be 'feared of runnin' at all.

YOUNG MAN: Sure certain of himself . . . wish I was so certain, one way or the other. Even if it weren't true certain, at least I'd know somethin'.

(*HARMONICA begins to play "All Quiet Along The Potomac."*)

BOY: Look! Across the river yeh can see the red dots of the enemy's campfires . . . like lightnin' bugs yeh can reach out an' cup in yer hand, holdin' them prisoner till yeh choose to let 'em go.

YOUNG MAN: The quiet's spooky tonight . . .

BOY: Are you tryin' to scare me?!

YOUNG MAN: Not intentional . . . it's a quiet kind of quiet, the kind of quiet you hear just before a thunderstorm . . .

BOY: I'm scared of thunder.

YOUNG MAN: Is there anything you're not scared of?

BOY: I'm not scared of you.

YOUNG MAN: (*Pause*) I am.

(*SOUND: The screech of a shell shattering through the silence and landing in an explosion, followed by whistling bullets.*)

LIEUTENANT: On your feet . . . Prepare for attack!

(*The SOLDIERS grab their rifles and take places behind posts, platforms, etc.*)

LOUD SOLDIER: A fine time to attack . . . I ain't ready for 'em . . . sneakin' devils.

DRUM: I can't see 'em in the dark.

HARMONICA: Then they can't see us either.

GLUM SOLDIER: I can't see what I'm shootin' at.

FLUTE: Just keep shootin'. You're bound to hit somethin'.

(*The BOY with his toy rifle crouches in the center of his toy army. The YOUNG MAN crouches near him behind the ramp.*)

HARMONICA: They certainly ain't got much sense attackin' in the pitch dark.

(*The shooting ceases.*)

DRUM: They stopped firin'.

LOUD SOLDIER: Probably jist tryin' tuh scare us.

BOY: (*Panicked*) Where are you? . . . Don't leave me alone.

YOUNG MAN: I'm here . . . Quiet! . . . Don't let 'em know you're scared . . . Try to be brave.

SCARED SOLDIER: What do we do now?

SINGING SOLDIER: They could outnumber us by hundreds.

FLUTE: If we could just see 'em.

(*LOUD SOLDIER rushes to YOUNG MAN.*)

LOUD SOLDIER: Are yeh okay?

YOUNG MAN: Fine . . . the fightin' took me unexpected.

LOUD SOLDIER: Me too. It's my first and last battle . . .

YOUNG MAN: What?

LOUD SOLDIER: It's gonna be my first an' last battle . . . I gotta feelin'. Somethin' tells me I ain't gonna see another.

YOUNG MAN: Don't be . . .

LOUD SOLDIER: Here . . . I want yeh to take these here things . . . to . . . my . . . folks.

(*Hands him an envelope*)

YOUNG MAN: Why, what the devil! . . .

LOUD SOLDIER: It's got my gran-pa's gold watch and . . .

SINGING SOLDIER: Somethin's movin' there in the bushes . . .

(Gunshot)

LOUD SOLDIER: I gotta get back . . . careful with it now.

(He returns to his spot. A SOLDIER enters from under the platform.)

TALL SOLDIER: It's Jackson, yeh shot Jackson.

(He rushes to him and helps him to a spot under the platform.)

LOUD SOLDIER: Fine Army we got here . . . shootin' their own men.

TALL SOLDIER: Shut up an' give me a hand here bandagin' him up . . . he's
  bleedin' bad in the arm.

(LOUD SOLDIER helps the other one bandage the SOLDIERS.)

WOUNDED SOLDIER: Stupid fool! Now I'll never be able to fight . . . waited
  all these months for the fight, to be shot by one of my own.

YOUNG MAN: They don't know what they're doin' . . . the whole bunch is
  crazy.

DRUM: Think they'll come back?

CHEERY SOLDIER: Sure of it. They know we're here now.

LIEUTENANT: All right, men, cozy into where yeh are an' be alert . . . they'll
  be back, an' you be read fer 'em . . . Jackson, yeh fool . . .

BOY: It was an accident. He didn't mean to hurt him . . . he'll be all right
  tomorrow.

LIEUTENANT: You're gonna have tuh fight anyhow. We need everyone we
  can get.

HARMONICA: I'm sure they'll wait till sun-up and come up on us full blast.

BOY: (To YOUNG MAN) Let's run . . .

YOUNG MAN: (To SOLDIERS) Let's clear out before they come . . . Why are we
  waitin' around just to be shot at?

TALL SOLDIER: They must have a reason.

BOY: How do yeh know they're right? . . . We've got to run or we'll be killed.

SINGING SOLDIER: Yeh was lookin' for fightin', weren't yeh? Better here than
  marchin' somewhere else to get it.

TALL SOLDIER: We'll be ready for 'em when they come back.

SCARED SOLDIER: Give us a chance to prepare.

LOUD SOLDIER: Again it's waitin' . . . waitin' . . .

BOY: I can't wait till it's over.

YOUNG MAN: All this waitin's makin' it worse.

BOY: I wanna gather up everythin' an' go back home . . . they ain't doin' it right.

YOUNG MAN: Wait . . . Wait an' see what happens next . . . I've got to find out what all this waitin' was for.

(SLIDE: Sunrise.)

(The lights brighten. Gunshots.)

TRUMPET: Here they come!

(SLIDE: A fiery dragon.)

(SOUND: A trumpet blast followed by music and battle sounds. The battle is in slow motion and pantomimed. Only the YOUNG MAN and BOY will break the pace and the quick flashing of the SLIDES. The SLIDES will show the toy soldiers in various stages of destruction . . . the stage after the first blast blacks out and spots of light pop up revealing individual SOLDIERS. A light remains up on the YOUNG MAN and BOY at all times.)

YOUNG MAN: There are hundreds of them . . . We'll never be able to hold them off.

BOY: They're expectin' too much of me.

(Spot on TALL SOLDIER tying red handkerchief around his neck.)

TALL SOLDIER: Oh, we're in for it now . . . we're really in for it now.

LIEUTENANT'S VOICE: Reserve your fire, boys . . . Don't shoot till I tell you . . . save your fire . . . wait till they get close up . . . don't be damned fools!

(The YOUNG MAN feverishly waits. He wipes his eyes with his coat sleeve. He lifts his rifle into position and fires. There follow other gunshots blending into the sound of fireworks.)

BOY: The fireworks are getting too close . . . I'll get hurt . . . I'll get hurt.

(SLIDE: A fireworks display.)

(SOUND: The spots will pop up to reveal a SOLDIER. A recorded sound or phrase will correspond with the SOLDIER. Following their initial exposure, the sounds will begin to blend, forming a chant, and the spots will cross blend, like a pinball machine at victory.)

SOLDIER #1: (Muffled) Please, God, don't let me die.

SOLDIER #2: Rotten Rebs!

SOLDIER #3: Yea! . . . Got yeh, damned devil!

SOLDIER #4: Our Father, who art in heaven . . .

SOLDIER #5: (Heavy breathing)

SOLDIER #6: They got Pete Johnson in the head.

SOLDIER #7: (*Muttering*) Be brave . . . be brave . . . be brave.

TALL SOLDIER: I ain't a liar . . . I said there'd be fightin'.

LOUD SOLDIER: Die, you stinkin' devils!

SOLDIER #8: Dear Lord, don't leave my side.

SOLDIER #9: I'm afraid . . . I'm afraid.

(*SLIDE: A toy soldier with broken off arm, followed by SLIDES of other toy soldiers with broken legs, head, torso, etc.*)

BOY: Stop it! . . . You ain't playin' fair . . . You're breakin' 'em . . . You're breakin' 'em!

(*SOUND: The chant begins to increase in tempo, a swirl of mismatched words. The BOY covers his ears. The YOUNG MAN swirls in all directions as a spot stops on a SOLDIER who clutches his head which is dripping red. It moves to another who clutches his stomach and falls to his knees, to another whose knee is splashed with red. He drops his rifle and clutches a post and cries out in silence. The BOY rushes to the YOUNG MAN and pulls at him.*)

BOY: Come on, you've got to run . . . You can't stay here. You'll be killed . . . Run! . . . Run!

(*YOUNG MAN rises and the BOY pulls him off up the ramp. The chanting combined with the music and battle sounds continue. They reach the center top platform and the YOUNG MAN stops and stands on the edge, teetering. He catches himself and turns and runs down the back ramp pulled by the BOY. The lights fade to black except for the . . .*)

(*SLIDES: Toppled over broken toy soldiers, a battlefield of strewn bodies, a close-up of a broken toy soldier, a close-up of a dead SOLDIER, a picture of a beautiful forest with red dripping down it.*)

(*SOUND: Chant fading to the distant sound of battle. The lights come up on the right ramp to reveal the YOUNG MAN and BOY running on. They are breathing heavily.*)

YOUNG MAN: I can't run any more.

BOY: You've got to . . . it will catch us.

YOUNG MAN: Why didn't the others run, the fools . . . Didn't they see what was happening? The stupid fools will be killed! They were as stiff as toy soldiers waiting for a giant hand to lift them out of there.

BOY: (*Crossing to toy soldiers*) They're all broken. They're no good any more . . . but you are, and I am . . . We're at least alive . . .

YOUNG MAN: Yes, I'm still alive to be used again . . . Someone had to live to tell about it.

BOY: You're the only one alive to be a hero . . . to tell stories about it.

(SLIDE: Toy soldier with huge oversized medal.)

(SOUND: SOLDIERS' voices cheering in the distance.)

YOUNG MAN: Listen.

BOY: What is it?

YOUNG MAN: Sounds like cheering . . . Ssh, someone's coming . . . Hide over here.

(They hide behind ramp.)

SOLDIER: (Far off) They did it! . . . They did it. They walloped the beejeezus out of 'em.

SOLDIER: The 304th?

SOLDIER: Sure 'nuf did . . . We'll take 'em for sure now. The war's nearly over.

(The distant cheering continues.)

YOUNG MAN. Those fools beat 'em!

(He rises and rushes to the tall platform to see.)

  Look, he's right . . . They beat 'em. I ran! You made me run!

(Grabs BOY)

  You stupid fool, you made me run!

BOY: (Crying) I had to. You're the only friend I have . . . I had to save you.

(The cheering fades.)

YOUNG MAN: Why? . . . What good am I now? . . . I could never go back . . . I'm a coward . . . I ran . . . just like I thought I might.

BOY: No, you were right . . . It's them who are the fools . . . They're all broken into a million pieces.

YOUNG MAN: They may be broken, but they ain't dead. They can be patched back together. They'll have proof of their courage. They'll wear their bandages like medals of courage. Look at me . . . I ain't even got a scratch to prove I was there.

BOY: They'll know you were there.

YOUNG MAN: How? . . . Are you gonna tell 'em? A silly kid . . . Who'd even believe yeh? I can't wait till I get rid of yeh. It's you who's keepin' me from bein' a hero.

BOY: No, I want to help!

YOUNG MAN: I don't want your help. I can do it by myself. Go play with your toys and leave me be.

(SOUND: *Battle sounds and chant.*)

YOUNG MAN: The fightin's started up again. The sound shames me . . . I've got to run and hide.

(*He starts to run. The BOY follows. He stops.*)

Where you goin'? . . . I said leave me be.

BOY: I'm scared . . . Take me with you.

YOUNG MAN: You're goin' to destroy me!

BOY: Please, just for a little longer . . . please!

YOUNG MAN: (*Pause*) Well, I guess I can't keep yeh from followin' me . . .

(*Grabs his head*)

That sound . . . I've got to find some place quiet to think this all out! Tell those voices to stop!

(SOUND: *The voices stop abruptly, replaced by sounds of nature — birds, etc. Shafts of light as if filtering through trees pour down.*)

(SLIDES: *Trees with rays of sun.*)

YOUNG MAN: What happened? . . . The voices stopped. I'm . . .

(*Looks around*)

I'm somewhere else.

BOY: We've been wandering through the woods for hours . . . I'm gettin' tired. Let's rest here for a spell.

YOUNG MAN: Where are we? . . .

BOY: It's as quiet as a church.

(*Organ music, very subdued*)

YOUNG MAN: The quiet's like a hazy wall shielding out all the awful sounds of life.

BOY: (*Quickly*) Look! . . . There's a squirrel . . .

(*He throws a pine cone at him.*)

Look. Look at him run.

(*Laughs*)

YOUNG MAN: He runs from fear of death . . . and he's just an ordinary squirrel, not a man like me. Nature prepared him to run. It's not cowardly for him to run from fear and the unknown. Does anyone shame the squirrel for running from attack? . . . Then why should they shame me?

BOY: You were right to run . . . just like the squirrel. You did what you had to at the time.

YOUNG MAN: Yes . . . I had to . . .

BOY: Come on, let's run and play . . . Chase me.

(*Starts to run*)

YOUNG MAN: I'm too tired for games.

BOY: Please? . . .

YOUNG MAN: All right, but be careful where you run.

(*BOY runs up one ramp and down the other, then under the back of the platform. He trips over something . . . a body. The body is leaning against a post, rotted and forgotten. A skeletal arm hangs loose from the sleeve of a once blue uniform now faded to a pale blue-gray. The BOY falls in such a way that he lays across it. He looks up and is face to face with the "once" SOLDIER and freezes. The YOUNG MAN enters, and seeing the BOY, freezes momentarily into a statue. He finally pulls the BOY from the body.*)

BOY: Who was he? . . . Was he a soldier like us?

YOUNG MAN: Quiet. Don't disturb his peace.

BOY: Did he run away too? . . . He seems lost.

YOUNG MAN: Leave him to his secrets.

BOY: (*Crying*) Did anyone tell his mother? . . . Does anybody know?

YOUNG MAN: You see, there's no running away from it . . . It will follow us wherever we go.

(*Pulls BOY*)

Let's get out of here . . . Stop crying . . . He's happy . . . he's dead! He knows his end.

(*BOY runs up the ramp.*)

BOY: Wait! Wait for me. Don't leave me here alone with him.

(*SOUND: Distant singing. "Battle Cry of Freedom" sung by the SOLDIERS, which stops the BOY on the center platform.*)

YOUNG MAN: Stop! . . . Listen, it's singin' . . . It's comin' this way.

BOY: It's soldiers. They're comin' to drag us back. Let's run.

YOUNG MAN: There's no place left to run. Wherever we run, we'll be haunted.

BOY: You ain't goin' back, are yeh?

YOUNG MAN: How else will I become a hero? . . . I don't want to die and lie rottin', a forgotten hero. Gotta let folks know I was a part of this whole thing. Gotta patch up the broken past an' move on.

BOY: It'll just be more of the same.

YOUNG MAN: Might not, but I've gotta stop runnin' some time before I run my whole life away.

(*SLIDE: Toy soldiers all pieced back together with bandages.*)

BOY: (*Looking down the back ramp*) They're all bloody an' hurt . . . They're comin' this way, at us.

YOUNG MAN: We'll just follow 'em. Maybe they'll lead us back to our camp.

(*The wounded SOLDIERS enter up the back ramp. Their uniforms are those of many wars. They are bloodied and bandaged and a terrible sight. They will cross down the right ramp and settle below the center platform around the body. SOUND: A funeral procession. SUGGEST: "Lincoln's Funeral March".*)

SINGING SOLDIER: (*Hopping on one leg, singing*)

> Sing a song a' vic'try,
> A pocket full a' bullets,
> Five an' twenty dead men
> Baked in a . . . pie.

FLUTE: (*Shot in the arm*) Durned General . . . if he knew how tuh run an army, never woulda been hit.

(*Two SOLDIERS carry a limp body on a stretcher. Another helps a SOLDIER who can hardly walk.*)

GLUM SOLDIER: Don't joggle me so, Johnson, yeh fool. Think m'leg is made of iron? If yeh can't help me decent, leave me be an' let someone else do it.

(*As they move down the ramp*)

> Say, make way there, can't yeh? Make way, dickens take it all!

SOLDIERS: (*As they pass*)

> —Think yeh're the only one hurt?
> —Watch who you're shovin'! . . .
> —If I had my arm back, I'd show yeh! . . .
> —Careful who yeh're trompin' on!

(*They bump into a SOLDIER walking in a daze, completely unaware of anyone or anything. They knock him down, off the ramp. A tattered SOLDIER helps him to sit up with his one good arm.*)

YOUNG MAN: Yeh see anyone from our regiment in the lot?

BOY: They're so patched up, couldn't tell if there was.

YOUNG MAN: They're like a funeral procession marchin' to their graves . . .

BOY: If they lost their bandages, they'd fall apart into a million pieces.

(*They walk slowly down the ramp looking over the mass of men.*)

They all know his secret grave now.

(*Referring to the body*)

YOUNG MAN: He'll have to move over to make room for more.

(*They settle on the ramp near the TATTERED SOLDIER who looks up at them.*)

TATTERED SOLDIER: Was a pretty good fight, wasn't it?

YOUNG MAN: What?

TATTERED SOLDIER: Was a pretty good fight, wa'n't it? Dern me if I ever seen fellers fight so. Laws, how they did fight! I know'd the boys'd fight when they oncet got square at it. The boys ain't had no fair chancet up t'now, but this time they showed what they was. I know'd it'd turn out this way. Yeh can't lick them boys. No sir! They're fighters, they be. I was talkin' with a boy from Georgia oncet, an' that boy, he sez, "Your fellers'll all run like hell when they oncet hear a gun," he sez. "Mebbe they will," I sez, "but I don't b'lieve none of it," I sez, "an' by jiminey," I sez to 'im, "mebbe yer fellers will run like hell when they oncet hear a gun," I sez. He laffed. Well, they didn't run to'day, did they, hey? No, sir! They fought an' fought an' fought!

(*The YOUNG MAN stands and starts to move.*)

Where yeh hit?

YOUNG MAN: What?

TATTERED SOLDIER: Where yeh hit?

YOUNG MAN: Why, I . . . I . . . that is . . . why . . . I . . .

(*Fidgets with a button on his coat. BOY grabs his hand and pulls him away.*)

BOY: C'mon . . . Let's set over here in the shade.

(*They move to the other side of the stage.*)

YOUNG MAN: It shows! . . . Even that old man could see right through me . . . They're all lookin' at me. They can see it burned on my face . . . Coward!

BOY: They look happy with their wounds . . . all torn and broken, but proud. I wish I had a wound like theirs . . . a red badge of courage.

YOUNG MAN: They make me feel guilty . . . but I'm not. I'm not guilty . . . I ran . . .

BOY: Like the squirrel, I ran. With all of the wounded, they'll need me now. They have only me left to fight.

(*The dazed SOLDIER moves his head toward us and we see he is the TALL SOLDIER. He recognizes the YOUNG MAN and makes his way toward him.*)

YOUNG MAN: Someone had to run, to run and come back later . . . I did right. They'll see.

(The TALL SOLDIER places his gory hand on the YOUNG MAN's shoulder. The YOUNG MAN turns slowly.)

Gawd! Jim Conklin!

TALL SOLDIER: *(Slight smile)* Hello, Henry.

YOUNG MAN: *(Helping him to sit)* Oh, Jim . . . Jim . . .

TALL SOLDIER: *(Monotonous voice)* Where yeh been, Henry? I thought mebbe yeh got keeled over. There's been thunder t'pay to'day. I was worryin' about yeh a good deal.

BOY: Jim! Gawd, not Jim. He's the best one of the bunch.

TALL SOLDIER: Yeh know, I was out there. An', Lord, what a circus! An' by jiminey, I got shot . . . I got shot. Yes, by jiminey, I got shot.

BOY: I'm afraid . . . I'm afraid!

TALL SOLDIER: *(Clutching YOUNG MAN's shoulder and whispering)* I tell yeh what I'm 'fraid of, Henry . . . I'll tell yeh what I'm 'fraid of. I'm 'fraid I'll fall down . . . an' then, yeh know . . . they likely as not'll tromp right over me. That's what I'm 'fraid of.

YOUNG MAN: *(Crying out)* I'll take care of yeh, Jim! I'll take care of yeh! I swear t'Gawd I will!

TALL SOLDIER: Sure . . . Will yeh, Henry?

BOY: *(Crying)* Yes . . . yes . . . I tell yeh . . . I'll take care of yeh, Jim!

TALL SOLDIER: *(Weakly falling into the YOUNG MAN's arms)* Please . . . please don't let 'em run all over me . . . promise me. I was allus a good friend to yeh, wa'n't I, Henry? I've allus been a good fella, ain't I? An' it ain't much t'ask, is it? Jest t'pull me along outer the road? I'd do it fer you, wouldn't I, Henry?

(YOUNG MAN cannot answer for the held-in sobs. SOUND: The funeral march begins again as the wounded men slowly get up, grumbling, and begin to move off. The TALL SOLDIER sees them and begins to rise.)

YOUNG MAN: Here, lean on me.

TALL SOLDIER: *(Shaking his head, protesting)* No . . . No . . . No . . . Leave me be . . . Leave me be . . .

YOUNG MAN: You're weak. You need help.

TALL SOLDIER: No . . . No . . . Leave me be . . . Leave me be.

(TATTERED SOLDIER moves in.)

TATTERED SOLDIER: Ye'd better take 'im outta the road, son. He's a goner anyhow in about five minutes . . . yeh kin see that. Ye'd better take 'im outta the road. Don't know where the blazes he gits his stren'th from.

YOUNG MAN: Lord knows!

(*Grasps shoulders of the TALL SOLDIER who has been wandering around aimlessly*)

Jim! Jim! Come with me.

TALL SOLDIER: (*Weakly attempting to wrench himself free*) Huh? (*He stares at the YOUNG MAN, then dimly realizing.*) Oh! In the th' fields? Oh! (*He starts blindly toward the ramp.*)

TATTERED SOLDIER: Gawd! He's runnin!!

YOUNG MAN: (*Rushing to him*) Jim! . . . Jim, what are you doing? You'll hurt hourself.

TALL SOLDIER: (*Gazing up toward the center platform*) No . . . No . . . Don't tech me . . . Leave me be . . . Leave me be.

YOUNG MAN: Where yeh goin', Jim? . . . What are you thinkin' about? . . . Tell me, won't yeh, Jim?

TALL SOLDIER: (*Nearly in tears*) Leave me be, can't yeh? Leave me be for a minnit.

YOUNG MAN: Why, Jim? . . . What's the matter with you?

(*He pulls forward, releasing himself from the YOUNG MAN's grasp and struggles forward to the center platform where he clings to a post. His chest begins to heave. It increases.*)

BOY: No! . . . No! . . . Don't take him away! . . . He didn't do no harm to nobody! . . . Stop! . . . Stop! . . . Don't take him!

(*YOUNG MAN starts up the ramp.*)

YOUNG MAN: Jim! . . . Jim!

TALL SOLDIER: (*Quietly gesturing*) Leave me be . . . Don't tech me . . . Leave me be.

(*He grasps the pole with several gasps, slithers to the ground. The YOUNG MAN rushes to the body and kneels. He touches his shoulder and then with livid rage shakes his fist at the battlefield.*)

(*SLIDE: A dead body.*)

YOUNG MAN: Hell! . . .

(*SLIDE: A grave marking.*)

TATTERED SOLDIER: (*Moving up the other ramp with the BOY*) Well, he was a reg'lar jim'dandy fer nerve, wa'n't he?

(*Softly*)

A reg'lar jim-dandy.

(*Pokes one of the hands with his foot*)

I wonder where he got his stren'th from? I never seen a man do like that before. It was a funny thing. Well, he was a reg'lar jim-dandy.

(*YOUNG MAN rises, and unable to screech out, grabs a post and clutches it, sobbing. The TATTERED SOLDIER watches for a moment.*)

TATTERED SOLDIER: Look-a-here, son. He's up an' gone, ain't 'e, an' we might as well begin t' look out fer ol' number one. This here thing is all over. He's up an' gone, aint' 'e? An' he's all right here. Nobody won't bother 'im. An' I must say I ain't enjoyin' any great health m'self these days.

(*Crosses to YOUNG MAN*)

There ain't no use in us stayin' aroun' here. He'll be jest fine.

BOY: He picked the spot hisself . . . he and the other feller here will keep each other company.

YOUNG MAN: 'Tis the quietest spot around.

TATTERED SOLDIER: Well, he were a jim-dandy, weren't he?

YOUNG MAN: (*Walking down ramp*) A jim-dandy.

TATTERED SOLDIER: (*Weakly*) I'm commencin' t' feel pretty bad . . . I'm commencin' t' feel pretty damn bad.

BOY: Are yeh goin' t' die like Jim?

TATTERED SOLDIER: Oh, I'm not goin' t' die yet! There's too much dependin' on me fer me t' die yit. No, sir! Nary die! I *can't*! Ye'd oughter see th' swad a' children I've got, an' all like that.

(*The YOUNG MAN turns to see him smile. The TATTERED SOLDIER and BOY come down the ramp.*)

Yeh know Tom Jamison, he lives next door t' me up home. He's a nice feller he is. An' we was allus good friends . . . smart too. Smart as a steel trap. Well, when we was a-fightin' this afternoon, all of a sudden he begin t' rip up an' cuss an' beller at me. "Yer shot, yeh blamed infernal!" . . . he swear horrible . . . he sez t' me. I put m' hand t' m' head an' when I looked at m' fingers, I seen, sure 'nough I was shot. I give a holler an' began t' run, but before I could get away another one hit me in the arm an' whirled me clean 'round. I got skeered when they was all a-shootin' behind me an' I run t' beat all, but I catch it pretty bad. I've an idee I'd a' been fightin' yit, if 'twasn't for Tom Jamison . . . I don't believe I kin walk much further.

BOY: Set for a minute . . . Yeh ain't lookin' good at all.

TATTERED SOLDIER: (*To YOUNG MAN*) Yeh look pretty peaked yourself . . .

I beg yeh got a worser wound than yeh think. Ye'd better take keer of yer hurt. It don't do t' let sech things go. It might be inside mostly, an' them plays thunder. Where is it located?

YOUNG MAN: Why don't yeh not bother me?

BOY: He's jest tryin' to be nice ... He's a nice man.

TATTERED SOLDIER: I seen a feller git hit plum in th' head when my regiment was a-standing' at ease oncet. An' everybody yelled out to 'im, "Hurt, John? Are yeh hurt much?" "No," sez he. He looked kinder surprised, an' he went on tellin' 'em how he felt. He sed he didn't feel nothin'. But, by dad, the first thing that feller knowed, he was dead. Yes, he was dead ... stone dead. So, ye want to watch out. Yeh might have some strange kinda hurt yerself. Yeh can't never tell. Where is your'n located?

YOUNG MAN: (Crying out) Oh, don't bother me!

(In pain)

Don't bother me!

TATTERED SOLDIER: Well, Lord knows I don't want ta bother anybody. Lord knows I've gotta 'nough m' own t' tend to.

(Loosens BOY's hand. BOY walks away.)

BOY: Good-bye.

TATTERED SOLDIER: Why ... Why, boy, where yeh goin'?

(He begins to act dumb-like, his thoughts floundering about in his head.)

Now ... now ... look ... a ... here, you. Tom Jamison ... now ... I won't have this ... this here won't do. I ... I see through you, boy ... where ... Where yeh goin'?

YOUNG MAN: (Pointing vaguely) Over there.

TATTERED SOLDIER: Well now, look ... a ... here ... now ... this thing won't do now, Tom Jamison. It won't do. I know yeh, yeh pigheaded devil. Yeh wantta go trompin' off with a bad hurt. It ain't right ... now ... Tom Jamison ... it ain't right. Yeh wantta leave me take keer of yeh, son. It ain't right ... it ain't fer yeh t' go ... trompin' off ... with a bad hurt ... it ain't ... ain't ... ain't right ... it ain't ...

(Falling to his knees beside the decayed SOLDIER, he delivers his final lines clutching him.)

YOUNG MAN: (To BOY) Come on ... We gotta find our way back.

TATTERED SOLDIER: Yeh need me tuh take keer of ya.

BOY: (To YOUNG MAN) We can't leave him here ... he's hurt bad ... he needs us.

YOUNG MAN: Well, I don't need him botherin' and pesterin' at me no more
. . . Yeh decide . . . him or me . . . I'm leavin'.

(*He starts up the ramp and down the back.*)

TATTERED SOLDIER: Look . . . a . . . here now, Tom Jamison . . . now . . . it
ain't . . .

(*The BOY runs after the YOUNG MAN as the lights fade. SOUND: Wind, lonely.*)

(*SLIDES: Deserted graves.*)

(*The lights come up on the right ramp as the YOUNG MAN and BOY enter.*)

BOY: How could yeh jest leave 'im there tuh die? . . . What'd he ever do tuh
you?

YOUNG MAN: He knew, he knew I was a coward . . . He could see right
through me. Yeh heard him say it.

BOY: It ain't right . . . It ain't right to desert him.

YOUNG MAN: If yeh care so much, why don't yeh go back? . . . If he means
that much to yeh . . . a complete stranger, go on ahead. Be glad to get rid of
yeh anyhow . . . It's your fault I'm in this mess.

BOY: Yer jest as much tuh blame as me.

YOUNG MAN: Go! . . . Get out of my life! Get out! Without yeh I can be what I
want . . . Without yeh, I'll be a man. There's no room in me for you any more.

BOY: Yeh really mean that? . . . Yeh don't want me around no more?

YOUNG MAN: (*Falling to his knees, sobbing*) I don't know . . . I don't know *what*
I am any more.

BOY: Then, I'll leave . . . I'll leave . . . then you'll see.

(*Starts to run up the ramp*)

YOUNG MAN: No! . . . Don't leave me alone . . . I didn't mean it.

BOY: Yah, yeh did . . . I know yeh. I know yeh did.

(*He runs off.*)

YOUNG MAN: (*Shouts*) You don't know me at all! . . . Nobody knows me!

(*SOUND: Gunfire, explosions.*)

(*SLIDES: Soldiers running.*)

YOUNG MAN: I'm hungry . . . thirsty and hungry. That's all it is.

(*Stands and dizzily moves about. He covers his ears.*)

That noise . . . the gunfire's blowing my head apart! Stop it! . . . Stop this war!
. . . I give up. You win! I surrender to you.

(*The lights fade slowly to a circle of light around him.*)

I can't run another step . . . Somebody find me.

(*SOUND: Recorded Voices.*)

"Where's Henry Fleming?"
"He run, didn't he?"
"He run like a coward, he did."

MOTHER: Henry, don't run, you'll fall.

"What are yeh 'fraid of, Henry?"

YOUNG MAN: Somebody find me . . . I surrender.

(*SOLDIERS begin to run through, passing the circle of light. The SOLDIERS are the same as in previous scenes. They wear the same jackets, but solid light-colored trousers to indicate they are from another regiment. They bump into him, knocking him about as they pass.*)

HARMONICA: There's hundreds of 'em in there . . . C'mon man, run.

BANJO: Where's the way out of here?!

YOUNG MAN: No, yeh can't run . . .

SCARED SOLDIER: We're outnumbered . . .

YOUNG MAN: Don't run . . . I'll help you. I'll help you . . . Stay!

GLUM SOLDIER: (*To YOUNG MAN*) Get outta the way . . . Run, yeh fool . . .

TRUMPET: (*Screaming*) Gawd, it's the walls of hell fallin' in . . .

YOUNG MAN: (*Grabbing SOLDIER by the arm and swinging him to him*) Why?
     . . . Why? . . .

TRUMPET: Let me go! . . . Let me go!

(*Heaving and panting, he struggles, pulling the YOUNG MAN along.*)

Let me go! . . . Let me go!

YOUNG MAN: Why? . . . Why?

TRUMPET: Well then!

(*He swings his rifle around and crashes the butt on the side of the YOUNG MAN's head. The YOUNG MAN falls to the ground and the SOLDIER runs off. The second the rifle strikes, the SOUND whirls like a plug pulled on a phonograph and the SLIDES blur. They heighten, then blur and fade along with the light on the YOUNG MAN to black.*)

ACT 2

(*The SLIDES and SOUND slowly fade up to where they were at the end of Act I. A light fades up on the YOUNG MAN: A bloodstain is now on the side of his head.*)

He clutches his head as he stands and weaves unsteadily on his feet. The SOUND develops into a recorded eerie, haunting version of "Battle Cry of Freedom.")

YOUNG MAN: The drums an' bugles are callin' me . . . They're callin' me to fight . . . *(Cries out)* I don't know the way . . . I don't know the way to run.

(Spot up on BOY)

BOY: Run to the castle and bolt all the doors . . . the dragon won't get you there . . . run to the castle.

(Spot up on the DECAYED SOLDIER, who rises)

DECAYED SOLDIER: Run to the grave and bury your secret beneath . . . Kill your confusion . . . Put your running to rest. Run to the grave.

(Spot up on TALL SOLDIER)

TALL SOLDIER: The war's in your hands now, Henry . . . Yer fightin' fer the both of us now . . . Get in there an' show 'em how a war is run.

(Spot up on MOTHER)

MOTHER: I told yeh yeh'd get bad hurt if yeh played that fightin' game . . . Run inside, Son, an' wash off that blood.

(Spot up on TATTERED SOLDIER)

TATTERED SOLDIER: Hold onto yer head . . . hold on fer dear life . . . death is fer the dead . . . don't let it run away with ye, son.

YOUNG MAN: I'm bleeding! . . . My head is lying open . . . Everyone get out! . . . Get out!

BOY: You can't get rid of me that easily . . .

MOTHER: Don't forget what I said, Son . . .

TALL SOLDIER: Don't let what I started go undone.

TATTERED SOLDIER: You can't escape what you are, boy.

DECAYED SOLDIER: I'll always be in your thoughts . . .

YOUNG MAN: Get out! . . . Get out!

(He starts to run, but bumps into them.)

BOY: Run to the castle!

MOTHER: Run inside an' wash off the blood.

TALL SOLDIER: Show 'em how a war is run!

TATTERED SOLDIER: Don't let it run away with yeh, son.

DECAYED SOLDIER: Put your running to rest!

BOY: *(Sing-song)* Henry's a coward . . . Henry's a coward.

MOTHER: Yeh gotta be brave to be a hero, Son.

TALL SOLDIER: Where's yer courage, Henry?

TATTERED SOLDIER: Ain't no place for cowards here.

DECAYED SOLDIER: Cowards die a thousand deaths.

YOUNG MAN: (*Falling to his knees. A piercing vibration as the spots fade and the YOUNG MAN cowers in pain.*) Somebody help me! . . . Please! . . . Somebody point me in the right direction!

(*The CHEERY SOLDIER, who has been watching in the background, walks up behind him.*)

CHEERY SOLDIER: Yeh seem t' be in a pretty bad way, boy.

YOUNG MAN: (*Not looking up*) Uh!

CHEERY SOLDIER: (*Taking his arm*) Well, I'm goin' your way. The whole gang is goin' your way. An' I guess I kin give yeh a lift.

(*Lifts him up, putting his arm around him to steady him*)

Yeh seem mighty troubled 'bout somethin' . . . been watchin' yeh. Oh, you'll make it . . . you'll make it jest fine. Fightin's a little harder fer some than fer others. Pretty nearly everybody got their share of fightin' t'day. By dad, I give myself up fer dead any number of times.

(*They move in to different light areas as they make their way up one ramp and down the other.*)

There was shootin' there, an' hollerin' there in the durn darkness until I couldn't tell t' save my soul which side I was on. It was the most mixed up dern thing I ever seen. These here hull woods is a reg'lar mess. How'd yeh get way over here anyhow? Well, I guess we can find yer way okay. Yeh know, there was a boy killed in my comp'ny t'day that I thought the world an' all of. Sure was a nice feller. By ginger, it hurt like thunder t' see ol' Jim jest git knocked flat. We was a-standin' purty peaceable fer a spell, though there was men runnin' ev'ry way all 'round us, an' while we was a-standin' like that, 'long comes a big fat fellow. He began t' peck at Jim's elbow, and he sez, "Say, where's the road to the river?" Jim was a-lookin' ahead all the time tryin' t' see the gray comin' through th' woods, an' he never paid no attention t' this big fat feller fer a long time, but at last he turned 'round an' he sez, "Ah, go t' blazes an' find the road to the river!" An' jest then a shot slapped him bang on the side of the head. Them was his last words.

(*SOUND: Faint strains of "Tenting Tonight," sung by the SOLDIERS offstage and played by HARMONICA.*)

SOLDIERS: (*Sung*)

We're tenting tonight, on the old camp ground.

Give us a song to cheer
Our weary hearts, a song of home
And friends we love so dear.
Many are the hearts, that are weary tonight
Wishing for the war to cease.
Many are the hearts, looking for the right
To see the dawn of peace.
Tenting tonight . . . tenting tonight,
Tenting on the old camp ground.

YOUNG MAN: Where are yeh takin' me?

CHEERY SOLDIER: Leadin' yeh to where yeh belong, jest like yeh asked.

YOUNG MAN: How do yeh . . . ?

CHEERY SOLDIER: Funny how yeh get instincts 'bout some things . . . Jest take it easy now . . . I'll help yeh find yer way.

(*They move off into the darkness as the SOLDIERS enter, their song building as they arrange themselves around the camp. The BOY is spotted near his toy soldiers.*)

(*SLIDES: A peaceful camp with fires, etc. A homelike and inviting picture.*)

(*At the end of the song, the HARMONICA continues and the YOUNG MAN and CHEERY SOLDIER enter up the rear ramp.*)

CHEERY SOLDIER: Ah, here yeh be! . . . See, they're all waitin' fer yeh 'round the fire. You'll be jist fine now. Willin' to bet all I own on it too. Good-bye, ol' boy, good luck to yeh.

(*He rests him by a post, then turns and cheerfully strides away whistling.*)

YOUNG MAN: Wait . . . I don't know who you are . . . I never saw yer face.

(*He clutches onto the post.*)

Why did you bring me here?

(*From below, the LOUD SOLDIER grabs a rifle and starts up the ramp toward him.*)

LOUD SOLDIER: Halt! . . . Halt!

YOUNG MAN: (*Recognizing the voice*) Wilson? . . . You . . . You here?

LOUD SOLDIER: (*Moving in closer*) That you, Henry?

YOUNG MAN: Yes, it's . . . it's me.

LOUD SOLDIER: Well, well, ol' boy, I'm glad to see yeh! I give yeh up for a goner. I thought yeh was dead sure enough.

YOUNG MAN: (*Clutching even stronger to the post*) I've . . . I've had an awful time. I've been all over. Way over on the right. Terrible fightin' over there. I had an awful time. I got separated from the reg'ment.

(*Spot up on BOY*)

BOY: We ran . . . we ran till we was clean outta breath.

YOUNG MAN: No! . . . Got separated! . . . Over on the right. I got shot . . . in the head.

(*Spot up on MOTHER*)

MOTHER: Son, I taught yeh never to lie . . . Tell the truth now, Son . . . Tell the truth.

YOUNG MAN: I got shot!

(*Light pops out on MOTHER*)

     In the head! I never seen sech fightin'. Awful time. I don't see how I coulda get separated from the regiment.

BOY: Yes yeh do . . . yeh ran . . . ran like the squirrel.

YOUNG MAN: I got shot too.

BOY: Ma told yeh never to lie.

(*Spot out on BOY*)

LOUD SOLDIERS: What? Got shot? Why didn't yeh say so first?

LIEUTENANT: (*Coming up the ramp*) Who yeh talkin' to, Wilson? Yer the darndest sentinel . . . Why I . . .

(*Sees YOUNG MAN*)

     Henry! . . . Why, I thought you was dead four hours ago. Where was yeh?

YOUNG MAN: Over on the right. I got separated . . .

LOUD SOLDIER: Yes, an' he got shot in the head. We'd best see to him right away.

(*Puts his arm about him*)

     Gee, it must hurt like thunder!

YOUNG MAN: Yes, it hurts . . . hurts a good deal . . .

LIEUTENANT: (*Taking YOUNG MAN's arm*) Come on, son. I'll take keer o' yeh.

(*Starts to lead him down the ramp*)

LOUD SOLDIER: Put 'im to sleep on my blanket. Look at his head by the fire an' see how it looks. Maybe it's a pretty bad 'un. When I git relieved in a coupla minutes, I'll be over an' see t' him.

LIEUTENANT: (*Leading him to fire by the BOY and his toy soldiers*) Now, let's have a look at yer ol' head.

(*The YOUNG MAN sits down and the LIEUTENANT fumbles through his hair, spots the wound and lets out a long whistle.*)

Ah, here we are! Jest as I thought . . . yeh've been grazed. It's raised a strange lump jest as if some feller had lammed yeh on the head with a club. It stopped bleedin' long time ago. The most about it is that in the mornin' yeh'll feel that a number ten hat wouldn't fit yeh . . .

(*Spot up on MOTHER*)

MOTHER: An' your head'll be all het up an' feel as dry as burnt pork. An' yeh may get a lotta other sicknesses, too, by mornin'. Yeh can't never tell. Still, I don't much think so. It's jest a hit on the head, Son . . . nothin' more . . . Yer always gettin' in some sort of scrap . . . always fightin' . . . Be a good boy, Son, and stop all this fightin' . . . Be a man . . .

(*Spot out*)

LIEUTENANT: Now, you jest sit here an' don't move. I'll send Wilson t' take keer a' yeh.

(*He exits up the ramp and relieves Wilson.*)

BOY: Yeh sure have 'em all fooled.

YOUNG MAN: I thought yeh left . . . preferred that tattered soldier t' me.

BOY: He's dead . . . died soon after I got to him. Yeh don't have to worry 'bout him . . . he won't say nothin' to no one . . . his suspicions died with him.

YOUNG MAN: Where was yeh when I needed yeh? . . . When I got hit.

BOY: Proves yeh can't get along without me.

YOUNG MAN: I don't need anyone but me.

(*The LOUD SOLDIER comes forward, carrying a canteen.*)

LOUD SOLDIER: Well now, Henry, ol' boy, we'll have yeh fixed up in jest about a minute.

(*Sits down and hands him the canteen*)

Here, drink some of this hot coffee.

(*Pours water from another canteen into a white scrap of cloth and ties it around the YOUNG MAN's head*)

BOY: They'll really take note of yeh back home now . . . a red badge of courage . . . Wow!

LOUD SOLDIER: Yeh sure are a brave one, Henry . . . Yeh don't holler ner say nothin'. Most men would a' been in the hospital long ago. A shot in the head ain't foolin' business.

(*YOUNG MAN makes no reply, but fidgets with the buttons on his coat*)

TALL SOLDIER: (*Entering*) I died fer doin' an honest deed . . . Yer makin' a fool a' me, Henry . . . Yer lies are laughin' at me.

TATTERED SOLDIER: (*Entering*) You ain't foolin' me none . . . I see right through yeh, an' soon enough they all will see through too.

MOTHER: (*Entering*) I raised yeh better than that, Son . . . I'm ashamed of yeh . . . I'm ashamed to call yeh my own.

YOUNG MAN: (*Frantically pulling on LOUD SOLDIER*) Tell 'em to go away . . . Tell 'em to leave me alone.

LOUD SOLDIER: Who? . . . What are yeh talkin' about? . . . Ain't no one there . . . jest darkness. That's all that's out there.

YOUNG MAN: They're haunting me . . . the darkness is . . .

LOUD SOLDIER: Calm yerself down now . . . yer jest tired . . . yeh need rest. Good night's sleep'll do yeh jest fine.

(*Lays him back on the ground and covers him with a blanket*)

   Tomorrow everythin'll be jest like before.

(*He rises and exits.*)

MOTHER: Tell the truth, Son.

BOY: Tell 'em yeh was only foolin'.

TALL SOLDIER: Let me die in truth, Henry.

TATTERED SOLDIER: Yer only foolin' yerself, son.

YOUNG MAN: I'll show yeh what courage I got in me . . . you'll see!

(*He becomes weaker and weaker but he grasps for strength. Finally, he falls back into sleep.*)

   You'll see! . . . You'll . . . You'll . . . You . . .

(*MOTHER comes to him and kneels.*)

MOTHER: Sleep well, my son . . . rest.

BOY: (*Moving in*) We can start all over again tomorrow.

TALL SOLDIER: Let me rest in peace, Henry.

TATTERED SOLDIER: *You* have another chance . . . Try again in truth, my son.

(*The lights fade on them, but remain up on the BOY and his soldiers.*)

BOY: One little, two little, three little soldiers . . . four little, five little, six little soldiers . . . seven little, eight little, nine little . . . ten little soldiers . . . dead!

(*He furiously topples them all over.*)

(*SLIDE: A mound of bodies.*)

   Dumb toys! . . . stupid game! . . . Where have all the dragons gone? . . . Castles are for kids . . . Heroes are for storybooks . . . Courage is a word for show-offs!

(*Starts to cry*)

I'm afraid of becoming a man!

(*The light fades on him. SOUND: Hollow rumble of drums and a distant bugle sounding faintly.*)

(*SLIDE: A new day.*)

(*The lights fade up slowly. The YOUNG MAN rises slowly and yawns.*)

YOUNG MAN: Thunder! . . . Mornin' already.

LOUD SOLDIER: (*Crossing to him*) Well, Henry, ol' man, how do yeh feel this morning'?

YOUNG MAN: I feel pretty bad.

LOUD SOLDIER: I hoped ye'd feel all right this mornin'. Let's see the bandage . . . I guess it's slipped.

(*He begins to fumble rather crudely with it.*)

YOUNG MAN: (*Pulling back*) Gosh-dern it! You're the hangdest man I ever saw! You wear muffs on yer hands? Why in good thunderation can't you be more easy? I'd rather yeh stand off an' throw rocks at it. Now, go slow, an' don't act as if you was nailin' down a carpet.

LOUD SOLDIER: Sorry . . . Come now an' git some grub. Then maybe you'll feel better.

(*They move to a fire where a group of SOLDIERS are pouring coffee.*)

BANJO: How yeh be, Henry?

HARMONICA: Welcome back . . . Sorry yeh got shot up.

CHEERY SOLDIER: Try to fight the whole war yerself?

GLUM SOLDIER: Some guys'll do anythin' to get themselves a badge fer courage.

(*Laughs*)

SINGING SOLDIER: Prob'ly jist fell an' hit his head on a rock while was runnin'.

(*Laughs. TATTERED SOLDIER enters.*)

TATTERED SOLDIER: They see right through yeh, son.

YOUNG MAN: (*Turning sharply to him*) You . . . You're dead! . . . You're dead . . . What do you know?

TATTERED SOLDIER: I'm dead . . . What do *you* know?

BANJO: (*Confused*) Who yeh talkin' to, Henry? . . . Got yerself a dead ghost?

(*They ALL laugh.*)

YOUNG MAN: (*To them quickly*) Jim Conklin's dead!

LOUD SOLDIER: What? . . . Is he? . . . Jim Conklin?

YOUNG MAN: Yes. He's dead. Shot in the head.

CHEERY SOLDIER: Yeh don't say so. Jim Conklin . . . poor cuss!

GLUM SOLDIER: One more gone . . .

TALL SOLDIER: (*Entering*) Don't let 'em chalk me off as jest another number . . .

BOY: (*Counting SOLDIERS around the fire*) One little, two little, three little soldiers . . . four little, five little, six little . . .

YOUNG MAN: (*Quickly*) He died real brave like . . . with courage!

HARMONICA: Courage ain't no good to a dead man.

LOUD SOLDIER: Gonna be hard to fergit ol' Jim.

YOUNG MAN: He was a hero! . . . With courage . . . He had no fears at all.

HARMONICA: Them's the kind always gettin' themselves killed . . . It's the cowards who live on to tell 'bout it.

(*Laughs*)

YOUNG MAN: (*Mad*) It ain't so! . . . I ain't no coward! You take that back or I'll kill yeh! . . . I ain't no coward! I got shot. Ain't that proof 'nuf fer yeh?

LOUD SOLDIER: (*Quieting him down*) Whoa there, Henry . . .

SINGING SOLDIER: Awf'lly touchy, ain't yeh, Henry?

BANJO: Can't yeh take a little ribbin'?

LOUD SOLDIER: Ain't no one callin' yeh a coward . . . Cheer up . . . Have some hard crackers . . . That'll take yer mind off from things.

CHEERY SOLDIER: Take yer appetite away too.

BANJO: Hard crackers an' coffee . . . 'nough to make yeh crave goober peas an' mush.

GLUM SOLDIER: They say an army travels on its stomach.

SINGING SOLDIER: Well, my innards have taken a mighty punishment.

HARMONICA: My stomach lost the battle months ago.

(*Hands cracker to YOUNG MAN*)

Have yourself a jaw breaker, Henry . . . Keep yer jaws busy on somethin' else fer a spell.

(*BANJO plunks several strings. HARMONICA joins in.*)

SOLDIERS: (*Sung*)

Let us close our talk of cowards.

Take our tin cups in hand.

While we gather round the cook tent's door

Where dried bundles of hard crackers are given to each man.
Oh, hard crackers come again no more.

'Tis the song and the sigh of the hungry
Hard crackers, hard crackers
Come again no more.
Many days have you lingered upon
Our stomachs sore . . .
Oh, hard crackers, come again no more.

(They ALL laugh as they move away.)

LOUD SOLDIER: Well, Henry . . . What d'yeh think the chances are? Do yeh think we'll wallop 'em?

YOUNG MAN: Day b'fore yesterday you would've bet you'd lick the hull kit-an'-boodle all by yourself.

LOUD SOLDIER: Would I? . . . Well, perhaps I would.

(Stares into fire)

YOUNG MAN: Oh, no you wouldn't either.

LOUD SOLDIER: Oh, yeh needn't mind, Henry . . . I believe I was a pretty big fool in those days . . . All the officers say we've got 'em in a pretty tight box.

(Clears his throat)

They all seem t' think we've got 'em just where we want 'em.

YOUNG MAN: I don't know about that . . . What I seen over on the right makes me think it was the other way about. From where I was, it looked as if we was getting' a good poundin' yesterday.

LOUD SOLDIER: D' yeh think so? . . . I thought we handled 'em pretty rough yesterday.

YOUNG MAN: Not a bit . . . Why, Lord, man, you didn't see nothin' of the fight like I did.

LOUD SOLDIER: Fleming.

YOUNG MAN: What?

LOUD SOLDIER: (*Putting his hand to his mouth, coughing and beginning to fidget*) Well, I guess yeh might as well give me back that envelope.

YOUNG MAN: All right, Wilson . . .

(Producing it from his jacket and handing it to him)

LOUD SOLDIER: (*Embarrassed*) Thanks, Henry, fer carryin' it fer me . . . Guess I can handle it myself now.

(Walks away)

YOUNG MAN: (*To himself*) Too bad! Too bad! The poor devil, it makes him feel tough.

BOY: How do *you* feel?

YOUNG MAN: A mite stronger than yesterday ... Poor ol' Wilson seems a bit jealous a' my courage.

BOY: Yeh mean yer beginnin' tuh believe it yerself?

YOUNG MAN: How do you know? You weren't there! ...

BOY: What's happenin' to yeh? ... I don't know yeh at all any more. Yeh can't go on livin' a lie ... Admit it ... at least to yerself.

YOUNG MAN: The whole regiment knows who I am fer the first time ... They know me by name. Before, I was jest one of the hundreds of thousands ... but now I'm somebody ... I can't ... I can't admit it! I feel part of this whole thing fer the first time ... Don't take that away from me.

BOY: You're cheating ... it ain't fair.

YOUNG MAN: Nothin' about this war is fair ... Look at ol' Jim Conklin. What was fair 'bout him dyin'?

BOY: He died honestly ... he *lost* fairly ... if yeh can't be truthful to yerself, be truthful fer Jim.

YOUNG MAN: I can't! ... I can't! ... He's gone. I'm still here ... I've gotta think of me now.

BOY: You'll never win, yeh know ... Someone somewhere'll see right through yeh ... jest like that tattered soldier.

YOUNG MAN: He's dead! ... Yeh jest want tuh take my courage away ... It was you who made me run.

BOY: Yeh can't go on blamin' me for yer mistakes forever.

YOUNG MAN: No! Yer trickin' me ... tryin' tuh get me to confess.

BOY: Yer trickin' yerself ... I'm goin'.

(*Starts to pick up toy soldiers*)

YOUNG MAN: You can't ... you can't go till I tell you to.

BOY: I'm ashamed I was ever a part of you.

(*Pleads*)

Why don't yeh become a man an' let me go away feelin' proud? ...

YOUNG MAN: I don't know what yer talkin' about ... Yer jest a crazy kid with a sackful of toys playin' a war game. It ain't real! ... This! ... This is real! They don't topple over ... They die!

BOY: An' lie?

YOUNG MAN: So do those storybooks yeh read . . . It ain't like that here . . . There are no knights an' shiny white horses . . . Here there ain't none of that . . . They lied too.

BOY: They were fer me tuh read an' believe in . . . not you.

YOUNG MAN: Go then . . . I'll do jest fine without yeh. You'll see things my way some day.

(The light fades on the BOY and the YOUNG MAN talks to the darkness.)

This ain't a storybook war . . . This is real! When are yeh goin' to realize it? Yeh dumb, stupid, idiot kid!

(LOUD SOLDIER walks up to him.)

LOUD SOLDIER: What's the matter, Henry? . . . Talkin' to yerself is supposed to be some sign of guilt, yeh know.

YOUNG MAN: Jest had tuh get rid a' somethin' on my chest, that's all.

LOUD SOLDIER: Well, is it gone?

YOUNG MAN: Disappeared . . . Don't know if it's gone, though.

LOUD SOLDIER: Wanta tell me about it? . . . I'm still yer friend, ain't I?

YOUNG MAN: I'll be fine . . . Thanks though, Wilson.

LOUD SOLDIER: Well, if yeh change yer mind yeh know where tuh find me . . . How's yer head?

YOUNG MAN: Fine . . .

LOUD SOLDIER: Good.

(He exits.)

YOUNG MAN: *(To where BOY was)* That dumb little kid's changed roles on me . . . He's suddenly made me into the boy an' he's walked away the man.

(MOTHER walks into the BOY's light.)

MOTHER: Yer such a bad boy, Henry.

YOUNG MAN: Ma . . . Man, yer goin' to be real proud of me, Ma . . . Look, I got shot . . . a badge of courage.

MOTHER: Courage ain't somethin' yeh wear like a badge, Son. Courage is somethin' only you can see . . . It's worn inside, outta sight.

YOUNG MAN: But I . . .

MOTHER: What do yeh have tuh prove, Son . . . except to yerself?

YOUNG MAN: I want *you* tuh be proud.

MOTHER: I always was, Son . . . Yeh don't need tuh win a badge fer me . . . Yeh don't need tuh lie fer me.

YOUNG MAN: He told you, didn't he? . . . That little . . .

MOTHER: This war yer fightin's in yerself, Son . . . You can win over it . . . with truth!

(*The light fades on her.*)

YOUNG MAN: I want to belong . . . to be part. Try an' understand, Ma, it's the only way.

(*Light up on DECAYED SOLDIER.*)

> No, I don't want to die! . . . Don't hang around waitin' fer me . . . You ain't gettin' me like yeh got Jim . . . Ain't yeh got enough by now? . . . What do yeh hang around lurkin' at me for?! Take those yeh already got and go away!

(*He turns and begins to run toward the right ramp.*)

> I can run faster than you . . . I'll manage to stay a step or two ahead!

(*The light fades on the DECAYED SOLDIER. SOUND: Cannons and guns. Lights flash and flicker. The SOLDIERS rush to their spots.*)

LOUD SOLDIER: Take cover, Henry . . . Protect yerself!

YOUNG MAN: What's happening? . . .

TRUMPET: Yer in a war, boy . . . Show yer courage!

YOUNG MAN: (*Dazed*) Show my courage . . . Show my . . .

(*Shouts*)

> It's here! . . . See! . . . See my red badge of courage.

FRIENDLY SOLDIER: Prove it!

YOUNG MAN: I have proof . . . See it . . . See the bandage.

HARMONICA: Live up to it then!

(*Throws him a rifle*)

> Here, put yer courage into action.

YOUNG MAN: Yes! . . . Yes, I'll prove it to you all . . . I'll show you.

(*Spot up on MOTHER*)

MOTHER: Show yerself, Son.

(*Spot up on BOY*)

BOY: Let me walk away proud.

LIEUTENANT: I was willin' t' bet they'd attack as soon as the sun got fairly up.

YOUNG MAN: (*Showing off*) Good Gawd! We're always bein' chased around like rats! It makes me sick. Nobody seems to know where we go or why we go. We jest get fired around from pillar to post an' get licked there, an' nobody knows what it's done fer. It makes a man feel like a durn kitten in a bag . . .

LOUD SOLDIER: It'll turn out all right in th' end.

YOUNG MAN: Oh, the devil it will! You always talk like a dog-hanged parson. Don't tell me! I know . . .

LIEUTENANT: You boys shut up! . . . You've been jawin' like a lotta old hens. All you've got to do is fight. Less talkin' an' more fightin' is what's best for you boys. I never saw sech gabblin' jackasses.

(SOUND: Battle roar settling into a single long explosion.)

(SLIDES: Civil War battle photos interspersed throughout the following scene.)

(The YOUNG MAN cowers behind a post as do the other SOLDIERS, stationed about the unit. A spot comes up on the BOY.)

BOY: Why are you drawing me back? . . . I left . . . Let me stay gone.

YOUNG MAN: I can't do it alone . . . I'm still afraid.

BOY: You're going to ruin everything . . . everything. Think for yourself. You don't need a boy to talk to any more . . . Talk it out with the man.

YOUNG MAN: (As he speaks, the DECAYED SOLDIER appears behind the BOY. The BOY smiles up at him and takes his hand. The BOY's spot slowly dims.) I don't know what to do. I can't let them see I lied . . . They're all watching to see . . . Their eyes are all glued to me, digging into me to find the truth.

BOY: Don't let them see it . . . Don't let them see me . . . Do something!

YOUNG MAN: (Looking out, searching for the BOY) What? Tell me what!

BOY: Quickly . . . This is your moment of truth. Tell yourself, Henry.

YOUNG MAN (As his voice fades into a recording. The recording, played over the sound system, becomes his newfound self. No longer is the BOY his conscience. He has become a man.) My moment of truth . . . my moment of proof.

(He begins to rise unconsciously.)

What's happening? . . . I'm being pulled up . . . A giant hand is lifting me like a toy soldier. I have no control. The hand is moving me.

(He starts to move down the ramp without control. He stumbles and falls.)

I've been shot! In the arm? . . . In the head? . . . Where?

(He rises.)

Where are you, death?

(He searches for the DECAYED SOLDIER.)

He's gone . . . I'm still here . . . I managed to slip through his boney fingers.

(*He rushes down the ramp and takes refuge beside it.*)

You won't get me like yeh got Jim . . . All right, yeh stinkin' devils, yeh ain't gonna take me! I'll fight yeh till my arms fall off . . .

(*He continually pumps cartridges into his rifle.*)

I'll show yeh I ain't no coward . . . I'll get eight of you for every Jim of ours yeh took . . .

(*He becomes a mad man.*)

Run! . . . Run back, yeh dragons of death . . .

(*He moves out, standing in the open.*)

Look at 'em! . . . What's the matter, are yeh afraid? . . . Run! . . . Run! . . . Run, ya stinkin' fools!

(*Everyone has stopped firing but him. They stare at him in amazement.*)

TRUMPET: (*Laughing*) Yeh infernal fool, don't yeh know enough t' quit when there ain't anythin' to' shoot at? Good Gawd!

(*The YOUNG MAN turns, the only one out front. They are all staring at him. He turns front again, seeing a deserted ground.*)

YOUNG MAN: Oh.

(*He returns to the group and sits.*)

LIEUTENANT: By Gawd, if I had ten thousand wildcats like you, I could tear the stomach outta this war in less'n a week!

LOUD SOLDIER: (*Crossing to YOUNG MAN*) Are yeh all right, Fleming? Do yeh feel all right? There ain't nothin' the matter with yeh, Henry, is there?

YOUNG MAN: No.

BANJO: By thunder, I bet this Army'll never see another reg'ment like us!

FLUTE: You bet!

HARMONICA: A dog, a woman, an' a walnut tree. The more yeh beat 'em, the better they be!

SCARED SOLDIER: That's like us.

WOUNDED SOLDIER: Lost a pile of men, they did. If an ol' woman swept up the woods, she'd get a dustpanful.

GLUM SOLDIER: Yes, an' if she'll come aroun' ag'in in 'bout an hour, she'll git a pile more.

(*SOUND: Rolling clatter of musketry.*)

YOUNG MAN: (*Recorded*) Yer wantin' more, are yeh? . . . Well, come on, quit hidin' like a bunch of scared boys . . . Show yerself! . . . Fight like men. Let us have it! . . . We'll give it back to yeh ten times better.

(The stage brightens suddenly in vibrant red. A SOLDIER falls. Others shield their eyes.)

Good Gawd, it's suddenly turned into the fires of hell!

(The men seem paralyzed. They lower their guns and stare bewilderedly at the sight.)

What's wrong with 'em? . . . They're frozen . . . Come on, raise those rifles and let 'em have it . . . Yeh durn fools, yer actin' like a bunch of rundown toy soldiers . . . Wind yerselves up or they'll charge in and trample yeh into the ground.

YOUNG MAN: (*Live*) Come on, yeh fools! . . . Come on! Yeh can't jest set there like a bunch of wooden men. Come on!

(The stare blankly at him. The LOUD SOLDIER rushes down, raises his rifle and shoots. The shot seems to awaken them and they come alive.)

YOUNG MAN: (*Recorded*) Good goin', Wilson . . . Fire death right back in their faces . . .

(The color bearer rises to the top level.)

Raise that flag high. Show 'em what we're fightin' for . . . the reason we're here riskin' our lives.

(Quietly, as if suddenly realizing)

The reason . . . the flag . . . of course that's what this is all about . . . the purpose. A flowing flag of truth and honesty. A badge of courage.

(The color bearer is hit and falls to his knees.)

It's been hit! . . . It's falling!

YOUNG MAN: (*Live*) The flag! . . . Someone grab the flag. It's been hit!

(They ignore his cry.)

YOUNG MAN: (*Recorded*) It's falling like Jim Conklin into a coward's grave . . . For Gawd's sake, someone save it!

(He starts up the ramp to the flag.)

That flag is the real meaning of all this fighting nonsense . . . Don't let it fall into a lie.

(He reaches the flag and pries it from the dying soldier. He holds it as if it were made of precious china.)

Here, here is the real badge of my courage.

(Suddenly he rises and waves it frantically over the men.)

YOUNG MAN: (*Live*) Look! . . . Look, all of you . . . Here is what we're here for . . . This is what we're fightin' for . . . Ripped and shredded, it still holds together . . . Fight like the flag, men . . . Fight for the right of the flag!

YOUNG MAN: (*Recorded*) They see it . . . It seems to be callin' to them like it called to me . . . Look at those bullets fly . . . Wahoo! Show 'em, men . . . Show 'em what this war is all about . . . Looky there, they're runnin' . . . They're runnin' like hell . . . We won 'em . . . We won 'em!

LOUD SOLDIER: (*Rushing to the YOUNG MAN*) I can't believe it . . . We did it . . . We did it! We fought like thunder! Yeh jest oughtta heard.

YOUNG MAN: Heard what?

LOUD SOLDIER: The Colonel . . . The Colonel, he says to Simpson, he says, "Who was that lad that grabbed the flag?" Yeh hear that, Henry? . . . An' Simpson, he says, "Why, that was Fleming, Sir, he's a real courageous lad." "He's a good un," says the Colonel, "a real brave lad he is." Put that in a letter an' send it home to yer mother, Henry.

YOUNG MAN: Yer lyin', Wilson.

LOUD SOLDIER: No, I swear to yeh, Henry . . . it's the truth . . . Yer a hero!

YOUNG MAN: Yeh mean, with all those men fightin' out there, they saw me?

LOUD SOLDIER: Sure 'nough did . . . Sure made me feel proud I knew yeh.

YOUNG MAN: (*Shouting out*) Yeh hear that, Boy . . . Yeh hear what Wilson's sayin' 'bout me? . . .

LOUD SOLDIER: Who yeh yellin' at?

YOUNG MAN: A boy I knew before I became a man.

LOUD SOLDIER: Well, yeh sure took hold a' that flag like a man. Heard 'em talkin' about us joinin' up with the 256th. They're needin' help bad.

YOUNG MAN: So soon? . . . Ain't we goin' to get a rest?

LOUD SOLDIER: Movin' out right away . . . Heroes don't rest. Don't yeh read yer storybooks?

(*He laughs.*)

Can I walk beside yeh, Henry?

YOUNG MAN: Yeh mean it?

LOUD SOLDIER: Sure, we're ol' school buddies, ain't we?

YOUNG MAN: Sure.

LOUD SOLDIER: Meet yeh on the road.

(*He runs off.*)

YOUNG MAN: Did yeh hear that, all of yeh? I ain't no coward . . . I've erased my lie . . . I'm a man . . . Yer all outta me now, back where yeh belong . . .

(*The spot fades up on the body of the TALL SOLDIER where he died.*)

You can rest in peace now, Jim . . .

(Spot up on body of TATTERED SOLDIER)

Yeh were right, ol' timer . . . I don't need to run no more.

(Spot on body of DECAYED SOLDIER)

Your secret's safe with me, dead man . . . You've got others to keep you company now . . . Share your deaths with each other.

(Spot up on BOY lying dead, a blood spot on his head. The sack of toy soldiers is spread about the ground around him.)

You! . . . No! . . . Not you . . . I didn't mean for you to die.

(He runs to him.)

I just wanted you to leave.

(Holds body in his arms)

You didn't have to die to make me a man . . . Or did you?

(The musicians begin to play "When Johnny Comes Marching Home.")

Do yeh hear the drums and bugles? . . .

(Brushes dirt from the BOY's uniform)

Yer new blue coat's gotten dirty . . . What's Ma gonna say?

(Holds him tightly)

I'll miss yeh. The castle will be lonely without yeh.

(LOUD SOLDIER rushes in)

LOUD SOLDIER: Come on, Henry, it's time to move on.

YOUNG MAN: Comin'.

LOUD SOLDIER: Another dead one? . . . Did yeh know him?

YOUNG MAN: Used to play war with him when I was a kid.

LOUD SOLDIER: Come on! . . . We've got a real war to win now.

(They join the others as the SOLDIERS in dim light begin to sing and march up the right ramp, down the left and off slowly. The spots remain up on the bodies.)

SOLDIERS: *(Sung)*

When Johnny comes marchin' home again,
Hurrah! Hurrah!
We'll give him a hearty welcome then,
Hurrah! Hurrah!
The men will cheer, the boys will shout,
The ladies they will all turn out,
And we'll all feel gay

When Johnny comes marching home.

Get ready for the jubilee,
Hurrah! Hurrah!
We'll give the hero three times three,
Hurrah! Hurrah!
The laurel wreath is ready now
To place upon his loyal brow
And we'll all feel gay
When Johnny comes marching home.

(*As they march off, the spots on the bodies fade slowly and out as the song fades to silence.*)

CURTAIN

Production credits from the premiere of *Courage!* and details concerning performance rights are included in the acting edition of the play as published by Dramatic Publishing.

Historical Drama

Mother Hicks

Johnny Tremain

Mother Hicks

Suzan Zeder

In a small Illinois town during the Depression, Mother Hicks, a mysterious recluse, healer, and midwife, is suspected by the townspeople of being a witch. Living with her is Tuc, a young man also cast as an outsider due to the fact that he is deaf. Tuc wants to befriend a child called only "Girl," who was found abandoned as an infant and has been passed from home to home ever since. When he sees her accidentally cut herself while delirious with fever, he carries Girl to Mother Hicks's house on Dug Hill. As Mother Hicks uses her knowledge of the natural world to nurse her back to health, Girl realizes that no one in the household has anything to do with witchcraft, or with the misfortunes the townspeople blame on "witching." Convinced that Girl has been captured against her will, the townspeople venture up Dug Hill to demand her return, and causing Girl to flee in fear. Mother Hicks tries to reason with the angry mob, but it is clear that the townspeople are more interested in a scapegoat for life's difficulties than the truth, and she finally frightens them away by threatening to "witch" them. When Girl returns several days later she is more at peace with her life; knowing she is accepted in this unusual trio that has given her a sense of belonging. Girl says that she is ready to name herself—and would like Mother Hicks to help her do so.

Characters

TUC: A deaf man, in his 20s

GIRL: A foundling, 13 years old

MOTHER HICKS: An ageless woman in her 40s

CHORUS

(who translate for TUC and play the following roles:)

RICKY RICKS: 12 years old

IZZY SUE RICKS: His mother

JAKE HAMMON: Farmer

HOWIE HAMMON: His son, 11 years old

CLOVIS P. EUDY: Shopkeeper

WILSON WAKER: Writer for the WPA

HOSIAH WARD: Mortician

ALMA WARD: His wife

Setting

The town of Ware, in southern Illinois

Act 1: Various locations in and around town

Act 2: Dug Hill, the store, a street, Cairo, the graveyard

TIME: Late Spring, 1935

ACT 1

The set consists of a large open area on a gently raked stage. Downstage there are two tall telephone poles with terminals and cables. The wires stretch diagonally upstage and connect with another smaller pole. There is a feeling of uncluttered vastness reaching toward a disappearing horizon.

Opening music is a folk song of the Depression: an upbeat kind of song: not too city, not too country; that reflects the tension and trouble of the time. House lights fade with the music and a tinkling bell is heard in the silence of the darkness. A rosey hued cyclorama floods the stage.

A figure is seen silhouetted against the cyclorama. TUC pulls a large wagon, ringing the bell as he crosses downstage. As lights come up we see that the wagon is loaded with odd pieces of furniture, hung with miscellaneous costume pieces, and rigged with a variety of props. From this wagon will come many of the costume and prop pieces used by the CHORUS as they take their

various roles and move the action from scene to scene. TUC pulls the wagon to
a spot center-stage, and steps into a bright pool of light. The CHORUS enters
behind him.

. TUC signs in silence for a beat or two, then the CHORUS speaks his words.

CHORUS:

Mother Hicks is a witch, people say.
And she lives all alone at the top of Dug Hill
And she works her magic on the town below.

When cracks is seen in the dry creek bed
When the corn burns up
When a calf's born dead
Mother Hicks is a witch, people say.

When a child falls sick
And there ain't no cause
And there ain't no cure
Then everybody knows that it's witched for sure.
Mother Hicks is a witch . . . people say.

(During the following, CHORUS members come forward, speak a few lines, take an
article of clothing from the wagon, and exit. TUC continues signing.)

CHORUS:

This time is Spring in 1935
A year of fear in the Great Depression.
This place is Ware. W.A.R.E.
The Mississippi River's over there.
This is southern Illinois,
But we call it Egypt.

(A single CHORUS member remains; comes forward and shares the edge of the
spotlight with TUC. All subsequent translations of sign language will be handled this
way: the interpreter shares the light, but gives focus to the sign.)

CHORUS:

My name is Tuc.
I cannot speak. I cannot hear.
I use my hands and the words appear.
I hang these words in the air for you
To tell a story that I know is true;
'Cause I heard every word with my eyes.

It is deep in the early,
Just before dawn.

(*Lights fade to blackout, a low throbbing electrical hum pulsates in the darkness. The sound is pierced by the shrill sound of a whistle. Lights come up on GIRL at the top of the telephone pole.*)

GIRL: A dare is a dare and done. Dare and double dare, to sneak over the fence at the power station and fetch the quarter that Ricky threw there. Up and over the fence and then drop down into the cool wet grass.

(*She drops down a rung.*)

Then I heard it, that stinging, singing sound; racing through them wires, and round them coils and cables; like the electricity wanted to be out like lightning bolts. It's true fact, that I do dares of mortal danger. Things that no one else in town would dare to do, or dare to tell they'd done 'em.

A dare is a dare and done!

(*From out of the darkness, a voice is heard off-stage. It is RICKY RICKS, a boy about GIRL'S age.*)

RICKY: Girl! Hey . . . You here, Girl?

(*GIRL ducks behind the pole and hoots like an owl. RICKY enters.*)

Dang it, Girl come out! If my Ma finds out I'm not in bed . . .

(*GIRL jumps out of the tree and startles him.*)

You just made me jump to Jesus!

GIRL: You should have guessed, Ricky, them hoot owls live in trees.

RICKY: It's five o'clock in the morning, and I don't exactly feel like guessing!

(*GIRL flips a quarter in the air and catches it.*)

GIRL: A dare is a dare and done!

RICKY: My quarter.

GIRL: Nope, my quarter.

RICKY: I was sure you'd get electrocuted doing that dare.

GIRL: A dare ain't a dare unless there's danger. You got the money?

RICKY: I don't know why we had to do this so early. Why couldn't we wait 'till . . .

GIRL: Cause I need the money now!

RICKY: Then hand 'em over.

GIRL: (*Evasive*) Uhhh Ricky, you know how you always wanted a pet, but your Mama wouldn't let you have a dog cause it'd slobber up the house?

RICKY: Yeah.

GIRL: Well, I decided to sell you my frogs.

RICKY: Your frogs?

GIRL: I raised them since they was squiggles, they're good hoppers, and they all got names.

RICKY: Names?

GIRL: I figure frogs with names is worth more than regular.

RICKY: A deal's a deal! You promised to sell me your Tom Mix Wrangler Badge, the Buck Rogers pocket watch, and the Orphan Annie Secret Society code book.

GIRL: I did a million dares to get all that stuff.

RICKY: ... AND all the seals you collected from the Ovaltine jars.

GIRL: I had to go through all the garbage in the whole City dump to get those...

RICKY: Deal's a deal! I also want the Jack Armstrong Whistle Ring!

GIRL: But Jake gave me that whistle, he sent for it with Wheaties box tops.

RICKY: No whistle, no deal.

GIRL: But it's the only thing that ever came through the mail just for me.

RICKY: (*Turning to leave*) Guess you don't want my money.

GIRL: I need that money, Ricky, I need it bad.

RICKY: Not bad enough.

GIRL: You can have the whistle! Hell-fire! You can have anything you want except my quilt piece.

(*GIRL takes off her whistle-ring and gives it to him. She unfolds her quilt piece which contains her treasures in a small bundle*)

RICKY: Who'd want that dirty old thing?

GIRL: That shows how much you know! This here's fine embroidery on these here initials: I.S.H. fine embroidery, by someone's own hand!

RICKY: Let's go see those frogs, maybe I'll buy 'em for a penny a piece.

(*RICKY starts out, GIRL follows.*)

GIRL: Penny? They's worth a least a nickel!

RICKY: I kin catch 'em myself.

GIRL: With names? Kin you catch them with names ... and trained?

(*GIRL and RICKY exit. Lights pick up as a CHORUS member signs.*)

CHORUS:
> A baby girl found in town,
> About thirteen years ago.

People took her in and raised her
Here, and there, and all around.
And so, she goes . . .
In and out of people's houses,
Like so many times before.
She rests a while inside a family,
Until they can't keep her anymore.
And then . . . she goes again.

(*There is the sound of distant thunder. From off stage JAKE is heard.*)

JAKE: Girl! You come here, Girl!

(*He enters carrying a duffle.*)

I want to get off before the storm!

(*GIRL enters at a run. She is clutching an old sock.*)

GIRL: I got it. Jake! I got it!

JAKE: (*Not listening to her*) Now, I told you, I need to be in Cairo by this afternoon and I can't go until I see you safely to the Wards.

GIRL: Sit down, Jake.

JAKE: Ellen and Becca packed up all your things, all they could find.

GIRL: Sit down.

JAKE: No, Girl. This one time you're not going to get me buffaloed I've got to
get going.

GIRL: No, you don't!

JAKE: Girl, I told you.

GIRL: I got it for you. I got the money.

JAKE: What?

GIRL: I been collecting bottles at a penny a piece; I run groceries for Mr. Eudy,
pulled weeds for Miz. Snipes, and sold some stuff. I got six dollars and
forty-three cents.

(*GIRL hands him the sock proudly. JAKE sits on a stump.*)

JAKE: Girl, that's real fine; and Ella and me, we're grateful, but I need a bit
more for the mortgage.

GIRL: How much?

JAKE: Two hundred and fifty six dollars.

GIRL: (*Simply*) That's a lot of frogs.

JAKE: Huh?

GIRL: I kin earn it. I kin get me a real job . . .

JAKE: It's over. They took the farm and they'll sell it for back payments. I can't stay where I can't work.

GIRL: Bob Ricks digs ditches on the county road, Ricky told me.

JAKE: That's a WPA job. WPA stands for "we piddle around!" I wouldn't take a handout from those crooks in Washington if my life depended on it. There are jobs in Cairo, real jobs.

GIRL: (*Pleading*) Take me with you.

JAKE: I can't.

GIRL: I could get a job in Cairo. I could give you and Ellen all the money.

JAKE: I wish we could take you. Hell, I like you better'n some of my own kids. But you're not kin and I can't take responsibility for another living soul right now.

GIRL: I won't take up much room and I won't eat hardly nothing.

JAKE: Girl, neither God nor nature ever sent me anything before that I couldn't handle. Last year, when the flood came, I built a wall with sandbags.

When we had that tornado, I knew how to get everyone in the shelter and wait it out. Even a war's got enemies with bullets; but there's something happening in this country now, like a terrible silent storm. I can't see it, or hear it, and I don't know how to fight it, and it scares me.

(*There is a pause. GIRL knows she can't change his mind. He hands her back her money.*)

GIRL: (*Very vulnerable*) I got used to your family, Jake.

JAKE: Hush, now.

GIRL: I never got used to anything before.

(*JAKE pulls out a plug of Red Man chewing tobacco, GIRL holds out her hand for some too.*)

JAKE: Chewing tobacco is one bad habit you'll have to break. Alma Ward will probably have a heart attack first time you spit.

GIRL: (*Suddenly angry*) I ain't going to live with no grave digger.

JAKE: Mortician.

GIRL: He digs graves, don't he?

JAKE: At least, Hosiah Ward will never be out of work.

GIRL: I won't go to the Wards. He smells like chemicals and she's got a face like somebody's foot.

JAKE: Alma Ward is a nice woman and they can afford to give you a good home.

GIRL: I won't go!

JAKE: They're the only one's in town who'll take you. You just about used up everybody else.

GIRL: I'll run away. I'll hitch me a ride to Cairo and I'll find my people.

JAKE: I told you, Girl, we can't . . .

GIRL: I mean my people!

JAKE: (*He has heard this before*) Oh, Girl . . . You better roll up that tired old dream and put it away. Your people are long gone, or never were.

GIRL: (*Very upset*) That's all you know! Maybe they're rich, Jake! Maybe they got a truck bigger'n yours; maybe they got a family, better'n yours! Maybe they got jobs and lots of money!

JAKE: If they're so rich, how come they never found you?

GIRL: 'Cause I'm hard to find!

(*She throws the money at him and runs off. He picks it up and takes off after her.*)

JAKE: Dang it, Girl! You come back . . .

(*Lights return to TUC and CHORUS member. TUC signs.*)

CHORUS:

> There's a certain kind of spell
> In the air, everywhere.
> You can tell, very well, that it's fear.
> Things begin to disappear.
>
> Gone is the money in the bank.
> Gone are the jobs.
> Gone are the homes, and the families and their plans.
> But they seemed so safe!
> But they seemed so sure!
> All of a sudden, everybody's poor.
>
> Where did it go?
> Who took it all away?
> Mother Hicks is a witch, people say.

(*RICKY RICKS enters at a run from the opposite side and nearly collides with TUC. RICKY backs off frightened, and ducks behind a tree stump. From off-stage his Mother, IZZY, calls.*)

IZZY: Ricky Ricks, you get back here and eat your oatmeal! You'll get it for supper, see if you don't!

(*She enters, sees TUC, shouts and waves to him.*)

TUC! Oh, Tuc, I've got something for you! Now you wait right there.

(*To herself*)

I don't know why I do that. I know perfectly well that boy is deaf as a fire plug, but I always call out to him!

(*IZZY exits back into her house as HOWIE enters looking for GIRL. RICKY pulls HOWIE down behind the stump hiding from TUC, who busies himself with his cart.*)

HOWIE: Ricky! You just about yanked my arm off.

RICKY: Sorry.

HOWIE: You seen the Girl, my Pa's lookin' everywhere for her.

RICKY: I thought you were leaving today.

HOWIE: That's why I'm lookin'. She's got the keys to his truck. I gotta go.

(*He starts off and RICKY yanks him back.*)

Ricky!

RICKY: You got time for one last dare.

HOWIE: Ricky!

RICKY: Dare and double dare, you owe me one!

HOWIE: I do?

RICKY: You remember that time you dared me to piss on the electric fan while it was running?

HOWIE: Oh yeah.

RICKY: Well, now, you gotta sneak up behind Tuc and touch him without him seein' you.

HOWIE: That ain't nothin'.

RICKY: But you got to use your whole hand and not just one finger.

HOWIE: (*Not so sure*) You do it.

RICKY: Go on, it's your dare.

HOWIE: I ain't got time, and my Pa's really mad, and . . .

(*HOWIE starts to rise and RICKY yanks him back again.*)

RICKY: You got time for this.

HOWIE: Okay! Okay!

(*HOWIE starts moving toward him and hesitates.*)

RICKY: What's the matter?

HOWIE: I'm going . . . I'm going . . .

(*HOWIE inches toward TUC, RICKY pulls back his sling shot and takes aim at TUC, HOWIE looks back and sees what he's up to.*)

HOWIE: Ricky Ricks, you dumb ass, if you hit him he'll probably kill you.

RICKY: I'm just giving you some cover.

HOWIE: Yeah, sure.

RICKY: Go on.

(*Slowly, HOWIE inches toward TUC and just as he gets there, almost touching him, RICKY lets the stone fly, which hits TUC who whirls around. TUC makes a face at HOWIE who screams and races back to the stump. RICKY doubles up with laughter. GIRL springs from nowhere and lands on RICKY, beating him up.*)

GIRL: The dare was to touch him, not to hurt him.

HOWIE: Girl!

(*TUC starts toward them as JAKE enters at a run and pulls them apart.*)

JAKE: It's Okay, Tuc. I got 'em.

(*TUC nods, gestures and crosses back to his wagon but continues to watch.*)

JAKE: (*To GIRL*) Wouldn't you know I'd find you fighting.

HOWIE: I found her for you, Pa! I found her!

GIRL: No you didn't.

HOWIE: Yes, I did.

GIRL: Shut up, Howie. (*To Jake*) They was throwin' rocks, trying to hit . . .

RICKY AND HOWIE: No, I wasn't.

HOWIE: It was Ricky, he's the one with the . . .

RICKY: Shut up, Howie . . .

JAKE: Now, Girl . . .

(*RICKY picks up the car keys which have fallen in the scuffle. HOWIE snatches them away.*)

HOWIE: I found 'em for you Pa, I found the keys!

RICKY: No, you didn't.

HOWIE: Yes, I did

JAKE: Shut up, Howie. Now, Girl, you are coming with me to the Wards, and you are coming, now.

HOWIE: (*Taunting*) We're going to Cairo, and you can't go! We're going to Cairo, and you can't go! We're going to . . .

JAKE, RICKY, AND GIRL: Shut up Howie!

HOWIE: Yes, sir!

JAKE: You get on home and tell your Mother I'll be right there.

HOWIE: Yes, sir.

JAKE: And round up all the other kids, I'm not waiting on ANYONE, under-stand me?

HOWIE: Yes sir!

(HOWIE exits and IZZY enters with an arm load of old clothes.)

IZZY: Well, Jake Hammond, I thought you and all those kids were long gone to Cairo.

JAKE: We're trying, Izzy, we're trying!

IZZY: Well, good luck to you.

JAKE: I figure I'm due a little good luck.

IZZY: I expect you are.

(JAKE nods and exits with GIRL, practically dragging her off.)

GIRL: Hellfire, Jake, it weren't my fault . . . It weren't my . . .

(IZZY crosses to TUC with the clothes.)

IZZY: *(Shouting)* This here's clothes . . . OLD CLOTHES.

(She pulls out a pair of overalls and shouts even louder.)

I swear you can see daylight through the knees of these overalls, but I ex-pect you'll find some use for them.

(She takes RICKY by the hand.)

They say he reads lips, but I ain't so sure.

(TUC smiles, indicates his thanks. IZZY exits. TUC comes forward and signs. A CHORUS member speaks for him.)

CHORUS:
Handed-down people and
Handed-down clothes
Passed from one to another
When the wear starts to show.
They give to feel good,
And then go on their way.
They don't know how it feels
To be given away.

(CHORUS sets up CLOVIS P. EUDY's GENERAL MERCANTILE: a counter with a cash register and candy jars, a few barrels, etc. CLOVIS enters with a crate. Whenever he talks to TUC, CLOVIS uses a loud exaggerated tone. TUC reads his lips.)

CLOVIS: And these crates here, move them over there. Here to there. Under-stand? Comprendez? Got it?

(TUC nods. WILSON WALKER enters, just as horn is heard off stage.)

WILSON: (*To CLOVIS*) Excuse me, could you tell me if this place is called Ware?

CLOVIS: This place is called Clovis P. Eudy's General Mercantile; the town's Ware...

(*Horn honks again.*)

...and that's the mail truck.

(*CLOVIS exits, WILSON crosses to TUC who is moving crates.*)

WILSON: I beg your pardon; my name is Wilson Walker and I'm from the University at Carbondale. I'm doing some research on folklore.

(*TUC continues to work, unaware that WILSON is talking to him.*)

I'm collecting tales and legends and stories and sayings, that kind of thing, for a book about this region.

(*TUC notices him and hands him a card which Wilson reads.*)

"My name is Tuc. I am deaf and mute."

(*Embarrassed, shouts at TUC.*)

WILSON: Oh, My God, I'm sorry!

(*TUC turns the card over and hands it back to him. Wilson reads.*)

"Please do not shout. If you speak slowly I can read your lips."

(*Clovis enters*)

CLOVIS: Leave him alone, he's working.

WILSON: I'm sorry, I didn't realize.

CLOVIS: What do you want?

WILSON: Information.

CLOVIS: Figures; information's free.

WILSON: My name is Wilson Walker and I'm from the Federal Writer's Project.

CLOVIS: From the government?

WILSON: Sort of.

CLOVIS: I've got nothing to say.

(*CLOVIS turns away. Before WILSON can respond, GIRL bursts into the store.*)

GIRL: Mr. Eudy, Mr. Eudy, afternoon mail here yet?

CLOVIS: Still in the bag.

GIRL: Anything for me?

CLOVIS: You think I got X-ray eyes?

GIRL: I'm expecting a very important letter from Jake Hammon; see he promised to send for me, just as soon as he got to Cairo...

CLOVIS: Girl, you seen the last of that dirt farmer and his family. Now, the Wards is nice people and you've got a good home . . .

GIRL: It ain't my home!

CLOVIS: Well, you go along there anyway.

GIRL: I can't!

CLOVIS: Why not!

GIRL: They sent me for groceries! Here's the list from the stiff house!

CLOVIS: Girl. . .

GIRL: And one more thing that should be on this list, a plug of Red Man.

CLOVIS: Girl. I can't sell you chewing tobacco. I'll check the mail.

(CLOVIS touches TUC and hands him the list. They exit. GIRL scopes out WILSON.)

GIRL: Hi.

WILSON: Hi.

GIRL: You're new around here.

WILSON: Just passing through.

GIRL: You chew?

WILSON: Huh?

GIRL: (Meaning tobacco) I don't suppose you chew, do you?

WILSON: Oh yeah, sure. . . . Have a stick of Wriggley's.

(WILSON hands her a stick of gum, she takes it but is obviously disappointed.)

GIRL: Thanks. What's your name?

WILSON: Wilson Walker.

GIRL: Two last names? That's dumb.

WILSON: (Amused by her) Oh, yeah? What's yours?

GIRL: Girl.

WILSON: I can see that, what's your name?

GIRL: (Touching her quilt piece) Iswa Shunta Ho.

WILSON: Huh?

GIRL: It's a Cherokee name, you know, like these initials here on this Cherokee Indian blanket. I'm practically three quarters Cherokee.

WILSON: So how'd you get over here to Illinois, Cherokee?

GIRL: In a trunk.

WILSON: A trunk?

GIRL: My people was Vaudeville and they was always having babies in trunks and. . .

WILSON: I thought you said they were Cherokee Indian.

GIRL: They was Cherokee vaudeville.

WILSON: Oh! . . . so, where is everybody today, or is the town usually this dead?

GIRL: They're all at the funeral. Zollie Phelps got himself witched.

WILSON: Witched?

GIRL: That's what everybody says.

WILSON: Looks like I came to the right place.

GIRL: Oh, yeah.

WILSON: I hunt witches.

GIRL: Oh, yeah?

WILSON: Yep, I figure I've hunted down fifteen, maybe twenty witches between Carthage and Karnack.

GIRL: What do you use to hunt them with? Cross, silver bullet, holy water, Bible?

WILSON: I trap 'em here in this notebook and hold 'em tight in these pages, so people can read about 'em forever.

GIRL: You talk like a loon.

WILSON: I'm with the WPA. . .

GIRL: WPA? I wouldn't take a handout from those crooks in Washington if my life depended on it!

WILSON: Handout? This is a job!

(WILSON sits as CLOVIS enters with a letter and package.)

CLOVIS: Hey Girl.

GIRL: He wrote! I knew he would!

CLOVIS: This letter's for Hosiah and the package from Chicago's for Alma. You might as well take it home with you.

GIRL: I told you it ain't my home.

(RICKY RICKS enters.)

RICKY: Afternoon, Mr. Eudy, is my Ma here yet? I'm supposed to meet her here after the funeral.

CLOVIS: She'll be along. I expect they're just getting to the Amens and Hallelujas.

(CLOVIS turns his back to RICKY who steals a licorice whip, CLOVIS turns just in time to see him.)

CLOVIS: Did you get any hail over to your place?

RICKY: Yes, sir. Hail stones big as knucklebones.

CLOVIS: Queer time of year for hail.

RICKY: "Hail in June is a Devil's moon," that's what my Ma says.

CLOVIS: I'll check on your order, Girl.

(CLOVIS, exits, RICKY swipes another piece of licorice. He sees GIRL and brandishes his Jack Armstrong whistle-ring with a flourish and blows it.)

RICKY: Hey, Girl, want to see a neat ring I got here?

GIRL: Not especially.

(RICKY blows it again just to tease her.)

   Hey, Ricky, how about if I come to live at your house for a while?

RICKY: You give me back my quarter?

GIRL: Yeah . . .

(GIRL tosses him the quarter. RICKY takes it.)

RICKY: You kin sleep with the baby. She don't do nothing but cry and make bad smells.

GIRL: I don't mind.

(RICKY sniffs in her direction.)

   You got a cold, boy?

RICKY: I just wondered if you smelled like the dead yet.

GIRL: Get out of here.

RICKY: Well, you've been staying over to the grave-diggers.

GIRL: Ricky, I'm going to bust you one if you don't. . .

(GIRL stops and sniffs herself.)

   Do I?

RICKY: *(Seriously)* Not so I can tell, of course I never smelled the dead.

GIRL: Neither have I!

RICKY: *(Teasing)* They make you sleep in a coffin?

GIRL: Shut up, Ricky.

RICKY: You ever see any . . . bodies?

GIRL: I'm warning you.

RICKY: Alright!

(*RICKY turns away, steals a licorice whip just as IZZY enters.*)

IZZY: Ricky, stop stealing those licorice whips, you know I always wind up paying for them later.

RICKY: I like snitching them better!

IZZY: Ricky!

GIRL: Miz Ricks, I'm going to come and live with you for a while. Ricky said it was okay.

IZZY: But you're staying over with Alma and Hosiah Ward.

GIRL: You don't want me, huh?

IZZY: (*Simply*) We can't afford you, not now. I'm sorry.

(*GIRL turns away. CLOVIS enters.*)

CLOVIS: Morning, Izzy. You feeling any better today?

IZZY: Oh, not hardly. I feel like I'm something sent for that couldn't come. If I didn't know better I'd swear I'd been hexed.

CLOVIS: How was the funeral?

IZZY: Poor old Zollie, he sure did look . . . oh, I don't know . . . dead. It was witch-work, Clovis, witch-work.

CLOVIS: You think?

IZZY: I know! Last time she came to town, Zollie cursed her for making his cows go dry. From that day on, he was a dead man.

GIRL: Zollie Phelps was a drunk.

IZZY: You watch your mouth, Girl. He was my cousin.

GIRL: Jake Hammond always said, witches was bunk.

IZZY: Well, Jake Hammond didn't know everything, young lady. There's not a sane person in this town would make light of witches, not in witch weather.

GIRL: Witch weather?

IZZY: When it's cold like this, long past time for summer; when the thunder clouds roll in and the hail comes like frozen pieces of lightning, then it's Mother Hicks, up to her old tricks.

(*WILSON crosses down to them.*)

WILSON: Excuse me, did you say Mother Hicks?

IZZY: What if I did?

WILSON: My name is Wilson Walker, I'm with the Federal Writer's Project.

IZZY: Federal Writer's Project. I've heard of that! I heard Mrs. Roosevelt talking about it on the radio!

WILSON: Yes Mam, I'm with the Folklore Division: my subject is witchcraft.

CLOVIS: Witchcraft, you say.

WILSON: I was on my way to Jonesboro but I decided to stop and see if I could find out about this Mother Hicks.

IZZY: Well, you better look up on Dug Hill. You won't find her down here in town.

WILSON: People say this Mother Hicks is a witch.

IZZY: Mother Hicks is a witch alright, and she lives all alone at the top of Dug Hill. And most every night at midnight she comes to the graveyard and casts spells with devil dolls and tiny little clothes and tiny little shoes.

WILSON: People say she used to be a midwife.

IZZY: Until she stopped birthing babies and started witching them.

CLOVIS: Babies got sick.

IZZY: Babies died!

CLOVIS: People say she used to have a child herself once.

IZZY: A little girl, but she gave that child to the Devil.

GIRL: Gaw!

(RICKY and GIRL listen, mouths agape.)

IZZY: (Tweeking RICKY'S ear) Now, don't these little pitchers have the biggest ears?

RICKY: Cut it out, Ma.

GIRL: What about you, Two Names. Do you believe in witches?

WILSON: I've collected five notebooks full of stories.

GIRL: Stories or lies?

WILSON: The people who told them, told them as true. I believe every voice in these notebooks.

(GIRL takes a notebook from WILSON and glances through it. TUC enters with a box. He works as they talk about him.)

CLOVIS: You see that poor unfortunate boy?

WILSON: Yes.

CLOVIS: Mother Hicks witched him, when she came to nurse him through the fever.

(A hooded figure with a walking stick slowly approaches the STORE. The others, wrapped up in IZZY's story, do not notice.)

IZZY: First she nursed him, then she witched him. When he cried that fever cry, she touched his throat and caught that cry; then she looked at him with the evil eye and sucked up his sounds into silence. Mother Hicks is a witch alright.

GIRL: Mother Hicks IS a witch!

WILSON: People say . . .

(*The FIGURE raps sharply on the counter with the walking stick. All look up, startled. The FIGURE walks directly to Clovis and hands him an empty box of shotgun shells. IZZY and RICKY turn away as she passes. GIRL is frightened but curious. WILSON is confused at first, then fascinated.*)

WILSON: What's going on?

IZZY: Shut up, you damn fool.

WILSON: That's HER, isn't it?

(*WILSON starts to speak to MOTHER HICKS, but she turns toward him and his mouth is dry as ash. She turns back to Clovis who hands her a full box of shells. She pays him and exits swiftly.*)

(*Starting after her*)

    I want to talk to her.

(*IZZY grabs his arm.*)

IZZY: Then you go up Dug Hill, all by yourself. Don't you see, she's down here because of the funeral. She must have smelled it all the way up witch mountain.

(*When TUC finishes he touches GIRL who is startled and yells.*)

GIRL: Ahhh!

(*They all jump.*)

GIRL: You just made me jump to Jesus!

CLOVIS: Your order's ready, Girl. You take the sack and I'll send Tuc along later with the heavy things. Now go straight home!

(*CLOVIS exits.*)

WILSON: How do I get to Dug Hill?

IZZY: Just up the Jonesboro road.

WILSON: Good, that's the way I'm headed.

IZZY: But you won't find her, unless she wants to be found. Come on, Ricky. Goodbye, Mr. Wilson.

WILSON: (*Correcting*) Walker.

IZZY: (*Flustered*) Walker . . . Wilson . . . whatever! Goodbye.

(IZZY exits.)

WILSON: Thank you, you've been most helpful.

(WILSON starts out. GIRL still has one of his notebooks.)

GIRL: Wait!

WILSON: What?

(GIRL makes a decision to keep the book and hides it.)

GIRL: Uhhhh, good luck, Two Names.

WILSON: So long Cherokee!

(WILSON exits. GIRL starts out.)

RICKY: Hey, Girl, I know the dare of dares, the dare of dares!

GIRL: What?

RICKY: Go to the graveyard late tonight and touch Mother Hicks if she comes.

GIRL: Shut up, Ricky!

RICKY: Dare and double dare? (He spits on his hand. Pause.)

GIRL: Dare and double dare!

(She spits on her hand and they shake. They exit.)

(TUC comes forward and signs. CHORUS member interprets.)

CHORUS:
>That Girl never does what she is told
>Instead she does a dare or two.
>Like going down to the railroad track
>When the Rock Island Rocket rips through,
>Or going down to the quarry pool
>Diving deep into cold black wells.
>And nobody tries to stop her
>Because there's nobody there
>To tell her to be careful.

(During this speech the CHORUS has set up the WARD'S DINING ROOM. ALMA puts the finishing touches on the dinner table. HOSIAH ties his tie, very precisely, looking in a mirror. He checks his watch.)

HOSIAH: That's it, Alma. We start without her.

ALMA: Just five more minutes, Hosiah. I'm sure she'll be along.

HOSIAH: I've got to be there for the memorial service by 6:55.

ALMA: I'm sure she'll be . . .

(GIRL enters clutching the bag and the package.)

Finally, Girl! I was getting worried.

GIRL: (*Heading straight for the table*) Oh, good! Supper's ready! I'm starved!

(*ALMA takes the package from her.*)

   Sorry about the package, it got a little ripped up on the barbity wire over to
   the quarry.

(*ALMA exits into the kitchen with the groceries, she leaves the package on stage.*)

HOSIAH: Do you have any idea what time it is?

GIRL: (*She doesn't.*) Uh uh.

HOSIAH: It's 6:08.

GIRL: So?

HOSIAH: In this house dinner is served exactly at six o'clock.

GIRL: Why?

HOSIAH: Because that's dinner time.

GIRL: At Jake's, dinner was whenever you got to the grub.

(*ALMA enters with a plate of food.*)

ALMA: Do you want to change for supper?

GIRL: Change what?

ALMA: (*A bit amused*) Never mind. You can wash up in the kitchen.

GIRL: Don't need to. I been swimming over to the quarry.

ALMA: (*On her way back to the kitchen*) But the quarry's closed.

HOSIAH: And there's a big sign saying "No Trespassing."

GIRL: I wasn't trespassing. I was swimming.

HOSIAH: (*Calling out to ALMA*) Remember that memorial service, Alma. They
   can't get started without the ashes.

GIRL: That's disgusting.

HOSIAH: It's a business.

GIRL: That's disgusting.

HOSIAH: What are we supposed to do, let people decompose wherever they
   drop dead?

(*ALMA enters with biscuits and hears this.*)

ALMA: That's disgusting.

(*HOSIAH starts to dish up food with a serving fork.*)

GIRL: I don't see how you can do that.

HOSIAH: Do what?

GIRL: Touch food with hands that have touched the dead.

HOSIAH: I use a fork.

ALMA: (*Heading off an argument*) Shall we say a blessing?

(*ALL take hands, except GIRL who reaches over HOSIAH'S hand to his wrist. They bow heads.*)

HOSIAH: Bless us, Oh Lord. . . .

(*GIRL isn't used to grace and starts for her food. ALMA catches her eye.*)

    . . . For these thy gifts. . .

(*GIRL starts for food again.*)

    Which we are about to receive through Thy mercy.

GIRL: Now?

ALMA: Now.

(*GIRL digs in and begins to wolf down her food.*)

ALMA: I heard a queer thing from Izzy today. Folks are having trouble with their milking. Cows have gone dry morning and evening.

GIRL: (*Talking with her mouth full*) I heard how a . . .

HOSIAH: Don't talk with your mouth full.

(*In all innocence, GIRL spits her food into her hand and finishes her sentence.*)

GIRL: I heard once how a witch can milk a cow a mile away by wringing milk out of a clean white dish rag.

(*She pops the food back in her mouth and wipes her hand on her knee. It does not go unnoticed by HOSIAH. ALMA just shakes her head.*)

ALMA: There is entirely too much witch talk in this town.

GIRL: Did you ever see Mother Hicks? People say she comes to the graveyard at midnight and does spells with. . .

ALMA: I don't want you going into the graveyard, Girl, not at night.

HOSIAH: Not at any time. You kids are always knocking over the gravestones and tearing up the plots. If I catch you in that graveyard, you're going to wish I hadn't.

(*GIRL pushes away from the table and pouts.*)

ALMA: Can I give you another biscuit, Girl?

GIRL: No.

HOSIAH: (*Prompting*) No what?

GIRL: No biscuit. I'm not hungry.

(*To break the tension ALMA hands GIRL the package.*)

ALMA: I was going to wait until after supper, but you might as well have this now.

GIRL: That package was for me?

ALMA: Since you've been so careless with this, I've half a mind not to give it to you.

(GIRL tears into the package and pulls out a new dress. She buries her face in it and smells.)

GIRL: This is new ain't it?

ALMA: Yes.

GIRL: I kin tell because it don't smell like somebody else yet. I never had a new one, not one of my own.

ALMA: You need a new dress before you start at the big school next fall.

GIRL: I got no use for school. I'm going to Cairo to sell costume jewelry at Woolworths.

HOSIAH: Oh?

ALMA: You'll do no such thing; and speaking of school, we'll have to do something about your name.

GIRL: What about my name?

ALMA: If you're going to the big school you'll have to have a proper name.

GIRL: Why are you always trying to change me?

ALMA: I'm not trying to change you.

(GIRL tosses aside the dress.)

GIRL: I like my old things better.

HOSIAH: (To GIRL) Pick it up.

ALMA: (Picking up the dress herself) I just want you to be comfortable here.

GIRL: How can I be comfortable with you pickin' and peckin' at me all the time. I feel like a bird feeder.

HOSIAH: Young lady, that is enough!

ALMA: It's alright, Hosiah . . .

HOSIAH: It is not alright! She comes into our house like a tornado and acts like a hooligan when you are just trying to give her something.

GIRL: I don't want anything! I don't want anything from YOU!

HOSIAH: Go to your room.

GIRL: It ain't MY room. I'm going out. There's something I've got to do.

HOSIAH: The only thing you're going to do is to get to your room, before I let a spanking teach you some manners! Do you understand?

(*There is a moment of stand-off before GIRL storms off.*)

HOSIAH: (*After a beat*) I told you this wouldn't work, Alma.

ALMA: It might if you weren't so hard on her.

HOSIAH: Hard on her?

ALMA: It will work, we just have to be patient.

HOSIAH: We are just too old to be starting again with children.

(*ALMA turns away, stung by his remark.*)

And that one will tear you up! Alma, that kid was born bad and there's nothing you can do to break her of it.

(*GIRL returns, sneaking out, but she hears the following.*)

ALMA: I can try.

HOSIAH: I give it another week, but then she goes.

ALMA: There's nowhere else for her to go.

HOSIAH: There's the State Home.

(*GIRL hears this, and exits.*)

ALMA: Not while I have breath.

HOSIAH: The State Home is where that child belongs.

ALMA: Not while I have breath.

(*Lights change and TUC steps into a spot. CHORUS member speaks.*)

CHORUS:
> So I go and follow her.
> I have followed her before,
> As she runs down darkening streets,
> Until she can't run anymore;
> Or climbs a huge pecan tree
> To try to touch a star.
> I am there below in shadow
> Never seen, but never far,
> Should she fall
> Or suddenly be frightened.
>
> Out late, deep into night
> She goes to the graveyard
> In the pale moonlight.

(During the last speech the stage has been cleared of everything but the telephone poles. This scene begins in deep shadow. In the distance there is the hooting of an owl and the cry of a loon. Crickets can be heard, softly at first, providing an understated tension. The lighting is eerie in the graveyard.

GIRL enters, slowly frightened. She moves through the graveyard with the utmost care. She stops for a moment and realizes that she is standing on a grave.)

GIRL: Oh, my Lord! I'm standing on one . . . sorry! (*She steps aside gingerly.*)
    There's no such thing as spooks! There's no such thing as spooks!

(Far downstage, to one side, GIRL sits and wraps herself in the quilt. She hums softly to herself. TUC enters and watches the following at a distance, from the shadows.)

(For a few beats there is only the sound of the crickets. Far upstage left the shrouded, hooded figure of a woman enters and crosses downstage. She walks neither quickly nor slowly through the graveyard to a specific spot. She carries a basket. Under her breath she is muttering; only the rhythm and an occasional sibilant sound can be heard. The chirping of the crickets grows louder.)

(The women kneels and carefully clears the ground in front of her, meticulously smoothing the earth. She removes a tiny baby dress from the basket, shakes it out, and places it on the ground. She removes a sweater from the basket, shakes it out and places it on top of the dress. A knitted cap, and two tiny soft moccasins are placed precisely in a human form. Suddenly, the woman stretches out her arms, catches her breath and slowly lowers herself onto the ground over the clothes. The cricket sound grows.)

(GIRL rises slowly and moves toward the woman with an outstretched hand. The woman starts to rise, is aware of the presence and stops. GIRL draws back into the shadow, but she drops her quilt piece. The woman kneels, GIRL makes two feeble attempts to reach the piece and pulls back.)

(The woman gathers up the clothes quickly and turns toward the GIRL'S hiding place. She crosses slowly to the quilt piece, stops and picks it up. GIRL is frozen with fear. The woman steps toward GIRL and holds the cloth out to her. The crickets are deafening.)

(GIRL reaches for the cloth and there is a split second when they both hold it. GIRL looks up and they make eye contact. The woman drops the cloth, turns and exits back where she came from. Gradually the cricket sounds lessen, GIRL steps out of the shadow, looks at the quilt piece and speaks.)

GIRL: My heart is pounding. Louder than thunder, louder than Jesus. I close
    my eyes and see her eyes, shooting sparks. A witch can kill with a look. But
    then I see it, like a match, flare up inside her eyes, like she recognized me,
    like she knew me forever. And then her eyes go deep as wells and fill up

with a kind of sadness. She recognized me and I recognized her, too. She looked at me and knew me all my life. (*She looks at the quilt piece.*) I.S.H. . . . H, for Hicks?

(*A loon cries in the distance. HOSIAH and the other CHORUS members appear in the shadows.*)

HOSIAH: I thought I told you to stay out of the graveyard!

GIRL: (*Startled*) Oh.

HOSIAH: Girl, I warned you.

(*HOSIAH turns her over his knee. He spanks her in a stylized manner. He mimes three or four blows; his hand stops short of hitting her as the others clap providing the sound of blows.*)

(*Lights dim, all but a spot on GIRL.*)

(*GIRL rises slowly and looks toward the spot where HOSIAH stands in shadow. She pulls out Wilson's notebook.*)

GIRL: Witches are never lonely or afraid because they got the power.

(*Lights dim. In the dark there is the sound of running water. Lights rise on TUC and a CHORUS member.*)

CHORUS:
> Early one morning, just before dawn,
> I hitch up my cart and come down the long road.
> Down to the town, from the hill where I stay.
> I don't usually see much, but on this one day
> I come to a clearing, near a stream and a tree,
> And I saw the strangest thing I ever did see.

(*The water sound is louder as GIRL comes down-stage with a sack. She carefully kneels and mimes the edge of the stream. She tests the cold water with her finger tips and shudders. She takes a white pan and a rusty knife out of the sack. She opens Wilson's notebook.*)

GIRL: (*She opens the notebook and reads.*) "This how you get to be a witch . . . Every morning just before dawn from Sabbath to Sabbath, go to a clear cold stream where the water runs east. Take a new white porcelain pan and an old knife gone red with rust. Wash that knife in water and pour a full pan of cold, clear water over your head and give your body to the Devil, saying . . ."

(*GIRL goes through the ritual as she speaks.*)

GIRL:
> I swear that I do give
> Everything betwixt me two hands

To the ways of witchcraft.
And I swear to do anything
The witch power asks of me.

(GIRL remains in her position and continues to mime the ritual as the scenes of her "witching" are played around her. It should be clear that she is responsible for the various tricks and pranks, but she need not go through the actual business. TUC signs. CHORUS member speaks.)

CHORUS:
That very next day.
I followed the Girl as she wandered around.
Strange things started happening
All over town.

Day One, Monday.

(GIRL reads from the notebook.)

GIRL: "To make a witchball, gather up some cow hair, licked with cow spit. Mix with salt and tallow. Get some ashes from a burned down church, gather moss from a tombstone, and roll it all, in a ball, around a little piece of razor."

(Upstage IZZY enters with a picnic basket. She looks in the basket and screams. ALMA enters quickly.)

IZZY: Oh, my Gawd! Oh, my Gawd!

ALMA: What in the world's the matter?

IZZY: Look there, what do you see?

ALMA: Why, Izzy, it looks like your supper for the church social.

IZZY: No, there, on top of the pecan pie! Look on top of the pie!

ALMA: Euuuuuuwwwwww, it looks like a bug, a big, hairy bug.

IZZY: It's a ball, it's a witch ball!

(GIRL laughs. She remains in her position and repeats the ritual as the scenes of her witching are played behind her. TUC signs each day as it passes.)

CHORUS: *(For TUC)* Day Two, Tuesday.

GIRL: *(Reading from the notebook)* "A spell is done by placing a witch wreath inside the hat of the person fer hex. The spell will grow around the person's head and he is sure to go mad."

(Lights up on HOSIAH and CLOVIS.)

HOSIAH: It's a what?

CLOVIS: A witch wreath, made with feathers from a black hen.

HOSIAH: And you pulled that thing out of my hat?

CLOVIS: I think those headaches will stop now, Hosiah.

HOSIAH: You mean to tell me that bunch of feathers did a spell that caused my headaches?

CLOVIS: Nope, made your hat fit too tight.

CHORUS: (*For TUC*) Day Three, Wednesday.

GIRL: (*Reading*) "A witch can turn herself into a black panther cat and prowl around unnoticed. If that cat steals something from someone, the witch will have power over them for sure."

(*GIRL looks devilish and meows. IZZY crosses to CLOVIS.*)

IZZY: I tell you it was a cat, a big black panther cat, an unnaturally large panther cat and I heard it prowling around my washline and it stole a pair of my . . . personals.

CLOVIS: Now, let me get this straight. A cat stole your drawers and ever since, your vision's blurred, there's a ringing in your ears, you've got the chills, the shakes, the faints, and gas?

IZZY: That's right, Clovis.

CLOVIS: But Doc Gunner says there's not a thing wrong with you.

IZZY: That's how I know I'm doomed. When the Doctor can't find a thing wrong it's a sign that a person is witched. She's up to her old tricks.

CLOVIS: Mother Hicks?

IZZY: Mother Hicks!

(*From here to the end of the scene, a low muttering of "Mother Hicks" begins to build.*)

CHORUS: (*For TUC*) Day Four, Thursday.

GIRL: (*GIRL pours the water over her head again in the ritual. She is ill and shows it.*)
I swear that I do give
Everything betwixt my two hands
To the ways of witchcraft . . .

(*ALMA crosses to CLOVIS.*)

ALMA: When I woke the Girl this morning, she was burning up with fever, her hair was all wet and she was cold and clammy.

CLOVIS: What does Doc Gunner say?

ALMA: He's afraid it's pneumonia.

CLOVIS: Put a silver bullet in a bag and tie it around her neck.

ALMA: Whatever for?

CLOVIS: To protect her from witches.

ALMA: Doc Gunner says it's pneumonia.

(*Muttering increases.*)

CHORUS: (*For TUC*) Day Five, Friday.

(*IZZY crosses to CLOVIS, ALMA turns away.*)

IZZY: It just has to be Mother Hicks, Clovis. We've all been hexed by Mother Hicks.

CLOVIS: It's just like it was in 1925.

IZZY: But in 1925 they all died!

(*Muttering increases, ALMA, very upset, crosses to HOSIAH.*)

CHORUS: (*For TUC*) Day Six, Saturday!

ALMA: Girl is going to the hospital, and she is going today!

HOSIAH: But Doc Gunner say's she's better off here at home.

ALMA: She's delirious! This morning she woke up screaming something about witchcraft!

(*Muttering increases to a chant: "Mother Hicks . . . Mother Hicks."*)

CHORUS: (*For TUC*) Day Seven, the second Sabbath!

(*GIRL is extremely ill as she kneels by the stream and forces herself through the ritual. Throughout the next few lines, TUC signs the numbers 1–7, one after another, as the scene builds in intensity.*)

GIRL:
> I swear that I do give
> Everything . . .

IZZY: It's a witchball!

GIRL: Everything . . .

HOSIAH: I got these headaches!

GIRL: Everything . . .

ALMA: It's pneumonia!

GIRL: Everything!

CLOVIS: They all died!

GIRL:
> Everything betwixt my two hands
> To the ways of witchcraft

(*Chanting builds to a crescendo.*)

> And I swear to do anything
> The witch power asks of me!

ALMA: (*Voice rising above the others*) THIS HAS GOT TO STOP!

(*Silence. GIRL picks up the notebook and reads, she is almost too ill to see the words.*)

GIRL:

>"Take a rust red knife
>And cut the head off a living thing
>Where the blood falls
>The Devil will appear
>And welcome you as a witch."

(*She is exhausted. She wraps her arms around her legs and holds herself together.*)

But I don't want to be that kind of witch, the kind of witch that kills things.

(*She spies a flower growing nearby.*)

A flower is a living thing!

(*She plucks the flower and holds it in front of her as she brandishes the knife above her head.*)

>I swear that I do give
>Everything betwixt my two hands
>To the ways of witchcraft.
>And I swear to do anything . . .

(*She brings the knife slashing down, misses the flower, but cuts a deep gash into her own leg. It is a serious wound and blood flows down her leg. She grabs at her leg in shock.*)

GIRL: I cut myself . . . bad! I cut myself . . . BAD!

(*TUC rushes from the shadows where he has been watching her. She sees him and screams. She faints, he catches her and lifts her up in his arms. Just as he turns upstage, a spot comes up on the shrouded figure from the graveyard. MOTHER HICKS holds her arms out as TUC turns toward her. BLACKOUT.*)

END OF ACT

ACT 2

MOTHER HICKS's cabin on Dug Hill. With the addition of poles and canvas panels, TUC's wagon is transformed into the cabin. All around are ceramic pots, baskets, jugs and small cages. Atop one of the poles is a wren roost. The area is lit by firelight from a large permanent campfire and several kerosene lamps around and about. A large smoking cauldron hangs above the campfire. Near the cauldron is a rocking chair.

Stage left is a makeshift pallet. GIRL is asleep, wrapped tightly in blankets. She wears an old flannel shirt and sleeps fitfully. Near the pallet, TUC squats on his heels and watches GIRL. He has been there some time, keeping a silent vigil.

(*GIRL stirs and moans and begins to cough deeply. TUC rises and fetches MOTHER HICKS from the cabin. She crosses to the steaming cauldron and stirs a smoking cupful of the brew into a bowl. She crosses to GIRL and hands the bowl to TUC who puts it to GIRL's lips.*)

MOTHER HICKS: Drink this.

GIRL: Don't hurt me.

MOTHER HICKS: Hush.

GIRL: Where am I?

MOTHER HICKS: Dug Hill.

GIRL: I know who you are! You're . . .

MOTHER HICKS: (*Cutting her off*) Drink!

GIRL: No!

MOTHER HICKS: Drink it or you'll strangle on your own phlegm.

(*MOTHER HICKS makes a sharp sign to TUC; together they make GIRL drink the brew. MOTHER HICKS strokes GIRL's throat the way she might help an injured animal to swallow.*)

GIRL: What is it?

MOTHER HICKS: Brew of scaley bark, pokeweed, and rattlesnake yarb.

GIRL: Tastes terrible.

MOTHER HICKS: Better'n dying.

(*MOTHER HICKS bends over her and loosens the blankets.*)

GIRL: This ain't my shirt. It smells foul.

MOTHER HICKS: Greased it good with hog fat and nutmeg.

GIRL: Why?

MOTHER HICKS: Reasons.

(*MOTHER HICKS draws back the cover and reveals the leg wound covered with a thick yellow mud. MOTHER HICKS draws a large hunting knife and passes the blade through the fire. GIRL sees this and struggles.*)

　　Hold her.

(*MOTHER HICKS signs as she speaks to TUC. She repeats both the sign and the words with urgency.*)

　　HOLD HER!

(*MOTHER HICKS approaches with the knife. GIRL struggles as TUC holds her down.*)

GIRL: Don't touch me! Don't hurt . . .

MOTHER HICKS: Hold Still!

(In one swift motion, MOTHER HICKS flips the mudpack off revealing a long healing scar. She crosses to the fire and reaches into a small bowl.)

GIRL: What's that?

MOTHER HICKS: Hot yellow mud and vinegar, to draw the poison.

(MOTHER HICKS slaps the poultice on GIRL's leg. GIRL cries out.)

GIRL: Owwwwww!

MOTHER HICKS: Hesh up, you're not hurt. You're not hurt are you?

(For the first time GIRL realizes that she isn't.)

GIRL: Some.

MOTHER HICKS: If I can't stop the festering, I'll have to cut it off.

GIRL: The mud?

MOTHER HICKS: The leg.

GIRL: No!

(GIRL struggles again. MOTHER HICKS signs to TUC to hold her.)

MOTHER HICKS: Now settle down and let that poultice dry. I'll have to tie you down if you don't.

(GIRL stops struggling and TUC and MOTHER HICKS wrap her up in the blankets. MOTHER HICKS rises and checks the sky. As she speaks to TUC, she signs.)

We'll leave her out here while the weather holds; inside smells like skunk.

GIRL: What are you going to do with me?

MOTHER HICKS: *(With a crooked grin.)* Girl, I am doing with you now.

(MOTHER HICKS exits into the cabin. GIRL sinks back down as TUC resumes his watch. Lights dim.)

(Pause)

(In the darkness a shrieking sound is heard. it is just dawn, the sky is a bluish-red. MOTHER HICKS is kneeling over a large box. TUC sits in the chair holding a lantern over her work. The shrieking sound comes from the box as does a thumping sound of struggle.)

MOTHER HICKS: Hesh, Sister Kicker, hesh. 1, 2, 3, 4, 5 alive and come this dead one, stuck. There ain't no help for it, Sister Kicker, there ain't no help.

(GIRL wakes and sits up. MOTHER HICKS pulls the lantern towards her and lifts the chimney, she passes the blade through the flame.)

GIRL: What are you doing?

MOTHER HICKS: Stay away!

GIRL: What's happening?

MOTHER HICKS: I said, stay. . .

(*TUC is distracted and pulls the light away, MOTHER HICKS jerks his arm back.*)

    Light, I need light!

GIRL: Stop it, please, whatever you're doing, stop it!

MOTHER HICKS: I can't.

(*At TUC's encouragement, GIRL inches toward them, horrified but fascinated at what is happening inside the box. MOTHER HICKS returns to the task at hand.*)

MOTHER HICKS: There, got it!

(*MOTHER HICKS hands the knife to TUC and returns her attention to the box.*)

    Now, let 'em come. Snip, snip, snip and clip 'em off. Clip 'em clean!

(*After a beat, the sound subsides. MOTHER HICKS wipes her hands they are covered with blood.*)

GIRL: There's blood.

MOTHER HICKS: There always blood at a birthing.

(*GIRL peers into the box.*)

GIRL: A rabbit?

MOTHER HICKS: Rabbits.

GIRL: I never heard a rabbit make such a sound before.

MOTHER HICKS: They only do when they're mortal scared or hurt.

GIRL: How many babies?

MOTHER HICKS: Five alive, three dead.

(*MOTHER HICKS tosses three tiny objects into a pail.*)

GIRL: (*Pulling at the box*) Can I see?

MOTHER HICKS: (*Protectively*) If she gets riled, she'll eat 'em.

GIRL: Eat her own babies?

MOTHER HICKS: (*Peering into the box*) Now, look at that, she's pushing them away, won't let them even get close to her.

GIRL: Why won't she nurse them?

MOTHER HICKS: Who knows why some critters don't take to their young? No reason, they just don't.

GIRL: Will she ever?

MOTHER HICKS: Likely not.

(*MOTHER HICKS stands and stretches.*)

MOTHER HICKS: Looks like the sky is getting ready to make itself a dawn. Come here!

(*MOTHER HICKS checks the fever. GIRL pulls away.*)

I said, come here! The fever's broke . . . Good. But get back to bed before it's light.

(*TUC carries her to the pallet.*)

GIRL: Can I name the rabbits?

MOTHER HICKS: No, but you can help.

(*TUC sets her gently down and hands her the quilt piece tucked under her pillow. She is very pleased to see it.*)

GIRL: My quilt piece!

MOTHER HICKS: Go to sleep!

(*GIRL goes back to sleep, lights dim.*)

(*Pause*)

(*After beat there is the sound of chirping birds, lights rise on a morning scene. MOTHER HICKS kneels with several basins and baskets near her. She lifts an article of clothing out of a basin and wrings white liquid out of it. She shakes it out and we see it is a baby dress.*)

MOTHER HICKS: (*To the dress*) So, there you are, all fresh and clean; all fresh and clean to go visiting. Tonight we'll go, just like I promised. Tonight we'll go.

(*Accidentally she squirts some water on herself. GIRL wakes and listens.*)

None of that splashing, you hear?

(*She splashes more water and laughs.*)

And no spitting either!

(*GIRL sits up.*)

Now, stop, I say, stop! If you can't keep from dousing your own . . .

(*She is suddenly aware of GIRL.*)

What are you peeping at?

GIRL: Nothing.

MOTHER HICKS: You call me nothing?

GIRL: I didn't see nothing.

MOTHER HICKS: And if lies was food, there'd be no hunger in the world!

(*MOTHER HICKS lifts out another article and wrings soapy water out of it.*)

GIRL: I know what you're doing!

MOTHER HICKS: What?

GIRL: You're milking a cow by magic!

(MOTHER HICKS pours a basin of soapy water into a bucket.)

MOTHER HICKS: (Gruff) This here's laundry! I save the soapy water for my
   yarbs!

GIRL: Oh . . . If it's laundry I can help.

(GIRL limps over to MOTHER HICKS and tentatively takes an article and wraps it in
a flannel cloth.)

   I can take these flannel pieces and use 'em to wring the water out . . . These
   is baby clothes!

MOTHER HICKS: They is.

GIRL: There was all kinds of babies over at Jakes. Jakes is where I used to
   stay, and I used to love to play with 'em. They was all soft and white and
   plumped up, like dough before it's baked; soft little bread babies.

(She works as she speaks.)

   This sure is fine linen, I can see right through it.

MOTHER HICKS: You be careful, mind?

GIRL: I mind.

MOTHER HICKS: Once there was a girl who wore that dress, and she had
   hair colored hair. You know how some folks go on about children and say
   they got hair blond as gold, or eyes blue as sky? Well, this little girl had hair
   colored hair, and eye colored eyes and she were beautiful.

GIRL: (The question is important to her.) What happened to that girl?

MOTHER HICKS: (Bitter) Gone, taken with the rest.

GIRL: Gone where?

MOTHER HICKS: Just gone!

GIRL: Taken by who? Where was she taken?

MOTHER HICKS: (Snaps at her) Watch how you touch that piece, you're stran-
   gling the life out of it.

GIRL: But I want to know!

MOTHER HICKS: Well, wantin' ain't gettin'!

(TUC enters at a run, laughing and gesturing to MOTHER HICKS.)

   What in the. . .

(TUC signs something to her.)

    I don't know.

(TUC signs something else and they both laugh.)

GIRL: *(Mystified)* What are you laughing at?

MOTHER HICKS: This here fool.

GIRL: Jake always told me it weren't nice to laugh at him just because he's
    afflicted.

MOTHER HICKS: He told me a riddle.

GIRL: What?

MOTHER HICKS: He just make it up.

(TUC signs as MOTHER HICKS speaks.)

MOTHER HICKS: What looks just like half a chicken?

GIRL: What?

MOTHER HICKS: *(As TUC signs)* The other half.

(They both laugh. GIRL is mystified.)

GIRL: He told you that?

MOTHER HICKS: He did.

GIRL: How?

MOTHER HICKS: With them air pictures.

GIRL: You mean, all that fingering around means things?

MOTHER HICKS: *(Signs as she speaks)* They teached him that over to the State
    School where he learned to lip talk. After he left the school and his people
    died, he came around here and just stayed. He teached me some he learned
    at School, and I teached him some, I made up, and we just built ourselves
    a talking way.

(TUC signs to her in a very animated manner, GIRL is a bit taken aback.)

GIRL: What's he doing now?

MOTHER HICKS: He's talking to you.

GIRL: To me?

MOTHER HICKS: He's trying to tell you something, but you're too ignorant
    to understand.

GIRL: I am not ignorant!

MOTHER HICKS: In his talk you are. He said. . .

(TUC signs and MOTHER HICKS translates.)

    You are my friend.

GIRL: Oh.

(*TUC continues signing.*)

   What's he saying now?

(*TUC signs the following speech as MOTHER HICKS translates. She places emphasis on what is being said rather than a word by word translation of the signs.*)

MOTHER HICKS: You look at me and only see things I cannot do, things I cannot be; but I can taste the cool spring water and know what month it is, I can smell the difference between the smoke of hickory and apple wood. I can see the sharp sting of honey, and I can taste the sunrise.

GIRL: Don't he mean he can taste the honey and see the sunrise?

MOTHER HICKS: He means what he says, that's the trouble with you town folks; you see and you hear, but you don't know nothing!

GIRL: Down in town, nobody knows he stays up here.

MOTHER HICKS: (*Suddenly bitter*) I don't much care what they know in town.

(*TUC signs something.*)

GIRL: What did he say?

MOTHER HICKS: He asked if we could put your old shirt on. You smell like a buzzard egg gone bad.

GIRL: (*Sniffing herself*) I do!

MOTHER HICKS: Fever's broke, so I guess it will be alright. Go in, it's in the cabin.

(*GIRL starts limping to cabin.*)

   And watch how you walk on that leg!

(*GIRL hops, on her good leg, into the cabin. There is the sound of geese and other animals. TUC signs, "Girl stay here" to MOTHER HICKS.*)

   No Tuc, as soon as she's well, she'll leave.

(*He signs it again.*)

   She's just here for a spell.

(*He signs, "I want her to stay."*)

   All critters come for the healing and then they go.

(*He signs, "I stayed," and MOTHER HICKS pats his cheek.*)

   I know, Tuc, you stayed.

(*GIRL comes out from the cabin wearing her own shirt.*)

GIRL: There's a whole zoo in there!

MOTHER HICKS: Just the geese, a squirrel or two, and a family of skunks.

GIRL: Skunks?

(*TUC signs, "You are my friend," to GIRL.*)

    Is he talking to me?

MOTHER HICKS: It appears that way.

GIRL: What's he saying?

MOTHER HICKS: I already told you that once! You got the memory of a piss
    ant.

GIRL: (*Understands*) OH!

(*She signs along with him.*)

    You are my friend.

(*TUC signs "yes."*)

MOTHER HICKS: Look, I can't sit around her jaw jacking with you two. I got
    work to do.

GIRL: (*Curiosity peaked*) Are you going to do . . . secret things?

MOTHER HICKS: (*Mysteriously*) I am going to hang up this here laundry . . .
    (*Sharply*) . . . if that is any of your business!

GIRL: I just wondered . . .

MOTHER HICKS: If you want to make yourself some use you can feed the
    rabbits and see if you can find their names.

GIRL: But I want to name them myself.

MOTHER HICKS: Every critter's got its own name inside 'em; you can't just
    make it up, but if you watch 'em close enough sometimes you can find it.

GIRL: I don't understand.

MOTHER HICKS: Don't matter, the rabbits do.

(*MOTHER HICKS exits with laundry. GIRL and TUC cross down to the rabbit box.
GIRL tenderly takes a tiny rabbit from the box and she and TUC feed it with an eye
dropper and a bowl of warm milk.*)

GIRL: (*To TUC, pointing to the bunny*) Sure is ugly, ain't it? Looks like a rat!

(*TUC teaches her the sign for "rat." With TUC'S help she feeds the bunny with an eye
dropper.*)

    Wouldn't it be something if you could remember that far back, when you
    was as young as they is? If you could remember lying there and all of a sud-
    den you see this big old milk nipple coming towards you and WHAM . . .
    supper!

(*She squirts the rest of the milk into her own mouth.*)

Sometimes I can remember back that far, I really can.

(*She puts the bunny back in the box.*)

I can just barely see hair colored hair and eye colored eyes . . .

(*GIRL turns directly to TUC.*)

You remember your people, Tuc? Your Paw and your Momma?

(*TUC signs "yes."*)

They're dead ain't they?

(*TUC signs "yes."*)

GIRL: You're lucky . . . Not on account of them being dead, that part's sad, but lucky you know where they are. You can close your eyes and see 'em live inside your mind. When you don't know about 'em . . . when you don't know, there's always something inside you that's hungry.

(*GIRL notices TUC staring at her.*)

When I see you staring at me, your eyes so big and round, I think I could fall right inside both your eyes and never be seen again.

(*TUC looks puzzled.*)

Oh, don't mind me, I'm just talking loon talk. Loon talk, that's me!

(*GIRL makes a circle near her ear and crosses her eyes, TUC copies her gesture, rolls over and laughs. MOTHER HICKS enters and spreads out the flannels, pours the soapy water into a bucket and generally busies herself. GIRL crosses to her.*)

Will you teach me things?

(*MOTHER HICKS does not respond.*)

Teach me secret things?

MOTHER HICKS: Don't know any secret things.

GIRL: Some people call this place witch mountain.

MOTHER HICKS: Some people are stupid.

GIRL: I want to show you something, something special.

(*GIRL fetches her quilt piece and holds it out to her. MOTHER HICKS focuses on her tasks.*)

Have you ever seen this piece before?

MOTHER HICKS: Yep.

GIRL: You have?

MOTHER HICKS: When you first came, I practically had to pry it out of your hand.

GIRL: I mean before that, have you ever seen this before that?

MOTHER HICKS: (*Uncomfortable*) I don't know, maybe, maybe not.

GIRL: I had this with me ever since I was born and see these initials here, these are sewn on with someone's own hand, and they stand for my name, see here I.S.H. . . . what do you think the H could stand for?

(*MOTHER HICKS crosses to the rabbit box, GIRL follows her.*)

MOTHER HICKS: (*Annoyed*) I told you, I don't know. Now, cut out the jaw jacking and feed these babies, all this jabbering's gettin' them rabbits riled.

(*MOTHER HICKS places the eye dropper in GIRL's hand and tries to get her to concentrate on the rabbits. GIRL still wants answers.*)

GIRL: You could teach me things.

MOTHER HICKS: (*Exasperated*) I wish someone had taught you how to feed a rabbit, you're squirting it up its nose! I swear of all the critters I got here you make the most noise and the least sense!

(*MOTHER HICKS stands and crosses to the bucket.*)

Now, I am going to water my yarbs and I want you to stay put!

(*She signs to TUC gruffly.*)

Watch her!

(*MOTHER HICKS exits, GIRL pouts and sits in the rocking chair.*)

GIRL: Is she always so mean?

(*TUC turns her face to look at his.*)

Is she always so mean?

(*TUC shakes his head "no," and signs something much more elaborate.*)

I don't understand.

(*TUC signs "MOTHER HICKS," but GIRL does not understand until he mimes her movements and GIRL figures it out.*)

GIRL: Mother Hicks!

(*TUC teaches GIRL the sign for "Mother Hicks."*)

Mother Hicks.

(*TUC does the sign for "earth." GIRL does not understand, so he gives her hints with gestures.*)

Dirt.

(*He continues with different hints until GIRL guesses correctly.*)

Dirt, ground, world, earth!

(*TUC repeats "Mother Hicks" and "earth."*)

Mother Hicks . . . earth!

(TUC nods and signs "and.")

　　And.

(TUC nods and signs "air.")

　　Wind, blow, all over, AIR!

(TUC nods and repeats all three signs.)

　　Mother Hicks. . . earth and air!

(TUC nods and signs "and.")

　　And . . .

(TUC signs "fire" and points to campfire.)

GIRL: FIRE!

(TUC signs "and.")

GIRL: And

(TUC signs "water" and gestures.)

　　Water!

(TUC nods and repeats all the signs. GIRL tries to copy but tries to go too fast. TUC laughs and slows her down.)

(TUC signs "and.")

　　And

(TUC signs "blood." GIRL finally guesses it.)

　　Cut, . . . blood!

(TUC signs "and.")

　　And.

(TUC signs "tears," tracing a tear down his cheek and then down GIRL's cheek.)

　　Tears.

(TUC and GIRL repeat the whole sequence, as they do, the words and signs take on meaning and deep significance for her.)

GIRL: Mother Hicks IS earth, and air, and fire, and water, and blood, and tears.
　　Mother Hicks is. . .

(TUC signs "everything." GIRL does not understand until he makes a more sweeping gesture.)

　　Everything!

(TUC signs "yes" as the lights dim.) (Pause)

(A spot comes up on TUC as he moves into it and signs. A CHORUS member enters and speaks.)

CHORUS:

> But soon there came the morning when
> It was time for me to go to town again.
> I didn't want to go.
> I was afraid somehow they'd know
> That Girl was here with us, and then
> They'd make me bring her back again.

(TUC moves a bit nearer to her and watches her sleep.)

> That morning, before I left,
> I stood and watched her sleep.
> I pressed my thoughts and feelings deep
> Inside my memory.

(Lights dim on GIRL.)

(Lights quickly come up on another area of the stage which indicates CLOVIS's store. The following scenes are played in fragmentary rapid succession similar to the witching scene at the end of Act 1.)

(TUC moves through the groups of townspeople catching fragments of their conversations.)

CLOVIS: *(To TUC)* And where in the blazes have you been? Take a little vacation did you? This whole town's been going to Hell and my stock boy decides to take himself a vacation!

(ALMA joins them.)

ALMA: Morning, Clovis, any news?

CLOVIS: I went to the highway patrol station on my way in this morning. They haven't seen her, but they suggested you call the State Home, they keep runaways there sometimes. I'll call if you like.

ALMA: Thank you, Clovis, I'm grateful for your help.

CLOVIS: *(To TUC)* I got a week's worth of stock piled up, get with it, Boy!

(Lights up on IZZY and ALMA.)

IZZY: So, where's Hosiah off to in such a hurry?

ALMA: He's going to Cairo, he figures that's where Girl went looking for the Hammons.

IZZY: The whole time she was with them, they just let her run wild, let all those kids run wild, just wild things! Now, I'm sure that's where she went!

ALMA: She had pneumonia, she wouldn't have made it as far as the county line!

(*HOSIAH enters. ALMA rushes to him.*)

   Did you find her?

HOSIAH: Fool's errand! I been to the Cairo employment office, the welfare department, and I called every Hammon in the whole city and not one has ever heard of Jake or the Girl.

(*She turns away.*)

   Alma, we've tried to find her.

ALMA: Not hard enough!

HOSIAH: There's nothing more we can do.

ALMA: When our boy was born dead, there was nothing we could do. When the scarlet fever took Sarah, there was nothing we could do, but this time, Hosiah, this time there *is* something we can do. We can keep looking!

(*TUC starts to exit and CLOVIS crosses to him and stops him.*)

CLOVIS: Hey, hey, hey! Where do you think you're going?

(*TUC tries to sign something.*)

   Don't you go waggling your fingers at me.

(*CLOVIS finds a plug of Red Man chewing tobacco in TUC'S top pocket of his overalls.*)

   Got yourself a new habit, Boy?

(*TUC shakes his head.*)

CLOVIS: Help yourself, did you?

(*TUC indicates he paid for it.*)

   What's the matter with you, Boy. What's the matter with you anyway?

(*Lights dim to a spot. TUC signs, CHORUS member speaks.*)

CHORUS:
   Home late, long into night,
   Winding up the trail in the pale moonlight
   With a feeling deep inside
   Makes me want to run and hide.
   So, I turn . . . nothing.
   And I turn . . . no one.
   Then I turn and I see
   There ain't no one there but me,
   But I run anyway.

(*Lights come up on the cabin. MOTHER HICKS sits near the fire, braiding GIRL's hair. We hear the sound of tree toads.*)

(*TUC enters at a run and grabs GIRL's blanket and runs into the cabin with it.*)

MOTHER HICKS: Hey!

GIRL: What's going on?

MOTHER HICKS: I don't know, but I aim to find out!

(TUC *runs out of the cabin again.*)

Whoa! Care to tell me what you're doing?

(TUC *signs, "Girl sleep in cabin."*)

She can't sleep in there 'cause I got a whole family of rackity coons that won't take too kindly to being disturbed just because you got the willies!

GIRL: What's the matter?

MOTHER HICKS: He's just got the jumps. (*To* TUC) Now come and eat, you got black beans . . . burnt black beans. Now, sit and eat before you start making me feel goosey.

(TUC *takes his bowl of beans but keeps a watchful eye all around.* MOTHER HICKS *sits in her chair and weaves a basket.* TUC *tosses* GIRL *the plug of Red Man.*)

GIRL: Hey, thanks! You was over in town today?

(TUC *signs "yes."*)

Anything going on? Anyone say anything, you know, about me?

(TUC *pauses and signs "no."*)

Nobody?

(TUC *repeats the "no."*)

My whole life, I lived in that town and now, they don't even notice once I'm gone.

MOTHER HICKS: Down in town is a mighty measly place.

GIRL: But it's different here.

MOTHER HICKS: Here, my walls is made of tar paper, so creatures can come and go. There ain't no keepin' out and there ain't no holdin' in.

GIRL: (*Starting to take a plug of tobacco.*) Why do the animals come here?

MOTHER HICKS: They come for the healing, when there's a fester to lance, or something broken to be bound up or cut away. They come when they can't do for themselves.

(MOTHER HICKS *crosses to* GIRL *and holds out her hand for the tobacco.* GIRL *gives it to her.*)

GIRL: And after? What happens after they's well?

MOTHER HICKS: Tuc and me, we watch 'em close and find their names, then they can go and we'll always know 'em again.

(To TUC)

MOTHER HICKS: Now you bring back that bedding, so this little chicken can roost!

(TUC exits into the house.)

GIRL: What if an . . . animal doesn't want to go?

MOTHER HICKS: Sooner or later they do, they all do.

(TUC enters with blankets and crosses back into the cabin.)

GIRL: Will you wrap me up tight in them blankets, like when I first came here?

MOTHER HICKS: Why?

GIRL: I kinda feel like I'm a little tiny worm, all wrapped up in a cocoon.

MOTHER HICKS: Well, I ain't going to be expecting no butterflies at breakfast.

(TUC enters with a shotgun.)

MOTHER HICKS: And what do you think you're doing with that?

(TUC signs "guarding.")

MOTHER HICKS: Guarding? Against what?

GIRL: Something's wrong isn't it?

MOTHER HICKS: Sleep tight, Little Rabbit, and don't worry about nothing, lessen it's Daniel Boone over there shooting his own foot off.

(There is a rustling sound.)

GIRL: I heard something.

MOTHER HICKS: What?

GIRL: I thought I heard something over there.

(CLOVIS steps out of shadow.)

MOTHER HICKS: Who's there? I said, who's there?

CLOVIS: So it is you, and you've got. . .

(TUC sees CLOVIS and shoots the shotgun in the air. CLOVIS turns and runs.)

MOTHER HICKS: Tuc, you damned fool!

(TUC starts to run after him and she snatches the gun away. TUC follows CLOVIS.)

Tuc, it ain't no use!

(Lights dim and come up immediately on the town. CLOVIS enters at a run. There is the sound of a bell ringing over and over. HOSIAH and ALMA cross over to CLOVIS.)

ALMA: Clovis, that's the night bell, we only use it for emergencies.

CLOVIS: This is an emergency. I found her. I found the Girl.

ALMA: Where?

CLOVIS: Up on Dug Hill.

ALMA: Was she all right?

CLOVIS: I didn't get a good look.

ALMA: I am calling the State Police.

HOSIAH: Them state troopers don't take too kindly to witch stories or to trespassing!

CLOVIS: Trespassing? We are talking about kidnapping.

(*Lights up on IZZY, she is holding a telephone receiver. ALMA and HOSIAH turn their backs.*)

IZZY: We are talking about witchcraft, Clovis.

(*CLOVIS steps into a pool of light. He also has a phone receiver.*)

CLOVIS: And then she said to Hosiah and me "You can sit around here jaw jacking, but I'm going up that hill."

IZZY: Tonight? She's going up there tonight?

(*ALMA turns around.*)

ALMA: And don't you dare try to stop me, Hosiah Ward!

(*HOSIAH turns around.*)

HOSIAH: How do we know she was taken up there? How do we know she didn't just go.

ALMA: We won't unless we go up that hill.

(*ALMA and HOSIAH turn their backs.*)

CLOVIS: (*Into the phone*) And then she asked me to show her the way. When I hesitated she said . . .

ALMA: (*Turning front*) Clovis, I do believe you're scared.

IZZY: (*Into the phone*) It just makes sense to be scared when you're dealing with a witch.

CLOVIS: (*Into the phone*) Dealing with a shotgun!

ALMA: If you won't come with me, I swear I'll go alone.

CLOVIS: (*Into the phone*) So, I told her I'd go.

IZZY: (*Into the phone*) Clovis P. Eudy! If you think I'm going to go traipsing up witch mountain in my condition . . .

CLOVIS: (*Into the phone*) Then stay behind.

IZZY: (*Into the phone*) And miss everything?

(*Lights out on CLOVIS and IZZY. There is tension between ALMA and HOSIAH.*)

ALMA: You don't want her to come back, do you?

HOSIAH: Oh, Alma.

ALMA: Do you?

HOSIAH: Not if she's just going to leave again. I don't want her to hurt you that way.

ALMA: I'll be alright and I have to know that she's all right.

(*She touches his cheek. He nods.*)

HOSIAH: I'll need my climbing boots.

ALMA: Better bring mine too . . . And Hosiah, you better bring your gun.

(*He nods and exits as lights change back to the cabin.*)

(*GIRL is asleep on her pallet. MOTHER HICKS paces. TUC enters, out of breath and signing wildly.*)

MOTHER HICKS: Slow down, I can't follow you . . . slow down.

(*TUC takes a breath and signs, "Many people come. Very angry."*)

    When?

(*TUC signs, "Now."*)

    But why?

(*TUC signs, "Find Girl. Have guns."*)

    But they ain't got no cause, they ain't got no right.

(*GIRL wakes and sits up.*)

GIRL: (*Alarmed*) What's going on?

MOTHER HICKS: (*To TUC*) And they've got guns? Damned fools!

GIRL: What is it? What's happened?

(*TUC runs into the cabin.*)

MOTHER HICKS: Tuc says some folks from town is on their way up here, he says they're riled and they got guns.

GIRL: But why?

MOTHER HICKS: Something to do with you.

GIRL: Let's witch 'em. All of 'em. Let's you and I witch 'em all.

MOTHER HICKS: What did you say?

GIRL: Let's throw them a spell to turn the road to slime and let 'em slide all the way back down to Main Street.

MOTHER HICKS: Hesh up, you fool.

GIRL: You can do it, and I can help. I know who I am.

MOTHER HICKS: You don't know anything!

GIRL: Yes I do! (*Mimes the witch ritual.*)
>I swear that I do give
>Everything betwixt my two hands
>To the ways of witchcraft.

MOTHER HICKS: (*Angry*) Stop that jabbering!

GIRL: I want to be a witch, like you!

MOTHER HICKS: I'll tell you witches, I'll tell you witchcraft! When the fever comes and makes the babies scream and burn up in their beds and die, that can't be scarlet fever, it's a hex. When a child's born all crippled up, or blind, or deaf, it can't be because its mother took no notice of the measles, it's a spell! When the hand of God strikes a good man down, or takes away his job, it must be someone's fault, it must be witchcraft!

GIRL: But, Mother Hicks . . .

MOTHER HICKS: (*Turns on her*) Don't you EVER call me that!

GIRL: Why not?

MOTHER HICKS: Don't you ever say that to me again.

(*She turns away from GIRL.*)

GIRL: (*Simply*) I know that I am your child.

MOTHER HICKS: My child was taken.

GIRL: They say you gave her to the Devil, but I . . .

MOTHER HICKS: (*Deeply grieved*) I never gave her up! I held her when she screamed. I held her all the time she cried. I held her until she died of fever!

GIRL: She died?

MOTHER HICKS: And after, I held her in my own two arms, and then I laid her in the ground all by myself.

GIRL: (*Showing her the quilt piece*) But look at this, you know you've seen this before, it's my name here and the H . . . the H it stands for Hicks!

(*GIRL shoves the piece into her hands. MOTHER HICKS looks at her squarely.*)

MOTHER HICKS: It stands for Home.

GIRL: What?

MOTHER HICKS: Illinois State Home.

(*There is a pause.*)

>I seen this piece before. I wrapped you in it just after you was born. Your Mother came here from the Sate Home, scared and all alone, hardly more than a child herself. I helped her with the birthing . . .

GIRL: (*In disbelief*) No.

MOTHER HICKS: She stayed a spell, but then one day she ran and took you with her. She must have left you in the town on her way to somewhere else.

GIRL: And so I am . . .

MOTHER HICKS: The orphan child of an orphan child.

GIRL: That's not true!

MOTHER HICKS: Yes it is, Little Rabbit.

GIRL: Witches is powerful, witches can make things happen, witches is never lonely or afraid, because they've got the power. I am your child and you are a witch!

MOTHER HICKS: I am not a witch!

GIRL: Then what are you?

MOTHER HICKS: I'm just a left over person, just like you!

(TUC enters with an empty box of shotgun shells.)

GIRL: That's not true!

MOTHER HICKS: (To TUC) I threw away the shells, I was afraid someone would get hurt! (To GIRL) Now, they are coming for you, and you'll go back to town with them, because that's where you belong!

GIRL: NO!

(GIRL runs into the darkness. TUC starts after her. MOTHER HICKS grabs the gun from him.)

MOTHER HICKS: Let her go, Tuc!

(MOTHER HICKS paces for a minute, crosses to the rocker and sits with the gun in her lap.)

  Let her go.

(Voices of the townspeople are heard coming up the Hill.)

RICKY: (Offstage) Look there, just ahead! There's a fire!

(CLOVIS, ALMA, HOSIAH, IZZY and RICKY enter clutching flashlights.)

ALMA: Oh my God, Hosiah, there it is!

(MOTHER HICKS stands at her doorway holding the shotgun in her arms.)

MOTHER HICKS: Stop right there. One more step and you're on private property.

CLOVIS: (Seeing the gun) Uhhhhhh, beg your pardon, Miz Hicks.

MOTHER HICKS: You got exactly three seconds to get your backsides down this hill.

ALMA: We understand that you're holding a child here against her will.

MOTHER HICKS: There ain't no one here.

ALMA: The Girl's been missing over a week and . . .

MOTHER HICKS: That's no concern of mine.

CLOVIS: We just want to look around.

MOTHER HICKS: You got a warrant?

ALMA: (*Advancing on her*) Please, I need to see for myself . . .

IZZY: Don't look at her, Alma! She'll witch you!

MOTHER HICKS: (*To IZZY*) You never change, do you? What did I ever do to you, except give you a place to put your hate?

IZZY: (*Praying as a protection*) You know what you did. In the name of the Father, and the Son . . .

MOTHER HICKS: (*Shouting*) Be quiet!

CLOVIS: Can't stand to hear the word of God?

MOTHER HICKS: Prayers used that way is blasphemy!

IZZY: You cry blasphemy after witching our children?

MOTHER HICKS: I never hurt a child!

CLOVIS: But they died, you touched those babies and they died.

MOTHER HICKS: It was the fever!

HOSIAH: (*Gun at the ready*) Stand aside or use that gun, but we are coming in.

MOTHER HICKS: (*Raising the gun slightly*) What gives you the right? What gives any of you the right, to talk, and talk, and talk, and call me a witch?

ALMA: We just want the Girl!

MOTHER HICKS: (*Putting her gun down*) What's the use? You'll take whatever you want. You'll come in here with guns and call ME criminal!

ALMA: We just want the Girl.

MOTHER HICKS: She's not here!

ALMA: Let me look. Please, I care for her.

MOTHER HICKS: (*After a long moment*) Then look, but just one. I won't have all of you trampling through my house.

(*HOSIAH starts.*)

Not the one with the gun.

(*ALMA starts, and HOSIAH pulls her back.*)

ALMA: Who then?

MOTHER HICKS: The child.

RICKY: MAMA!

IZZY: Lord, no. No child of mine . . .

ALMA: Izzy, please. She can't hurt you, Ricky. Do it for the Girl, Ricky. Dare and double dare.

RICKY: If you ever find the Girl, you gotta swear you'll tell her I did this.

(RICKY slowly approaches the door. Animal sounds are heard as he enters. Immediately, he comes out.)

RICKY: I'm dead, I'm killed, I'm killed, I'm dead.

ALMA: No you're not, but you smell like . . .

HOSIAH, CLOVIS, ALMA: Skunk!!!

RICKY: She ain't there. There's nothing in there but eyes, hundreds of eyes shinin' in the dark.

IZZY: Her incubus! The Devil animals!

MOTHER HICKS: (This is the last straw.) That's right! You want a witch? Then witch I'll be! When you look, you see what you want to see.

IZZY: It's a spell!

MOTHER HICKS: (Every bit a witch) Get out of here, before I lock your jaw and turn your blood to poison.

CLOVIS: We don't want any trouble.

MOTHER HICKS: Then get off my property!

(She lunges at them. HOSIAH aims and cocks his gun. She faces him squarely.)

And you better have a silver bullet in that gun!

(There is a moment of tension.)

ALMA: Hosiah.

(He puts the gun down.)

MOTHER HICKS: I'll count to five, and if you're not halfway down that hill by then, I'll spell you all to Sunday! ONE!

IZZY: Come on, Ricky.

(IZZY and RICKY bolt and exit.)

MOTHER HICKS: TWO!

CLOVIS: We don't want any trouble.

MOTHER HICKS: THREE!

(CLOVIS exits.)

HOSIAH: Come on, Alma.

MOTHER HICKS: FOUR!

ALMA: I'll be right there.

(*HOSIAH steps aside but remains in shadows.*)

MOTHER HICKS: FIVE.

ALMA: She was ill. She had pneumonia.

MOTHER HICKS: Not anymore.

ALMA: (*Relieved*) She was here! When did she leave?

MOTHER HICKS: Not long ago.

ALMA: Where . . .

MOTHER HICKS: I don't know.

ALMA: If she comes back, if you see her . . . please tell her I want her to come back.

MOTHER HICKS: I know . . . now, go.

(*There is a moment of understanding between the two women. ALMA turns and walks to HOSIAH who takes her hand as they exit together. TUC steps into a spotlight. A CHORUS MEMBER interprets.*)

CHORUS:

Four days come, and four days gone
And she ain't here, and she ain't there.
This time the Girl has disappeared
I know, cause I've looked everywhere
And I am used to shadows, but she's not there
Or anywhere.

(*During the end of TUC's speech there is the sound of a train whistle and an on-rushing train. Lights come up on shadowy figures of TWO MEN warming their hands above an oil drum with a fire in it. Their tattered coats are pulled up around their faces, the glow from the drum casts weird shadows. GIRL enters and approaches the men. Tentatively, she pulls on one of the men's coats.*)

GIRL: Excuse me, sir I . . .

MAN 1: Yeah?

MAN 2: (*Gruffly*) Whad'da want, kid?

GIRL: Uhhh, never mind . . . nothing . . . sorry.

(*She pulls away from them, and crosses to a group of trash cans, lifts the lid, and rummages through the trash. She finds an apple core, which she devours, and a can of beans. She runs her fingers along the inside of the can to see if there is any left. After a bit, a BOY approaches the cans from the opposite side. He does not see GIRL. He rifles through the trash, tossing it out, and showering GIRL. He comes up with a glass milk bottle.*)

Hey, watch what you're doing!

(GIRL comes up swinging. She gets a good look at him. It is HOWIE HAMMON. He drops the can lid and runs. GIRL chases him.)

Hey! Hey! Howie!

(They run past a few shanties of a "HOOVERVILLE." GIRL finally catches him.)

I always could outrun you, Howie Hammon!

HOWIE: GIRL!

GIRL: Why did you run?

HOWIE: Around here, if someone yells, I always run. What are you doing here?

GIRL: I hopped me a freight train, Howie. It slowed down over to the depot to drop off the mail and I just reached out, grabbed me an armful of wind, and blew right down here to Cairo. I was scared, but I made it.

HOWIE: You come here? On purpose?

GIRL: I been lookin' all over this blamed city for you. Last four days I see things to make you to weep to think of them. People are starving here, Howie.

HOWIE: Why'd you come?

GIRL: I told you. I was lookin' for you. For you, for all your brothers and sisters, for Ella . . . for Jake.

HOWIE: Come on.

GIRL: What are you doing here?

HOWIE: I live here.

GIRL: Here? All of you?

HOWIE: Come on.

(He leads her a short distance to an odd dwelling that has been fashioned from Jake's truck. All that can be seen is one side of the cab with a canvas roof which extends like a lean-to.)

HOWIE: Hey, Dad?

(A voice comes from inside the cab.)

JAKE: Did you find any?

HOWIE: Dad.

JAKE: I hear they are paying a penny a piece for milk bottles.

HOWIE: Look who's here.

(JAKE emerges from the inside of the cab. He is disheveled; a bottle sticks out of his hip pocket.)

JAKE: Girl!

(*GIRL runs to him and hugs him hard. He barely responds.*)

GIRL: I knew I'd find you. I just knew it!

JAKE: How are you, Girl?

GIRL: I'm fine.

JAKE: It's good to see you, really good. Howie, what have we got to eat?

HOWIE: (*Alarmed*) Dad you know we don't . . .

JAKE: (*Ignoring him*) See what we got to eat. I'm sure we got something to . . .

HOWIE: Dad . . .

GIRL: That's okay . . .

JAKE: (*To GIRL*) You must be tired; you look tired.

GIRL: I'm tired, but I'm here! I thought you'd be living in a big house with two
     porches, Jake.

JAKE: Howie, see if we got something, some beans or some . . .

GIRL: (*Sharply*) I'm not hungry!

(*JAKE turns away. There is an uncomfortable pause.*)

     Where are the others?

JAKE: Gone.

GIRL: Gone? Gone where?

JAKE: Different places.

GIRL: What?

JAKE: Ella and Becca and the baby are over at my sister's. Libby went to
     my aunt in Memphis. Margaret is working for some folks in Mound City.
     Frank's joined the CCC and is off in California or some place, and Sarah . . .
     God, where is Sarah?

GIRL: You don't remember?

JAKE: I'll remember in a minute. Howie, where is Sarah?

(*HOWIE takes some bottles out of his coat.*)

HOWIE: St. Louis.

JAKE: That's right. She went with a family. They wanted her to take care of
     their baby. Sarah was always good with babies. You remember.

GIRL: Sarah weren't no older than me!

JAKE: Anyway, they seemed like nice folks.

HOWIE: Dad, I got ten bottles; that's good, isn't it, Dad?

JAKE: Howie and I . . . we've just been camping out here in the car until something better comes along, eh, Howie?

HOWIE: Ten bottles is good, isn't it?

GIRL: How could you do it, Jake?

HOWIE: Last night, I only got six. Ten's much better than six.

GIRL: How could you do it?

JAKE: Do what?

GIRL: Let 'em all go like that?

JAKE: I couldn't help it.

GIRL: What about your job?

JAKE: There wasn't any job.

(JAKE takes a swig out of the bottle.)

GIRL: What about the WPA?

JAKE: I wouldn't take a hand out from those crooks in . . .

GIRL: (Angry) I heard that already, Jake!

JAKE: (Desperate) There wasn't money for food.

GIRL: But there was money for that! (Points to the bottle)

JAKE: (Defensive) Don't judge me. You haven't got the right!

GIRL: You had a family, but you just threw it away!

JAKE: (Starting to cry) I just couldn't hold on to them.

HOWIE: Don't you talk to my Dad like that!

GIRL: You just threw it away.

HOWIE: (To JAKE) We're doing okay. Aren't we Dad?

JAKE: There was nothing I could do.

GIRL: You could've held on to them, no matter what. That's what I'd do.

HOWIE: Get out of here.

(GIRL turns to walk away.)

JAKE: Where are you going?

GIRL: (Turns back) What the Hell do you care?

(She walks away without looking back. HOWIE turns to JAKE who is weeping.)

HOWIE: We're doing okay, aren't we, Dad? We're doing okay.

JAKE: Yeah, Howie!

(They exit back into the car as lights fade and the sound of the train is heard. Lights
come up on TUC who signs, as a CHORUS MEMBER speaks.)

CHORUS:
>It was just before midnight
>I was passing the graveyard
>On my way *home.*

(Lights are dim. The crickets, a distant owl hooting, and the sound of a loon are heard. TUC crouches in shadow. GIRL enters and moves to her hiding place as before.)

(MOTHER HICKS enters the graveyard and moves to the same spot she went to before. As she places the baby clothes on the ground, she speaks softly, but her words are audible.)

MOTHER HICKS: So there you are, and don't you look something all dressed up to Sunday. Mind you don't get this pretty little dress dirty; I just washed it.

(GIRL sits up.)

>The rabbits is fine and we got ourselves a whole family of raccoons.

(GIRL moves slowly, carefully near her.)

>Them coons got into rat poison, I reckon; but they're doing fine on sour milk and apple peelings . . . Oh, I wish you could see them.

(With great grief and infinite tenderness, MOTHER HICKS starts to lower herself onto the ground. She is suddenly aware of GIRL and stops.)

GIRL: I was afraid you wouldn't be here.

MOTHER HICKS: *(Without looking at her)* I didn't come looking for you. I had other reasons.

GIRL: I'm sorry for what I said to you.

(No response from MOTHER HICKS)

>I just needed it to be true.

(No response from MOTHER HICKS)

>Please, look at me.

(MOTHER HICKS looks at her.)

>She's there isn't she? What was her name?

MOTHER HICKS: May-ry.

GIRL: Mary.

MOTHER HICKS: It ain't Mary and it ain't Marie. It's May-ry.

GIRL: May-ry.

>*(There is a pause.)* I'm sorry I ran away.

MOTHER HICKS: They always go when they's healed.

GIRL: But I'm not healed, not yet. But I do know one thing, I know one thing for positive sure; someday things are going to belong to me and I'm going to belong to them. But there's something I need first and I won't be healed until I find it.

MOTHER HICKS: You look all right to me.

GIRL: I'm talkin' about something inside me, like a piece of me left out and wanting.

MOTHER HICKS: (*Looks at her evenly*) You'll never find her. No matter how hard you look, you'll never find that poor scared rabbit that gave you birth.

GIRL: I know, that part of me isn't hungry anymore, it's just sad.

MOTHER HICKS: That woman, Alma, she cares. She wants you back.

GIRL: I know, but I can't go back there until I find what I need.

MOTHER HICKS: What?

GIRL: A name. I need a name. So, I wonder, could I have her name? Could I be May-ry?

MOTHER HICKS: That's her name, it ain't yours.

GIRL: But I wish it were.

MOTHER HICKS: (*Simply*) Well, you can wish in one hand and spit in the other and see which gets full first.

GIRL: Could you help me find my own name?

MOTHER HICKS: (*Looks at GIRL*) I reckon I could.

GIRL: Then I can stay with you 'til we find it, just for a while?

MOTHER HICKS: Creatures come when they need a healing spell, but when it's done, they go.

GIRL: I know.

(*TUC comes forward and signs. The CHORUS enters as a group as at the top of the play. As they speak, MOTHER HICKS gathers up the baby clothes. GIRL carefully folds the quilt piece and places it on top of the grave. She looks to MOTHER HICKS who nods. GIRL pats the quilt piece and leaves it behind.*)

CHORUS:
> Mother Hicks is a witch, people say
> And she lives all alone at the top of Dug Hill
> And she works her magic on the town below.
> When a child falls sick
> And there ain't no cause
> And there ain't no cure

Then everybody knows, that it's witched for sure
Mother Hicks is a witch, people say.

(MOTHER HICKS extends her hand to GIRL who reaches for it just as the CHORUS finishes their lines.)

(Lights dim to black.)

CURTAIN

Production credits from the premiere of *Mother Hicks* and details concerning performance rights are included in the acting edition of the play as published by Dramatic Publishing.

Johnny Tremain

Dramatized by Lola H. and Coleman A. Jennings

Based on the youth novel of historical

fiction by Esther Forbes

It is 1773, and an orphan named Johnny Tremain is apprenticed to a well-known Boston silversmith in hopes of becoming one himself. But when a severe burn to his hand makes it impossible for him to continue learning the trade he is forced to find another job. Determined to find a place for himself in the rapidly changing colonies he does not give up his search, even as he is rejected by numerous other tradesmen. Johnny eventually accepts a position as a delivery boy for the *Boston Observer*, a newspaper known to side with the Whig party's stance against the British. It is here that he befriends another young man, Rab, who introduces him to the cause of colonial independence. As Johnny gradually becomes involved with the Patriots and the turbulent early days of the American Revolution, he encounters such famous figures and events as Samuel Adams, Paul Revere, the Boston Tea Party, and even the battles of Lexington and Concord. Rab is mortally wounded at Lexington, leaving Johnny to reconsider the cause and their struggle. Inspired by the words of a veteran member of the Sons of Liberty—"We give all we have— lives, property, safety, skills—we fight, we die, for a simple thing. Only that a man can stand up."—Johnny seeks out an operation that will repair his hand and allow him to take up Rab's musket and continue in the fight for independence.

Characters (in order of appearance)

JOHNNY	MR. LORNE
CILLA LAPHAM	SAMUEL ADAMS
MRS. LAPHAM	JOSEPH WARREN
JOHN HANCOCK	PAUL REVERE
MR. LAPHAM	BOY ONE AS "INDIAN"
DOVE	BOY TWO AS "INDIAN"
RAB	BOY THREE AS "INDIAN"
SEWALL	BRITISH ADMIRAL
MERCHANT LYTE	BRITISH OFFICER
SHERIFF	DESERTER

Offstage Voices
MERCHANT
INSTRUMENT MAKER
CLOCK MAKER
NIGHT WATCHMAN
JUSTICE DANA
Non-Speaking Roles
THREE "INDIANS"
SIX TOWNSPEOPLE
FOUR BRITISH SOLDIERS
NINE MINUTEMEN

Johnny Tremaine

(As audience enters theatre, curtain is up, revealing unit set and some furniture pieces which will be used throughout production. Recorded period MUSIC sets mood of play in one-minute overture to action.)

Lapham's silversmith shop.
Boston. Morning, early July, 1773.

(CILLA enters as JOHNNY is busy at silver work area.)
CILLA: Johnny!
JOHNNY: *(Arrogantly)* What is it, Cilla?

CILLA: Ma sent me. Johnny, it's Mr. Hancock himself. He's coming here to order something. Stand by and listen or Grandpa will get it wrong.

(MRS. LAPHAM enters, followed by DOVE)

MRS. LAPHAM: Johnny, straighten up! It's Mr. Hancock. He's ordering a sugar basin. Shake a leg. (CILLA offers him her clean apron for towel to wipe charcoal off his hands.)

(MR. LAPHAM ushers JOHN HANCOCK into room and offers him armchair. DOVE stands nearby.)

JOHNNY: (Straightening work bench, he pushes DOVE out of way.) Get back, Dove. You're always in the way.

JOHN HANCOCK: (Speaking, as he is ushered in by MR. LAPHAM) And it is to be done next Monday—a week from today. I want it as a birthday present for my venerable aunt Lydia Hancock. (Sits in armchair) This is the creamer of the set. (Handing cream pitcher to MR. LAPHAM) Only this morning a clumsy maid melted the sugar bowl. I want you to make me a new one, about so high . . . so broad . . . (Indicating the size of sugar bowl with his hands. JOHNNY crosses to MR. LAPHAM, carefully eyeing beautiful basin.)

JOHNNY: Is this the work of John Coney, sir?

JOHN HANCOCK: Look at the mark, boy. (JOHNNY turns basin upside down to see smith's mark.) Your master . . . (Gesturing to MR. LAPHAM) . . . made that creamer . . . forty years ago. He made the entire set.

JOHNNY: (To MR. LAPHAM) You made it!

MR. LAPHAM: I remember when your uncle, Mr. Thomas Hancock, sir, ordered that set. "Make it big, and make it handsome, bigger and hand-somer than anything in Boston. As big and handsome as my Lady is. Make it as rich as I am."

JOHN HANCOCK: (Laughing) That is just the way my uncle used to talk. (Standing up) But you have not as yet said whether you can make my sugar basin for me . . . and have it done by Monday next. (Crossing to exit, stops, turns to MR. LAPHAM) Of course, I thought of you first because you made the original. But there are other silversmiths. (MR. LAPHAM hesitates in his response.) Perhaps you would rather not undertake . . .

MR. LAPHAM: I've got the time, materials, and the boys to help. I can get right at it, but honestly, sir . . . I don't know. Perhaps I haven't got the skill anymore. I've not done anything so fine for thirty years. I am not what I used to be . . . (MRS. LAPHAM nods to JOHNNY encouraging him to speak up.)

JOHNNY: (Rushing to HANCOCK) We can do it, Mr. Hancock.

JOHN HANCOCK: *Bless me.* (*Surprised*) An apprentice speaking for his master?

JOHNNY: Yes, sir. And you shall have it delivered to your own house in one week. It's going to be just exactly right.

MR. LAPHAM: (*Looking at JOHNNY gratefully*) Certainly, sir. I'm humbly grateful for your patronage.

(*HANCOCK bows slightly, tossing silver coin to JOHNNY, another to DOVE.*)

JOHN HANCOCK: One for each of you boys. I hope you will be diligent at your work. (*MRS. LAPHAM curtsies as he exits.*)

MR. LAPHAM: He is hoping you two will vote for him when you are grown up and have enough property.

JOHNNY: Don't you ever vote for Mr. Hancock, sir?

MR. LAPHAM: No, I never do. I don't hold much with these fellows that are always trying to stir up trouble between us and England. Maybe English rule ain't always perfect, but it's good enough for me. Fellows like Mr. Hancock and Sam Adams, calling themselves patriots and talking too much. Not reading God's Word . . . like their parents did . . . which tells us to be humble. But he's my landlord and I don't say much. (*General stage illumination decreases to half except for spot on JOHNNY who silently studies cream pitcher in his hands as MR. LAPHAM, MRS. LAPHAM and CILLA exit*)

Early evening, the next day.

(*As lighting returns to normal JOHNNY crosses to work area, puts cream pitcher away and starts working with piece of wax, trying to shape it into handle for silver bowl. CILLA enters with slate, designing silversmith mark for JOHNNY.*)

CILLA: I'm designing you a beautiful mark so when you are man-grown and a master smith, you can stamp your silver with it.

JOHNNY: I've five more years to work under your grandpa. I'm just an apprentice who earns no wages. No matter how good my work may be, I have to stamp it with your grandpa's mark.

CILLA: Look. I've got your "J" and "T" sort of entwined.

JOHNNY: Too hard to read. Then, too, when I'm a master smith I'm going to use all three of my initials.

CILLA: *All three?*

JOHNNY: J. L. T.

CILLA: (*Almost respectfully*) You're not making it up? I've heard tell of folk with three names, but I never saw one before.

JOHNNY: (*Walking away from her*) Look at *me*, my girl.

CILLA: Wait, Johnny. What is that middle name? It begins with "L."

JOHNNY: (*Not sure whether or not to tell her*) As far as *you* are concerned, it ends with "L," too.

CILLA: I'll bet it's something so awful you are ashamed of it, like "Ladybug" or "Leapfrog." I'll bet it's "Lamentable." (*JOHNNY grins.*) What is your middle name, Johnny?

JOHNNY: (*After long pause*) My middle name is Lyte.

CILLA: So you are really John Lyte Tremain?

JOHNNY: No. My baptized Bible name is Jonathan. I've always been called Johnny. That's the way my papers were made out to your grandpa. But I am really Jonathan Lyte Tremain.

CILLA: Why, that's just like the rich Merchant Lyte.

JOHNNY: Just like. My mother told me.

CILLA: You don't suppose you are related?

JOHNNY: I *do* suppose. But I don't know. Lyte's not a common name. And we are both Jonathan.

CILLA: You never speak of your mother, Johnny. She hadn't been dead more'n a few weeks when you first came here. You never talked about her. Was that because you liked her so much? Or not at all.

JOHNNY: (*Long pause*) Liked her so much. We had been living in Maine. She earned enough for us both by sewing. But when she knew she had to die, she wanted me taught skilled work, and all I wanted was to be a silversmith. That's why we came to Boston, so's to get me a proper master. She could still sew, but she coughed all the time. Even when she was so weak she could hardly hold a needle, she kept on and on, teaching me reading and writing and all that. She was determined I shouldn't grow up untaught. She wanted me to be something.

CILLA: That's why you work so hard?

JOHNNY: That's why. Mrs. Lapham promised her that your grandpa would take me on just as soon as she was buried. She died . . . and he did. That's all.

CILLA: What was her name? And how come she . . . a poor sewing woman . . . was so well learned?

JOHNNY: Roundabout here she called herself just Mrs. Tremain, but she was born Lavinia Lyte. She came of gentlefolk.

CILLA: Johnny, didn't she ever go to her rich relatives and say, "Here I am?"

JOHNNY: No, and she told me not to . . . ever. Unless . . . only, if I'd got to the end of everything. Then I should go to Merchant Lyte, show him my cup and tell him my mother told me before she died that I was kin to him. In pity, he might help me.

CILLA: Your cup?

JOHNNY: She said I wasn't to sell it . . . ever. I was to go hungry and cold first.

CILLA: Where is your cup?

JOHNNY: If you swear by your hope of Heaven and your fear of Hell, never, never to mention any of this to anyone. Never tell my true name, nor that I have a cup. (*Very serious, CILLA nods in agreement and follows him to chest. JOHNNY carefully takes cup from chest and hands it to her.*)

CILLA: (*Looking at it in wonder*) The same markings as Merchant Lyte.

JOHNNY: And the same motto. Look.

CILLA: (*Reading in halting manner*) "Let there by Lyte."

JOHNNY: (*Whispering*) Just like the sun coming up yonder out of the sea, pushing rays of light ahead of it.

CILLA: (*In sour manner, thinking JOHNNY is getting beyond himself*) Might it not just as well be a *setting* sun?

JOHNNY: No, no. My mother said it is a rising sun. But I was to keep whist and mum about it . . . unless even God has turned away His face. And Cilla . . . you promised.

CILLA: By my hope of Heaven and my fear of Hell. (*As general stage illumination changes to half, JOHNNY is left in spotlight. CILLA exits.*)

JOHNNY: (*Thinking aloud, slowly to himself*) Yes, you swore never to mention any of this . . . to anyone by your hope of Heaven and your fear of Hell.

Mid-afternoon, several days later.

(*DOVE enters slowly as lighting returns to normal. He is carrying basket filled with worst looking charcoal JOHNNY has ever seen.*)

DOVE: Johnny, I got the charcoal.

JOHNNY: (*Annoyed, looking around*) Where have you been? I sent you to get charcoal hours ago. (*Crosses to DOVE to examine charcoal*) This isn't what we silversmiths use. This is fourth-rate . . . fit for iron . . . maybe. You know that, Dove.

DOVE: Naw. Not me. I don't know anything. (*Crossing away from JOHNNY*)

You're always telling me that. You always like to take charge of things 'round here.

JOHNNY: I want willow charcoal.

DOVE: You never said so.

JOHNNY: I'll go myself, but this delay means we'll be working in lamplight and up to midnight. (*Crossing to DOVE*) You are the stupidest animal God ever made. Why your mother didn't drown you when you were a pup, I can't imagine.

(*MR. LAPHAM enters.*)

MR. LAPHAM: (*Mildly*) Boys, you quarrel all the time.

JOHNNY: (*Furious*) He is a lazy, good-for-nothing pig of a louse.

MR. LAPHAM: (*Seeking to calm JOHNNY*) Johnny. (*Then to DOVE*) Dove, I want to speak to Johnny alone. (*DOVE, giving JOHNNY a triumphant look, exits.*) Johnny, I don't want you to be riding him so hard. Dove tries, but he's stupid. If God had wanted him bright He would have made him that way. We're all poor worms. You're getting above yourself. God is going to send you a dire punishment for your pride.

JOHNNY: Yes, sir.

MR. LAPHAM: One trouble with you is you haven't been up against any boys as good as yourself . . . or better. Because you're the best young one on this wharf, you think you're the best one in the world. (*Anxious to be on with his work, JOHNNY hardly listens.*) And boy, don't you go get all fretted up over what's after all nothing but an order for silver. It's sinful to let yourself go on over worldly things. Work's over for the day.

JOHNNY: *What?*

MR. LAPHAM: Yep. It always was the old-fashioned way to start Lord's Day at sunset on Saturday, and I've decided to re-establish the habit in my house.

JOHNNY: Mr. Lapham, we've *got* to work this evening. We've promised Mr. Hancock.

MR. LAPHAM: I doubt God cares even a little bit whether Mr. Hancock has any silver. It's better to break faith with him, isn't it, than with the Lord? (*MR. LAPHAM exits as JOHNNY disobediently returns to his work.*)

(*Having overheard previous conversation, MRS. LAPHAM enters from opposite side of stage.*)

MRS. LAPHAM: Sabbath or no Sabbath, that sugar basin is going to be done on time. Johnny, how many more work-hours will you need?

JOHNNY: Seven . . . maybe. I can get two Monday morning.

MRS. LAPHAM: You shall have them. I'm not letting any old-fashioned, fussy notions upset the best order we've had for ten years. And if Mr. Hancock is pleased, he may come again and again. Tomorrow, Papa is to be at church all day. That's where you get them five hours, Johnny . . . tomorrow afternoon. (*Urgently*) Darest to, Johnny?

JOHNNY: (*Hesitating only slightly*) I darest. (*To himself as lighting changes to his spotlight*) But working on the Sabbath is against the law as well as the Bible. I might very well go to the stocks or to Hell for it!

Next morning, Sunday.

(*CILLA rushes into shop as lights return to normal.*)

CILLA: Ma, there's a man looking at our chimney.

MRS. LAPHAM: (*Frightened*) How's he dressed?

CILLA: Seafaring man.

MRS. LAPHAM: No seafaring man ever objected to a little Sabbath-breaking. (*Then, firmly*) But mind if you see any deacons or constables. (*CILLA quickly exits to return to her guard post. MRS. LAPHAM goes to work station. JOHNNY is busy with his two wax models for handles as he stands by piping hot furnace. MRS. LAPHAM is trying to help.*)

(*DOVE enters and stands at distance watching them.*)

JOHNNY: (*In commanding manner*) Not the draft yet, Mrs. Lapham . . . now get to work with the bellows. (*JOHNNY embeds his wax models in wet sand and checks fire, as she pumps bellows.*) Look sharp, Mrs. Lapham!

MRS. LAPHAM: Yes, Johnny.

JOHNNY: Now fetch me the crucible.

MRS. LAPHAM: (*Crossly, to DOVE*) Don't just stand there. You know which crucible he needs, boy?

DOVE: I'll get her down. (*Goes to crucibles, choosing one after looking to see if JOHNNY is watching. Takes it to JOHNNY, who puts silver ingots in it and sets it on top of furnace so silver can melt.*)

JOHNNY: (*To MRS. LAPHAM*) Look sharp. Hold the master's old watch where I can see it. (*MRS. LAPHAM holds chain so JOHNNY can see watch.*) The silver will soon be ready. (*Watching JOHNNY, DOVE is snickering to himself out of way of action.*)

MRS. LAPHAM: (*Watching silver*) Johnny, isn't it time to pour? Look, the silver is melted and begun to wink. (*His right hand outstretched, JOHNNY moves* toward crucible. Just as he touches it, crucible breaks apart and silver spills over furnace like milk. As JOHNNY instinctively reaches toward it, his hand comes down into molten silver on furnace. Jumping back, screaming and holding his stiffened right arm, he faints on shop floor. MRS. LAPHAM kneels next to JOHNNY and pats his cheeks.) Johnny, Johnny! Can you hear me?

(Having heard screams, CILLA rushes in and stops horror-stricken by what she sees.)

MRS. LAPHAM: Quick, get a pan of flour from the barrel. (CILLA numbly, but quickly, obeys, scooping out flour into nearby pan. DOVE's snickering has turned to cowering fear. CILLA takes pan to JOHNNY's right side, and MRS. LAPHAM plunges his burned hand into it. To CILLA) Get him some brandy. (CILLA runs to jug of brandy, quickly fills cup and rushes back to JOHNNY's side. MRS. LAPHAM grabs the cup from her and lifts his head to pour down draught.)

CILLA: Ma, (Terrified) shall I run for Dr. Warren?

MRS. LAPHAM: No . . . no . . . oh, wait, I've got to think. I don't want any of them doctors to know we was breaking the Sabbath Day. And we don't need no doctor for just a burn. Cilla, you run along the wharf and you fetch that old midwife, Gran' Hopper. These old women know better than any doctor how to cure things like this. Johnny, how you feel? (DOVE watches in silence.)

JOHNNY: All right.

MRS. LAPHAM: Hurt yet?

JOHNNY: Not yet.

MRS. LAPHAM: It will . . . Johnny . . . it will . . . later. (JOHNNY looks away from her. As general lighting changes to half, CILLA is left in single spotlight.)

CILLA: (To herself, full front) Oh, Johnny, I'm sorrier than I was ever sorry before.

Afternoon, six weeks later, late August, 1773.

(As lighting slowly returns to normal, MRS. LAPHAM and DOVE exit, MR. LAPHAM enters. JOHNNY, whose burned hand has now grown together, rises and crosses to MR. LAPHAM as he is called. JOHNNY's thumb crosses his palm, with forefingers bent over thumb in a loose fist, forming a hook. His hand must remain in this position throughout play.)

MR. LAPHAM: (Calling) JOHNNY! Come boy, over here. Sit down. (Sits) Soon it will be September. Summer is over. I promised your mother to feed and clothe you, keep you in good discipline, and as far as your ability permitted to teach you the silversmith's arts and mysteries . . . I . . . I never had a boy so quick to teach, but now . . . I can't keep my contract with you. I can't teach a cripple-handed boy to be a silversmith. (*JOHNNY quickly puts his right hand behind his back or in his pocket.*) You're a bright boy, Johnny. Maybe a rope-maker or a butcher could teach you his craft. That hand of yours will soon be strong enough.

JOHNNY: But I want to be a craftsman who makes *beautiful* things.

MR. LAPHAM: Don't you see, Johnny? With that hand sort of doubled in on itself, it's not possible. You must be content to find a respectable trade where a bad hand won't matter too much. You've got to learn a way to support yourself. (*JOHNNY starts to look at his hand, but quickly thrusts it into his pocket.*)

JOHNNY: You're right. I have to find something I can do.

MR. LAPHAM: I don't want you to feel hurried about leaving us, Johnny. You're just about earning your keep here by the odd jobs you do. You look about you quietly and find a trade to your fancy and a master you think you'd like. (*Stands, starts to exit*) And one more thing I have on my mind.

JOHNNY: Yes, sir.

MR. LAPHAM: I want you to forgive Dove like a Christian.

JOHNNY: Forgive him? Why?

MR. LAPHAM: Why, when you asked for a crucible he handed you the old cracked one.

JOHNNY: You mean . . . (*Standing*) . . . he did it on purpose?

MR. LAPHAM: No, no, Johnny, he only meant to humiliate you. He tells me that he was so offended by your Sabbath-breaking he thought it fitting that you should learn a lesson. I can't help but admit I'm encouraged to see that much piety in *one* of my boys.

JOHNNY: (*In strangled voice*) Mr. Lapham, I'm going to get him for that . . .

MR. LAPHAM: Hush, hush, boy. I say, and the Bible says, forgive. He was real repentant when he told me. Never meant to harm you. He was in tears.

JOHNNY: He's going to be in a lot more of those tears before I'm done with him. That scabby, white louse, that hypocritical . . .

MR. LAPHAM: Hold your tongue, boy. I thought misfortune had taught you patience.

JOHNNY: It has. If I have to, I'll wait ten years to get that scoundrel, Dove.

(*DOVE enters unexpectedly. He and JOHNNY stare at each other in silence. MR. LAPHAM shakes his head in disappointment.*)

JOHNNY: I will find another place for myself.

DOVE: Will Mr. Johnny Tremain be so kind as to fetch us a bucket of drinking water? Mrs. Lapham says I am too valuable to leave my workbench. She told me I was to send you. Look sharp, boy. Look sharp. (*JOHNNY moves to another area as the lighting changes to half. DOVE exits.*)

JOHNNY: (*In spotlight, thinking aloud, determined*) I will find a place for myself . . . the newspaper . . . *The Boston Observer* . . . Mr. Lapham says they are trying to stir up discontent in Boston, but maybe the paper's not as wicked as he says. (*As lighting returns to normal, JOHNNY crosses to another area.*)

The Boston Observer newspaper and printing office, Boston. Late morning, late September, 1773.

(*RAB, wearing cloth apron similar to leather one JOHNNY wore as apprentice, enters carrying package of food.*)

JOHNNY: Does your master need another boy to help with the newspaper?

RAB: Perhaps. (*Sitting down and taking from package his claspknife, bread and cheese, he studies JOHNNY briefly.*) Are you hungry? (*JOHNNY nods.*) Sit down. (*Sits*) My master's wife . . . she's my aunt . . . always sends over more than I can eat. (*Extending knife toward JOHNNY*) Here, help yourself to bread and cheese. (*JOHNNY hesitating, finally removes his bad hand from his pocket to steady bread while he awkwardly cuts left-handedly.*)

JOHNNY: I'm looking for some sort of work I think I could do well in . . . even with a bad hand.

RAB: (*As JOHNNY begins eating*) That's quite a recent burn.

JOHNNY: I did it last July. I am . . . I *was* apprenticed to a silversmith. I burned it on hot silver.

RAB: I see. So everything you are trained for is out?

JOHNNY: Yes. I wouldn't mind so much being a clock maker or instrument maker. But I can't and I *won't* be a butcher nor a soap-boiler.

RAB: No?

JOHNNY: I've *got* to do something I like, or . . . or . . .

RAB: Or what?

JOHNNY: I just don't know. I can't think.

RAB: More cheese? (*JOHNNY nods and takes proffered cheese.*) I don't know how you'll make out. Of course, you can get work . . . if you'll take it.

JOHNNY: I know . . . unskilled work.

RAB: Yes, work you don't want.

JOHNNY: (*Confidence renewed after eating*) But I feel sure I'll get something. By the way, I'm Johnny Tremain.

RAB: (*Nods to JOHNNY*) Name's Rab. My uncle, Mr. Lorne, owns this printing office. He is the master here. There is some work here you could do. Not the sort that teaches a boy a skilled trade. Just horseback riding for us . . . delivering newspapers all over Boston and around. Nothing you'd want.

JOHNNY: Mr. Lapham used to say your newspaper is wicked.

RAB: Wicked? (*Chuckling at thought*) Why?

JOHNNY: He thinks *The Observer* is trying to stir up discontent here in Boston, so that the people will revolt against England.

RAB: But, don't you think we should be ruling ourselves?

JOHNNY: I hadn't thought about it.

RAB: The Whigs and Tories of these colonies are in the midst of a big disagreement about freedom.

JOHNNY: What's the difference between a Whig and a Tory?

RAB: The Whigs think that we shouldn't be taxed by the King of England, that we should choose our own leaders. Right now England is forcing us to pay a tax on tea, threepence the pound. But the Whigs say that we shouldn't be taxed at all, unless we vote for the men who tax us. That's what I think, too.

JOHNNY: What do the Tories stand for?

RAB: They believe that all differences of opinion can be settled with time and patience. Some of the Tories think it's all right to let the British Parliament break us down, stamp in our faces, take all we've got by taxes and never protest. They say we American colonies are too weak to get on without England's help and guidance.

JOHNNY: That's what Mr. Lapham thinks.

RAB: But, a lot of other people in Boston think the tax on tea is wrong. Three English ships loaded with tea are due in the harbor soon. I look for trouble.

JOHNNY: What will happen?

RAB: I don't know. But whatever does happen, I intend to be part of it. Some of us Whigs are members of the Sons of Liberty. (*Showing JOHNNY medal hung round his neck from string*) This medal means I am a member. We are willing to do whatever is necessary to have our own government, free of England. Even die. (*Pause, as his thoughts return to JOHNNY'S situation*) You haven't any folks?

JOHNNY: No.

RAB: I've got lots of relatives, but my parents are dead. (*As he clears away the rest of the food)* Well, you come back again. Here. (*Handing him his own coat)* To wear when you go looking for a new master.

JOHNNY: Thanks, Rab. (*Offers his left hand to shake. RAB takes it with his right.)* I'll come back all right . . . but not until I can tell you what a good job I've found for myself. (*As lighting changes to special on JOHNNY, RAB exits.)*

Shops along the wharf, Boston. October, 1773.

(*JOHNNY, standing full front, silently reacts to increasingly harsh rejections. Male VOICES are heard from different offstage locations.)*

MERCHANT: I cannot read your writing. You do not write clearly enough with your left hand. No work here, boy.

INSTRUMENT MAKER: We have no apprentice positions for you. Instrument makers must have two whole hands.

CLOCK MAKER: A crippled hand is of no use to a clock maker. Be gone, boy. (*JOHNNY becomes more and more discouraged. In his depression, he walks counter-clockwise, making small, full circle, ending in same spot where he stood when heard the VOICES.)*

Backstreet, Boston. Late night, October, 1773.

NIGHT WATCHMAN: (*Calling from offstage)* One o'clock and a warm fair night.

JOHNNY: (*Glances up toward sky)* Oh, Mother, Mother, how sorry you would be if you knew that I can't get decent work. With this ruined hand, I can't ever be a silversmith. I go into a shop and ask, "Do you need another boy?" The master asks why I no longer am apprenticed to the silversmith. When I tell him . . . I have a bad hand, he insists that I show him . . . other people in the shop want to see . . . I hate it . . . I thrust it out and everyone stares. (*Grimaces at memory)* The master always says he has no place for me . . . that I should know better than to waste his time. (*Weeping)* Where shall I go? What is to become of me? (*He lies down, weeping begins to subside.)* God has turned away from me. (*As the weeping stops, he falls asleep. NIGHT WATCHMAN calls from offstage after few seconds of silence.)*

NIGHT WATCHMAN: Six o'clock in the morning and all's well. (*JOHNNY awakens and sits in silence for brief moment with his arms hugging his knees.)*

JOHNNY: (*Stands)* There is no other way. I must go to Merchant Lyte as Mother told me. He will help me, for I am Jonathan Lyte Tremain, his kin. (*Lighting turns to day, JOHNNY exits.)*

Merchant Lyte's counting house, Boston.
Mid-morning, several weeks later, mid-October, 1773.

(*SEWALL enters from opposite direction, carrying large ledger and quill pen, sits and begins busily writing. Almost immediately JOHNNY enters, crossing to SEWALL who ignores him.*)

JOHNNY: (*After pause, nervously clears his throat*) Excuse me. Is Merchant Lyte here?

SEWALL: What do you want?

JOHNNY: It is a personal matter between myself and Mr. Lyte.

SEWALL: (*Pleasantly*) Well, even if it is personal, you'd better tell me what it is.

JOHNNY: It is a family matter. I cannot, in honor, tell anyone except Mr. Lyte.

SEWALL: (*Shrugs*) Look here, boy. (*Indicating offstage room*) He'll be coming in here with work for me. You can speak to him then. (*He returns to his writing, quill pen scratching. JOHNNY sits down to wait.*)

(*MERCHANT LYTE, papers in hand, enters and crosses to SEWALL.*)

MERCHANT LYTE: Enter these today, Sewall. (*Handing him the papers, turns around to return to his office without seeing JOHNNY, who jumps up and crosses behind LYTE. SEWALL continues to write during scene, trying to ignore mounting conflict between JOHNNY and LYTE.*)

JOHNNY: Merchant Lyte, sir?

MERCHANT LYTE: (*Surprised and annoyed at intrusion*) What is it? And who, for heaven's sake, are you?

JOHNNY: Sir, I'm Jonathan Lyte Tremain. (*LYTE pauses to study JOHNNY and opening jeweled snuff box, he takes snuff.*)

MERCHANT LYTE: Well?

JOHNNY: My mother, sir. (*Voice shaking slightly*) She told me . . . she always said . . .

MERCHANT LYTE: (*Sneezes and blows his nose*) I can go on from there, boy. Your mother on her deathbed told you that you were related to the rich Boston merchant?

JOHNNY: Yes, sir, she did. But, I didn't know you'd know.

MERCHANT LYTE: *Know?* I didn't need to *know.* It is a very old story . . . a very old trick, and will you be gone . . . or shall I have you flung out?

JOHNNY: (*Stubbornly*) I'll stay.

MERCHANT LYTE: (*Not raising his voice*) Sewall. (*SEWALL comes instantly to his side.*) Show him out, Sewall, and happens he lands in the water, you . . .

ah! Can baptize him with my name . . . ah . . . ha, ha! (*Picking up a handful of papers, he turns to go.*)

JOHNNY: I can prove to you one thing, Mr. Lyte. My name is Jonathan Lyte Tremain.

MERCHANT LYTE: (*Turning to face JOHNNY*) What of it? Any back-alley drab-tail can name her child for the greatest man in the colony. There should be a law against it, but there is none.

JOHNNY: (*His temper beginning to go*) You flatter yourself. What have you ever done except be rich? Why, I doubt even a monkey mother would name a monkey child after you.

MERCHANT LYTE: (*Gives long whistle*) That was quite a mouthful. Sewall!

SEWALL: Yes, sir.

MERCHANT LYTE: You just take this monkey child of a monkey mother out, and drown it. (*SEWALL, grabbing JOHNNY by shoulder, pulls him to door.*)

SEWALL: Yes, sir. (*JOHNNY fiercely shakes himself free and rushes back to LYTE.*)

JOHNNY: I don't want your money. Now that I've met you face to face, I don't much fancy you as kin. (*LYTE signals to SEWALL to run for help. SEWALL exits.*)

MERCHANT LYTE: Your manners, my boy, are a credit to your mother.

JOHNNY: But facts are facts, and I've a cup with your markings on it to prove what I say is true.

MERCHANT LYTE: (*Very interested*) You've got a cup of mine?

JOHNNY: No, of *mine*.

MERCHANT LYTE: So . . . so you've got a cup. Will you describe it?

JOHNNY: I can do better than that. I can show you. (*Drawing bag from inside of his coat, hands cup to LYTE*) Here it is.

MERCHANT LYTE: (*Carefully examining cup*) This cup is one of my set. It is perfectly obvious that this cup is now in the hands where it belongs. The question is how was it ever separated from its fellows?

(*SEWALL and SHERIFF enter quietly, unbeknownst to JOHNNY.*)

MERCHANT LYTE: In fact . . . (*LYTE'S voice is louder.*) I declare this to be the very cup which was stolen from my home on Beacon Hill on the twenty-third of last August. Sheriff, I order you to arrest this boy for burglary. (*SHERIFF steps forward and grabs JOHNNY by one shoulder.*)

SHERIFF: What is your name, boy?

JOHNY: Johnny Tremain. That is, Jonathan Lyte Tremain.

SHERIFF: Johnny Tremain, alias Jonathan Lyte Tremain, of King and Bay

Colony, I accuse you of stealing a standing cup that was taken away from the home of the most respected Jonathan Lyte on the twenty-third day of August in the year of our Lord one thousand seven hundred and seventy-three.

JOHNNY: This is not true.

SHERIFF: A boy can be hanged for stealing a silver cup. You can explain to the judge.

JOHNNY: (*Full horror; accusation is now very real*) Very well, I can and I will.

MERCHANT LYTE: Boy, where did you get that coat?

JOHNNY: It was lent me.

MERCHANT LYTE: Lent you? By whom, pray?

JOHNNY: A printer's boy. I don't know his last name. Down at *The Observer* office . . . he's called Rab.

MERCHANT LYTE: That coat is worth money. Do you think someone whose last name you admit you don't know would lend you a coat?

JOHNNY: It doesn't sound like . . . but happens it's true.

MERCHANT LYTE: Sheriff, look into this.

SHERIFF: I certainly will, Mr. Lyte. (*As he snaps handcuffs on JOHNNY'S wrists*) Good day, Mr. Lyte. I'll get this scamp locked up. (*LYTE and SEWALL exit as SHERIFF and JOHNNY cross to another area where SHERIFF places JOHNNY in imaginary cell, closes and locks cell door.*)

Jail cell, Boston. Morning, the next day.

SHERIFF: Now, boy, you've got some rights. Who do you want notified? Got any kin except the Lytes? Relatives? Parents?

JOHNNY: I've no one. But will you please tell that boy down at *The Observer?* He's a tall boy . . . all I know is that his name is Rab.

SHERIFF: The one you stole the coat off? I was going to look him up tonight.

(*SHERIFF exits, passing RAB who quickly crosses to cell door.*)

RAB: (*Seeing exhausted, defeated JOHNNY seated on low stool*) Johnny? I'm here. (*JOHNNY crosses to jail cell door. Both he and RAB are filled with sense of urgency about situation.*) The sheriff came by the newspaper office today. I told him that I had *given* you that jacket. But he said Merchant Lyte is accusing you of stealing a silver cup. (*JOHNNY nods.*) That's a serious charge.

JOHNNY: But, I didn't steal it. It's *my* cup. My mother gave it to me the day she died. She said if ever there was nothing left and God Himself had turned away His face from me, then I was to go to Mr. Lyte and show him the cup. He would know by the markings on it that I was a member of his family. I couldn't find a job and there was nothing else to do.

RAB: We need to think what we can do *now*. Lyte's crooked, you know.

JOHNNY: That's what I've heard.

RAB: Did you show your cup to any living soul sometime before August twenty-third? If there *is* someone, that person's testimony could prove you had owned the cup before Mr. Lyte's was stolen.

JOHNNY: (*Thinking; then, triumphantly*) Cilla Lapham. I told *her* . . . that was July. Come to think, it was the very day Mr. Hancock ordered his sugar bowl. It was the second day of July . . . that was a Tuesday.

RAB: That's all you'll need. Mr. Lyte was a fool to bring so flimsy a charge against you.

JOHNNY: What do you suppose he meant when he said he had expected something like me turning up as soon as that cup was stolen?

RAB: I don't know what goes on in that clever, bad head, but perhaps he thinks you are an imposter and stole the cup first to back up some claim of kinship. Will Cilla come to court for you?

JOHNNY: If her mother will let her.

RAB: Lyte may have already found out you were Mr. Lapham's apprentice. If he has, he'll go to them and make sure no one will come to your defense.

JOHNNY: How could he do that?

RAB: You said your master gets little work these days, didn't you? Well, Lyte may place a large order for silver in exchange for a promise that all the Laphams stay away from your trial.

JOHNNY: You mean *bribe* them? I could hang!

RAB: (*His thoughts racing ahead as he plans strategy*) Now for a lawyer. I'll talk to Josiah Quincy. He often writes for *The Observer.*

JOHNNY: Josiah Quincy? But . . . Rab, you can't do that . . .

RAB: You don't want him? He's the best young lawyer in Boston.

JOHNNY: I could never pay him.

RAB: You don't understand. If he agrees to help you, he'll give you his time for nothing. I'll ask him to come see you. I'll also meet Cilla, behind her mother's back, if necessary.

JOHNNY: It all depends on Cilla, doesn't it?

RAB: Well . . . pretty much.

JOHNNY: What if Mrs. Lapham locks her up?

RAB: Lock her up so I can't get her out? Boy, I could even get her out of this jail.

JOHNNY: Rab, do you think I have a chance of winning against Lyte?

RAB: I hope so, Johnny. He's sly, though. When the merchants agreed not to import any English goods until the Stamp Act was repealed, he was one of the first to sign . . . then imported secretly. Sold through another name and made more money. Sam Adams spoke to him privately . . . scared him. He says he won't do that again. He's trying to ride two horses . . . Whig and Tory. I can't stand men like Lyte, who care nothing for anything except themselves and their own fortunes. Playing both ends against the middle.

JOHNNY: I'd never have picked him for a relative.

RAB: Nor I. I will find Cilla and Mr. Quincy. If I can get her to testify, your case will be dismissed. Good luck, Johnny. (RAB rushes off.)

JOHNNY: (Afraid, he calls after RAB) Rab! (As JOHNNY stands alone in pool of light, he is surrounded by VOICES from his trial which create one speech, moving quickly and building in intensity.)

Courtroom, Boston. Two days later.

(Offstage VOICES.)

JUSTICE DANA: (After pounding of gavel) Do you swear to tell the truth, the whole truth . . . so help you God?

MERCHANT LYTE: This is the stolen cup; I've tied a red ribbon on it.

JUSTICE DANA: Mr. Lyte, could it not be possible that this boy is related to you? Could his story be true?

MERCHANT LYTE: There is too much thieving going on in Boston. These apprentices are getting out of hand.

JUSTICE DANA: Is there proof that Johnny had the cup before August 23rd?

CILLA: Weeks before Mr. Lyte said his cup was stolen, Johnny showed it to me, sir.

JUSTICE DANA: There is not the slightest evidence that the accused stole the cup. Johnny, you may take the one with the red ribbon. It is yours to keep. (Pounding of gavel. With great joy, JOHNNY runs offstage.)

The Observer office. Morning, two days after the trial.

(*RAB enters and begins working, followed almost immediately by JOHNNY who rushes in, relieved and out of breath.*)

JOHNNY: I was hoping you'd be here. (*Checking outside door to see if his pursuer is in sight*) I think I outran him.

RAB: Who?

JOHNNY: One of Merchant Lyte's sea captains.

RAB: What happened?

JOHNNY: I was just in Lyte's counting house on the wharf. I went there to sell him my cup, but he grabbed it away from me. He ordered a sea captain to take me far away from Boston on one of his ships. I slipped away from them and ran here.

RAB: Why did you go there of all places? You saw how angry Lyte was in court when the judge dismissed his case against you.

(*MR. LORNE enters behind JOHNNY and stops to listen.*)

JOHNNY: I needed money. I was going to sell the cup to a silversmith, but I thought Lyte would pay more since it's a cup from his own family.

RAB: Uncle Lorne, this is Johnny Tremain. (*LORNE shakes JOHNNY's left hand as RAB continues.*) He's the one who came here looking for work last week . . . I told you about him.

MR. LORNE: The boy who went to court and won his case against Merchant Lyte? (*RAB nods. To JOHNNY*) Rab told me it was quite a trial. Old Lyte was very unhappy about losing his case.

JOHNNY: How did you convince Mrs. Lapham to let Cilla come to court?

RAB: I just showed her a letter from the governor. I pointed to the seal on it and said, "Governor's orders." Since she can't read, she didn't know it wasn't about Cilla. It was really an order to all printers in Boston to quit their rebellious publications. I didn't give her time to find someone who could read it. Cilla and I just ran to the trial.

MR. LORNE: So after the trial you returned to Lyte to sell him your cup?

JOHNNY: Yes. But he took it away from me and kept it. He refused to pay me anything. Do you still want a horse boy, Mr. Lorne?

MR. LORNE: Why, yes . . . sometime . . . but there's no hurry.

JOHNNY: Will I do?

MR. LORNE: Will he do for a rider, Rab?

RAB: Yes.

MR. LORNE: Very well, Johnny. Of course, you know how to ride?

JOHNNY: I've never been on a horse in my life.

MR. LORNE: Well, then I'm not sure . . .

JOHNNY: (*Interrupting*) I can learn.

MR. LORNE: What do you think, Rab?

RAB: He can learn, Uncle Lorne.

MR. LORNE: All right, boy. (*Gently guiding him to stool, LORNE gestures for JOHNNY to sit.*) I can't do more than sleep you, feed you, and clothe you. But you'll have the first four days of the week to pick up money for yourself, or to go on with your learning. I've got a fine library. You can sleep in the loft above the shop where Rab sleeps. *The Observer* is out every Thursday and the papers are delivered in Boston on that day. For the next two days, you will ride through the surrounding towns. Rab will draw you a map.

JOHNNY: (*Eagerly standing up*) I'm ready to start.

MR. LORNE: Rab, go over to Queen's stables and show Johnny that horse you bought. Take the afternoon off and give him a lesson in falling off without getting hurt.

RAB: (*Pushes JOHNNY down on stool to get friendly head start*) Come, Johnny, I'll race you to the stables. (*Exits with JOHNNY close behind*)

(*As LORNE exits, loud, sharp knocking is heard at door and continues until JOHNNY returns from different area, sleepily tucking shirt in breeches.*)

Early morning, six weeks later, Sunday, November 28, 1773.

JOHNNY: (*Calling back over his shoulder*) I'll see who it is, Rab.

(*JOHNNY opens door to SAMUEL ADAMS.*)

SAMUEL ADAMS: (*Radiant with happiness*) Look you, Johnny. I know it's Lord's Day, but there's a placard I must have printed and posted secretly tonight. The Sons of Liberty will take care of the posting, but Mr. Lorne must see to the printing. Could you run across and ask him to step over? And Rab . . . where's he?

(*RAB enters sleepily as JOHNNY quickly exits in another direction.*)

RAB: Mr. Adams—What's happening?

SAMUEL ADAMS: (*Very excited*) The first of the ships, the *Dartmouth*, is entering the harbor.

RAB: (*Now fully awake*) So they really dared send them?

SAMUEL ADAMS: Yes.

RAB: And the first has come?

SAMUEL ADAMS: Yes. God give us strength to resist. That tea cannot be allowed to land. (*Handing RAB text for placard*) Here 'tis, Rab.

RAB: I can set that in no time. Two hundred copies?

SAMUEL ADAMS: (*Nodding*) Good.

RAB: They'll be fairly dry by nightfall.

(*JOHNNY returns with LORNE.*)

SAMUEL ADAMS: (*Shaking hands with LORNE*) Ah, Mr. Lorne, you do realize that you are in grave danger, for everyone knows you are a Whig printer and a leader in this revolt against England.

MR. LORNE: I will go on printing, begging the people of Massachusetts to wake up and resist this tyranny before it's too late.

SAMUEL ADAMS: Without you printers, the cause of liberty would be lost forever.

MR. LORNE: (*His voice shaking with emotion*) Without you, Sam Adams, there would not have been any belief in liberty to lose. I will, as always, do anything . . . you wish.

SAMUEL ADAMS: The Boston selectmen will meet today and I am calling a mass meeting for tomorrow. This is the placard I will put up. (*Taking text from RAB's hands and reading*) "Friends! Brethren! Countrymen! The detested tea shipped for this port is now arrived in the harbor. Every friend to his country is now called upon to meet at Faneuil Hall, at nine o'clock this day, so we can make united and successful resistance against the English who expect us to pay tax on this tea." (*Quietly, in explanation of the situation*) Up to the last moment, we will beg the governor's permission for the ships' return to London with their cargo. We have twenty days.

MR. LORNE: Shouldn't the members of *The Observers*' group meet here tonight?

SAMUEL ADAMS: Most definitely. There are *private* decisions to be made before the mass meeting tomorrow at nine.

MR. LORNE: Johnny, you know who the members are. (*Anxious to please ADAMS, he urges JOHNNY to leave.*) Why don't you go now?

SAMUEL ADAMS: (*Stopping him*) No . . . noon tomorrow will be better. That will give the members time to get home from church. And as usual, Johnny, make no stir. Ours is a secret group. No outsider must know who we are. (*Preparing to leave*) Until tonight, Mr. Lorne.

MR. LORNE: (*Seeing ADAMS out*) Until tonight. (*ADAMS exits.*)

RAB: Come, Johnny, we've work to do. (*In dim light, RAB and JOHNNY exit. LORNE is alone in spotlight. He studies text he is to print, realizing gravity of situation, he reads aloud.*)

MR. LORNE: "...The detested tea shipped for this port is now arrived in the harbor ... a united resistance against the English who expect us to pay tax on this tea ..." It must be done.

(*Carefully protecting paper, LORNE exits as JOHNNY and RAB enter from other direction with stools and supplies for their task.*)

Room above The Observer office. That night.

(*JOHNNY and RAB sit, add slices of oranges and lemons to bowl of punch that they are preparing for Observers' meeting. As they stir mixture, ADAMS, HANCOCK, JOSEPH WARREN, PAUL REVERE and LORNE enter another part of the stage in dimmed light, and sit on crates or stand about, engaged in mimed conversations. As full lights come up on JOHNNY and RAB, sounds of men fighting are heard in street outside. JOHNNY goes to window and looks down.*)

JOHNNY: Look, Rab. (*RAB continues his work.*) What's happening out there?

RAB: (*Looking, too, but less concerned than JOHNNY*) A Tory probably refused to let the Sons of Liberty post one of Sam Adams' placards on his property. (*Shrugs shoulders*) So, they are beating him.

JOHNNY: (*As he returns to his place near RAB*) Do they have to *beat* him?

RAB: Yes, sometimes.

JOHNNY: Why?

RAB: (*Impatiently*) I don't know. Some people can't be persuaded any other way. (*The sounds of the beating stop.*)

JOHNNY: What will they decide ... (*Gesturing toward them*) ... those men in the meeting?

RAB: You heard Sam Adams. If *possible*, the ships will sail home again with their tea. We've got twenty days.

JOHNNY: But if the governor won't agree?

RAB: He won't. Least that's what Sam Adams thinks.

JOHNNY: And then ... what next, Rab? (*Blows and oaths are heard from outside, and then, noises stop. JOHNNY crosses again to window and looks down.*)

RAB: (*Looks at JOHNNY. Pauses, then as if to distract him*) As soon as we go in with our punch, we'll know. Look at Sam Adams. If he looks pleased as an old fox with a fat chicken in his mouth, we'll know they've agreed to violence if everything else fails. He doesn't care much anymore about our patching up our differences with England.

JOHNNY: But the king's warships are in the harbor. They'll protect the tea. They'll fight.

RAB: We can fight, too. Farmers and craftsmen in towns all over Massachusetts are preparing for war.

JOHNNY: Are those the "Minutemen"? (*RAB nods.*) Why are they called that?

RAB: Because we will stop anything we are doing at a minute's notice to go fight. (*RAB is finishing punch by pouring in wine, sprinkling in clove and nutmeg and breaking up cinnamon bark, and stirring bowl with ladle. After tasting and approving it himself, he offers ladle to JOHNNY.*) Taste it, Johnny. That Madeira Mr. Hancock brought with him is first-class. (*Low moaning and sobbing comes from beaten Tory in street. JOHNNY listens to moans, then seeing ladle, pushes it aside and walks away.*)

JOHNNY: No. (*Shaking his head*) I can't now, Rab. (*RAB pours proffered drink back into bowl and lays ladle inside. LORNE calls, as lights come up on meeting room.*)

MR. LORNE: Boys, ready with your punch?

RAB: (*Quietly to JOHNNY as he lifts up bowl*) They made up their minds fast tonight. I rather thought they would. (*Moving to meeting area, RAB places bowl near HANCOCK, MODERATOR OF MEETING. Adams, who was whispering in HANCOCK's ear, stops as JOHNNY and RAB enter.*)

SAMUEL ADAMS: Aha! And here, my good men, is the finest punch in Boston. (*RAB and JOHNNY begin ladling out punch into cups.*)

JOHN HANCOCK: Yes, thanks to Rab and Johnny. Come all. Paul Revere, I've never known you to hesitate about a good punch. (*REVERE takes cup and nods to HANCOCK.*) And Joseph Warren, do have a cup. (*WARREN takes cup and LORNE follows.*)

PAUL REVERE: First, we must drink to the day on which the tea must be destroyed or returned to England.

SAMUEL ADAMS: I do not believe that there can be any permanent, friendly agreement with the British Parliament. Gentlemen, we may be embarked on the path to war. And I am for it!

JOHN HANCOCK: (*Raising cup in toast*) Here's to December the sixteenth, the day we will destroy the tea!

ALL: Hear! Hear!

JOSEPH WARREN: Johnny? (*Crossing to him as some watch, others confer*) You

know I am a doctor . . . I've been noticing your hand. May I see it? (*Instantly,*
JOHNNY thrusts it behind him, backs away and says nothing.) You don't want me
to look at it? (*JOHNNY shakes head again, unable to talk about accident. Crossing*
to JOHNNY, WARREN grasps JOHNNY's upper arms in gesture of encouragement.)
Never mind, Johnny. God's will be done.

SAMUEL ADAMS: (*Clapping slightly for attention*) Gentlemen, tonight we have
made our decision and know how the tea can be destroyed, if the ships are
not allowed to return to England. Here we have with us two boys in whom
we have implicit trust. If it is the wish of the assembled members, I suggest
we tell them of our plans tonight. The time will be up before we know. All
who agree say, "Aye."

ALL: Aye, aye. (*Several sit.*)

SAMUEL ADAMS: (*To RAB and JOHNNY*) First, raise your right hands. (*RAB does*
so. JOHNNY raises his left hand, then lowers it as he slowly raises his right hand.)
Swear never, for as long as you live, to tell anyone of the secret matters now
trusted to you. Do you so swear?

RAB and JOHNNY: (*Not in unison*) I do.

SAMUEL ADAMS: There's no chance . . . not one . . . those ships will be allowed to return. The mass meetings which will be held almost daily de-
manding the return of the tea are to arouse public opinion and to persuade
the world we did not turn to violence until every other course had been
blocked to us. When the twenty days are up, those ships are going to be
boarded. That tea will be dumped in Boston Harbor. For each ship, the
Dartmouth, the *Eleanor* and the *Beaver,* we will need thirty stout, honest,
fearless men and boys. Will you be one, Rab?

RAB: Of course, sir.

SAMUEL ADAMS: Could you find other boys for the night's work? Strong
and trustworthy boys . . . for if one ounce of tea is stolen, the whole thing
becomes a robbery . . . not a protest. Boys who can keep their mouths shut?

RAB: (*Nodding*) Yes, Mr. Adams.

PAUL REVERE: I can furnish twenty or more from my neighborhood.

SAMUEL ADAMS: Not one is to be told in advance just what the work will be,
nor who the others are, nor the names of the men who instigated this tea
party . . . that is, the gentlemen gathered here tonight. Simply, as they love
their country and liberty and hate tyranny, they are to gather in this shop
on the night of December sixteenth, carrying with them such disguises as
they can think of, and each armed with an ax.

RAB: It will be as you say.

JOHN HANCOCK: Each of these groups must have a good leader, a man who can keep discipline.

PAUL REVERE: I'll go, for one.

JOSEPH WARREN: Look here, Paul, it has been decided this work must be done by apprentices, strangers , . . folk little known about Boston. Many people here know Paul Revere. If you are recognized . . .

PAUL REVERE: I'll risk it.

MR. LORNE: Come boys. Leave us to our planning. (*As JOHNNY and RAB cross to another area, MEN exit with their cups, whispering together in pairs. LORNE carries off the bowl. Preparing for sleep, JOHNNY and RAB unroll their pre-set pallets next to each other. RAB lies down immediately.*)

JOHNNY: (*Standing by pallet*) Rab?

RAB: Uh?

JOHNNY: Those boys you promised to find. (*Sitting, looking at RAB*) I'm going to be one.

RAB: You're the first one I'd choose.

JOHNNY: (*Urgently*) But my hand . . . What will we have to do?

RAB: Chop open tea chests. Dump tea in the harbor.

JOHNNY: Rab?

RAB: Hummmm?

JOHNNY: How can I ever chop?

RAB: You've twenty days to practice. Logs in the backyard need splitting. Do those. Now get to sleep. (*Pause. JOHNNY looks over at RAB ready to continue conversation.*)

JOHNNY: Rab . . . ? (*Realizing RAB is already asleep, JOHNNY sighs, looks at him once again, then turns over to go to sleep.*)

(*As lights dim to "night" actors playing "INDIANS" enter from all directions, criss-crossing stage, cautiously on the alert. In ensuing action JOHNNY exits as three BOYS cross to RAB who has rolled up pallets and picked up soot and red paint for their faces.*)

The Observer office. Night, December 16, 1773.

(*Over their costumes, three BOYS have pulled on nightcaps, old frocks, torn jackets or blankets with holes cut for their arms, speaking occasionally to each other in whispers. They wait excitedly to have their faces streaked with soot and red paint after RAB streaks his own.*)

BOY ONE: (*Pointing to another BOY in disguise and laughing*) Look at John there.

BOY TWO: (*As if in competition*) Look at me! (*Struts about for all to see*)

RAB: (*In commanding whisper*) Quiet! All is lost if we are discovered. (*Immediately quiet, BOYS listen as RAB continues with quiet intensity that rivets their attention.*) Remember, we are listening for a whistle from Johnny Tremain. He is at the meeting at Old South Church waiting for a signal from Sam Adams. When that comes, you will go quickly to the group of men near one of the ships. The leader will be wearing a white handkerchief around his neck and a red string about the right wrist. To him you will each say softly, "Me know you." He will know you are there to help. From then on, you will do as he says. Do you understand? (*ALL nod.*) Good. (*A low WHISTLE sounds.*) There it is! (*BOYS are instantly alert.*) Get your axes and to the ships . . . may God protect us! (*With overlapping lines, BOYS excitedly exit.*)

BOY THREE: Boston Harbor a teapot tonight!

BOY ONE: Salt-water tea!

BOY TWO: Hi, Mohawks, get your axes and pay no taxes! (*As RAB watches them exit, JOHNNY rushes in.*)

JOHNNY: (*Crossing immediately to RAB*) I came as fast as I could. I was afraid you would already have gone. (*RAB streaks his face with soot.*)

RAB: We're late, Johnny. Come, follow me . . . we'll go through the backways. Run.

(*As JOHNNY and RAB quickly exit, three BOYS, REVERE and "INDIAN" enter, carrying axes, looking for boxes of tea to destroy. JOHNNY and RAB do not return to participate in Tea Party action, so they have time to remove their "Indian" face paint for next scene. Six TOWNSPEOPLE enter to form silent, watching, anonymous crowd.*)

Deck of ship. Later that same night.

(*Tea Party participants break open boxes, some with great effort. REVERE gives brief commands in gesture. Played in dim light, scene is generally quiet as "INDIANS" and BOYS split crates and dump tea into harbor. MUSICAL UNDERSCORING can be used to enhance urgency and danger of situation.*)

PAUL REVERE: (*As their work nears completion*) Clean the deck.

(*After hurried cleaning of the deck with blankets or hats, "INDIANS" and BOYS with axes on their shoulders march in triumph. A "hurrah" goes up from TOWNSPEOPLE, and FIFE MUSIC from offstage plays them home.*)

(*As "INDIANS" near exit, BRITISH ADMIRAL enters and takes C stage. FIFE MUSIC stops.*)

BRITISH ADMIRAL: Well, boys, (*In cold, ominous voice*) you've had a fine, pleasant evening for your Indian caper, haven't you? But hear me . . . you've got to pay the fiddler yet. (*Slight pause as REVERE and "INDIANS" return stare of ADMIRAL, and then, along with TOWNSPEOPLE, gradually begin to exit silently as though in rejection of ADMIRAL's lines. ADMIRAL, alone on stage, stands face front.*) Not one ship will enter or leave the port of Boston until the tea is paid for, except His Majesty's warships. Merchants' counting houses will be closed; hundreds of sailors, rope-makers and dockhands will be out of work, because the great ships which have been bringing wealth to Boston will be idle. The paralysis will soon spread out and include everybody. No one will have money to live, because there will be no jobs. (*ADMIRAL, still standing alone in spotlight*) Boston will be starved into submission. The leaders of your revolt will be hanged. Mark my words, you will live to regret this tea party of yours. (*Loud beat of DRUM accents end of his sentence, followed by drum roll which continues as he exits.*)

(*Simultaneously, as ADMIRAL exits, and from opposite side of stage four, BRITISH SOLDIERS, muskets on shoulders, march on stage, commanded by the OFFICER. RAB and JOHNNY enter after them to watch their maneuvers and breaking of ranks.*)

Boston Common. Afternoon, about six months later, June 1, 1774.

RAB: Uncle Lorne is upset. He says the printers will not be able to go on with the newspapers. He won't be able to collect subscriptions, or get any advertising. He won't be able to buy paper or ink.

JOHNNY: Mr. Lorne won't give up. He'll find the paper and ink to keep on printing about our wrongs . . . and our rights . . . until he drops dead at the press . . . or gets hanged. (*Watching SOLDIERS*) I wonder how many British soldiers are here.

RAB: (*Also watching*) *Too* many. Boston is full of them, sent over on warships. General Gage is in charge now. It's all because of the dumping of the tea, you know. (*JOHNNY nods.*) But, we're getting ready for them.

JOHNNY: Like going home to Lexington every week to drill with the Minutemen.

RAB: (*Nods*) We have no uniforms, but we don't need uniforms. Not like we need guns. Our muskets are so old and unreliable that we can't hit rabbits ten feet away from us. And we can't buy any decent guns, that's the worst. (*Pause. SOLDIERS have left their muskets leaning against box, near RAB and JOHNNY.*) Just look at these. (*Pointing, and then, touching lock on one*) This lock is a new ... (*SOLDIER leaps over to RAB, grabs a gun and knocks him down. After hitting RAB with the butt of the rifle, SOLDIER stands next to him.*)

JOHNNY: (*Kneels down to other side of RAB*) Rab, are you all right?

BRITISH OFFICER: (*Crossing to them*) Spectators are not to intrude. (*To JOHNNY*) Get back! (*JOHNNY stays beside RAB. The SOLDIERS either watch action or silently converse among themselves.*) What was he doing?

JOHNNY: Just looking at a gun. (*Still kneeling as he helps RAB*)

BRITISH OFFICER: Touching it?

JOHNNY: Well ... yes.

BRITISH OFFICER: And only got hit? He got off easy. Filching a soldier's arms is a serious misdemeanor. It's a wonder my soldier didn't kill him. (*Gestures to SOLDIER to relax and join others*)

RAB: (*Thickly*) I hadn't thought to filch it. Not a bad idea. Guess I'll ... guess I'll ... (*JOHNNY grabs RAB's arm as he attempts to strike OFFICER.*)

BRITISH OFFICER: (*Laughing at him*) Now boys, you forget talk like that. You remember that *we* don't like being here in Boston any better than you like having us. I'd rather be with my wife and children in London. We're both in a tight spot. But if we keep our tempers and you keep your tempers, why, we can fix things up between us somehow. We're all one people, you know.

JOHNNY: Yes ... (*Softly*) ... we are. (*JOHNNY and RAB turn to leave.*)

BRITISH OFFICER: By the way, do either of you know a boy with a good horse who'd ride for me? I've a cousin who lives over in Cambridge. Haven't had a chance to send him a letter. I'll pay well. (*RAB nods at JOHNNY.*)

JOHNNY: I've got a good horse.

BRITISH OFFICER: Fine. Come to me at noon today. (*JOHNNY nods.*) I'm living with the Shaw family in North Square. (*Returning to his SOLDIERS*)

JOHNNY: If I can get started carrying messages for him, others may follow. Could be we'd learn things Sam Adams and the others would like to know. They wouldn't dare send their own men to carry letters ... they'd be afraid somebody might kill them.

RAB: And did you hear him saying he was staying with the Shaws? Of course, the Shaws had no choice. It isn't fair. We shouldn't be forced to take England's soldiers into our homes. Sam Adams is right, Johnny. (*As JOHNNY and RAB exit*) We must stand up for our rights!

BRITISH OFFICER: 'Tention. Hup, forward, march. (*As they march off, drums are heard, underscoring action. Volume of off-stage drums increases to heighten feeling of impending conflict.*)

(As SOLDIERS exit, RAB and JOHNNY enter immediately, placing crates in room for meeting of the Observers.)

Room above The Observer office. Night, five months later, November 1774.

JOHNNY: I wonder how long it will be before the British soldiers march out of Boston . . . and war begins.

RAB: God knows, God and General Gage. Maybe not until next spring. Armies always move in the spring. But before then, I must have a good gun in my hands. I almost bought one from a farmer yesterday.

JOHNNY: (Interested) A farmer? How?

RAB: He thought he had tricked a soldier into selling his musket. When the farmer came with the money, they arrested him. They caught me, too, because the farmer told them he was going to sell it to me.

JOHNNY: How'd you get away?

RAB: Colonel Nesbit said I was just a child. "Go buy a popgun, boy," he said. They told me to go home.

JOHNNY: (Laughing) So all he did was hurt your feelings.

RAB: (With wry grin) Luckily, I didn't give my money in advance. I returned it to Uncle Lorne. (Absentmindedly) Their red coats will make good targets, all right.

JOHNNY: (Sobered by RAB's observation) I can't think of them as targets . . . yet.

RAB: I can. (Lights up on rest of stage as ADAMS, HANCOCK, WARREN, REVERE and LORNE enter meeting room. RAB and JOHNNY follow and remain in room, listening to men.)

JOHN HANCOCK: (To ADAMS) General Gage is surely getting ready to make war. He must think we are an easy enemy to outwit after his men seized our cannon and gunpowder. They simply got in their boats, rowed to Charlestown, and then, back to Boston. Not one shot was fired. It was all too late when thousands of armed farmers had arrived. The British by then were safe home again.

SAMUEL ADAMS: Yet, this rising up of an army of a thousand from the very soil of New England badly frightened General Gage.

JOSEPH WARREN: In other words, gentlemen, it was our fault. If we could only have known but two hours in advance what the British were intending . . . Then our men would have been there before the British troops arrived . . . instead of a half-hour after they left.

PAUL REVERE: We must organize a better system of watching their movements, but in such a way that they will not realize they are being watched.
(*WARREN crosses to REVERE, and they talk between themselves.*)

MR. LORNE: We must wish success to Mr. Adams at the Continental Congress
in Philadelphia. It begins tomorrow!

JOHN HANCOCK: But there must be some hope we can still patch up our
differences with England. Sir, you will work for peace?

SAMUEL ADAMS: No. That time is past.

JOHN HANCOCK: Well, then, if not for peace, what *will* we be fighting for?

SAMUEL ADAMS: To free Boston from these infernal redcoats . . .

JOHN HANCOCK: No, that's not good enough reason for going into a war.
Did any occupied city ever have better treatment than we've had from the
British? Has one rebellious newspaper been stopped . . . one treasonable
speech? I hate those infernal British troops spread all over my town as
much as you do. But we are not going off into a war merely to get them out
of Boston. Why are we going to fight?

SAMUEL ADAMS: (*After embarrassed silence*) We will fight for the rights of
Americans. England cannot take our money away by taxes.

JOHN HANCOCK: No, no. For something more important than the pocket-
books of our American citizens.

JOSEPH WARREN: For the rights of Englishmen . . . everywhere.

JOHN HANCOCK: Why stop with Englishmen? For men and women and
children all over the world. A man must be able to choose who shall rule
over him.

SAMUEL ADAMS: (*Bored, but pretending agreement*) Yes, yes, Hancock, but we
must end this meeting soon. I must have a good night's sleep so I will be
rested for my journey.

JOSEPH WARREN: (*Transfixed by HANCOCK's words*) Let him speak, Sam.

JOHN HANCOCK: (*Softly*) We are lucky men, for we have a cause worth dying
for. This honor is not given to every generation. (*Pause, as GROUP intently
listens, lost in his spell.*) You, Paul Revere, you'll give up that silvercraft you
love. God made you to make silver, not war.

PAUL REVERE: (*Smiling*) There's a time for the casting of silver and a time for
the casting of cannon. If that's not in the Bible, it should be.

JOHN HANCOCK: Doctor Warren, you've a young family. You know quite
well, if you get killed they may literally starve.

JOSEPH WARREN: I've thought of all that long ago.

JOHN HANCOCK: And some (*Turning to RAB*) will give their lives. All the years of their maturity. All the children they will never live to have. (*RAB looks straight back at HANCOCK, with arms folded across his chest and head flung back a little.*) We give all we have, lives, property, safety . . . we fight, we die, for a simple thing. Only that a man can stand up. That's all I have to say.

SAMUEL ADAMS: (*Standing, preparing to leave*) And well said, indeed. After tonight we will not meet again as a group. (*Shaking hands all around*) It is too dangerous, for I believe Gage knows all about us. (*Shaking hands with REVERE last*) What about that spy system you think you can organize here in Boston?

PAUL REVERE: Yes, Sam, I know of thirty craftsmen whom we can trust.

SAMUEL ADAMS: (*Nodding*) Get it set up! (*Then, to ALL observers*) May you get to your homes in safety. We will stay in contact by messenger. (*ALL exit, leaving JOHNNY and RAB, who then carry crates to one side.*)

RAB: (*Pausing in his work*) Johnny?

JOHNNY: Yes.

RAB: What was it he said?

JOHNNY: That a man can stand up.

RAB: Yes . . . that a man can stand up. (*Sighs*) As simple as that.

(*Lights out. RAB exits with some of crates. As JOHNNY starts off in other direction, he is greeted by BRITISH SOLDIER who will become DESERTER.*)

Street near stables. Afternoon, four months later, March, 1775.

DESERTER: (*Calling to JOHNNY*) Boy, haven't I seen you delivering *The Observer?*

JOHNNY: (*apprehensive*) Yes.

DESERTER: (*In confidential manner*) Come closer . . . you tell Mr. Lorne that many British soldiers are on your side. That's why there has been so much deserting.

JOHNNY: But deserters get shot . . . at the foot of the Common.

DESERTER: If they get caught. I'd leave the army if I could get a disguise and find a farmer who'd swear that I was his hired man as he took me past the guards at the edge of town.

JOHNNY: I think I can get you that . . . in exchange for your musket . . . (*To himself*) . . . for a friend of mine. (*To DESERTER*) But will you really leave the army?

DESERTER: Yes, I'd like to live here forever, have a farm of my own with cows. Poor folk can't have that in England.

JOHNNY: You'll get shot if they catch you.

DESERTER: Getting shot is what you have to expect in the army!

JOHNNY: Wait near the stables until I return. (*JOHNNY and DESERTER exit in opposite directions.*)

The *Observer* office. Afternoon, late March, 1775.

(*RAB, in apron, enters with stack of papers. JOHNNY hurriedly enters and crosses to him.*)

JOHNNY: (*Out of breath*) Rab! I just met a man who will give you his gun. He's a British soldier.

RAB: Shhh! (*Crossing to see if anyone was within earshot, JOHNNY follows, they whisper. Then, aloud.*) We can get him all that.

JOHNNY: That's what I told him! But in exchange, I wanted his musket.

RAB: Well?

JOHNNY: He's agreed. He's no soldier; he wants to be a farmer. What he likes is manure!

RAB: My uncle from Lexington comes in every Thursday for market. He'd take him out.

JOHNNY: We can get him clothes and a wig for a disguise, and I can hide them in hay at the stables. He can leave his musket and uniform in exchange. Where shall I tell him to meet your uncle?

RAB: At the market near Faneuil Hall . . . just at dusk, any Thursday. I'll tell Uncle to be watching for him.

JOHNNY: I'll go now. He promised to wait at the stables until I came to tell him about his ride. (*Starting to go*) Can we have the clothes hidden for him by tomorrow?

RAB: Yes, yes. You are a clever fellow! (*Beaming, JOHNNY exits. Calling after him*) Hurry, Johnny. Thank God, I may soon have a decent weapon in my hands!

(*Lights out and up immediately as CILLA, then JOHNNY, enter from opposite directions.*)

Boston common. Mid-day, one week later, early April, 1775.

JOHNNY: Cilla!

CILLA: (*Rushing to him*) Why, Johnny! I haven't seen you for so long. I thought I would see you often when I was getting our water at North Square.

JOHNNY: Are *you* carrying the water now? What about Dove?

CILLA: I don't live at home now. Merchant Lyte's daughter hired me to be her maid, so I am living with the Lyte family.

JOHNNY: Do you like them?

CILLA: Sometimes.

JOHNNY: I think all the Lytes are very disagreeable.

CILLA: But you *are* a member of the Lyte family. Merchant Lyte's daughter told me you are, that she did some checking, and she knows you are the grandson of Mr. Lyte who built their house.

JOHNNY: Does Merchant Lyte know?

CILLA: Now, he does. He's too sick to talk to you, but his daughter says she will write out the whole family history and give it to you.

JOHNNY: I want nothing of that family. Neither their blood nor their silver cup. There are more important things.

CILLA: They may be moving to London. They are very frightened in Boston . . . ever since the tea was dumped overboard from the ships. They think there will be a war.

JOHNNY: Will you go with them?

CILLA: Oh, no. I'll stay here and live in their house with the other servants.

JOHNNY: If they go, they won't ever return, because there *is* going to be a war, and we'll win. The Tories and England will lose. This is the end of one thing and the beginning of something else.

(*Somber roll of drums as BRITISH OFFICER enters, followed by two SOLDIERS, DESERTER, and behind him, one more SOLDIER. DESERTER's hands are tied behind his back, and hat partially covers his face. JOHNNY and CILLA watch transfixed as MEN march across stage and stop UC. OFFICER stands erect as SOLDIER removes hat from DESERTER and replaces it with black hood that covers his head and face. One SOLDIER leads DESERTER offstage.*)

JOHNNY: (*Stunned by reality of war*) Oh, Cilla, that prisoner is the man who gave me his musket for Rab. They *caught* him! He hated being a soldier. He just wanted to have a little land . . . to be a farmer. (*SOLDIER returns to formation without DESERTER. Immediately they arrange themselves in a firing line and take aim with their muskets. OFFICER quickly lowers his extended arm. Second roll of drums as shots are fired. JOHNNY and CILLA react to shots and turn away.)*

BRITISH OFFICER: Hurrup! Hep! Hep! (*SOLDIERS march offstage as JOHNNY and CILLA watch.*)

JOHNNY: (*Overwhelmed by situation*) But he only wanted his own farm and cows. (*CILLA sobs. JOHNNY comforts her.*) Rab got the musket he needed, but that soldier won't get his farm . . . only a grave on the Common. That much he'll have till Judgment Day.

CILLA: Oh, Johnny.

JOHNNY: I have never been afraid of a fight, Cilla. I've always been the first one to raise my fists. But now, I wonder if I have the courage for war . . . with its bloody death and terrible destruction. In a way, I'm glad my hand cannot pull a trigger. I'm afraid I'm a coward at heart. (*Pause*) Do you understand, Cilla?

CILLA: I do understand, Johnny. (*Pause*) But you are *not* a coward!

JOHNNY: (*Getting hold of himself*) I must go now. Can we see each other again soon?

CILLA: I hope so.

JOHNNY: Good. (*Slight nod and smile, exits as CILLA watches him go. As lighting changes, CILLA is left in spotlight.*)

CILLA: Oh, Johnny, I'm afraid, too. What is to become of us? (*After pause of reflection, CILLA exits as lighting returns to normal.*)

Joseph Warren's office, Boston. Night, ten days later, April 14, 1775.

(*REVERE and WARREN enter, deep in mimed conversation. As they cross to C stage, JOHNNY enters from other direction.*)

JOSEPH WARREN: Come in, my boy. (*Gesturing for JOHNNY to join them*) Any news!

JOHNNY: (*Breathless from running*) The British troops on the Common may be getting ready to move.

PAUL REVERE: How do you know?

JOSEPH WARREN. Did you overhear any orders from the officers?

JOHNNY: No, but the soldiers are drilling all the time, and they are sharpening their bayonets.

PAUL REVERE: That may mean something, Johnny . . . but it may not.

JOHNNY: They're even preparing their boats for a trip. Maybe over to Charlestown.

JOSEPH WARREN. Gage might have ordered the work on the boats to confuse the people of Boston. We really don't know where and when they are going to attack or how they'll get there.

JOHNNY: I still think something's going to happen soon.

PAUL REVERE: It seems likely. Since Hancock and Adams are both in Lexington, I'll row over to Charlestown, and then, borrow a horse to ride to Lexington, so I can tell them that a sizeable force may soon move. They had best hide themselves for a few days.

JOSEPH WARREN: And get word to Concord. The arms and ammunition there need to be hidden.

PAUL REVERE: That's right.

JOSEPH WARREN: Tell them that the moment the troops begin to move, either on foot or into those boats, we will send them warning in time to get the Minutemen into the field.

PAUL REVERE: But suppose none of us can get out? Gage knows we'd send word if we could. He may guard the town so well it will be impossible. (Thinking) The spire . . . (Exhilarated by his idea) . . . the spire of Christ's Church here in Boston can be seen clearly from Charlestown. Joseph, if the British go out by land, we must tell the sexton of the church to show one lantern. If they are in the boats . . . two. From Charlestown, I'll watch that spire. And come what may, I'll do my best to get a horse and tell all in Lexington and Concord what's happening. If I get caught as I row to Charlestown, another man should be ready to try to get out of Boston by land.

JOSEPH WARREN: What about Billy Dawes? He can impersonate anybody from a British general to a drunken farmer. That might help him get through the gates.

PAUL REVERE: (To JOHNNY) Do you know Billy Dawes?

JOHNNY: Yes.

PAUL REVERE: (Stands and turns to JOHNNY) You go ask him, Johnny. (JOHNNY stands, ready to depart.) He must leave soon. When the British move, we won't have a moment to lose. Tell him to watch the church spire for the lantern signal. And keep your ears open! (JOHNNY nods, shakes hands with REVERE and then WARREN, who stands. JOHNNY exits.) I must leave immediately myself!

JOSEPH WARREN: And I to Christ's Church to find the sexton. (Shaking hands with REVERE) Good luck, brave friend!

PAUL REVERE: May God help us get through this! (*He and WARREN exit in opposite directions.*)

Room above *The Observer* office. Morning, two days later, April 16, 1775.

(*JOHNNY enters, noticing that RAB is preparing to go to war.*)

JOHNNY: What are you doing, Rab?

RAB: I'm packing to leave Boston. I must report to Lexington.

JOHNNY: (*Feeling deserted and very unhappy*) But why do you go now? Nothing has started yet. I just saw (*Gesturing outside*) British soldiers going to church services. Everything is the same.

RAB: Don't be fooled. It isn't. I am leaving Boston for good, because I'm certain that the fighting will begin before the week is out. I intend to be in it.

JOHNNY: But how do you know? Maybe it won't even start . . .

RAB: You know it's coming, Johnny. As soon as the first shot is fired, no man of military age will get out of Boston. They'll see to it. It's now or never. (*RAB rolls extra stockings and shirt together into bundle.*)

JOHNNY: (*Hoping RAB will agree with him*) Then, I'll go, too.

RAB: No, you can't. You've got your work to do right here in town.

JOHNNY: There's not one reason why I can't leave for Lexington, except you don't want me. (*RAB laughs as JOHNNY gazes at him sullenly.*) You *want* to go.

RAB: Yes.

JOHNNY: Well, then—go!

RAB: I'm going as fast as I can. (*Begins humming to himself as he crosses to his pallet to get his jacket, then crosses to JOHNNY and puts hand on his shoulder.*) Good-bye, Johnny. I'm off.

JOHNNY: Good-bye, Rab. And good luck.

RAB: (*Smiles*) You're a good friend, Johnny Tremain. (*They start to shake hands but stop, briefly stare at each other, and then embrace "goodbye." RAB exits. JOHNNY hurries to watch RAB go. Lights dim partially except for spot on JOHNNY*)

JOHNNY: (*Speaking his thoughts aloud*) Oh, Rab, Rab! Don't you go. Don't you go! (*After few seconds of silence, knocking sound is heard.*)

(*WARREN enters as lighting returns to normal.*)

JOSEPH WARREN: I'm glad you are here, Johnny. We've just had word that the British will move out tonight by sea. They are planning to go no more than thirty miles away, so that means they are heading for Lexington and

Concord. They think they'll be back in Boston in two days, with the war over and the Minutemen defeated.

JOHNNY: Did Mr. Revere make it through the harbor to Charlestown?

JOSEPH WARREN: We think so, and Billy Dawes, too, since neither one has been brought back to Boston as a prisoner. I wanted you to know that I am leaving now to go to Lexington.

JOHNNY: I can go with you! Although . . . with my hand, I won't be of much use in the fighting.

JOSEPH WARREN: Let me see it, Johnny. (*Unhesitating, he extends his hand toward WARREN, who crosses to JOHNNY. WARREN examines hand, bending fingers and twisting thumb that has grown attached to palm of his hand in its healing.*) This hand is not so bad as you think. Burned, wasn't it?

JOHNNY: Yes.

JOSEPH WARREN: Was it kept flat while healing?

JOHNNY: No.

JOSEPH WARREN: I suppose your master called in some old herb woman to care for it.

JOHNNY: (*Nods*) A midwife, I think.

JOSEPH WARREN: These midwives! Any doctor in Boston would have known . . . you see, the thumb is pulled about like that, not because of injury, but by scar tissues.

JOHNNY: What do you mean?

JOSEPH WARREN: I mean that if you have the courage, I can cut through the scar to free the thumb.

JOHNNY: My hand good and free once more?

JOSEPH WARREN: I can't promise too much. I don't know whether you can ever go back to your silver work. But not even Paul Revere is going to make much silver for a while.

JOHNNY: Will it be good enough to hold a gun?

JOSEPH WARREN: I think I can promise you that.

JOHNNY: The silver can wait. When can you do it, Dr. Warren? I've got the courage.

JOSEPH WARREN: When you come to Lexington. I'll get some men to hold your arm still while I operate.

JOHNNY: No need. I can hold it still, myself.

JOSEPH WARREN: (*Putting hand on JOHNNY's shoulder*) I believe you can,

Johnny. But I must go now. Stay on in Boston a day or so longer to learn what you can about the plans of the British who are still here. Then, make your way to Lexington as you can.

JOHNNY: I'll be there. (*As they start to shake hands, JOHNNY offers his left one which WARREN does not take. WARREN then nods toward his crippled hand, which after pausing, JOHNNY offers. They shake.*) And if you see Rab, tell him I'm coming to fight, too.

JOSEPH WARREN: I will, Johnny. (*Lighting dims as soldiers rush to battle.*)

Lexington Green, Lexington, Massachusetts. Morning, April 19, 1775.

(*Sounds suggest battlefield with drum rolls, gun shots, battle cries. Criss-crossing stage, rushing to battle, BRITISH SOLDIERS run from UR to DL, exiting; MINUTEMEN run from UL to DR. Once offstage, MINUTEMEN immediately run back onstage and exit UL. One is shot and falls on second cross. Running in with MINUTEMEN, WARREN stops C stage to give medical aid to fallen MINUTEMAN. Battle is not seen, only men rushing to fight and wounding of one MINUTEMAN. JOHNNY enters as WARREN, kneeling, helps the MINUTEMAN.*)

JOSEPH WARREN: (*Noticing JOHNNY*) Johnny? I *knew* you would make it to Lexington somehow!

JOHNNY: (*Astonished*) Did they fight in this small place? (*In dim light as WARREN speaks, RAB, seated in a chair, is carried in by two MINUTEMEN who then exit. Dim spotlight remains on RAB.*)

JOSEPH WARREN: This is it. Seventy men stood up to face 700 soldiers. The British major called to the seventy: "Disperse ye rebels, ye villains, disperse! Why don't ye lay down your arms?" But they stood their ground. The British fired one shot, and then, a volley. Eight died and more were wounded. (*Wounded MINUTEMAN helped to his feet and exits.*) The others fled to join a larger group of Minutemen at North Bridge near Concord. The British had to face 1,000 of our men at that bridge. The Redcoats were soon in retreat, and our men fought them all the way back to Charlestown.

JOHNNY: As I left Boston, I saw boats full of wounded soldiers and officers coming back.

JOSEPH WARREN: The British will never again dare underestimate what our Yankee farmers can do!

JOHNNY: Do you know anything of Rab, Dr. Warren? Was he in the fight here in Lexington? I've got to find him. No one has been able to tell me.

JOSEPH WARREN: (*Sighs*) I'll tell you, Johnny. (*Pause*) Rab stood here . . . just about where we are standing now. He did not go when Major Pitcairn told them to disperse; he kept on standing with his musket in his hands.

JOHNNY: But after that, did Rab follow the British to Charlestown?

JOSEPH WARREN: No. He was wounded in that first volley. He got it pretty bad.

JOHNNY: You mean very bad, don't you?

JOSEPH WARREN: Yes, very.

JOHNNY: (*Full of grief, but in control*) I see. Where . . . ?

JOSEPH WARREN: He was carried to Buckman's Tavern. I saw him yesterday. I was about to go there now. But . . . don't expect too much.

JOHNNY: No.

JOSEPH WARREN: Rab played a man's part. Look that you do the same.

JOHNNY: I will.

(*JOHNNY and WARREN walk together into DR area as lights come up on RAB in armchair propped up with pillows and coverlet over lap. His musket is on floor next to chair.*)

Room in Buckman's Tavern, Lexington. Same day.

RAB: (*Smiling*) You got out of Boston all right?

JOHNNY: Yes. The British there are furious that we licked them so.

RAB: (*Coughs*) I've had a lot of time to think. Colonel Nesbit . . . remember? And he told me, "Go buy a popgun, boy." Well . . . a popgun would have done me just as well in the end. (*WARREN wipes his forehead with handkerchief.*) I thought I might have to stand up to them without a good gun in my hands. But thanks to you, I had it all right. And I never did get to fire it. They shot first. (*As JOHNNY sadly stares at RAB, WARREN wipes RAB's mouth.*)

JOSEPH WARREN: Steady, boy. Is it better so?

RAB: (*Whispering*) It is . . . better. (*Then quite naturally*) Johnny? (*JOHNNY crosses to RAB, kneels next to chair and puts his hand on RAB's arm.*)

JOHNNY: Yes, Rab?

RAB: I want you to have the musket. (*Gestures toward the gun*) That way, I can think of its going on.

JOHNNY: I'll take good care of it.

RAB: And there's another thing you can do for me.

JOHNNY: Anything.

RAB: Go find out if my cousins here in Lexington are well and safe.

JOHNNY: (*Remaining at his side*) I will.

RAB: Now, Johnny . . . now.

JOHNNY: Yes, Rab. (*As JOHNNY exits, he sees RAB smile at him and JOHNNY smiles in answer. Dim light remains on RAB as JOHNNY leaves Buckman Tavern area and enters Lexington Green with his head down, carrying RAB's musket.*)

JOSEPH WARREN: (*Bending over RAB*) Did you really want to send him away?

RAB: Yes . . . it is better that he leave.

(*RAB dies. WARREN carefully covers RAB's face with coverlet and stands a moment with head bowed. Exits from tavern to Lexington Green entering behind JOHNNY, who hears him and turns to face him.*)

Lexington Green. Moments later.

JOHNNY: Rab?

JOSEPH WARREN: (*Crossing to JOHNNY*) He's gone, Johnny. (*In sorrow, JOHNNY and WARREN hug briefly, then JOHNNY steps back.*)

JOHNNY: He sent me away because he knew he had to die?

JOSEPH WARREN: Yes. He knew. You remember the last Observers' meeting? I can't remember much of what John Hancock said, but I remember how his words inspired us. He said . . . (*Hesitating to remember*)

JOHNNY: I'll never forget it! He said . . . so a man can stand up. (*In silence, MINUTEMEN enter slowly from all areas, to frame JOHNNY in a half circle who, at DC, is facing front. Dim light remains on RAB's body until play's end. JOHNNY continues after MINUTEMEN are in place. Softly an offstage FIFE begins to play "Yankee Doodle."*) We may have to give up everything . . . even our lives . . . so that people may choose who it is shall rule over them. A great many are going to die for that. God grant that there will always be men good enough. Boys like Rab . . . No, *men* who will fight so that a man can stand up. (*Determined to carry on as Minuteman himself, JOHNNY with musket in hand is in pose reminiscent of famous Minuteman statue. Volume of FIFE MUSIC increases, filling silence as lights dim to darkness.*)

CURTAIN

Production credits from the premiere of *Johnny Tremain* and details concerning performance rights are included in the acting edition of the play as published by Dramatic Publishing.

Diverse Themes

la ofrenda (the offering)

The Transition of Doodle Pequeño

la ofrenda (the offering)

José Casas

Nine-year-old Alex Smith's parents were both in the Twin Towers on September 11, 2001. Now, even though he hasn't seen his *abuelita* (grandma) Marta since he was very young, Alex has to go live with her in Los Angeles. Alex is constantly reminded how different his life will be without his parents: *abuelita* makes Mexican food, which he doesn't like; he can't speak Spanish; and he thinks the traditional *calaca* skeleton that hangs in his new bedroom (named Califas by his mother when she created him as a young girl) is creepy. Though Marta tries to help Alex learn more about his heritage in order to stay connected to the spirit of his parents, he remains distant and disdainful; Alex would rather spend time alone with his baseball cards than with Marta making an *ofrenda* altar for the Day of the Dead. But Alex gets some unexpected lessons when the street-smart Califas comes alive and begins speaking to him. Through their tough love conversations Alex gains a deeper understanding of his family, his Chicano heritage, and himself. For the first time he talks with his grandma about his parents' deaths, and helps her make an *ofrenda* to honor them. Together Alex and Marta agree to embrace their memories, each other, and whatever might come next as they learn to live again.

la ofrenda (the offering)

characters

alex smith: a nine-year old boy; biracial: chicano and white.

marta torres: alex's abuelita (grandmother). she is chicana and is in her late fifties. she is a bus driver for the city of los angeles.

califas: calavera (skeleton). he is part history, part fantasy. he speaks in calo (urban spanglish). he wears a white oakland raiders football jersey and khaki pants.

time and place

los angeles, california, the fall of 2001.

scene 1

(*sitting in a recliner, located in her living room, is MARTA TORRES. she is a chicana in her late 50s. she is a bus driver for the city of los angeles. her recliner contains side pockets where items such as magazines, remote controls, etc., are contained. she is enjoying the show that is playing on the television.*

marta's phone rings. the phone lies in one of the side pockets, but marta is enjoying the show so much that she is ignoring the call. after a few moments, the phone rings again. an annoyed marta grabs the [cordless] phone and checks the caller i.d.; realizing who it is, she ignores the ring again and places the phone back in the pocket. the phone rings a third time. marta figures she will watch the show without any interruptions, but, this time, the ringing doesn't stop so marta finally succumbs to the noise and answers the phone.)

marta. yes, yes, comadre. ya se. it's just that i recorded last weekend's show of *sabado gigante* and you know much i love don francisco . . . the tape's been sitting in the vcr since sun— (*it is apparent that the voice on the other line is becoming frantic.*) calmate, comadre! no te aguites. it's too early in the morn-ing. drink your café. why are you acting so crazy!? (*beat; worried*) que? what are you talking about? that can't be. what? what channel? todos!? (*marta reaches into the side pocket and clumsily gets the remote control. she is struggling to turn off the vcr so she can watch the breaking news. she finally does so.*) how could this be happening? i don't understand. no entiendo. (*beat*) lupe, that's where— (*marta drops the phone; extended beat. in shock; to herself.*) jason. (*beat*) estrella . . .

(the room goes dark with the only light being that of the television screen. as marta stares at the television screen, the sounds of news reports [of the 9/11 tragedy] can be heard. after a few moments, the stage fades to black as the sounds linger and, eventually, fade.)

scene 2

(the sounds of rustling keys can be heard. after a few moments, we hear a door open, then close. marta enters and then crosses the living room and throws her keys on the magazine stand.)

marta. well . . . what do you think?

alex. . . .

marta. *(turning toward the door)* alex?

(beat. a young boy, ALEX SMITH, enters. he is holding a new york yankees lunchbox. alex looks stoically around the room. there is a noticeable tension in the air; beat.)

marta. it's all right, mijo . . . we're here. *(marta exits and returns with two suitcases. she places them on the floor.)* i know it's not much, but it suits me just fine. are you thirsty, mijo? i can get you some pepsi or maybe a little bit of water?

alex. . . .

marta. you know, sooner or later you're going to have to say something.

alex. . . .

marta. *(annoyed)* que vamos hacer con este muchachito? *(beat)* we need some light.

(marta opens up the blinds as light filters throughout. as she does the light from outside immediately "hits" alex's eyes. he responds by covering his eyes; dropping his lunchbox. marta crosses to pick up the lunchbox, but alex quickly gets in her way and blocks her; extended beat. alex picks up his lunchbox and begins looking around the house.)

marta. i see . . . well, why don't we put away our things? *(marta grabs her suitcase and exits to her bedroom. from offstage:)* this will have to do for right now, mijo. the rest of your things will get here by next week. *(beat)* you'll see . . . everything will turn out for the best. leave your bag in your room and i'll help you unpack later.

(marta returns. alex remains standing in the middle of the living room. he has no "real" recollections of the place. marta can sense this and is a bit saddened by the fact; beat.)

marta. si, como no . . . it's been so long, mijo. how could you remember. (*marta picks up alex's suitcase and takes it to the door of alex's bedroom. she places it on the floor.*) this room is yours. es para usted y para nadien mas. tu eres el rey de este espacio. entiendes?

alex. . . . (*extended beat*)

marta. haven't you been keeping up with your spanish?

alex. . . .

marta. but . . . your mama said she was teach— (*awkward beat*) well, mister. let's make sure that doesn't continue. we can't let that happen . . . not in los angeles. that's for sure. there are too many people in this city and they all speak a different language, mijo. you need to discover how to talk to the gente. (*proudly*) look at me. i do it all the time when i'm driving my bus . . . i know bits and pieces of, at least, ten languages: english, spanish, chinese, korean y chicano; que lo que sea. i'm going to teach you . . . okay?

alex. . . .

marta. como no, then . . . that's the plan, stan. (*alex looks away toward the window that looks over the backyard. marta notices and crosses to the window. encouraged:*) it's the backyard, alex. (*alex hesitantly crosses to the window.*) alejandro . . . it's not so bad, you'll see. (*beat*) this is your backyard, mijo . . . your own space.

alex. (*quiet desperation*) i miss home. (*extended beat. alex touches the window.*) when can i go back home?

scene 3

(*alex is sitting on his bed, his lunchbox is open. he is looking over some baseball cards. his abuelita knocks on the door. he quickly closes his lunchbox.*)

marta. it's abuelita, can i come in?

alex. i guess.

marta. it's such a beautiful day, alejandro. why don't you go out a—

alex. (*annoyed*) my name is alex. i told you a million times already.

marta. i'm sorry, alex . . . you're right. you did tell me. (*beat*) would you like some menudo? or some handmade tortillas? why don't i make you a special treat?

alex. i don't eat mexican food.

marta. then . . . how about a peanut butter and jelly sandwich?

alex. no . . . mom is the only one who makes my sandwiches. she does it a special way.

marta. okay, then i won't ask until you do . . . you're the boss, mijo. (*beat*) i like your lunchbox. where did you get it?

alex. . . .

marta. did your mama get it for you?

alex. i got it with dad . . . at the ball game.

marta. (*beat*) pues, like i said before, it's a beautiful day today. why don't we go out back and throw the baseball around? i know you like baseball.

alex. you're a girl.

marta. and . . . you're a boy. what's your point?

alex. . . .

marta. who do you think taught your mama to throw?

alex. yeah, right.

marta. de veras. she played with the boys until she was thirteen. she made all-stars every year. she was that good.

alex. no, she didn't!

marta. she loved baseball . . . and, she loved the dodgers. (*beat; excited*) that's it! why don't you and i go to a dodgers game? there's still a few more games lef—

alex. (*offended*) the dodgers suck!

marta. alejandro! we don't use that type of language . . . not in this house!

alex. sorry. (*beat*) the yankees are my team.

(*extended beat; marta begins looking around the room.*)

marta. i'm impressed, mijo. every time i come in your room it's always so neat.

alex. (*annoyed*) it's not my room.

marta. well, then, mr. smart mouth. whose is it then?

alex. it's mom's room . . . right?

marta. (*quietly*) it was . . . once.

alex. that's what i said.

marta. (*playing along*) i suppose you're right.

alex. i know i am.

marta. it belongs to your mama . . . until you decide that you want it.

alex. what?

marta. look around. the room's the same color it's always been—pink! (*beat*) i can't imagine a proud muchacho like you would enjoy sleeping in a pink girl's room.

alex. i don't care.

marta. estrella's dolls are still on the dresser. (*beat*) you know, i'm glad you don't want this room. these dolls make me happy. they should stay.

alex. whatever.

marta. (*pointing to the calavera*) well, then, i guess i'll just leave you and your friend alone.

alex. what? that thing?

marta. that thing is not a thing . . . that is califas.

alex. who?

marta. califas the calaca . . . the skeleton.

alex. i don't care what his name is.

marta. your mama built him in the fifth grade.

alex. i don't like it.

marta. she did it all by herself. califas was her best friend.

alex. that's lame!

marta. (*to califas*) that's all right, califas. he doesn't understand, but don't worry. no te preocupes . . . you are staying put.

alex. no way!

marta. si, como no que no way . . . i don't think so.

alex. but, he gives me the creeps, grandma.

marta. you called me gra . . .

alex. what?

marta. (*beat; pleased*) oh, nothing, mijo.

alex. so . . . you'll get rid of this thing.

marta. sorry, buddy. since this isn't your room. you have no say. you said so yourself.

alex. that's not fair!

marta. neither is life, mijo . . . lesson number one. (*beat*) i believe i will let you borrow this room . . . for the time being. (*marta exits the bedroom.*)

scene 4

(*alex is lying on his bed staring at the ceiling. marta is running around the other areas of the house in a mad dash — trying to get ready for work, preparing alex's lunch, and searching for her keys; all at the same time. she is dressed in her work uniform.*)

marta. (*yelling*) alex! hurry up, mijo. i'm going to be late for work. (*looking at her watch.*) chihuahua! i'm already ten minutes late. alex! do you hear what i'm saying!?

alex. . . .

marta. don't make me go in there!

alex. (*annoyed*) i'm coming!

marta. what do you want for lunch? ham sandwich. a burrito? que quieres!?

alex. nothing!

marta. you didn't want breakfast, so you have to eat lunch. it's important to be healthy, mijo!

alex. i'm not hungry!

marta. aye, muchacho! you're going to be the death of me! (*marta's search for her keys becomes more desperate and she begins to look in every available space possible; to herself:*) my keys! i can't believe this. cada mañana. every morning. it never fails. (*making the sign of the cross*) what i need is my own personal saint anthony, patron saint of lost keys and, in my case, lost causes. aagh! (*beat*) alex, come on! the school doesn't run on chicano time!

alex. what's chicano time!?

marta. aye, que la— (*marta finally finds her keys: the keys which are on a chain that connect to marta's belt loop. annoyed; to herself.*) no me digas! (*beat; yelling*) alex! let's go!

(*alex meanders into the living room. he is carrying his lunchbox.*)

marta. i thought you said you weren't hungry.

alex. i'm not.

marta. then . . . porque con el lunchbox?

alex. i don't use it for lunch. i just use it. (*beat*) for stuff.

marta. i don't have time to argue with you now. here. (*marta pulls out some money and then shoves it into alex's pocket.*)

alex. what's that for?

marta. for lunch.

alex. i said i wasn't hungry.

marta. just in case . . . okay. let's go.

(*marta walks out of the living room. alex's mood has changed from annoying to nervous. he just stands there in silence like a deer in headlights; extended beat. marta reenters.*)

marta. what's the problem?

alex. please don't make me go.

marta. alex . . . you have to go. it's your first day in the new school and you're already behind as it is. if you miss any more, they'll make you repeat the fourth grade.

alex. but . . . i don't know anybody.

marta. june from next door is in your class. you said, "hi" to her a few days ago.

alex. it's not my school.

marta. it is now.

alex. no . . . i don't feel so good. i think i got a fever.

marta. alex . . . no more games. andale! (*marta grabs alex by the arm. alex doesn't budge.*)

alex. (*yelling*) don't make me go! i don't want to go!

marta. alex, grandma's boss isn't going to be happy! do you want me to get fired!?

alex. i don't care!

marta. no more joking around!

alex. please, grandma!

marta. alex! you're going to school whether you like it or not!

alex. you can't tell me what to do! you're not my moth—

(*marta slaps alex across the face; the regret instantly sets in; awkward and extended beat. alex, face red, stares silently at his grandmother.*)

marta. (*tearing up*) mijo, i'm sorry! i didn't mean . . . please, tell me you forgive me?

alex. . . . (*extended beat*)

marta. mijo . . . things are different. they are never going to be the same . . . sabes? your parents are not coming back. (*beat; solemnly*) this is not a vacation.

alex. . . .

marta. we are the only ones left, mijo. entiendes que te digo? it's just me and you.

alex. (*takes a couple of steps back from marta, coldly*) i hate you.

(*before marta can finish her sentence, alex storms out of the living room to the outside world, leaving a distraught marta, alone with her thoughts; extended beat. marta exits.*)

scene 5

(*marta is talking on the phone with her comadre. she is upset. sympathy cards litter the floor. alex is lying on his bed and throwing a baseball into the air.*)

marta. what can i do? que hago, lupe?

(*alex throws the baseball up, but it drops and rolls onto the floor near the door of his room which is slightly opened. alex picks up the ball and hears that marta is talking on the phone. he quietly stands by the door and begins to eavesdrop on the conversation.*)

marta. what was estrella thinking? alejandro no sabe espanol . . . not one single word. lo puedes creer? a grandson of mine not knowing his own language? a daughter of mine not teaching him? it's a sin . . . and, that husband of hers. he wasn't even chicano. (*beat*) honestly, lupita. i can't believe you said that. (*angrily*) no! you don't understand. i am not overreacting! out of all the nice mexican boys in the barrio she could've chosen, she had to go out and find him . . . ese huerito. (*beat*) do you remember josé lopez? yes! juanita's son. si, the doctor. did you know that he was madly in love with estrella? the pobrecito would come to me, almost in tears. that's how much he loved her, but estrella only had eyes for him as a friend. such a respectful and intelligent boy and he turned into such a good-looking man, as well. how could estrella not marry that boy!? (*resentful*) jason was the one who took them away from me, lupe, and now look . . . my nieto wants nothing to do with me. his own abuelita. his flesh and blood. (*beat; fondly*) i can still remember holding alejandro in my arms on the day he was born, he was so small and beautiful and brown . . . my little angelito. (*beat*) i don't know what to think anymore. (*marta begins to tear up. she takes out a tissue and dabs her eyes; extended beat.*) it feels like i'm living with a stranger.

(*alex is "stung" by these last few words. he dejectedly crosses back to bed and sits down. he opens up his lunchbox and pulls out a picture of his parents; staring at it.*)

scene 6

(*it's late at night. the sounds of a rainstorm can be heard. alex is in his bed, but he is nowhere close to falling asleep. the audience can see the rain visualized on the clothesline. the silhouette of a tree swaying can also be seen. it is obvious that alex is*)

a little scared so he begins to stare at the ceiling; talking to himself in an attempt to
fall asleep.)

alex. old old yankee. willie randolph. second baseman. was on yankee cham-
   pionship teams of seventy-seven and seventy-eight. mariano rivera. greatest yankee reliever of all time . . . should have a cy young award, but doesn't.
   (*thunder is heard. alex covers up a little more.*) derek jeter. shortstop. drafted by
   the yankees in the first round. scored a hundred and four runs in his rookie
   season . . . dated mariah carey like for a few weeks.

(*louder thunder can be heard. all the lights on the street go out, leaving the bedroom*
pitch black; beat. the lightning begins. the light from the storm is reflecting
on califas, causing a "spooky" type of atmosphere. alex wants to call out for his
grandmother, but doesn't. the lightning and thunder get worse and alex becomes
more scared as it does. he notices califas shaking during one of the bursts of lightning.
after a few moments, alex gets out of bed. he slowly walks toward the papier-mâché
figure. he gets within inches of califas; beat. he touches califas, then jumps back a
few steps; beat. he walks up to califas and touches him again.)

alex. you're not so bad. you don't scare me. (*another round of thunder. alex jumps;*
   begins looking around the room as if he is checking for something. he walks back to
   califas, then pushes him.) you ain't so tough.

(*thunder. CALIFAS comes to life.*)

califas. hey, vato . . . what's your problem!?

alex. (*screaming at the top of his lungs.*) grandma!!!

(*alex runs away from califas and goes to the door but is having problems opening it*
so he runs back into bed and pulls the cover over his head. for a few moments, there is
nothing but silence, then the tapping of a tree against the window is projected. marta
enters disheveled.)

marta. alex. que pasa? what's the matter!?

alex. . . .

marta. digame . . . tell me.

alex. (*pointing to califas*) that thing . . . it's alive.

marta. what in god's sake are you talking about?

alex. mom's skeleton . . . it's alive.

marta. alex, mijo, this isn't funny. it's late and i'm tired.

alex. i'm not lying. it's true. he talked to me.

(*marta crosses toward califas and for the sake of alex, touches califas to prove to him*
that califas is not real. she looks at alex, shaking her head.)

alex. but, grandma . . . i saw it with my own two eyes!

marta. (*unconvinced*) if you say so. (*the wind gets a little louder and the tree branch begins hitting the window again. marta crosses to the window.*) aye, alex . . . look! it was the branch hitting the window, mijo. it's nothing to worry about. this big old tree scared your mama tambien when there was a storm . . . you were just imagining things.

alex. no, i wasn't, grandma.

marta. (*sits next to alex on the bed*) it's all right. i know how storms can be scary. it happens to all of us. it still happens to me once in a while.

alex. i know what i saw.

marta. in fact, i'm a little scared right now. how about you keep your abuela company and bunk up in my room tonight?

alex. no way . . . i'm not a little kid.

marta. all right, then. (*marta gets up and crosses to the dresser and pulls out a small flashlight. she goes and gives it to alex.*) like i said . . . your mama went through the same thing, but i'm leaving the door open all the same.

alex. (*annoyed*) i'm not scared.

marta. you're very brave, mijo. (*beat*) but . . . you know where i am if you need me. (*beat. alex nods his head.*) que dios de bendiga, mijo.

(*marta exits. the sound of the rain is still present. the scene ends with a vigilant alex pointing the flashlight directly at the inanimate califas.*)

scene 7

(*spotlight on an answering machine. VOICES can be heard.*)

marta's voice. (*os*) hola . . . you've reached the torres household. marta and alex are not in at the moment. por favor deja su mensaje y numero . . . please leave a message and a number where we can reach you. have a nice day. (*perky*) adios!

(*a series of messages can be heard.*)

message 1. (*os*) aye, comadre . . . the compadre and i just got back from zacatecas. doña elena told us what happened to estrella and her esposo. we are so sorry . . . if there is anything we can— (*message erased.*)

message 2. (*os*) hello . . . my name is thomas and i am a representative of rockford communications with a great offer for your entire family. for only thirty dollars a month you can g— (*message erased.*)

message 3. (*os*) is johnny in? johnny? can you hear me? johnny? who's the old broad on the answering machine? johnny, is this even your numb— (*message erased.*)

message 4. (*os*) hello . . . miss torres. this is matthew debarry from the offices
   of randle, miller and duncan. this message is in regards to the estate of
   jason smith and estrella torres-smith. we've made numerous calls to your
   residence but have not been successful in reaching you. please, miss torres,
   i know that this must be a difficult time for you, but these matters have to
   be addressed in a timely fashion. you can fax over the documents i fed-exed
   you last week or you can call our office if you have any questions. our number again is 212— (*the machine stops. the play button is pressed.*)

answering machine voice. (*os*) you have one saved message.

scene 8

(*in the darkness, the smell of incense fills the stage. a mexican corrido can be heard in
the background. lights go up. there is an altar in honor of dia de le muertos/day of the
dead in the living room. it's partially built. marta places a picture on the altar, alex
enters as the music fades away.*)

marta. how was school, mijo?

alex. . . .

marta. okay, i won't ask. (*beat*) what do you think?

alex. about what?

marta. about our ofrenda . . . our altar.

alex. it smells.

marta. that is the sage and copal, mijo. it helps purify our space.

alex. it still smells.

marta. haven't you ever seen an altar before?

alex. nope.

marta. your mama never told you the stories of our altares? never built one?

alex. no.

(*extended beat. marta places another item on the altar.*)

marta. how was school today?

alex. you just asked me that?

marta. yes, yes . . . of course, i forgot . . . i'm sure you have a lot of homework
   to take care of. if you need anything, well, ya sabes, you know the deal.

(*marta turns her back to alex and begins working on the altar again. alex begins
walking to his room and turns around curiously; beat.*)

alex. i don't get what the big deal is?

marta. the yearly offering to the ancestors is very important, mijo.

alex. you do this every year?

marta. si dios quiere. (*beat*) so . . . are you interested in helping your abuela?

alex. i didn't say that.

marta. your mama used to help me all the time. she was a great helper. i think you would be, too.

alex. i'd mess it up.

marta. nonsense.

alex. plus . . . it's just a bunch of junk anyways.

marta. junk? junk means trash and this is not trash. (*annoyed*) entiendes, muchachito.

alex. all right. what's this stuff? whatever.

marta. it's not whatever . . . these are the treasures we offer up in prayer.

alex. like in church?

marta. almost, but not quite.

alex. what's the point?

marta. it's for dia de los muertos . . . the day of the dead. (*marta grabs a sugar skull and places it on the altar.*)

alex. you do all this for halloween?

marta. no, alex . . . halloween has nothing to do with this day and has nothing to do with this altar . . . this is different. (*beat*) this is a part of who we are. get my drift? (*alex shrugs his shoulders.*) entonces . . . enough talking. it's time for you to help me with the altar.

alex. do i have to?

marta. no, but what would you rather be doing right now, helping me with this or doing your times tables?

alex. good point.

marta. (*pointing*) can you go over to the counter and get me that bowl of fruit, mijo? (*alex crosses and retrieves the bowl. he gives it to marta who begins strategically placing each piece of fruit on the altar. after a moment, she gives alex a pear.*) here . . . find the perfect spot for this.

alex. why are you asking me? i don't know where to put it.

marta. don't think about it . . . just feel where it should go.

alex. but . . . it's just a pear.

marta. to you, maybe . . . to me, this little piece of fruta is a picture i see every time i close my eyes. (*beat; fondly*) i place pears on the ofrenda in honor of your grandfather. it was his favorite fruit. when we were first courting—

alex. courting? you like basketball.

marta. courting is dating, mijo.

alex. (*embarrassed*) oh.

marta. your grandfather was so poor that he picked pears from his neighbor's casa and gave them to me as a gift because he couldn't afford flowers. aye, your abuelito. he may not have had a lot of money, but he sure was a charmer. (*beat*) you do remember your abuelito, don't you?

alex. no.

marta. not even a little?

alex. i don't remember.

marta. como no, mijo . . . you were just a baby. i forgot.

alex. (*hands the pear to marta*) i think, maybe . . . you should be the one who puts this on.

(*marta nods and then meticulously finds a space for the pear.*)

marta. alex . . . this is a time for remembering, this is why we are here. this altar . . . it is a remembering space.

alex. why remember?

marta. so . . . that we never forget.

alex. (*beat*) forgetting isn't such a bad thing.

(*marta crosses to alex and tries to hug him, but he steps away in refusal; extended beat.*)

marta. you must never think that, mijo.

alex. i don't want to re— (*beat*) never mind.

marta. it's okay to talk, alex.

alex. that's all anyone ever wants to do nowadays . . . talk.

marta. talking is what connects us.

alex. no it doesn't.

marta. that's not true, mijo.

alex. yes, it is. people talk all the time. i see it on the news. but, people talk so much they start to fight. when they start to fight, they hurt each other . . . and, then things change forever.

marta. it's not that simple, mijo. it's more complicated than that.

alex. i'm tired of talking. i'm tired of people thinking i'm weird because i don't want to talk. i'm tired of people i don't know asking me questions . . . why can't they just leave me alone!?

marta. alex.

alex. why do you let them do that to me, grandma? i thought you liked me.

marta. mijo . . . i love you.

alex. (*quietly pleading*) then . . . make them stop talking to me.

marta. i can't, mijo . . . it's for your own good. they need to talk to you.

alex. no more talking.

marta. they're trying to help you.

alex. they make everything . . . worse. (*beat; dejectedly*) are we done with this thing yet?

(*extended beat. marta picks up a small transistor radio. she hands it to alex.*)

marta. this is the last thing for the day. it belonged to your mama . . . she would sneak this into her room after her bedtime when she wanted to listen to the dodgers play on the radio.

alex. (*fidgets with the transistor radio. angrily*) this doesn't belong on your stupid altar!

(*alex runs into his bedroom with the transistor radio. a worried marta makes no attempt to talk to him. she begins to sob quietly.*)

scene 9

(*alex is sitting at his school desk and is aggressively coloring a picture. marta is in her living room dusting. she picks up a picture of her late husband: carlos.*)

marta. aye, viejo . . . i wish you were here. necesito to ayuda. i'm scared for our little alejandro. the school counselor says alex should be in therapy. he needs to figure out about all the things running around in his head. i feel so helpless. i don't know what to do or what to say. i'm just a bus driver. nada mas. i'm too old. i have a thousand dollars in the bank. es todo . . . how will i manage? (*extended beat*) aye, querido . . . alex drew this picture in school. it was as if he was drawing a nightmare. a child should never have to experience such cosas in a lifetime. when his teacher showed me the drawing, i wanted to cry, but i couldn't . . . not in front of him. i need to be strong. i need to protect my little angel. he's the only thing i have left of estrella. he's the only thing i have in this world. (*beat*) how can i be both mama and papa to him? viejo, if you were around maybe things would be different. a boy needs a man in his life, sabes? (*beat*) mi amor, please send me the strength i need to raise our grandson.

(*marta kisses the photo and returns it to its place. she exits; beat. alex finishes coloring his picture. projected on the clothesline is a drawing: two large buildings exploding with clouds surrounding the top portions of the building. the drawing also includes birds flying away, stick people figures running away from the buildings and, finally, the letters c.n.n. on the bottom. alex stares at the drawing for a bit, then crumples it up in a ball; throwing it to the ground. he dejectedly lays his head on the desk. lights fade to black.*)

scene 10

(*the stage is dark. war's "slippin into darkness" begins playing. lights up, but the room is still dimly lit. alex is sleeping. califas is dancing his slow "homeboy"-style dance; grooving to the music. little by little, the music gets louder to the point that it wakes up alex. a startled alex stands up in his bed.*)

alex. (*scared*) grandma said you weren't real!

(*califas ignores him; continues to dance. alex tries to yell out to his grandmother, but for some reason, the words won't come out. alex jumps off his bed and grabs a wiffle-ball bat and begins swinging madly even though he is across the room. califas finally notices alex and is amused by his horrible batting style; beat. califas snaps his fingers and the music abruptly ends.*)

califas. hey, little vato . . . don't playa hate the old school. simon . . . like take a chill pill . . . for real.

(*alex ignores califas and charges after him. alex begins swinging at califas with the wiffle-ball bat, but califas holds him away at arm's length. califas feigns being hurt.*)

califas. ouch . . . ooch . . . please, ese, stop . . . you're killin' me. (*alex continues swinging. after a few moments, a bored califas steps to the side and alex falls to the floor.*)

califas. (*looking down*) really, little vato . . . violence is no way to solve your problems.

alex. leave me alone!

califas. i can . . . but, i won't.

alex. please, mister.

califas. mister . . . i like the way that rolls off the tongue. it makes me sound respectable.

alex. (*standing up*) i'm gonna get my grandma.

califas. knock yourself out . . . she likes me better anyway.

alex. this has to be a nightmare. (*closing his eyes; to himself*) wake up. wake up. wake up!

califas. that ain't gonna help.

alex. who are you?

califas. boy, you better recognize! (*beat*) what's my name again?

alex. (*beat; cautiously*) califas.

califas. yeah . . . that's what i thought.

alex. what do you want with me?

califas. you bein' in this room. you're crampin' up my estilo . . . my style, homeboy.

alex. this is my room.

califas. it's not.

alex. it is.

califas. it's not.

alex. it is!

califas. it's estrella's room!

(*extended beat. alex walks over to the window and stares out into the sky.*)

alex. (*sadly*) estrella.

califas. estrella.

alex. she's my mom.

califas. she . . . was your mom, ese.

alex. (*angrily*) stop it!

califas. your dad, too.

alex. shut up!

califas. don't bite my head off, carnalito . . . i'm just the messenger.

alex. they're coming back . . . i know they are.

califas. this ain't no book, carnalito . . . you can't rewrite the ending.

alex. they could still be ali—

califas. they aren't.

alex. how can you be so sure?

califas. trust me on this one, little homey.

alex. maybe, someone will see her flier. maybe, they'll recognize their picture. (*beat; defeated*) maybe . . . they'll call me.

califas. they won't.

alex. you're lying!

califas. you can't live the rest of your life hopin' for something that ain't never gonna happen, carnalito.

alex. i want my mom and dad here with me.

califas. sorry, vato. those are the breaks. como se dice . . . es la vida.

alex. they can't be gone, i won't let them.

califas. all you're left with are the memories, carnal.

alex. don't say that.

califas. don't trip out, carnalito. it ain't such a bad thing . . . that's the beauty of memories. no one can take them away from us. not even the tax man . . . nobody.

alex. it hurts so much.

califas. chale, no one said the system was perfect. (*extended beat*)

alex. (*quietly*) so . . . you knew my mom?

califas. simon . . . the girl was all that and a bag of chips.

alex. can you tell me something about her? something i don't know.

califas. you shouldn't hear it from my lips.

alex. why?

califas. i'm not the family photo album, ese. i got responsibilities, sabes? i'm a popular vato this side of town.

alex. i want to know.

califas. you got a whole lifetime to find out, carnalito . . . besides, what you are askin' is not my job . . . that chore, little man, belongs to your abuelita.

alex. who says?

califas. this ain't burger king, carnalito . . . you can't have it your way.

alex. i don't want to. (*beat; sadly*) talk to her.

califas. that ain't an option.

alex. who says?

califas. destiny says so, ese . . . you know, blood is thicker than water and all that jive.

alex. you can't make me believe that!

califas. don't worry, little alejandro. i wasn't going to try. (*beat; annoyed*) shoot . . . do i look like a babysitter to you?

alex. . . .

califas. you need to keep your eyes on the road ahead of you, homey.

alex. what road?

califas. the one you must walk . . . it's the path from birth to death and all that lies in between.

alex. i don't get it.

califas. no one . . . ever really truly gets it, vato . . . that's the problem. we all gotta have a little faith and wing it. if you want to wing it alone, well, that's on your shoulders.

alex. i don't know her.

califas. really, carnalito . . . this is your abuelita we're talking about. i don't know why you're turnin' this into a mexican novela.

alex. where was she when i was growing up, huh?

califas. it doesn't work that way, carnalito . . . things aren't always what they seem.

alex. if my grandma really loved us she would've moved closer to us.

califas. and . . . leave her home? the only home she's known her entire life?

alex. yeah.

califas. you make it sound so easy, carnalito.

alex. it is.

califas. did you want to leave the only home you've known your entire life?

alex. (*beat; hurt*) no.

califas. see, little alex. that's the point. everybody has reasons for doin' the things they do. whether or not you know what those reasons are don't matter . . . you just gotta learn to respect those decisions.

alex. what do i do now?

califas. only you can answer that, carnal.

alex. but . . . i have so many questions.

califas. don't we all? (*checking an imaginary watch*) orale pues, vato . . . i gotta go. my girl's waitin' for me.

alex. please, don't go.

califas. (*begins to exit*) stay . . . go . . . chale, ese, you gotta make up your mind.

alex. my mom! (*beat; quietly*) my parents.

califas. (*stops; facing away from alex*) now is not the time, homey.

alex. (*unconvincingly*) we're going to be a family again.

califas. is that what you think?

alex. i hope so.

califas. hopin' doesn't pay the bills, alejandro.

alex. califas?

califas. yeah?

alex. just one thing. (*beat*) tell me one thing about my mom . . . anything.

califas. (*turns around toward alex*) just one thing? (*alex nods his head.*) i probably shouldn't be sayin this . . . pero, i do remember this one thing your mom used to do. she was about the same age you are right now.

alex. what? what was it?

califas. (*pointing*) look at the wall. what do you see?

alex. it's just a bunch of scribbling.

califas. i think not, ese . . . take a closer look.

alex. (*steps toward the wall, struggling to read what is on it.*) who is fer . . . ferna . . . fernando . . . valen . . . valentine?

califas. fernando valenzuela, fool!

alex. sorry . . . jeez. (*beat*) who is he?

califas. chale, little man. you're goin' to be the life of me! who is fernando valenzuela!? he's only the greatest pitcher in dodgers history.

alex. okay . . . so what?

califas. so . . . look at what's written underneath that.

(*a baseball box score is projected on the clothesline. it reads as follows:*)

4/27/81
SF 1 3 1
LA 5 9 0

alex. whoa . . . mom wrote down the box score. the dodgers beat the giants five to one.

califas. your grandparents loved takin' your mom to the ballgame . . . just like your parents liked takin' you, que no?

alex. (*sadly*) yeah. (*beat*) we went to a lot of them.

califas. sounds nice.

alex. i remember this one time. (*beat*) against our biggest enemies . . . the boston red sox.

califas. was estrella there?

alex. yep. (*extended beat*)

califas. something wrong?

alex. my dad caught a foul ball in his glove and he handed it to me. (*beat; fondly*) then . . . he kissed my mom in front of the whole stadium . . . they got their pictures shown on the video scoreboard.

califas. sounds nice . . . did the bronx bombers win?

alex. i don't remember. (*beat*) that was the last game we ever went to . . . we were supposed to go to the final home stand of the season against the orioles, but . . .

califas. i know, carnalito.

alex. the game was cancelled.

califas. even life gets rained out, alejandro.

alex. (*barely audible*) i guess.

(*califas pulls out a pen and crosses to alex; handing it to him. califas walks to the window. he stops.*)

califas. (*tenderly*) remember, homey . . . don't let the one game that wasn't . . . erase all those games . . . that were. (*beat*) it's not worth the effort.

(*califas quietly exits; extended beat. alex walks to the wall and begins writing a box score on the wall which is projected on the clothesline. it reads as follows:*

PPD RAIN
9/10/01
BAL 0 0 0
NY 0 0 0

lights fade to black except for a spotlight on the box score; beat. the light on the box score slowly fades away.)

scene 11

(*alex opens the door to the living room. he's just gotten out of school. he places his lunchbox and backpack on the floor, he looks around the room.*)

alex. (*calling out*) hello? is anybody home? grandma!?

(*alex begins searching the rest of the house. there is still no sign of his grandmother; beat. alex begins to look around at the ofrenda; truly looking at it for the first time. he looks at the pictures and candles. he begins circling the altar for a better glimpse. as he does, califas enters, but he follows behind alex; making sure not to be seen. after a moment, califas grabs a stash of tamales that are on top of the altar. califas makes a gesture and a silhouette of a coyote can be seen on the clothesline. a howling sound soon follows. a scared alex witnesses this and hides behind the altar. an amused califas exits.*)

alex. grandma?

(*no response; beat. alex relaxes. he notices a toy plane on the altar. he picks it up and begins playing with it. after a few moments, marta enters, holding a white plastic shopping bag. she remains silent as she watches alex play. at one point, alex crashes the plane. it is obvious by the expression on marta's face that this is a source of concern for her.)*

marta. hola, alejandro.

(a startled alex stops playing with the plane.)

alex. where were you?

marta. i was across the street at connie's house, mijo. i needed to borrow some things.

alex. i didn't see anybody . . . and—

marta. i know, mijo . . . i know.

(extended beat. alex attempts to give his grandmother the toy plane.)

alex. here.

marta. you hold onto it, mijo . . . i'll let you find a spot for it on la ofrenda.

alex. you sure?

(marta nods her head. alex meticulously begins to walk around the altar. he wants to make sure he finds the perfect area to place the plane on. as he does, the shadow of a plane can be seen flying on the clothesline.)

marta. mijo . . . we build this ofrenda to honor those who have come before us. it must always be respected. sabes?

alex. . . .

marta. we honor our ancestors . . . our people.

alex. what do you mean our people?

marta. well . . . i mean our parents.

(alex stops; beat. he resumes walking.)

marta. our parents' parents. our grandparents' parents . . . a long line that traces back to the beginning . . . it's to celebrate the lives of those we've loved . . . and, even for those we didn't.

alex. that doesn't make any sense.

marta. it means we should never . . . not love anybody, mijo.

alex. oh.

marta. that is why our ofrenda is here, it's filled with bits and pieces of the past—pictures, favorite foods; just about anything. these things remind us that time stops for no one. entiendes?

alex. i think so.

marta. it's all right, mijo . . . rome wasn't built in a day . . . there's no rush.

alex. grandma?

marta. si?

alex. (*staring at the toy plane*) why do people hate each other so much?

marta. not everybody hates ea—

alex. but . . . some do.

marta. yes . . . i suppose they do. (*alex finally finds a spot for the plane; beat.*) why that spot, mijo?

alex. (*looking at the ofrenda*) it's on a runway . . . see, those skull things are surrounding it, making sure it's safe . . . and if you look at their eyes it looks like they're waiting for it to take off. (*beat*) that's where it belongs.

marta. i think you're right, mijo. (*extended beat*)

alex. this plane is more than just a toy, isn't it, grandma?

marta. si, mijo . . . we must honor the people who were on those planes that day . . . and, for the people who were in those buildings that day, as well. they need to know that they are still in our hearts.

alex. (*somberly*) can i go to my room, grandma?

marta. if you want, but i was hoping you could help me with just one more thing.

alex. okay, i guess.

(*marta crosses to the plastic bag she had entered with. she walks to the front of the stage area, standing at the end of the marigold petal trail started from the back of the audience. a curious alex follows; beat.*)

marta. close your eyes.

alex. what?

marta. close your eyes and reach into the bag.

alex. i don't know about this.

marta. aye, calmate . . . the bag won't bite.

alex. okay, okay. (*alex closes his eyes and reaches into the bag.*)

marta. don't pull out anything . . . enjoy it.

alex. enjoy what?

marta. (*closing her eyes; pleased*) shh . . . smell.

alex. (*taking a sniff*) it smells nice.

marta. (*opening her eyes*) reach out of the bag.

alex. (*opening his eyes*) they're flowers.

marta. they are the leaves of the cempasúchil.

alex. man . . . i'm not even going to try and say that.

marta. it's nahuatl for marigolds.

alex. what am i supposed to do with them?

marta. you and i are going to make a trail of them . . . all the way to the altar.

alex. why?

(*at this point, a lit trail of marigolds can be seen on the clothesline; almost appearing like a string of bright orange-yellow christmas lights. we also see the silhouettes of the ancestors following the trail. marta grabs some petals. she begins dropping them as she slowly walks toward the ofrenda.*)

marta. just do what i do. (*alex begins to follow marta's instructions.*) the spirits need all the help we can give them if they are to reach the ofrenda.

alex. why would ghosts nee—

marta. spirits, mijo, not ghosts . . . ghosts are for cartoons.

alex. what's the difference?

marta. ghosts are meant to scare. spirits are meant to protect.

alex. if they're protecting us, why are we helping them out?

marta. that's the funny thing, mijo . . . for some reason, the sweet smell of the petals guide the spirit of our ancestors to the ofrendas.

alex. that's sorta cool.

marta. i know . . . you know what else?

alex. what?

marta. they're blind, too.

alex. (*amused*) get out of here!

marta. de veras! (*gesturing*) cross my heart.

alex. no way!

marta. the marigolds form a pathway for them.

alex. like the yellow-brick road?

marta. i never thought about it that way but, yes, in some sort of strange way.

(*marta and alex reach the altar. they use the final marigold petals and spread them around the altar. once they complete this, the trail of marigolds and the ancestors fade away from the clothesline. alex and marta step back and admire their work; beat.*)

marta. i think we did a pretty nice job. what do you think?

alex. i guess it looks all right.

marta. alex?

alex. yeah?

marta. (*curiously*) did you take the tamales off the altar?

alex. nope.

marta. are you sure? maybe, when you put the plane on?

alex. i swear, grandma . . . i didn't touch a thing.

marta. hmm . . . that's strange. ni modo. (*beat*) me . . . you . . . us talking. this is nice? isn't it? (*marta puts her arm around alex. alex quickly pulls away.*) alex . . . mijo. what's wrong?

alex. nothing.

marta. (*beat*) i see so much of your mama in you. you know that?

alex. . . .

marta. you both share the same smile. (*beat*) you know, alex, it's all right if you want to talk to me about your mama—

alex. no.

marta. it's all right, mijo . . . that's what she would want us to do. don't you

alex. . . .

marta. your mama is always watching over you.

alex. i don't want to talk about her.

marta. pero, alex . . . why not?

alex. i just don't, okay . . . it doesn't matter anyway.

marta. that's not true.

alex. it's not going to change anything.

marta. it will make her happy.

alex. then . . . you talk to her.

marta. she wants to talk to us.

alex. no.

marta. the ofrenda will make sure of it.

alex. (*pointing*) no, it won't . . . because if this thing was special, my mom and dad would've built one, too . . . but, they didn't believe in it and if they didn't, why should i!?

marta. alex!

alex. we don't need an altar and i don't want to talk to any spirits.

marta. you need to talk to your mama.

alex. stop acting like that!

marta. like what, alex?

alex. (*angrily*) like i only have a mom!

marta. que que?

alex. i heard you talking on the phone . . . about my dad.

marta. mijo . . . i didn't mean t—

alex. what did he ever do to you!?

marta. . . .

alex. you talk about how we should love each other, but you're not telling the truth! you didn't like my dad. i'm part of my dad so if you don't like him, you don't like me!

marta. that's not true, alejandro.

alex. alex! my name is alex!!!

(*alex rushes into his bedroom; slamming the door. marta is stunned.*)

marta. (*to herself; ashamed*) i'm sorry.

scene 12

(*alex sits on his bed; looking down, his head between his legs. after a few moments, califas appears. he is enjoying the tamales that he had taken from the altar.*)

califas. (*mouth full*) man . . . i love your abuela's tamales! i swear, vato. this is my favorite time of the year!

alex. (*not looking up*) those don't belong to you.

califas. they do now, carnalito.

alex. she thought i took them.

califas. then . . . you better tell granny it's not cool to perpetuate the negative stereotype of the male chicano man.

alex. (*lifting his head*) what . . . are you talking about?

califas. in a few years when you're leadin' the grape protests, you'll understand. simon?

alex. (*annoyed*) whatever.

califas. hey . . . what's with the attitude? i thought we were becomin' friends. you know, like chico and the man . . . loooooookin' good!

alex. who?

califas. you're killin me, carnal . . . now i feel like an old man. do i look like a senior citizen to y—

alex. leave me alone. (*beat; somberly*) am i going to die?

califas. way to change the subject little—

alex. (*scared*) am i? (*extended beat*)

califas. yeah . . . you are. (*beat*) one day.

alex. when?

califas. don't ask me.

alex. why?

califas. it's not in my job description.

alex. i want to know.

califas. so does everyone else.

alex. it scares me sometimes . . . thinking about dying. (*beat; overwhelmed*) i don't want to die.

califas. simon. i can understand that.

alex. you can?

califas. it's a big deal, ese. it ain't no joke . . . goin' from one world to the next.

alex. what about god?

califas. what about him?

alex. is there a heaven?

califas. it depends on how you look at it.

alex. what do you mean?

califas. what i'm sayin', carnalito, is that not all people see it the same way, sabes? different strokes for different folks. buddhists. catholics. muslums . . . take your pick.

alex. how do i know which way is the right way?

califas. it ain't a competition, ese.

alex. how do you see it?

califas. death is as much a part of life as life is a part of death.

alex. huh?

califas. one depends on the other.

alex. i still don't get i—

califas. don't be afraid.

alex. but, you said it was all right for me to be scared.

califas. bein' scared and livin' your life in fear are two entirely different things, little man . . . but, in time, you'll figure it out.

alex. how?

califas. how? why? what? where? who? chale, vato. trust me . . . okay? (*beat*) this is the way it was meant to be.

alex. (*defeated*) but, what about—?

califas. stop chasin' your tail, carnalito. (*extended beat. califas puts his hands together; forming a butterfly. he begins flapping his hands. he does this for a few moments. alex is mesmerized by this action. califas motions for alex to copy his hand gestures.*) they've been linked with the spirits of the dead. their images were carved in stone on many aztec monuments . . . flyin' thousands of miles . . . millions of them . . . arrivin' for dia de los muertos.

alex. who?

califas. the mariposas. the coolest. the baddest. the most firme butterflies of them all . . . the monarchs. (*beat*) they're comin'.

alex. here?

califas. of course . . . they're invited guests. (*beat*) check it, little man . . . the day of the dead is about invitin' the past.

alex. why?

califas. because you can't know where you're goin' if you don't know where you've been . . . sabes?

alex. what does that mean? .

califas. it means we all have stories, vato.

alex. (*looking at his hands*) nothing's happening.

califas. i wouldn't be so sure of that.

(*the silhouette of a butterfly flapping its wings is projected on the clothesline. alex notices.*)

alex. cool!

califas. simon . . . it's a beautiful sight, ese. (*beat*) the picture in front of us . . . the myth.

alex. myth?

califas. the thin line between fact and fiction.

(*more butterfly silhouettes can be seen on the clothesline.*)

alex. more butterflies!

califas. all the way from mictlan . . . the land of the dead.

(*a flurry of butterfly silhouettes flapping their wings can be seen on the clothesline. califas stops moving his hands. alex notices; beat. he stops as well.*)

alex. check it out!

califas. the monarchs bear the spirits of the departed.

alex. departed?

califas. the dead.

alex. my . . .

califas. (*beat*) simon.

alex. i don't want them to be dead.

califas. they're not . . . not exactly.

alex. what does that mean?

califas. there are three deaths . . . los tres muertos.

alex. three?

califas. the first death is when our bodies no longer function. when our hearts no longer beat. when our gaze no longer has depth . . . when the space we occupy slowly loses its meaning.

(*some of the butterfly silhouettes disappear.*)

alex. the second?

califas. it comes when the body is lowered into the ground and returned to la tierra. to mother earth . . . out of our sight.

(*more butterflies disappear leaving only the silhouette of a lone butterfly flapping its wings.*)

alex. (*beat*) and . . . the third one?

califas. the third death. the one that truly matters . . . is when there is no one left alive to remember us. (*califas raises his palm, face up and blows away the final butterfly from the projection; to alex*) if you don't want to remember them . . . then, your parents truly are dead.

alex. they might not—

califas. not again, vato.

alex. my parents were nice people!

califas. simon. yes . . . and, those two nice people were inside those two buildings when they fell.

alex. why?

califas. i hate to break it to you, carnalito, but what happened on that day was a tragedy and tragedies happen all the time.

alex. why . . . them?

califas. why not? (*extended beat*)

alex. (*angrily*) why couldn't those guys take someone else!? someone bad!

califas. it's not my place to say, carnalito.

alex. why do the bad people get to live for such a long time!?

califas. even i don't have the answer to that one. (*extended beat. califas slowly walks to the window and opens it. he begins exiting and stops; half of his body is outside, half is inside.*) adios, carna—

alex. (*quietly*) my parents . . . are good people.

califas. (*shaking his head; frustrated*) whatever you say, little alex.

scene 13

(*marta is staring at the scribbling on the wall in alex's room; lost in thought. califas is standing behind her. after a few moments, califas walks over to the bed. he opens alex's lunchbox; beat. califas snaps his fingers. marta hears it and looks around the room, but she can't see califas. she does, however, notice that alex's lunchbox is open; beat. she decides to see what is inside. she notices the baseball cards and baseball. she also finds a picture of alex with his parents at a yankees game. she is about to cry, but she manages to keep her composure; extended beat. she closes the lunchbox and keeps the picture. marta and califas exit alex's bedroom and cross toward the ofrenda. she decides that she will place the picture on a prominent location on the altar. she does so and then she kneels in front of the ofrenda and begins praying; beat. the living room door opens; alex enters. he begins crossing to his bedroom.*)

marta. (*hurt*) not even a "hi" grandma.

(*alex stops, but doesn't bother to turn around.*)

alex. (*sulking*) hi.

marta. what do you think, mijo!?

alex. (*turning around*) about what?

marta. your picture on the altar.

alex. (*shocked*) what!?

marta. the one with you and your mama y papa.

alex. no . . . how could you!? (*alex runs to the altar and "rips" his photo off the altar.*)

alex. how did you get this!?

marta. mijo, calmate.

alex. it was in my lunchbox!

marta. it was open, mijo . . . i just thought you would like your pic—

alex. don't you ever touch it again! this is my picture . . . not yours!

marta. si, mijo . . . lo siento.

alex. i don't want it on your altar . . . ever!

marta. alejandr—

alex. i never asked to come here! i want to go home!

marta. mijo, this is your home.

alex. no! don't say that!

marta. por favor, mi nieto . . . no te —

alex. why did my parents have to leave me!?

marta. alex, they did not leave you.

alex. yes, they did!

marta. they loved you.

alex. if it wasn't for them, i wouldn't be here!

marta. (*pleading*) it wasn't their fault, mijo!

alex. they left me all alone.

marta. pero, mijo . . . you are not alone.

alex. yes, i am.

marta. you have me.

alex. no, i don't. don't lie to me!

marta. alex . . . que dices!?

alex. you're going to leave me, too . . . just like everybody else!

marta. alex, i'm never going anywhere.

alex. you can't say that! you can't make that promise! everybody dies!

marta. mijo —

alex. i hate this place!

marta. alex, please!

(*califas snaps his fingers. alex and marta freeze.*)

califas. do what you gotta do, ese. (*califas snaps his fingers. alex and marta unfreeze.*)

alex. i wish i was never born!!!

(*alex rushes to the the ofrenda and begins to throw items to the floor. a stunned marta begins to cry. as alex continues to destroy the ofrenda, marta kneels on the floor picking up a picture. alex finally stops fighting with the ofrenda and himself. he notices his grandmother on the floor crying, clutching a picture of her deceased husband.*)

marta. (*to herself*) aye, mi esposo querido . . . my carlos.

(*alex is stunned by this sight; not knowing what to do or what to say; extended beat. califas helps her up.*)

alex. (*apologetic*) grandma . . . i'm — (*to califas*) califas?

califas. (*solemnly*) don't look at me, ese . . . this is an a and b conversation . . .
    i'm c-ing my way out of it.

(*califas kisses marta on the forehead and disappears. alex crosses toward marta, but he stops. he is not quite sure what to do; extended beat. alex rushes off into his room with marta still clutching the picture of her deceased husband.*)

scene 14

(*alex is sitting on his bed. marta is next to her destroyed ofrenda. they are both praying. an old picture of marta holding alex as a newborn is projected on the clothesline. note: the dialogue in this scene is staggered; one on top of the other.*)

alex. god—

marta.   —dios santo—

alex. —are you listening—

marta.   —i need your guidance—

alex. —what's going to happen to us—

marta.   —now more than anytime—

alex. —if things get worse—

marta.   —turns his back—

alex. —stops loving me—

marta.   —what to do, what to say—

alex. —i don't want her to think—

marta.   —mi alejandro—

alex. —i don't love her—

marta.   —mi vida. my life—

alex. —because i do—

marta.   —my link to mija—

alex. —she's all i got—

marta.   —lo quiero. i love him with all my heart—

alex. —and, dad—

marta.   —jason—

alex. —i promise you i—

marta.   —please forgive me. i—

alex. —am never ever ever—

marta.   —going to—

alex. —forget you—

marta.   —blame you—

alex. —you and me, dad—

marta.   —put you—

alex. —yankees forever—

marta.   —in the middle of everything—

alex. —but, i keep having the same bad dream—

marta.   —what happened to our familia that morning—

alex. —i keep thinking that—

marta.   —it was just our imaginations—

alex. —that you and mom are—

marta.   —fooling us and that you two are—

alex. —going to walk through the door—

marta.   —hiding the pain—

alex. —and that we would be—

marta.   —living together as—

alex. —one big happy family again—

marta.   —una familia unida—

alex. —like we used to be—

marta.   —a family united as one—

alex. —mommy—

marta.   —estrella— (*extended beat*)

alex & marta. i miss you.

(*scene fades to black.*)

scene 15

(*alex is sleeping. he is clutching his yankees lunchbox. califas is writing on the "scribble" wall. the low hum of traffic can be heard in the background. after a few moments, it is apparent that alex is in the midst of a nightmare. he wakes up in a cold sweat; beat. he composes himself a bit; noticing califas at the same time.*)

alex. what are you doing?

califas. . . .

alex. i don't blame you. i wouldn't talk to me either.

califas. why is that, little man?

alex. you know why.

califas. simon.

alex. i'm sorry.

califas. you're talkin' to the wrong person, homey.

alex. (*beat*) maybe . . . i'm the bad person.

califas. chale, little vato . . . no need to go drama queen. you're only human, sabes?

alex. . . .

califas. you're a chavalito . . . just a kid.

alex. still. (*extended beat. alex gets up from the bed and crosses to califas. he stands by him.*) you're taking up the entire wall.

califas. not much . . . considerin' the size of the project.

alex. (*begins to read off a few names.*) judith jones. michael ivory. scott powell. kip taylor . . . el, el, elk—

califas. elkin yuen.

alex. oh. (*beat*) califas . . . what is this?

califas. a list.

alex. what kind of list?

califas. a list that lists names.

alex. there must be a couple of hundr—

califas. a couple of thousand . . . names.

alex. who are they?

califas. they're players in the box score of life, my man.

alex. i don't get it.

califas. just names, ese . . . nothing special.

alex. why bother?

califas. my thoughts exactly. (*califas turns toward alex and hands him the pen.*)

alex. what do you want me to do with this?

califas. complete the list.

alex. but . . . it looks finished.

califas. looks can be deceiving, que no?

alex. why me?

califas. because it's about your heritage . . . your warrior aztec blood . . . the blood runnin' through your veins . . . through the veins of your abuelita. the blood you share.

alex. you're not making any sense.

califas. (*sternly*) it's your responsibility . . . your time to start livin' the rest of your life, carnalito. (*beat*) but, you can't do that until you finish the list.

alex. i still don't get—

califas. the list! it's missin' two names and your parents aren't around to sign on the dotted line, homey.

(*alex ponders these words; beat. he walks up to the wall and begins to run his hand down the wall; touching it gently.*)

alex. (*defeated*) i can't, califas.

califas. sorry to hear that, vato.

(*alex attempts to hand califas the pen back, but califas does not accept.*)

alex. (*quietly pleading*) please . . . don't make me do it.

califas. if you don't want to sign it . . . fine. who am i to say anything. i don't care either way.

alex. (*angrily*) but . . . i do! (*extended beat*)

califas. then, prove it, little man.

(*extended beat. alex slowly inches up to the wall. he takes a deep breath and slowly begins writing. a picture of the wall is projected on the clothesline.*)

alex. (*to himself; subdued*) jason erik smith. (*beat*) estrella torres-smith. (*the projection of the list fades away.*)

califas. your parents were proud of you . . . i'm proud of you, ese.

alex. when will it stop hurting?

califas. it never will . . . but, it gets better.

alex. better?

califas. yeah.

alex. how soon?

califas. ain't no timeline for something like that.

alex. i wish it would stop hurting right now.

califas. simon, ese. lo siento, but life unfolds in its own way . . . you'll know when you know.

alex. know what?

califas. the answers to your questions.

alex. which questions?

califas. the ones—

alex. (*solemnly*) that matter.

califas. (*beat; proudly*) simon, carnalito . . . i think you're startin' to get the hang
of it.

(*califas starts to exit. he crosses to the window. alex crosses to him and then stops;
extended beat. alex stands there not saying a word, but knowing he doesn't have to.*)

califas. (*tenderly*) you're the man of the house now. take care of your abuelita.
entiendes, mendez?

(*alex nods; beat. califas extends out his hand. califas slowly and respectfully shows
alex the chicano handshake, then disappears.*)

scene 16

(*marta is sweeping up the living room. the virgen de guadalupe is projected on the
clothesline. after a few moments, alex enters cautiously.*)

alex. grandma?

marta. . . .

alex. abuelita?

(*marta is surprised by alex. she turns around and smiles at him; extended beat.*)

marta. you wouldn't mind helping an old lady . . . would you?

(*alex nods his head; beat. he crosses next to marta. they both discard items into a
plastic bag for a few moments without saying one word to each other.*)

alex. i'm sorry.

(*extended beat. the image of the virgen fades away.*)

marta. alex . . . grown-ups sometimes have trouble talk— (*beat; apologetic*)
about your papa. it was just that— (*marta crosses to another area of the living
room to pick up something; partly out of guilt.*)

alex. (*cautiously*) you can call me alejandro . . . i mean, could you call me alex
once in a while? i kinda like that name, too.

marta. okay, mijo . . . i'll do that.

alex. grandma?

marta. yes?

alex. what are we going to do?

marta. i'm not sure.

alex. i'm confused.

marta. that's all right, alejandro. at least, we'll be confused together . . . que
no? (*alex nods his head; extended beat.*) today is the second day of november.

alex. day of the dead.

marta. (*beat*) we must rebuild this ofrenda . . . make it even better.

alex. okay.

marta. thank you for reminding me, mijo.

alex. about what, grandma?

marta. that sometimes i need to talk, too.

alex. grandma?

marta. que, mi angelito?

alex. i remember.

marta. que, mi angelito?

alex. i remember one thing about when i was really young . . . your hugs. how warm they were . . . they're just like mom's hugs.

marta. you mean that, mijo?

alex. (*nods his head; beat*) what next, grandma?

marta. we survive, mijo . . . can't ask for anything more.

alex. grandma . . . what if i forget?

marta. no, mijo . . . impossible. your parents are part of you forever. they are your protectors now . . . your angels. (*extended beat*)

alex. mom and dad are safe now . . . aren't they?

marta. si, mijo . . . they are at peace.

(*marta opens her arms. alex dives into them. it is the first time alex has allowed marta to touch him. marta embraces her grandson as the stage goes dark except for a lone spotlight which is focused on alex and marta; extended beat.*)

alex. grandma?

marta. yes?

alex. (*on the verge of tears*) i can still miss my mom and dad . . . right?

marta (*tenderly*) always, mijo.

(*alex, in his grandmother's embrace, begins to sob loudly. it is the first time he has cried for his parents. marta is trying to keep her composure but, after a few moments, she begins sobbing alongside her grandson. lights fade to black and in the darkness, their crying can be heard as it slowly fades into silence.*)

CURTAIN

Production credits from the premiere of *la ofrenda* and details concerning performance rights are included in the acting edition of the play as published by Dramatic Publishing.

Dramatic Publishing, Inc.
311 Washington Street
P. O. Box 129
Woodstock, Il 60098

The Transition of Doodle Pequeño

A play for audiences of all ages by Gabriel Jason Dean

It is Halloween, but fifth-grader Doodle Pequeño won't be trick-or-treating. His mamá is working the late shift (again), Papá was sent back to Mexico, and his only friend is an imaginary goat named Valencia. Plus, old Mr. Baumgartner is outside in a weird face mask mixing up creepy potions. Why can't things just be "normal"? The fact that a boy named Reno has come over to invite Doodle to trick-or-treat doesn't help: Reno is wearing a tutu like a girl—and suggests Doodle make a costume of a clown wig and one of mamá's old skirts! Definitely not "normal." In fact, he says, the idea is "stupid" and "gay." With some nudging—literally—from Valencia, Doodle starts to think more about his choice of words, and what "normal" even is (after all, he *does* have an imaginary goat). Though he tries to make amends with Reno, Doodle faces an ever bigger decision when sixth grade "tomboy" Marjoram and her little brother see the boys together and start calling *him* strange names like "pansy," "homo," and even one he has used: "gay." When Mr. Baumgartner offers an unexpected opportunity to do the right thing Doodle realizes all the bad that can come from letting ignorance and peer pressure guide his thinking. Proud of their friendship and the unique identities that make them who they are, Doodle, Reno, and Mr. Baumgartner are able to work together to help the bullies see the error of their ways.

The Transition of Doodle Pequeño

Characters

DOODLE: a fifth-grade boy
VALENCIA: Doodle's imaginary goat
VOICE OF MAMÁ: voiced by Valencia
RENO: Doodle's fifth-grade neighbor
BAUMGARTNER: a mysterious old man
MARJORAM: a sixth-grade tomboy
TOPH: a third-grader, Marjoram's little brother

Character Notes

The vocal inflection of a native "Goat" speaker sounds a lot like a Mexican
     accent. In fact, maybe they're even the same.

< > is a beat for the actor.

The Voice of Mamá should be performed live offstage by the actress playing
     Valencia.

Setting

A quadruplex in Southern California on Halloween.

AT RISE: *The jack-o'-lantern 6 o'clock Pacific sun is beginning to set on a hilltop
stucco quadruplex in Southern California. Leafy trees in the courtyard cast eerie
shadows. The Santa Ana winds blow and we hear the low murmur of many wind
chimes. BAUMGARTNER, wearing a nuclear waste-style getup with a fumigating
mask, grumbles through the courtyard. He's fertilizing plants, weeding his beds,
examining his trees and hanging a few Halloween decorations.*

(*DOODLE, wearing his school uniform and a backpack, sprints into the courtyard,
seemingly carried by the wind.*)

DOODLE: Trick-or-treat! Smell these feet! Gimme somethin' good to eat! If you
     don't, then I don't care . . . (*Forgets words.*) If you don't, then I don't care . . .

BAUMGARNTER (*peeking out from a bush*): I'll pull out your ugly hair! (*Laughs
     raucously.*)

(*The wind howls. DOODLE and BAUMGARTNER regard each other. DOODLE runs
toward his apartment. BAUMGARTNER watches him. Lights rise on DOODLE and*

Mamá's cramped, one-window, studio apartment crammed with unpacked boxes. A message machine lets out a lonely beep.)

DOODLE: ¡Mamá! ¡Ya llegué de la escuela! < > ¡Mamá! < > Oh no.

(DOODLE presses a button on the message machine.)

VOICE OF MAMÁ *(via the answering machine)*: Hola, Doodle Pequeño. This is Mamá. Are you home? < > Ohhh ... lo siento mucho, cariño. La otra cajera renunció hoy. Y ahora tengo que cubrir su turno. < > I know, mi amor, you are going to be angry, pero este trabajo nuevo nos va a ayudar a pagar los gastos. Pero, llegaré a casa by nine of the clock—

DOODLE: You promised—

VOICE OF MAMÁ: I so sorry, niño. Pero, I bringing 25 PayDay candy bars home para tí— *(To customer.)* I be right with you, sir. Necesito regresar a trabajar, Doodle.

DOODLE: I want to go trick-or-treating. Like normal kids!

VOICE OF MAMÁ: Llegaré a la casa a las nueve—

DOODLE: All the candy'll be gone by then!

VOICE OF MAMÁ *(to customer)*: One second, sir. Doodle—I almost forgetting—por favor, take the monies upstairs to the landlord.

DOODLE: That man is super scary!

VOICE OF MAMÁ: Él es muy agradable. Ahora eres big boy. La renta se tiene que pagar hoy.

DOODLE: You're the adult! You pay for things. Not me.

VOICE OF MAMÁ *(to customer)*: I be right with you, sir. Oh, estoy emocionada por verte en tu disfraz de diablo!

DOODLE: I'm not wearing that stupid devil costume!

VOICE OF MAMÁ: < > Doodle ... things will be better for us.

(Singing.)

    NARANJA DULCE

    LIMÓN PARTI—

(BEEEEEEEEP! DOODLE slumps, unwraps a PayDay candy bar, eats it miserably.)

VALENCIA *(from inside the cabinet)*: B-eh-eh-eh-eh-eh!

(DOODLE casually opens the cabinet and VALENCIA, the goat, emerges.)

VALENCIA: Hola hola, Doodle Pequeño ...

DOODLE: Hola, Valencia.

(VALENCIA takes the PayDay from DOODLE, chomps it.)

DOODLE: Heeey—por qué estas eating my candy bars? Aren't you supposed to be eating grass or something?

VALENCIA: Ay, give me break. I *your* imaginary goat. I eat what *you* eat, mijo.

(*DOODLE slumps.*)

VALENCIA: Ay, you are one cloudy little Doodle.

DOODLE: I hate this stupid place so stupid much! We haven't unpacked yet! I've been wearing the same underwear for *three days*! I am not paying the stupid rent! (*Finds his devil horns, tail and bow tie. As he speaks, he rips them up.*) Y no voy a ir a stupid trick-and-treat o usar estos cuernos estúpidos estúpidos!

VALENCIA (*stomps and kicks some boxes, which fly across the room*): Espera. Why are we so much angry?

DOODLE: Mamá's stupid job!

VALENCIA: Stupid stupid stupid! Wait. What does that mean?

DOODLE: It means we hate it.

VALENCIA: Stu-u-u-u-u-u-u-pid!

DOODLE: Mamá's going to be mad at us.

VALENCIA: These things could be worse. (*Scratching herself.*) At least *you* no have fleas. < > Ah, maybe instead of your devil horns, you wearing my horns instead.

(*VALENCIA lifts her horns off her head, places them on DOODLE's head. DOODLE giggles in spite of himself and VALENCIA goat-leaps.*)

VALENCIA: You be the goat. I will be the *chupacabra*!

DOODLE: Chupahuh?

VALENCIA: Chupacabra. You know, mijo . . . goat vampire.

DOODLE: Vampire?

VALENCIA: Sí. The chupacabra comes out at night when cabritos like you are asleeping. He bites them on the neck with his muy grande fangs—

DOODLE: Fangs!?

VALENCIA: Sí, and then he drinks all their blood like it was Kool-aid! < > Mwah-ah-ah-ah-ah!

(*Silence.*)

VALENCIA: Now, you be the goat.

DOODLE: Why do *I* have to be the goat?

VALENCIA: Because you wearing the horns.

DOODLE: < > Fine. But *no* biting!

VALENCIA: Yeah, yeah. OK. Now, channel your inner goat.

(*DOODLE strikes his best goat pose.*)

VALENCIA: This is your best goat?

DOODLE: Yeah, what's wrong?

VALENCIA: Goats have four legs.

(*DOODLE goes down on all fours.*)

VALENCIA: That's a little better.

(*VALENCIA adjusts DOODLE to make him more goat-tastic.*)

VALENCIA: Sí, now you are a real goat.

DOODLE (*unconvincingly*): Bah-ah-ah-ah-ah.

VALENCIA: Más o menos. Now, pretend you are asleeping.

(*DOODLE snores.*)

VALENCIA: Cierra los ojos!

DOODLE: If I close my eyes, then you'll attack me.

VALENCIA: Sí.

DOODLE: I don't wanna be attacked.

VALENCIA: Are you scared of the chupacabra?

DOODLE: No!

VALENCIA: Then, cierra los ojos!

(*DOODLE closes one eye.*)

VALENCIA: Both eyes!

(*DOODLE nervously closes both eyes. VALENCIA hides in a small box. A loud grinding noise comes from the courtyard where BAUMGARTNER is fiddling with an uncooperative machine.*)

DOODLE: Valencia? What is that noise? Valencia? (*Opens his eyes, looks around for VALENCIA.*) Valencia?

(*DOODLE goes to the window to investigate the noise and sees BAUMGARTNER.*)

BAUMGARTNER: Blasted technology!

(*VALENCIA emerges from the small box and stalks behind DOODLE chupacabra-style. VALENCIA looks as though she is going to ferociously bite DOODLE's neck. DOODLE turns to see her.*)

DOODLE: AHHHHHHHHH!

(*VALENCIA goes for DOODLE's neck, but instead of biting him, she makes a fart noise on his neck with her lips.*)

DOODLE: Hey! Hey! No flurbling, Valencia!

VALENCIA: ¿Qué?

DOODLE: No flurbling my neck meat.

VALENCIA: What is *flu-u-u-u-rbling*?

DOODLE: Farting on my neck.

(*VALENCIA flurbles DOODLE. DOODLE flurbles VALENCIA.*)

VALENCIA: Be-eh-eh-eh-eh-eh!

(*DOODLE chases VALENCIA. She goat-leaps on boxes, chairs, counters. They chase until they are out-of-breath exhausted.*)

VALENCIA: Ayaya! The sugar from the PayDays making me bouncing off the floors!

DOODLE: You mean bounce off the walls —

VALENCIA: BAHFOOGEE.

DOODLE: What did you say?

VALENCIA: < > Bahfoogee.

DOODLE: Is that Spanish?

VALENCIA: No. It's Goat.

DOODLE: You speak Goat?

VALENCIA: Por supuesto, Doodle. I am goat, so I speak goat.

DOODLE: What's it mean?

VALENCIA: It's a curse word in Goat. Not meant for cabritos like you to be hearing.

DOODLE: I'm not a cabrito anymore. What's it mean?

VALENCIA: Is a b-a-a-a-a-a-d word to say — como when you lose something importante. I say it when I mixing up my Goat and English phrases. When I *lose* my words. I say it lots of the times.

DOODLE: Teach it to me!

VALENCIA: < > You can no say it front of Mamá. Do we have a deal?

DOODLE: Deal.

VALENCIA: Repite, por favor: *BAAAAHHHHFOOOOGEEE!*

DOODLE: *BOOOOOOOOOOOFAAAAAAAAAAHHHHGEEEEEEEEEE!*

VALENCIA: Um, your accent's a little funny. It sounded like you saying I have a big nose.

DOODLE: You do have a big nose.

VALENCIA: Besides the point. < > Try again. *BAAAAAAHHHHHFFFFFFOO OOOOOGEEEEEEEE!*

DOODLE: *BAAAAAHHHHFFFFOOOOOOGEEEEEEEE!*

VALENCIA: Very good!

DOODLE: *BAAAAAA—*

(*BAUMGARTNER grinds in the courtyard. DOODLE and VALENCIA cautiously approach the window. The two are amazed by BAUMGARTNER's every move. He smashes something underfoot, picks it up and examines it.*)

BAUMGARTNER: Looks like your run-of-the-mill Drosphila melanogaster. Not a Drosphila suzukii, thank goodness. (*Ritualistically puts things from the grinding machine into his sprayer.*) A bit of bone meal, kale, clay, shark fin, garlic—

(*BAUMGARTNER pours a red liquid from the machine into his sprayer. He slowly drags a big ladder across the courtyard. It makes horrendous noise. He climbs, grumbling with every step. He stands on top of a ladder, grunting and spraying the trees with a frightening mist.*)

DOODLE: *WHAT* . . . is that? Is it el chupacabra?

VALENCIA: No, it's worse. It's the *L-A-A-A-A-A-ANDLORD.*

DOODLE: What do you think he's *doing?*

VALENCIA: He say something about bones.

DOODLE: So?

VALENCIA: Maybe he's doing an ancient vo-oo-oo-oo-oo-oo-oo-doo magic spell cursey thingy. Maybe he's a *brujo?*

DOODLE: Witches are usually girls.

VALENCIA: Boys can be witches, too.

(*A gust of wind. BAUMGARTNER is shaky on the ladder. Wind chimes roar.*)

BAUMGARTNER: BWAH! Confound Santa Ana! Stay in Mexico!

DOODLE: I don't think I can give him the money.

VALENCIA: You no pay, we no stay.

DOODLE: ¿Y qué? This place is a dump.

VALENCIA: This place is our new casa, Doodle Pequeño!

DOODLE: You sound like Mamá.

VALENCIA: Fine. This place is stu-u-u-u-upid.

DOODLE: Much better.

(*VALENCIA kicks a box across the room. DOODLE throws a small box marked "fragile." Major breakage.*)

VALENCIA: Oopsy. Mamá is going to grind us for good.

DOODLE: *Ground* us.

VALENCIA: BAHFOOGEE.

(*DOODLE picks up the box.*)

VALENCIA: If you no open it, then you can deny it was you.

DOODLE: Sí, tienes razón. (*Hides the box in the cabinet.*)

VALENCIA: Out of the mind, out of the sight.

DOODLE: No, out of sight, out of mind.

VALENCIA: Ay, Bahfoogee!

(*DOODLE stares worriedly at the cabinet. After a moment, he opens the cabinet and pulls out the box.*)

VALENCIA: Ay, Doodle. No abras esa caja.

(*DOODLE pulls a bit of the tape off the top. VALENCIA gasps and shudders. DOODLE pulls again.*)

VALENCIA: Be-eh-eh-eh-eh-eh-eh!

(*DOODLE pulls again. VALENCIA faints.*)

DOODLE: You are so dramatic.

(*DOODLE digs inside the box, spilling packing peanuts on the floor. VALENCIA suddenly uprights.*)

VALENCIA: Oooooo—what are those?

DOODLE: Peanuts.

VALENCIA: ¡Ay, delicioso! (*Eats one, violently spits it out.*)

DOODLE: ¡No, cabra tonta! Packing peanuts. For to pack things.

VALENCIA: Yuck! Phew! Ewwwww. Gr-o-o-o-o-o-ss!

(*VALENCIA takes the box, dumps it. A broken picture frame falls out. DOODLE picks it up. It's a photo of Doodle, Mamá and Papá.*)

DOODLE: Oh no. (*Sitting.*) Oh no.

VALENCIA: Who is that funny-looking muchacho? He looks like you with a mustache.

DOODLE: Ése es mi papá.

VALENCIA: I never meet this papá.

DOODLE: He's in México.

VALENCIA: ¿Por qué?

DOODLE: He didn't have the right papers.

VALENCIA: For to eat?

DOODLE: No. For to stay. < > I can't believe we broke this!

VALENCIA: *We,* big man?

DOODLE: Sí, we!

VALENCIA: No, no, no, Doodle Pequeño. I am no real. How can I be breaking things? (*Picks up another packing peanut, eats it.*) Is an acquired taste. Be-eh-eh-eh-eh.

(*A loud knock on the door. VALENCIA goat-leaps onto the countertop.*)

VALENCIA: Expecting a visitor?

DOODLE: No.

(*Another knock.*)

VALENCIA: You should maybe be thinking about answering the door.

DOODLE: Mamá says never open the door a los extraños.

VALENCIA: How you know is a stranger?

DOODLE: Do *you* know who it is?

VALENCIA: You are the only person I am knowing, Doodle. So how do I know? (*More knocking. For longer this time.*)

VALENCIA: I no think this stranger—who may not be a stranger—is leaving.

DOODLE: Ay, what if it's el brujo wanting his money?

VALENCIA: Pues, you give him the monies!

(*DOODLE carefully approaches the curtainless window, hoping not to be seen. Suddenly, RENO, dressed in full old-school vampire regalia, appears in the window.*)

DOODLE (*screaming*): AAAAAAAHHHHHHHHH!

RENO (*screaming back*): AAAAAAAAHHHHHHHHHH!

VALENCIA (*bleat screaming*): B-EH-EH-EH-EH-EH-EH! < > Espera. Why are we screaming?

DOODLE: El vampiro at our window!

VALENCIA: ¿Chupacabra?

DOODLE: No—vampire . . . like a regular people vampire.

RENO (*knocks on the window and holds up his trick-or-treat bag*): Trick-or-treat?

DOODLE (*yelling*): Mamá says I can't open the door for strangers.

RENO (*yelling*): I'm not a stranger.

DOODLE: How do I know?

RENO: Because I live here. *You're* the new kid. *You're* the stranger.

DOODLE: You *look* strange.

RENO: I'm in your class at school!

DOODLE: You are?

RENO: Yeah, I look different without the cape.

(*DOODLE opens the door slightly.*)

RENO: Trick-or-treat!

(*RENO is wearing a ballet tutu.*)

DOODLE: ¿Qué se supone que eres?

RENO: What?

DOODLE: What are you supposed to be?

RENO: I'm Count Chaos, a vaudeville vampire.

DOODLE: What is that?

RENO: Vaudeville was a type of theatrical entertainment popular in the days
   of old.

DOODLE: < > You're wearing a dress.

RENO: Tutu actually.

DOODLE: It's still a dress.

RENO: So?

DOODLE: You're a boy. I think.

RENO: I think so too.

DOODLE: You *think* so?

RENO: Yeah. < > But vaudeville vamp, she's definitely a girl.

DOODLE (*to VALENCIA*): No entiendo—

RENO: In vaudeville, boys dress like girls and vice versa. < > So—trick-or-treat?

DOODLE: I don't have any candy.

RENO: What's that goat eating then?

DOODLE: ¿PUEDES VER MI CABRA?

RENO: I don't speak—

DOODLE: *YOU* CAN SEE MY GOAT?

RENO: Duh. I have an imagination too.

VALENCIA & DOODLE: ¡Ay, dios mío!

(*VALENCIA flurbles RENO.*)

VALENCIA: That is what's known as a flurble.

RENO: Cool.

(*RENO flurbles VALENCIA.*)

VALENCIA: Cool.

(*RENO almost flurbles DOODLE, but DOODLE puts a hand up to stop him.*)

RENO: What's your name again?

DOODLE: < > Doodle.

RENO (*laughing*): That's what my grandpa calls it when the cat misses the litter box. A *doodle*. The cat's really old. And kinda blind. I'm Reno.

VALENCIA: Like the city in Nevada?

RENO: Totally.

VALENCIA: Mi nombre es Valencia. Nice to be meeting you, Reno like the city in Nevada.

RENO: B-eh-eh-eh-eh-eh-gup.

DOODLE: You speak Goat?

VALENCIA: Actually—he speaking Sheep.

RENO: They sound similar. I used to have an imaginary sheep.

VALENCIA: Used to?

RENO: The Santa Ana winds blew Sigmund away last year.

(*A big gust of wind.*)

VALENCIA: I be staying en la casa. Just in case.

RENO: Soooo—about that candy—

VALENCIA: Want a PayDay?

RENO: Um, does a goat have horns?

DOODLE: No, not every goat has horns.

RENO: Ohhhhh—OK . . . (*Grabs horns from DOODLE's head.*) Mister Smarty Pants Kitty Doodle—now they do.

(*RENO puts the horns on VALENCIA. VALENCIA laughs and tosses RENO a PayDay.*)

DOODLE: ¿Por qué te estás riendo?

VALENCIA: Oh, I laughing because he said—he called you a . . . never mind.

(*BAUMGARTNER grinds.*)

VALENCIA: < > Reno like the city in Nevada, what's that noise?

RENO: You mean . . . the troll?

VALENCIA: ¿Un ogro? We thought he was el brujo.

RENO: El what?

DOODLE: Witch.

RENO: Does he look like a witch?

VALENCIA: Oh, this is no good. I knew a troll once. Very temperamental.

(*BAUMGARTNER grinds louder.*)

VALENCIA: What's he doing?

RENO: Grinding little boy bones for his pumpkin trees.

(*VALENCIA faints. DOODLE catches her.*)

DOODLE: Those are not pumpkins! Those are naranjas!

RENO: Come again?

VALENCIA (*waking*): Oranges.

RENO: They are *definitely* pumpkins. Blood pumpkins. Trust me.

(*The three move to the window to watch BAUMGARTNER.*)

RENO: The blood pumpkins are for evil children.

VALENCIA: ¿*Evil* niños?

RENO: Bullies and pranksters . . .

DOODLE: ¡Mentiroso!

RENO (*overlapping*): *And* the troll makes evil children swallow the blood pumpkins WHOLE!

VALENCIA: B-eh-eh-eh-eh-eh-eh! They no choke?

RENO: The pumpkins make your belly stick way out like a basketball. And it churns and turns until all the evil is gone. Sometimes it lasts for days—*weeks*—*YEARS*!

VALENCIA: How you knowing so much about this troll?

RENO: Back in the day when I was a first-grader, there was a boy in my class who lost his two front teeth and every time he talked, he (*whistling*) whistled.

(*VALENCIA laughs.*)

RENO: Beware of laughing, Valencia. I laughed and made up funny names for the whistling boy, which I won't repeat because one night as I was sleeping, the troll yanked me out of bed, dragged me by my hair and made me swallow *three* blood pumpkins—*AT THE SAME TIME*!

VALENCIA: Say is no so!

DOODLE: ¡Qué estúpido!

RENO: You wouldn't want to find out, right?

VALENCIA: No, no, no! We no want to be finding out.

DOODLE: How can you believe this payaso?

VALENCIA: This clown is very convincing.

RENO: Believe what you want, but don't say I didn't warn you.

DOODLE: Whatever.

RENO: It's your funeral. < > So why aren't you dressed up, *Doodle?*

DOODLE: Porque no. < > Halloween is for weirdoes. Like you.

RENO (*paces around the apartment, sizing up the place*): I'm the weirdo, huh? Don't you think fifth grade's a little late to have an imaginary friend?

VALENCIA: Cut him break. He just moving here. Sometimes you needing the imaginaries when you going through the tough times.

RENO: You moved here from Mexico?

VALENCIA: Sí, he come from—

DOODLE: Shhh!

VALENCIA: ¿Queeé?

RENO: It's cool. I mean, I just thought 'cause you don't speak English—

DOODLE: I speak English! I'm speaking English now!

RENO: Oh, I'm sorry, I mean because you speak Spanish—

DOODLE: I moved here from the East Side! I was born here, OK!

RENO: It's cool, Doodle. Wherever you came from. < > When I moved here— that's when I found Sigmund.

VALENCIA: When he come here, Doodle reaching out the car window and hooking me by the horns and pulling me inside. Tell him, Doodle.

DOODLE: No quiero.

RENO: < > You live here *alone?*

DOODLE: I have a mom!

RENO: Not everybody's so lucky.

VALENCIA: Mamá's at work. She just got a job at a convenience store. It's convenient for everyone but us.

RENO: Where's your dad?

DOODLE: You ask too many questions!

RENO: Geez—I'm just trying to be friendly. < > Fine. You ask me something.

DOODLE: Why you wear that dress?

RENO: Tutu.

DOODLE: OK. *Tutu.* < > It's not normal.

RENO: Neither is an imaginary goat.

VALENCIA: Hey hey hey. Be nice.

DOODLE: Boys shouldn't dress like girls.

RENO: < > I do sometimes.

DOODLE: Even when it's not Halloween?

RENO: < > Yeah.

DOODLE (*laughs*): Whoa. That's . . . that's weird.

RENO: Yeah. It is. Kinda. I guess. So?

DOODLE: I bet you get made fun of all the time.

RENO: I don't wear dresses at school. Do you take your goat to school?

(*VALENCIA sadly shakes her head. RENO takes off the tutu.*)

RENO: Wanna try?

DOODLE: No, gracias.

VALENCIA: Oooo — oooo! I will! Me me me! < > Hey, me por favor!

(*RENO gives VALENCIA the tutu. VALENCIA twirls.*)

VALENCIA: I feeling so fancy. (*Goat-leaps and frolics.*) Doodle! You should be trying this! Come on — it's so much of the funs!

(*VALENCIA makes it too hard to resist. DOODLE caves, tries it on.*)

DOODLE: This is kinda dumb.

RENO: Twirl.

DOODLE: No!

RENO: Just twirl.

(*DOODLE half-heartedly twirls.*)

RENO: Now with gusto!

(*RENO takes DOODLE's hand and spins him. Spin, spin, spin. DOODLE laughs.*)

RENO: Really fun, right?

DOODLE: < > It's not so bad.

RENO: Hey! Maybe you could go trick-or-treating with me!

DOODLE: I have to wait for Mamá to get home.

VALENCIA: She is no getting here till nine.

RENO: Whoa! All the candy will be totally gone by then.

DOODLE: Sí, I know, right?

RENO: We'll be back before nine. Your mamá will never know.

DOODLE: Pues, I don't think —

VALENCIA: We could get the candies —

DOODLE: She's already gonna be mad because we broke stuff.

VALENCIA: But the ca-a-a-a-andies!

RENO: You know, rolling with Reno has its privileges.

VALENCIA: O-o-o-o-o, privileges!

RENO: I know all the candy hot spots. This one lady on Carson gives out king-sized Reese's Peanut Butter Cups! *King-sized Reese's Peanut Butter Cups.* Just saying it makes your mouth water.

(*They imagine the king-sized candy.*)

DOODLE: I don't have a costume.

RENO: No problem . . . amigo.

(*RENO opens a box marked "Las ropas." He wildly throws clothes around the apartment. VALENCIA joins in.*)

RENO (*Holding up a Davy Crockett hat*): What about this?

(*VALENCIA is appalled.*)

DOODLE: Too much dead animal.

(*More rummaging.*)

RENO (*holding up clown wig*): What about this?

DOODLE: Too much rainbow.

RENO (*holding up a pirate sword*): What about this?

DOODLE: Too . . . Espera un momento. That's . . . ¡perfecto!

RENO (*holding up a bandana*): And this! Tie it on your head. You could be a pirate!

DOODLE: Ése es Papá's.

RENO: He won't mind.

DOODLE: Give me that. (*Holds the bandana. Puts it on his head.*)

RENO: You look totally cool. (*Holding up a flowery skirt.*) What about this?

DOODLE: It's a dress.

RENO: It's perfecto!

DOODLE: It's Mamá's.

VALENCIA: She won't be minding. You can be she-pirate.

DOODLE: I don't wanna be a she-pirate. Doodle is a he-pirate.

VALENCIA: But Reno like the city in Nevada is wearing a tutu.

DOODLE: Reno is . . . special.

RENO: Hey—the troll will hear you. He's like Santa Claus. He hears everything.

DOODLE: Lo siento, pero I'm not wearing a dress. < > It's *stupid* and it's *gay*.

(*RENO leaves without a word. BAUMGARTNER slowly follows RENO through the courtyard.*)

VALENCIA: You have hurt Reno like the city in Nevada.

DOODLE: ¿Y qué? He's a weirdo.

VALENCIA: You are having an argument with a goat. You are weirdo too.

DOODLE: Pero, he's a boy and he wears girl clothes!

VALENCIA: He was our friend.

DOODLE: We work better alone.

VALENCIA: You saying something before—una palabra . . . a word . . . it was a curse word in human . . . How you say it? Ga-a-a-a-a-ay? < > What this curse mean?

DOODLE: It's not a curse word.

VALENCIA: You say it like one.

DOODLE: It's . . . it's—you wouldn't understand. It means raro . . . weird. Or stupid. Like a boy who wears girls' clothes.

VALENCIA: I thinking is weird you wear clothes at all. I no wear the clothes and nobody is minding.

DOODLE: Animals don't wear clothes.

VALENCIA: You are animal.

DOODLE: I don't have fur to keep me warm.

VALENCIA: You no need to keeping warm. Vives in sunny California!

DOODLE: I have to wear clothes! And they have to be pants. No skirts with stupid flowers on them.

VALENCIA: Says who?

DOODLE: Says the whole world.

VALENCIA: Even the whole world can be wrong, Doodle. I thinking you should apologize. You make Reno like the city in Nevada sad.

DOODLE: You are *my* imaginary cabra. You are supposed to *agree* with me.

VALENCIA: Says who?

DOODLE: Says me!

VALENCIA: OK—I am liberated goat! I am free to express my own opinions.

DOODLE: Your opinions are gay.

(*VALENCIA kicks a box. It flies!*)

VALENCIA: Take that back, Doodle Pequeño.

DOODLE: No.

VALENCIA: Take it back or, te prometo, I will charge.

DOODLE: Stupid stupid smelly gay goat!

(*VALENCIA charges! Headbutt! Goat battle! It's epic. As they fight, RENO walks matter-of-factly through the courtyard. VALENCIA pins DOODLE against the wall.*)

VALENCIA: Reno's your only friend. He wants to take you trick-and-treat. He tells you about the horrible blood pumpkins. He is helping you for to make a new costume after you rip yours— (*Bends DOODLE over her knee, spanks him.*) Tenga, tenga, tenga, tenga, tenga . . .

(*RENO enters without being invited, doesn't close door behind him. He carries his tutu in hand.*)

RENO: If it makes you feel better, I won't wear the tutu. < > Oh, um, uh, sorry. I can come back later—

VALENICA (*releasing DOODLE*): Is OK, Reno like the city in Nevada. < > You want to be saying something, Doodle?

DOODLE: Um. Yeah. It's cool. I guess. Because it's Halloween. (*Grabs his skirt, puts it on.*) I'm . . . I'm . . .

VALENCIA: You are Princess Peg-leg and he is Countess Chaos.

(*RENO and DOODLE consider their new names.*)

RENO: Sweet! Let's crush this quadruplex's candy supply! Brought you a bucket.

(*A burst of wind through the door.*)

VALENCIA: Oh no! I can no go to trick-and-treat! Santa Ana will be blowing me away like it did the Sigmund!

RENO: You can hold onto me.

(*Another wind burst.*)

VALENCIA: I stay here. < > I can no risk it.

(*Before DOODLE closes the door, he looks back to see VALENCIA. DOODLE and RENO exit into the courtyard. The moon is rising. For the first time, we see blossoms on the trees and huge orange orbs hanging from the limbs.*)

DOODLE: Whooooooooa!

RENO: Dare you to pick a pumpkin.

DOODLE: Me?

RENO: No, the other pirate princess.

(*DOODLE looks behind him.*)

RENO: Double dog dare you!

DOODLE: Pero—

RENO: Triple dog!!!

DOODLE: I don't have a dog. I have a goat.

RENO: It's a dare, Doodle.

DOODLE: Pero—

RENO: Don't be a punk.

DOODLE: You said name calling makes the troll angry.

RENO: Punk isn't so bad. Come on! Pick a pumpkin. Halloween deserves as many tricks as treats.

DOODLE: What's in it for me?

RENO: Fame. Fortune. Bragging rights for infinity.

DOODLE: No sé. What if—

RENO: I thought you weren't scared of the troll.

DOODLE: I'm not.

RENO: So pick a pumpkin. The window of opportunity's closing, Peg-leg. You *could* be a legend.

DOODLE (*giving Reno his pirate sword*): Hold this.

(*DOODLE quietly pulls the ladder to the tree, carefully climbs and struggles to remove one of the biggest orbs. TOPH, a cowboy bandit, rushes onstage whirling a pumpkin flashlight.*)

TOPH: Put 'em up! Give me all your candy! Give me those chocolates, your caramels, your gummies, your sours, your toffees and brittles, candy corns, tootsies, lollies and jawbreakers, chewing gums, malted balls, vanilla chocolate strawberry lime, any flavor's fine. Except licorice. I hate licorice. (*Spits, cowboy style.*)

DOODLE: You didn't say anything about the pumpkin police.

RENO: I didn't know.

TOPH: Hand over the goodies, fellows.

RENO: Get out of here, Toph.

TOPH: Who is this Toph character of which you speak?

RENO: This is Toph. Toph meet Doodle.

TOPH: Oh, so you're the new kid in the quad. < > The Candy Bandit is growing impatient. Now—hand over the goods! I ain't afraid to shoot.

RENO: Scram, Yosemite Sam.

TOPH: Aww, come on, Reno . . . I'm just fooling. Can't you play along? < > What are *you* supposed to be anyway?

RENO: I'm a vaudeville vampire and this is Princess Peg-leg.

(*TOPH roars with laughter.*)

DOODLE: What's so funny?

(*TOPH is still roaring.*)

DOODLE: What's so funny . . . you, you—

RENO: Punk!

DOODLE: Punk!

TOPH: You're wearing dresses! (*Laughs.*)

(*MARJORAM, a tomboy, enters. She is wearing everyday clothes, except for her t-shirt which reads, "This is my costume."*)

MARJORAM: Who are you harassing now, you little nightmare?

TOPH: They're . . . they're wearing—look at 'em—they're wearing dresses!

MARJORAM: So what?

TOPH: But—they're boys.

MARJORAM: So?

TOPH: Well—you know.

MARJORAM: It's Halloween. < > So, it's OK to dress different today.

TOPH: Oh yeah. Right.

MARJORAM: Little brothers are so stupid. < > Who're you? < > You deaf?

DOODLE: I'm Doodle.

MARJORAM: Kinda name is that?

DOODLE: A nick.

MARJORAM: What?

DOODLE: A *nick*name.

TOPH: He's the new kid.

MARJORAM: Don't you think I know that? < > Welcome to the quad. Reno-Teeno showing you the lay of the land?

RENO: Marjoram, just go home.

MARJORAM: Can't I make friends too?

RENO: Doodle—don't listen to her. She's . . .

MARJORAM: I'm what? What am I?

RENO: < > Nothing.

MARJORAM: So. Doodle. You're Reno's new friend, huh?

DOODLE: Um, we just met, so—

MARJORAM: Didn't Reno tell you? About his problem.

RENO: I don't have a problem, Majoram! Just go home.

MARJORAM: Reno's gay.

RENO: I am not! Shut *up*, you stupid little idiot!

MARJORAM: Hey now—enough name calling. You don't want to get in trouble with the old man, right Reno?

RENO: You better just go home or I'll tell him what you said and he'll make you swallow—

MARJORAM (*overlapping*): He'll make you swallow three pumpkins at the same time. Can it, Reno-bambino.

RENO: Keep calling me names and see what happens.

MARJORAM: Pansy. < > Doofus. < > Homo. < > See. Nothing. Do it, Toph. (*Pushes TOPH.*) Go.

TOPH (*hesitantly*): Pansy. (*Runs back to MARJORAM.*)

MARJORAM: Keep going.

(*TOPH goes back to RENO.*)

TOPH: Doofus. < > HOMO!

MARJORAM (*laughs*): Nice. Hey Doodle . . . did Reno *make* you wear that dress or what?

TOPH: Maybe he's a *gay* too.

DOODLE: No. No. < > He made me. I didn't wanna wear it. (*Takes off the dress.*)

MARJORAM: That's what I thought. You don't look like— well, you look normal.

RENO (*to MARJORAM*): I hate you.

(*MARJORAM laughs. TOPH laughs. DOODLE laughs . . . sort of.*)

RENO: Shut up! You're all stupid, stupid . . . morons and, and . . . you don't know anything . . . about anything! I hate you all!

MARJORAM: Are you gonna go cry to the old man now?

TOPH: Yeah. What's 'a matter, Reno? You scared?

MARJORAM: I think I want that dress.

TOPH: Maybe you should take it.

MARJORAM: That's the first good idea you've had.

TOPH: Thanks.

MARJORAM: You wanna give it to me and make this easy?

RENO: Just leave me alone, OK? Tomboys don't wear tutus.

MARJORAM: What did you call me?

(*MARJORAM rips off RENO's tutu, pushing him to the ground. RENO does not resist. MARJORAM puts on the tutu, giggles. A light comes on upstairs. TOPH and MARJORAM hide.*)

BAUMGARTNER (*offstage*): Reno? Is everything all right?

RENO: Everything's . . . yeah . . . everything's *normal*.

(*RENO and DOODLE exchange a look. RENO exits. DOODLE looks around, takes off the bandana and slinks back into his apartment. VALENCIA is lounging diva style on the countertop.*)

VALENCIA: Hola hola. I can no wait to taste this king-sized Peanut Cupper Reese's Butt.

DOODLE: Reese's Peanut Butter Cup.

VALENCIA: BAH—

DOODLE: Bahfoogee! Get outta here, Valencia. I'm not in the mood. I feel sick to my stomach.

VALENCIA: Too much PayDay.

DOODLE: Just go.

VALENCIA: What's wrong, *glo-o-o-o-o-o-my* Doodle? Where's the candy?

DOODLE: There is none.

VALENCIA: What happened?

DOODLE: I think I did a bad thing.

VALENCIA: ¿Cómo?

DOODLE: It wasn't my fault.

VALENCIA: You can tell the Valencia.

DOODLE: I think I might have to swallow pumpkins.

(*A knock on the door. DOODLE freezes.*)

VALENCIA: The troll! Oh no!

(*Another knock.*)

MARJORAM & TOPH: Dooooooooodle! Trick-or-treat!

DOODLE: ¡Pá arriba! Your hiding place!

VALENCIA: No, por favor, don't make me go in there! You always forgetting Valencia when she goes into hiding.

DOODLE: It's the kids I just met.

VALENCIA: What? You are embarrassed of the Valencia?

(*Knocking!*)

DOODLE: If they find out I have an imaginary goat—

VALENCIA: You *are* embarrassed of the Valencia!

DOODLE: ¡Por favor, Valencia!

(*Knocking!!!!! VALENCIA mopes and jumps inside the mirror hanging on the wall, disappears. DOODLE opens the door. No one is there.*)

DOODLE: Hello?

MARJORAM & TOPH (*jumping out*): AAAAAHHHHHHH!

DOODLE: AAAAAAHHHHHHHHHHHHHHHHHHHHH!

TOPH: Hiya, Doodle noodle.

(*TOPH and MARJORAM enter the apartment uninvited.*)

MARJORAM: Whoa. This place sucks.

TOPH: Yeah. It sucks.

MARJORAM: Don't say that word.

DOODLE (*looks up to the window, then closes the door*): Um, we haven't unpacked yet . . .

MARJORAM (*looks through all the cabinets*): Got anything good to eat?

(*TOPH checks himself out in the mirror. VALENCIA jumps up, makes a chupacabra face. TOPH sees her.*)

TOPH: AAAAHHHH!

(*DOODLE laughs.*)

MARJORAM: Why you freaking out, little bro?

TOPH: Um, um . . . it was a . . . it's nothing.

MARJORAM (*to DOODLE*): What's so funny?

DOODLE: Nothing.

TOPH: Um, hey Doodle, you got any delicious Halloween candy?

DOODLE: I have PayDays!

TOPH: GROSS! Who eats PayDays? That's like the worst candy bar ever invented ever.

DOODLE: Oh. They're mi mamá's.

MARJORAM: Mamá, huh? Are you an alien?

TOPH (*alien voice*): My name is Doodle and I am from the planet Ooodle Ooodle Ooodle.

MARJORAM: No, idiot. Like from another country.

DOODLE: Mamá is . . . no, we were born here.

MARJORAM: You don't sound very American.

TOPH: Our dad says aliens are taking all the jobs.

DOODLE: Pues, tu papá es un estúpido.

MARJORAM: What'd you say?

DOODLE: I say . . . aliens only take . . . the crappy jobs. Like convenience stores.

TOPH: Yeah. Convenience stores.

MARJORAM: Do you have any food? *Besides* PayDays.

TOPH: It's OK, the last kid who lived in this apartment was really poor too.

(*VALENCIA makes angry faces in the mirror behind TOPH.*)

DOODLE: We're not poor! Papá is still—we're in transition. That's what Mamá says.

MARJORAM: Why are you hanging out with Reno?

DOODLE: He's nice, I guess—

TOPH: He's kinda weird.

MARJORAM: Trust me. You don't want to hang out with the wrong crowd here. Reno's trouble.

DOODLE: He seems OK.

TOPH: He made you wear a dress.

DOODLE: Just for Halloween.

MARJORAM: Not for Reno. Reno takes dress-up *very* seriously.

TOPH: You sure you're not an alien?

DOODLE: I'm from Earth. (*Imitating TOPH's alien voice.*) No Doodle oodle noodle.

(*DOODLE and TOPH invent a robot alien dance.*)

MARJORAM: Hey, morons, let's pull a Halloween prank!

TOPH: I like pranks.

MARJORAM: We'll have to be very quiet.

DOODLE: Because of the troll?

MARJORAM: You don't believe that stuff, do you?

DOODLE: No.

MARJORAM: You should.

TOPH: Really?

MARJORAM: Yeah really. < > You know about the blood pumpkins?

DOODLE: Just what Reno said—

MARJORAM: They're filled with the blood of kids who lived in *this* apartment.

(*VALENCIA is very concerned.*)

MARJORAM: D'you hear him using that machine thingy?

(*MARJORAM imitates the grinding sound. MARJORAM nods. TOPH nods. VALENCIA is terrified.*)

MARJORAM: But, I know something that might save you.

(*VALENCIA is excited.*)

MARJORAM: Aren't you interested?

(*VALENCIA nods fervently.*)

DOODLE: OK. Sure. Whatever.

MARJORAM: We have to shake the trees till all the blood pumpkins fall to the ground.

DOODLE: What's that supposed to do?

MARJORAM: No more pumpkins, no more problems.

TOPH: Come on, Doodle, it'll be fun! Bloody pumpkin guts everywhere!

(*TOPH opens the door. Wind rushes in. He and MARJORAM dash into the courtyard.*)

TOPH: You coming, (*Alien voice.*) Doodle ooodle noodle?

(*VALENCIA makes a chupacabra face at TOPH.*)

TOPH: AHHH!

(*TOPH scurries out. DOODLE looks to VALENCIA. DOODLE goes into the courtyard and VALENCIA vanishes in the mirror.*)

MARJORAM: The trick is to be perfectly quiet.

(*TOPH rushes over to one of the trees, shakes it slightly. A few orbs fall. He giggles.*)

MARJORAM: Toph. Shut up. (*Shakes a tree. More orbs fall.*)

TOPH: Come on!

(*DOODLE hesitantly shakes the tree. TOPH joins. MARJORAM joins. Orange orbs flood the courtyard. A few beats of anxious silence.*)

MARJORAM: PUMPKIN THIEF! PUMPKIN THIEF! PUMPKIN THIEF! (*Hurls orbs at DOODLE.*)

DOODLE: ¿Qué? ¡Ay, cállate! Shhh! ¡Párale!

TOPH: PUMPKIN THIEF! PUMPKIN THIEF! PUMPKIN THIEF!

(*DOODLE runs into the apartment. An offstage noise. MARJORAM and TOPH dash off. Some silence. DOODLE looks out the window. BAUMGARTNER, wearing his fumigating mask, grumbles into the courtyard wielding a rake. DOODLE gasps. BAUMGARTNER surveys the damage, sees DOODLE in the window. DOODLE gasps again, ducks down. BAUMGARTNER sees the trail of orbs leading to DOODLE's door. He picks one up. It's dripping red. He knocks on DOODLE's door. VALENCIA pops*)

up. DOODLE motions for her to stay down. Knock. DOODLE peeks out the window.
DOODLE is perfectly still. BAUMGARTNER opens the door.)

DOODLE *(screaming)*: AAAAAAAAHHHHHHHHH!

BAUMGARTNER *(screaming back)*: BWWWAAAAHHH!

(DOODLE runs and hides in an open moving box. VALENCIA is perfectly still,
mimicking a painting. BAUMGARTNER stomps over to the box, opens it.)

BAUMGARTNER: Are you the one who shook my trees?

DOODLE: ¡No, por favor!

BAUMGARTNER: Then why are you hiding?

DOODLE: ¡Por favor, no me lleves!

BAUMGARTNER: I'm not going to *take* you. Why would I take you?

DOODLE: Because you're a troll and Mamá owes you money!

BAUMGARTNER: Where is your mother?

DOODLE: 7-Eleven.

BAUMGARTNER: Your father?

DOODLE: Por favor, don't make me swallow pumpkins!

BAUMGARTNER: Come out of that box.

DOODLE: No, gracias. I think I'll stay here.

BAUMGARTNER. We need to talk about my trees.

DOODLE: Lo siento, Señor Ogro. I'm really really really really sorry for shaking your trees.

BAUMGARTNER: So it *was* you.

DOODLE: ¡Ay, no! Not *just* me.

BAUMGARTNER: Let me guess—Marjoram and Toph?

DOODLE: They *made* me.

BAUMGARTNER: They *made* you?

DOODLE: That's right.

BAUMGARTNER: You didn't shake my trees willingly?

DOODLE: No exactamente . . .

BAUMGARTNER: Come out of that box.

DOODLE: If I'm in here and you're out there, then no pumpkins get in my belly.

BAUMGARTNER: Pumpkins?

DOODLE: Por favor, Señor Ogro, I'm really sorry for everything I did.

BAUMGARTNER: Tell me what it is you've done.

DOODLE (*fast*): I left the apartment without Mamá's permission, I wore a dress, I told a lie, I said a curse and I shook your trees—*willingly*.

BAUMGARTNER: You've been busy.

DOODLE: And now you want to make me swallow your pumpkins porque that's what happens to evil niños in this quadruplex.

BAUMGARTNER (*takes off his mask*): See? You're safe. Come out of the box. Please.

DOODLE (*slowly exits the box*): Why do you wear that mask? And that suit?

BAUMGARTNER: Protection.

DOODLE: Protection against what?

BAUMGARTNER: Fumes from the chemicals I spray on the trees.

DOODLE: You mean the blood of evil ninos! (*Makes for the box.*)

BAUMGARTNER: No, no . . . My boy, what is your name?

DOODLE: I don't think I should tell you.

BAUMGARTNER: Why ever not?

DOODLE: Well . . . isn't there some kind of rule? If a troll knows your name, then—

BAUMGARTNER: There's no rule.

DOODLE: < > Me llamo Doodle.

BAUMGARTNER: Reno told me about what happened with you.

DOODLE: Oh no—

BAUMGARTNER: Interesting moniker. Doodle. That's what it's called when a cat misses—

DOODLE: Misses the litter box. Sí, I know.

BAUMGARTNER: A doodle is also something you draw without thinking.

DOODLE: I do a lot of things without thinking.

BAUMGARTNER: Is that why you're called Doodle?

DOODLE: Maybe. I think Mamá likes the way it sounds.

BAUMGARTNER: We should discuss my oranges.

DOODLE: You mean pumpkins?

BAUMGARTNER: Pumpkins are of the genus Cucurbita.

DOODLE: Cook my what!?

BAUMGARTNER: They grow on vines. Not trees. These are oranges.

DOODLE: I knew it. Reno said they were pumpkins.

BAUMGARTNER: He was getting your goat.

DOODLE: He met my goat.

BAUMGARTNER: No—*getting* your goat—

DOODLE: No, enserio, he *actually saw* her.

BAUMGARTNER: Who?

DOODLE: My goat.

BAUMGARTNER: You have an actual goat?

DOODLE: Sí.

BAUMGARTNER: In this apartment?

DOODLE: Sí.

BAUMGARTNER: Your mother did not pay a pet deposit.

DOODLE: She's imaginary.

BAUMGARTNER: Your mother?

DOODLE: My goat!

BAUMGARTNER: Ahhhhh. (*Peels an orange, reveals the blood red inside.*) My *oranges* are delicious. Take a bite. You'll see.

DOODLE: Oh, no no no! That's what all trolls say when they want the kid to eat the poison fruit.

BAUMGARTNER: It's not poison.

DOODLE: But they are rojas. Oranges are not red. That's why they're called oranges. Because they are orange.

BAUMGARTNER: Taste it.

DOODLE: How do I know it's not poison?

BAUMGARTNER (*eats a slice*): See? Try it.

DOODLE: You could have immunity to the poison.

BAUMGARTNER: Trust me. They're not poison.

(*DOODLE takes a slice.*)

BAUMGARTNER: Go ahead.

(*DOODLE eats it.*)

BAUMGARTNER: Pretty tasty, huh?

DOODLE: Hmmm. It tastes like . . . sabe como . . . like wind and sunshine. (*Takes another slice.*) ¡Qué rico! (*Takes another.*)

BAUMGARTNER: Slow down.

(*DOODLE takes another.*)

BAUMGARTNER: Whoa!

DOODLE: Perdon, I'm kinda hungry.

BAUMGARTNER: Eat slower. You'll get a tummy ache.

(*DOODLE shoots BAUMGARTNER a suspicious look.*)

BAUMGARTNER: *From eating too fast!* < > This is a hybrid orange I've been developing. It's a cross between giant grapefruit—*Citrus paradisi*—and a Spanish blood orange—*Citrus sinensis*.

DOODLE: So, you're not a troll?

BAUMGARTNER: I'm a retired botanist.

DOODLE: Is that some type of troll?

BAUMGARTNER: No—I study plants. Citrus precisely. I look for unique features in plants. Things that make them different from the rest. And when I find those things, well . . . I celebrate them.

DOODLE: I *knew* you weren't a troll.

BAUMGARTNER: If you *knew*, why did you hide in that box?

DOODLE: Maybe I didn't know *for sure*. Reno is very convincing.

BAUMGARTNER: Reno has an active imagination. He likes to tell stories. He's my nieto.

DOODLE: Your grandson?

BAUMGARTNER: That's right.

DOODLE: < > Hey . . . Señor . . . um . . .

BAUMGARTNER: Señor Baumgartner.

DOODLE: Bomb Gardener . . . do you know if Reno . . . is Reno angry with me?

BAUMGARTNER: You should ask him that question.

DOODLE: Maybe. < > Why does Reno call you a troll?

BAUMGARTNER: Reno feels safer if I'm a troll.

DOODLE: It doesn't bother you to be called a troll?

BAUMGARTNER: If Reno feels safer, then, no, it doesn't bother me. < > What's your *real* name, Doodle?

DOODLE: Martín.

BAUMGARTNER: That's a very grown-up name.

DOODLE: It's Papá's name.

BAUMGARTNER: It's a very nice name. Maybe you should use it.

DOODLE: Mamá used to call me Martín whenever I was in trouble. < > But now it makes her sad to say it. Ever since Papá . . .

BAUMGARTNER: Oh. I see. < > You know, you and Reno have something in common.

DOODLE: No, Reno likes to wear girls' clothes.

BAUMGARTNER: That's just a costume.

DOODLE: No, that's who Reno *is*. He doesn't just wear dresses on Halloween.

BAUMGARTNER: He told you that?

DOODLE: Yeah.

BAUMGARTNER: Hunh. < > I didn't mean you were similar because of how you dress. < > Reno lost his father too. And his mother. That's why he lives with me.

DOODLE: Bahfoogee.

BAUMGARTNER: What?

DOODLE: Bahfoogee. It's a curse word.

(BAUMGARTNER grumbles.)

DOODLE: In goat. You say it when something is lost.

BAUMGARTNER: < > I like it.

DOODLE: Señor Bomb Gardener—I didn't *lose* my father. He is . . . he was sent back.

BAUMGARTNER: I see.

DOODLE: Please don't tell anybody.

BAUMGARTNER: Trolls are very good at keeping secrets.

(DOODLE fetches the envelope of money from the cabinet and hands it to BAUMGARTNER.)

DOODLE: It's the rent. Mamá asked me to give it to you.

BAUMGARTNER: Thank you. < > We should discuss the consequences for shaking my trees.

DOODLE: Lay it on me.

BAUMGARTNER: There are several baskets in the courtyard. Put all the oranges in them. Take a couple out. Para tu mamá.

DOODLE: You won't tell her about the trees?

BAUMGARTNER: What you meant as a prank was actually very helpful. The oranges are obviously ripe and ready to eat. You saved this old troll hours of ups and downs on that rickety ladder.

(DOODLE and BAUMGARTNER shake hands and BAUMGARTNER exits. VALENCIA jumps out of the mirror.)

VALENCIA: Ay, is so very bo-o-o-o-o-o-ring in there, Doodle Pequeño.

DOODLE: Maybe you shouldn't call me that anymore.

VALENCIA: WAIT! Did the troll place a curse on you like he did his pumpkins?

DOODLE: He's not a troll! He's a grandpa. And those aren't pumpkins. They're oranges. Things aren't always what they seem. < > I got a job to do. Wanna help?

VALENCIA: I can no go outside —

DOODLE: You can hold onto me.

VALENCIA: You promise not to be letting go?

DOODLE: Sí, te lo prometo.

(DOODLE opens the door. A gust of wind. VALENCIA jumps on DOODLE's back.)

VALENCIA: I hold on very tight.

DOODLE: Maybe not *so* tight.

(VALENCIA and DOODLE enter the courtyard.)

DOODLE: I can't do this job with a goat on my back. I have an idea.

(DOODLE and VALENCIA go to a tree.)

DOODLE: Hold this. It has roots and isn't going anywhere.

VALENCIA: Are you sure?

DOODLE: Sí, estoy seguro. (Guides VALENCIA to hold the tree.) You good?

VALENCIA: No, but I'll be a brave Valencia!

DOODLE (finds the basket and begins to work. Sings to comfort VALENCIA):
> NARANJA DULCE
> LIMÓN PARTIDO
> DAME UN ABRAZO
> QUE YO TE PIDO.

DOODLE & VALENCIA:
> SI FUERAN FALSOS
> MIS JURAMENTOS,
> EN UN MOMENTO
> SE OLVIDARÁN.

(DOODLE works for a few moments before RENO enters. He is no longer wearing the vampire makeup or costume. He is now wearing an everyday dress.)

VALENCIA: Reno like the city in Nevada returns!

(DOODLE stands. Silence. Then RENO and DOODLE speak simultaneously.)

RENO: I'm sorry for —   DOODLE: I am sorry —

DOODLE: You're sorry?

RENO: I shouldn't have made you wear the dress.

DOODLE: You didn't *make* me. I said that because of the other kids. I wore it porque . . . I thought we could be amigos. < > Sorry about your tutu.

RENO: It's cool. I've got lots more.

DOODLE: ¡Esos cabritos son unos pingos!

RENO: What?

DOODLE: Pingos.

RENO: Pingos?

DOODLE: That's right. Punks. Those kids are punks.

RENO: Pingos. Cool. Reno spoke Spanish. < > Hey, you need help?

(*DOODLE offers RENO a basket. They pick up the oranges. DOODLE starts to sing. RENO listens and tries to join in.*)

DOODLE:	RENO:
NARANJA DULCE	
LIMÓN PARTIDO	
DAME UN ABRAZO	. . . UN ABRAZO
QUE YO TE PIDO.	. . . YO TE PIDO.
SI FUERAN FALSOS	SI . . . FALSOS
MIS JURAMENTOS,	MIS . . . MENTOS,
EN UN MOMENTO	. . . UN MOMENTO
SE OLVIDARÁN.	SE . . . DARÁN.

(*A big wind blows. VALENCIA floats a little.*)

VALENCIA: Ooooh, I starting to feel a little light in the head.

(*A light comes on in another window. MARJORAM and TOPH lean out the lit window.*)

MARJORAM: Oh, look, Toph. It's Reno-Homo and Doodle Dandy doing a little late-night gardening.

TOPH: Yeah. Gardening.

DOODLE: Hey!

TOPH: Hey yourself!

DOODLE: You can't talk to us that way anymore.

RENO: Yeah . . . pingos!

TOPH (*to MARJORAM*): What's a pingo?

MARJORAM: Shut up. You're both homos!

TOPH: What's a homo?

MARJORAM: Shut up.

DOODLE: ¿Y qué? So what if we are? What are you going to do about it?

RENO: Doodle—

MARJORAM: Don't make me come out there!

DOODLE: If you do, then you better be ready to fight us both! And just so you know, I'm a black belt in Tae Kwon Do. (*Strikes a pose.*)

TOPH: What's Tae Kwon Do?

MARJORAM: Come on!

(*MARJORAM and TOPH disappear from the window.*)

RENO: This is not good.

VALENCIA: No good.

DOODLE: Hold your ground.

RENO: Are you really a black belt?

DOODLE: Not at all.

VALENCIA: Ay.

(*A few moments pass. DOODLE and RENO stand back-to-back, ready to be ambushed. MARJORAM and TOPH come out of nowhere, lobbing Sweet Tarts.*)

TOPH & MARJORAM: Sweet Tarts for the sweethearts!

(*Sweet Tart war! TOPH and MARJORAM back DOODLE and RENO into a corner. When they run out of Sweet Tarts, they hurl oranges. When they run out of oranges, the kids standoff.*)

DOODLE: Just leave us alone!

MARJORAM: Aren't they cute, Toph?

TOPH: Yeah, *Princess* Peg-leg and *Countess* Chaos.

DOODLE: Get out of here! This is our courtyard. (*Picks up an orange.*)

MARJORAM: Oh, look, Toph—Doodle's got a blood pumpkin. So scary!

DOODLE: I'll make you swallow it!

RENO (*picks up an orange*): Yeah.

DOODLE (*picks up another orange*): And then another one.

RENO (*picks up another orange*): And another one . . .

DOODLE & RENO: AND ANOTHER ONE!!!

(*DOODLE and RENO charge, DOODLE wrestling MARJORAM to the ground, RENO wrestling TOPH. They begin to cram the oranges into TOPH and MARJORAM's mouths.*)

TOPH: Get off me, you stupid vampire!

MARJORAM: Boys cannot hit girls! Boys cannot hit girls!

(*During the battle, a gust of wind lifts VALENCIA to the top of the tree. BAUMGARTNER roars in, full nuclear suit, carrying his sprayer.*)

BAUMGARTNER: BWAAHHHHHHHHHHHHHHHH!

(*The kids jump to their feet. TOPH screams with an orange in his mouth. BAUMGARTNER backs them into a corner.*)

BAUMGARTNER: Who dares to eat my blood pumpkins? < > Answer me! This old troll will not be toyed with! (*Holds the sprayer wand close to their faces.*)

TOPH (*spitting out the orange*): I'm-Toph-please-don't-eat-me!

MARJORAM (*spitting out the orange*): Marjoram, but you already know that, old man.

BAUMGARTNER: < > And who are you, young man?

DOODLE: I'm . . . I'm . . . Martín.

BAUMGARTNER: Martín, huh? < > Well, you're *all* trespassers! < > There's only one thing I can think of as punishment. (*Growls.*)

RENO: Grandpa, stop.

BAUMGARTNER: Quiet! The troll is thinking of punishments! (*Growl.*)

RENO: No, Grandpa. There's no troll. (*Lifts BAUMGARTNER's mask.*) It's just you and me. You asked me not to wear my dresses outside of the apartment but I did it anyway. I'm sorry. Toph, Marjoram . . . I'm sorry we crammed oranges down your throat. Come on, Grandpa . . . let's go.

DOODLE: Wait. < > You shouldn't apologize.

RENO: It's OK, Doodle—we shouldn't have fought back. It only makes it worse.

BAUMGARTNER: That's right.

MARJORAM: Just wait till we tell our dad—oh, he's gonna be fierce!

RENO: I said I was sorry.

DOODLE: No! Stop saying that. You shouldn't be sorry. These pingos are the ones who should be apologizing. They can't just call you names 'cause you're different.

RENO: Doodle—

DOODLE: They can't just steal your clothes and . . . trespass in your courtyard!

MARJORAM: We're not trespassing, god!

DOODLE: They can't kick you out 'cause you're different. This is your home too, Reno. *You don't have to apologize.*

BAUMGARTNER: < > He's right. You shouldn't have to apologize.

RENO: OK. Well. Then. I'm *not sorry* for wearing a dress.

DOODLE: Sí, tienes razón.

RENO: I'm not sorry at all!

MARJORAM: Oh my god. YAWN. Toph, let's go.

RENO: At least I'm brave enough to be who I am, Marjoram.

MARJORAM: Who are you? *What* are you?

RENO: I'm Reno. Like the city in Nevada.

(*MARJORAM laughs.*)

RENO: I remember how those girls at school picked on you last year. They called you those names—

MARJORAM: Can it, Reno!

RENO: You didn't have to be embarrassed.

MARJORAM: Reno—I'm warning you—

RENO: You don't have to be afraid, Marj—

MARJORAM: Stop it! (*Stepping closer.*) If your troll-grandpa wasn't here, you wouldn't be so brave.

TOPH: Leave him alone, Marj.

MARJORAM: Shut up, you little . . . pingo.

TOPH: How come you're so mean *all* the time?

MARJORAM: Keep talking and I'll show you mean!

TOPH: You're so gay!

(*MARJORAM is speechless. She looks to RENO.*)

MARJORAM: Toph, that's not . . . you shouldn't . . . (*Looks to BAUMGARTNER. She heads offstage.*)

TOPH: Marj—wait. Marj—I didn't mean it! I don't even know what gay is.

MARJORAM (*turning back*): Toph . . . just don't say that word, OK?

TOPH: Is it a swear word or something?

MARJORAM: It's not a swear. It just hurts like one.

RENO: It doesn't have to hurt, Marj.

MARJORAM: Yeah, well . . . he shouldn't say it, OK?

TOPH: But you said it.

MARJORAM: That was different.

TOPH: How?

MARJORAM: It just was! < > Come on. Let's go. Halloween's over. (*Almost offstage.*) Hey Reno! That dress is so . . . that dress is . . . that dress . . .

(*MARJORAM and TOPH exit.*)

RENO (*to DOODLE*): Thanks for sticking up for me like that.

DOODLE: I wish I could be that brave all the time.

RENO: You are, Martín. Grandpa told me you ate the oranges. Even though you thought they were blood pumpkins, you still ate 'em. That's brave. ‹ › It's official. Welcome to the quad.

(*DOODLE and RENO shake hands.*)

RENO: There's no more troll, Grandpa.

BAUMGARTNER: Those kids won't stop what they're doing.

DOODLE: Señor Bomb Gardener, we'll do it like Papá says . . . un día a la vez.

RENO: Huh?

BAUMGARTNER: One day at a time.

VALENCIA: B-ah-ah-ah-ah-ah-ah-ah!

DOODLE: What are you doing up there?

(*Wind.*)

BAUMGARTNER: Who's he talking to?

RENO: His goat.

BAUMGARTNER: Oh. Right.

VALENCIA: Is time for me to go.

DOODLE: Pero—

VALENCIA: Once I am letting go of this branch, I riding the Santa Ana winds.

DOODLE: Where will you go, Valencia?

VALENCIA: When someone need me, they grabbing me by the horns, just like you.

(*DOODLE tosses an orange up to VALENCIA. BAUMGARTNER looks for it to fall back. It never does.*)

DOODLE: Don't forget me, por favor.

VALENCIA: Imposible, mi Martín.

(*The Santa Ana blows hard and the wind chimes fill the Halloween air. VALENCIA floats away, framed by the bronzed, full moon. DOODLE—now Martín—stares at the sky until VALENCIA is gone.*)

DOODLE: BAAAAHHHFOOOGEEEE!

RENO: BAAAAHHHFOOOGEEEE!

DOODLE & RENO: BAAAAHHHFOOOGEEEE!

CURTAIN

Production credits from the premiere of *The Transition of Doodle Pequeño* and details concerning performance rights are included in the acting edition of the play as published by Dramatic Publishing.

Friendship

In the Garden of the Selfish Giant

In the Garden of the Selfish Giant

Sandra Fenichel Asher

Eleven-year-old Maggie and her mother are spending the summer at the home of Maggie's dying grandmother. Irritated by her mother's grief, Maggie finds her own unhappiness at this unexpected "vacation" lightened by Allison, a kind hospice worker, and Brianna, a young neighbor with a vivid imagination. As the girls become friends, Maggie begins to make sense of her grandmother's notorious unfriendliness as well as her mother's grieving. Just before her grandmother dies, Maggie and Brianna act out Oscar Wilde's story *The Selfish Giant*. Brianna says, "If that Oscar Wilde guy can make up a story about a giant who dies, I can make up a story about a giant who lives!" Unhappy endings, however, cannot always be avoided.

In the Garden of the Selfish Giant

Characters

MAGGIE: 11, bright, attractive, moodily teetering between childhood and adolescence

BRIANNA: 9, precocious, energetic, sensitive, imaginative, unusual

SUSAN: Maggie's mother, 30s, wrestling with unresolved anger, but good-hearted

ALLISON: RN and Hospice worker, a few years younger than Susan, warm and funny

Time: The present; summer days and evenings.

Place: One set, depicting the back porch and yard of Maggie's grandmother's house in a small town. The setting is a state of mind as well as a place, representing the prevailing atmosphere among the characters: at first, closed and weed-choked, but slowly opening up, healing and clearing. The set may be realistic or suggested, but Maggie's tree must be a climbable object.

Scene 1

AT RISE: MUSIC. LIGHTS up. A summer afternoon. MAGGIE is seated UC in a tree in the backyard of her grandmother's house, sulking. Wooden steps UL lead to a porch and screen door at the back of the house. At DR, there is a section of a tall wooden privacy fence, with a knothole at child's eye level. Upstage of the knothole is a gate, now closed. The rest of the fence need not be seen, but encloses the entire backyard. An alley runs alongside the fence at right, outside the gate. Downstage of the unseen portion of the fence running along the apron is a sidewalk. On another small section of the fence, DL and visible to the audience, is a handmade sign in block letters: TRESPASSERS WILL BE PROSECUTED. The "climbing tree" is in full leaf. Beside the porch steps and along the fence at left, a neglected but still-blooming rose garden fights masses of weeds for sun and space. The garden continues, invisible but referred to by the actors, along the unseen downstage section of the fence, marked, perhaps, by fallen trellises, shards of broken pots and other signs of neglect. MUSIC fades as BRIANNA enters DL. She is wearing shorts over a bathing suit and has a towel draped across her shoulders. Pretending to be a tightrope walker and chanting her own version of circus music, she inches her way along the sidewalk, "balancing" herself with outstretched arms. Once or twice, she executes a particularly daring turn or leap—after which she interrupts her chanting to provide the sounds of her private audience with sotto voce "yays" and "bravos." Finally, she leaps off the "tightrope" at DR and strikes a triumphant pose.

BRIANNA: TADA! (*She bows to her "audience," blowing kisses with wild abandon.*) Ah, zank you, zank you, zank you. You are all zo verrrry kind! (*She accepts a pretend bouquet.*) Ah, ze flowers! Zank you, zank you!

(*She turns to exit grandly into the alley at right, stops, drops her circus pose, glances around to check that she's alone, and treats herself to a peek through the knothole into the forbidden yard, unaware that MAGGIE has been watching her from the tree with amazement and disdain.*)

MAGGIE: What are *you* looking at? (*BRIANNA gasps in surprise and jumps back, covering her mouth to stifle the sound. She looks around, but there's no one with whom to share this incredible discovery except MAGGIE herself.*)

BRIANNA: (*Calling softly through the knothole*) Hey! (*MAGGIE slides out of the tree, but doesn't respond, except to squint suspiciously toward knothole. BRIANNA calls a little louder.*) Hey, you! What are you *doing* in there? Can't you *read*?

MAGGIE: Read? Read what?

BRIANNA: The sign on this fence! "Trespassers will be prosecuted"!

(*A mirror image of BRIANNA, MAGGIE closes one eye and peers through knothole with the other. For a moment, she and BRIANNA freeze, eye to eye, equally fascinated, suspicious and unwilling to draw back. Finally—*)

MAGGIE: Who *are* you?

BRIANNA: Who are *you*?

MAGGIE: I asked first.

BRIANNA: (*Hesitates, then pulls back so MAGGIE can see more than her eye*) My name's Brianna Morgan, and I'm nine years old. Almost ten. (*A beat to let that news sink in, then, at knothole—*) Your turn.

MAGGIE: I'm Maggie Campbell. And I'm . . . nearly twelve.

BRIANNA: (*Truly impressed*) Twelve! Wow! You're almost a teenager!

MAGGIE: (*Likes the idea*) Almost.

BRIANNA: *Cool!* But . . . what are you doing in *there*, Maggie?

MAGGIE: (*Reminded to sulk*) None of your business.

BRIANNA: Is, too.

MAGGIE: Is *not*!

BRIANNA: Is *too*! This is *my* neighborhood, and we have Neighborhood Watch. We're supposed to report suspicious strangers.

MAGGIE: Well, you can report that I'm not suspicious and I'm not a stranger. This is my grandmother's house.

BRIANNA: (*Aghast*) Really?

MAGGIE: Yes.

BRIANNA: That explains a lot.

MAGGIE: What? Explains what?

BRIANNA: Why you're allowed in there. (*Beat*) And why you're acting like such a snot.

MAGGIE: I am not a snot!

BRIANNA: Well, you're not exactly friendly—

MAGGIE: Why should I be friendly? *You're* the stranger, not me—and you're pretty suspicious, too, peeking into my grandmother's private garden like that. Go away!

(*At this point, BRIANNA may step away from the knothole and continue the conversation from in front of the downstage, invisible portion of the fence. If so, she and MAGGIE must "create" the fence between them by never looking directly at each other and by raising their voices slightly as if calling back and forth over the barrier between them.*)

BRIANNA: Runs in the family, I guess.

MAGGIE: What runs in the family?

BRIANNA: (*Striking a shriveled, squinting pose as she explains*) Squinchedness.

MAGGIE: What?

BRIANNA: My mom says your grandmother's heart is all *squinched* up— always has been. Only now, it's finally *squinching* itself to death.

MAGGIE: There is no such word as "squinch."

BRIANNA: There should be. *Your* heart's probably all squinched up, too.

MAGGIE: It is not!

BRIANNA: Yeah, well. I was just trying to warn you to get out of that garden before she *prosecuted*, which means she would take you to court and have you thrown in jail. And she would, too. She's *that mean.*

MAGGIE: No, she isn't!

BRIANNA: Maybe not to you, since you're her granddaughter and all. So, never mind. I'm going swimming. Bye. (*She runs off.*)

MAGGIE: (*Goes to the gate and opens it*) Hey! Hey, wait a minute! (*BRIANNA is gone. MAGGIE kicks gate shut in frustration.*)

SUSAN: (*Comes out onto porch through screen door*) Maggie?

MAGGIE: (*Sullenly*) What?

SUSAN: Are you talking to someone out here?

MAGGIE: (*Technically telling the truth, since BRIANNA is now gone*) No.

SUSAN: (*Laughs, trying to jolly MAGGIE out of her mood*) Were you talking to yourself?

MAGGIE: NO!

SUSAN: Could've sworn I heard your voice. (*MAGGIE turns away, leans against the far side of the tree, trying to shut SUSAN out. SUSAN sighs, tries another tack.*) Pretty day, isn't it? (*MAGGIE ignores her.*) It's warm enough to go swimming. You'd meet the neighborhood kids at the pool. (*MAGGIE is silent. SUSAN tugs at a tangled vine.*) Or, we could spend some time trying to clean up Grandpa's rose garden. What a mess. I can't believe how she's let it go . . .

ALLISON: (*Steps out onto porch*) Susan? I'll be leaving in a few minutes. (*Sees MAGGIE, who has peered out at her from behind the tree, suddenly brightening in spite of herself*) Hey, Pepperoni! Didn't see you lurking behind that tree. (*MAGGIE gives her a shy wave and can't help smiling a little.*)

SUSAN: (*Crossing to porch to say goodbye*) Thank you, Allison. Thank you for everything.

ALLISON: You don't have to keep thanking me like that. I'm glad I can help. Your mother's had her bath and her medication. She's resting now.

SUSAN: I don't know how I could manage this without you. Without Hospice. I couldn't, that's all there is to it.

ALLISON: (*Gently*) That's why we're here. I'll stop by tomorrow. (*She starts to go inside.*)

SUSAN: But tomorrow's your day off—

ALLISON: Unofficial visit. Friend of the family.

SUSAN: (*Ruefully*) My mother has no friends—

ALLISON: (*With a sweep of her arm that includes MAGGIE and SUSAN*) I meant the family. The *entire family?*

SUSAN: Oh. Thank you. (*Catches herself, laughs*) I mean . . . well, *thank you*, Allison! What else can I say? Merci. Gracias. Danke schoen!

ALLISON: (*Laughing*) You're welcome, Susan. In any and all languages. (*A little louder, to MAGGIE*) See you tomorrow, Tamale! (*MAGGIE almost laughs at this, but just waves shyly. Her smile disappears as soon as SUSAN turns toward her.*)

SUSAN: (*Turning away from house and refocusing on MAGGIE*) Any plans for today, Maggie? (*MAGGIE is silent, sullen.*) I said, do you have any plans? (*No response. SUSAN sighs.*) Are you going to keep this up all summer? (*No response*) Look, I know you're angry at me. You've made your point. I know you didn't want to come here. *Neither did I!* But we're here, and we're both going to have to make the best of it.

MAGGIE: She's your mother, not mine. And you always *used* to say the two of you were better off staying out of each other's lives. So what are you doing here now? And why should I be stuck here with you? We've never been here *before*!

SUSAN: Look, she's the only mother I've got, okay? And she's dying. Whatever's gone on between us all these years . . . well, it really doesn't matter anymore.

MAGGIE: (*Not trying to get it*) I don't get it.

SUSAN: *She's my mother!* I've got to be here.

MAGGIE: She has Allison and the other people from Hospice.

SUSAN: Hospice only comes if there's a family member willing to help. I've been trying to explain this to you, Maggie—at home, in the car coming down . . . If you weren't so busy feeling sorry for yourself, for your "ruined summer," maybe you *would* get it. (*Beat, during which MAGGIE doesn't budge*) She's my *mother*. (*No response*) And I'm *your* mother. (*No response; a beat— then, in exasperation—*) So we're all stuck here together.

MAGGIE: I could've gone to camp like last year—

SUSAN: We've been through this before, Maggie. We have extra bills to pay—

MAGGIE: Then I could have stayed home with Daddy.

SUSAN: Your father's at work all day. He doesn't get summers off like I do—

MAGGIE: I could've stayed home by myself. I'm old enough—I'm nearly twelve!

SUSAN: Maggie, you're here . . . because . . . *I want you here!*

MAGGIE: For *what*? (*Overwhelmed by her own unacknowledged neediness and her fury, SUSAN is unable to answer. Teeth clenched, she groans and throws up her hands, then runs inside, letting the door slam behind her. MAGGIE turns away, jaw set, refusing to cry. MUSIC. LIGHTS fade.*)

Scene 2

AT RISE: *MUSIC. LIGHTS up. A couple of hours have passed. MAGGIE is on the porch steps, sipping from a cold can of soda and occasionally rubbing it across her forehead. BRIANNA enters alley at right, hair damp from her swim, deep in thought, mentally "revising" what happened at the pool to her own satisfaction. Suddenly realizing where she is, she stops, can't resist, peeks through knothole. MUSIC fades.*

BRIANNA: Hey! Maggie Campbell! It's me, again! (*MAGGIE jumps, betrays eagerness for a moment, quickly sinks back into sullenness.*) You'll never guess what happened at the pool! (*MAGGIE is curious, but hesitates.*) It was really funny!

MAGGIE: (*Saunters over to fence, slumps against it without looking through knot-hole*) What happened?

BRIANNA: I can't see you!

MAGGIE: So?

BRIANNA: It's hard to tell a good story if I can't see you.

MAGGIE: (*Shrugs, then—*) You want to come in?

BRIANNA: (*Jumps back in alarm*) No!

MAGGIE: Why not?

BRIANNA: Kids aren't allowed in there. Or even out here! Your grandmother chases them away with her cane! I've seen her!

MAGGIE: My grandmother's in bed. She can't even walk by herself.

BRIANNA: That's hard to imagine.

MAGGIE: Well, it's true. She had a stroke. A bunch of them. She can't walk or talk or feed herself or take a bath or anything.

BRIANNA: Oh. Doesn't she . . . stink?

MAGGIE: No. The lady from Hospice bathes her. Or my mom does it.

BRIANNA: What's a "lady from Hospice"?

MAGGIE: She's a kind of nurse. For people who are dying.

BRIANNA: (*Her voice hushed in awe*) Oh. Is your grandmother dying?

MAGGIE: (*As much annoyed at the fact as saddened by it*) Yeah. Only Allison says she's *living*, too, and we have to remember that. Dying is part of living, she says.

BRIANNA: Who's Allison?

MAGGIE: The lady from Hospice. There are three of them, but she's my favorite.

BRIANNA: Why?

MAGGIE: I don't know. She just is. She's funny.

BRIANNA: She works for dead people and she's funny?

MAGGIE: My grandmother isn't dead yet!

BRIANNA: Yeah, but she's *dying*. What's so funny about that?

MAGGIE: That's not the *funny* part! It's Allison. She calls me funny names.

BRIANNA: Like what?

MAGGIE: Something different every time. Lollipop. Lamb Chop. Cheese Danish.

BRIANNA: She sounds *hungry*.

MAGGIE: Oh, never mind! Look, do you want to come in or not? The house stinks, all right. But not like dirt. Like *old* . . . and *sick* . . . and—I don't know—just old and sick, I guess. But you could come in the yard, if you want. She won't hurt you.

BRIANNA: (*Eager, but still too afraid of Grandmother*) I . . . better not. Maybe another time. I'm all wet from the pool, and I need to get home.

MAGGIE: (*Resigned*) Yeah. Okay.

BRIANNA: Maybe I'll see you tomorrow.

MAGGIE: Sure. I'll be here. I have to stay as long as my mom stays. I'm not going anywhere.

BRIANNA: Guess not. (*Sensing MAGGIE's unhappiness*) Maggie?

MAGGIE: What?

BRIANNA: I'll tell you what happened, okay—at the pool?

I don't have to see you. I'll just tell you.

MAGGIE: (*Shrugs, but is glad in spite of herself*) Okay.

BRIANNA: (*Quickly warming to the tale*) Well, there's this kid, Ricky O'Malley. He's in my class at school. He calls me "Brenda." (*Imitating his goofy, mocking tone, with exaggerated emphasis on the "duh."*) "Bren-DUH, Brennnnn-DUHHHHH."

MAGGIE: I thought your name was Brianna.

BRIANNA: (*As herself*) It is! He's just being *stupid*! My mom says it's because he likes me.

MAGGIE: Or maybe he hates you.

BRIANNA: (*Accepts this possibility, but with regret*) Yeah. That's what I think. (*Eager to get on with the story, with dramatic flair—*) Anyway, he was at the pool and he was saying it—"Bren-DUH, Brennnnn-DUHHHH." (*At this point, she may use the downstage area to act out her story in front of the invisible portion of the fence, and MAGGIE may climb the tree to watch her.*) So I accidentally-kind-of-on-purpose splashed him. And he started splashing me back. I mean, *really* splashing—like a windmill, like a *tidal* wave, like *Niagara Falls*. I was trying to get away and I was laughing and choking and yelling "Quit it! Quit it!"—all at the same time. But I made it out of the pool and I started running. And he started chasing me. And the lifeguard blew his whistle and yelled, "No running around the pool!" So I stopped. But Ricky—he was going too fast and he *couldn't* stop. He shot right past me and out over the water! (*Really pouring on the high drama now*) It was just like . . . like one of those cartoons, with his arms and legs flapping like crazy, and when he hit the water, it was like an explosion! He practically drowned everybody—even the people lying out on the grass! Everybody laughed and laughed at him! (*MAGGIE is grinning, in spite of herself.*) It was so funny! (*BRIANNA presses her eye to the knothole.*) Are you laughing?

MAGGIE: (*Reluctantly*) Yes.

BRIANNA: (*Pleased with her success*) You should've been there, Maggie. The lifeguard made him get out of the pool and go home.

MAGGIE: (*Slides out of tree, approaches fence*) I'll bet he really hates you now.

BRIANNA: Who cares? It was his fault: "BrennnnDUHHHH!" Well, I gotta go. Talk to you tomorrow, okay?

MAGGIE: Yeah.

BRIANNA: Maybe I'll come in. I'll ask my mom.

MAGGIE: Aren't you going to the pool tomorrow?

BRIANNA: Oh . . . maybe not.

MAGGIE: Are you afraid of that kid? Ricky O'Malley?

BRIANNA: No! I just . . . look, if you don't want me to ask my mom if I can come in, I won't.

MAGGIE: I didn't say that. You can ask her—if you want.

BRIANNA: Okay, then, I will.

MAGGIE: Okay.

BRIANNA: Bye . . . Maggie.

MAGGIE: Bye . . . Brianna.

BRIANNA: (*Clumps across stage like Frankenstein and exits L, loudly imitating Ricky O'Malley*) "Bren-DUHHHH! Brennnn-DUHHHH! (*Quickly—*) Bren-duh. Bren-duh. (*Really drawn out—*) Brennnnnnnnnnnnnnnnnnn-DUHHHHHHHHHHHHHHH." (*MAGGIE leans a shoulder against the fence, smiling. MUSIC. LIGHTS fade.*)

Scene 3

AT RISE: *MUSIC. LIGHTS up. Early evening. Sunset bathes the porch and garden in shadow and cozy, intimate light. MAGGIE is nearly hidden up in the tree. SUSAN comes out through the screen door, sits on the porch steps, sighs deeply, and sips from a glass of iced tea. MUSIC fades.*

MAGGIE: (*A pause, then—*) Mom?

SUSAN: (*Looks around, startled*) Maggie?

MAGGIE: I'm up here.

SUSAN: (*Locates MAGGIE in tree*) Oh, there you are! What is it, sweetheart? Come down and sit with me.

MAGGIE: (*Doesn't move yet*) Can I ask you something?

SUSAN: Sure. Anything.

MAGGIE: It's something weird.

SUSAN: No problem.

MAGGIE: (*Slides out of tree, but remains leaning against its trunk*) Before Grandma got sick—did she really chase kids down the alley with her cane?

SUSAN: (*Taken aback*) Who told you that?

MAGGIE: A girl. From the neighborhood. Is it true?

SUSAN: (*Ruefully*) I wouldn't be surprised. What else did this girl tell you?

MAGGIE: That her mom said Grandma's heart is all squinched up, that it always has been, only now it's killing her.

SUSAN: "Squinched up"? If that's a medical term, I'm not familiar with it.

MAGGIE: That Grandma's always been grouchy and mean to people.

SUSAN: Ah. That's true. But it's not why she's ill. Grandma had something called rheumatic fever when she was a little girl. She didn't get proper treatment for it, and it ended up damaging her heart.

MAGGIE: Couldn't anyone fix it for her?

SUSAN: Maybe. If she'd gotten help in time. But she didn't.

MAGGIE: Why not?

SUSAN: I don't know. Maybe her parents didn't trust doctors. A lot of people didn't back then. But having a bad heart has nothing to do with being grouchy and mean.

MAGGIE: I'd be grouchy and mean if I were a sick little kid and nobody took me to the doctor.

SUSAN: (*Stunned by MAGGIE's insight*) I never thought of it that way. (*Beat, taking a moment to consider this, then—*) They tell me now she could've had surgery years ago, *should've* had it. But she kept putting it off, and by the time she was so sick she *had* to go to the doctor, it was too late.

MAGGIE: Doesn't *she* trust doctors either?

SUSAN: (*Shrugs, shakes her head*) She's always been ... distrustful ... of people. Work, she could rely on; money in the bank, she understood. *Things.* Not people.

MAGGIE: (*Moves closer, but still doesn't sit beside SUSAN*) Why?

SUSAN: (*Shakes her head and shrugs*) Who knows? She was never one for *ex-*

plaining anything. The rest of the world either let her have her way, or . . . escaped down that alley. I escaped every chance I got, and after your grandpa died, I made it permanent.

MAGGIE: Did Grandpa chase kids with a cane?

SUSAN: (*Laughs at the thought*) No. Your grandpa was a gentle man. He was a teacher—

MAGGIE: Like you!

SUSAN: Uh-huh. So he was home in the afternoon and all summer, while Grandma was still at work. There were lots of kids in the yard, then. Even in that tree. Like you!

MAGGIE: How come . . . when we're at home . . . you never talk about Grandma and Grandpa?

SUSAN: (*Shrugs, fighting tears; stands up and begins tugging at weeds*) Still hurts too much, I guess. (*A beat, pulls herself together, then—*) And your dad and you came later. You were part of a whole separate life. (*A pause, then, admiring a rose—*) I wish you'd known your grandpa, though. I wish he'd known you.

MAGGIE: (*Joining SUSAN in pulling weeds*) Why did he marry Grandma?

SUSAN: I suppose he had his reasons.

MAGGIE: But if she was so *mean*? (*SUSAN shrugs. A beat, then—*) Grownups are weird.

SUSAN: (*Laughing*) Yeah, a lot of them really are!

MAGGIE: Did Grandpa *love* her?

SUSAN: (*A pause, as she considers this*) Yes, he did. (*Beat*) I think he poured his love into these roses. (*Beat*) She liked roses.

MAGGIE: I don't. They have thorns.

SUSAN: Do they ever! *I'd* never plant them. Talk about fussy and ungrateful! But your grandpa spent hours caring for them. He knew everything there was to know about roses. (*Beat*) And look at them now . . . choked with weeds. (*She shakes her head in disgust and dismay, sighs, then forces her attention back on MAGGIE.*) Are you going to invite her over . . . that girl from the neighborhood? (*MAGGIE shrugs, sullenness creeping into body language again. She moves back toward tree, unwilling to share any positive developments.*)

MAGGIE: I don't know.

SUSAN: How'd you meet her?

MAGGIE: She peeked through that hole in the fence. She was going swimming.

SUSAN: See? I told you all the neighborhood kids go swimming. You could, too—

MAGGIE: I don't want to go swimming!

SUSAN: (*Draws back, then tries again—*) Does she have a name—this girl who peeked through the fence?

MAGGIE: Brianna.

SUSAN: Is she your age?

MAGGIE: No. She's only nine.

SUSAN: That's not so bad. And she probably knows some older kids—

MAGGIE: I don't think so.

SUSAN: Why not?

MAGGIE: She's kind of . . .

SUSAN: What?

MAGGIE: Weird.

SUSAN: Okay, so everybody's a little weird. Big deal. Why not get to know her? Invite her in.

MAGGIE: (*Snapping at SUSAN, irritated at feeling pushed*) I don't know if I want to or not!

SUSAN: There's no need to snap at me! I just thought it would be nice for you to make friends while we're here.

MAGGIE: If I want to get to know her, I will. And if I don't, I won't. Stop bugging me about it!

SUSAN: Suit yourself. Stay in this yard and be lonely and miserable, if that's what you want. (*She starts toward screen door, stops, turns back to MAGGIE.*) I know what you're doing, Maggie—you're punishing me for bringing you here. But it's foolish—because you're punishing yourself, too. And it's not fair. I've got enough to deal with without you going out of your way to make things worse. It's just not fair! (*She enters house and lets the screen door slam behind her. Again, MAGGIE refuses to respond. MUSIC. LIGHTS fade.*)

Scene 4

AT RISE: *MUSIC. LIGHTS. The next morning. MAGGIE is plucking at the weeds and debris among the roses gingerly, without too much sense of purpose, mostly out of boredom. BRIANNA enters L, pretending to ride a galloping horse. MAGGIE stops to listen. BRIANNA wears a towel or sheet tied around her neck like a cape and has a story printed out from the Internet stuffed in her pocket.*

BRIANNA: Giddyup, boy! Atta boy! Giddyup! Giddyup! (*Reaches R: reins in*) Whoa! (*She whinnies and snorts, both horse and rider at once, paws at the air with her hands like a rearing horse, then dismounts, pats the horse's nose.)* Good boy. Stay right here. *(She peeks through knothole.)* Maggie! Hey! It's me, again!

MAGGIE: *(Saunters toward the fence, glad for the company, but trying hard to be nonchalant about it)* Hey, Brianna.

BRIANNA: My mom says if it's okay with your mom for me to come in, it's okay with her, too.

MAGGIE: My mom's at the supermarket. But it's okay. She said to invite you. *(She opens gate; BRIANNA hesitates, takes a deep breath, then enters both eagerly and cautiously, expecting danger.)*

BRIANNA: Are you alone? What if your grandmother needs a bath?

MAGGIE: Allison is with her. And my grandma doesn't *always* need a bath. Sometimes Allison just comes over so my mom can run errands and stuff.

BRIANNA: Oh. *(A beat as she steps in more boldly)* Guess what? My mom says we know Allison.

MAGGIE: You do?

BRIANNA: Everybody knows everybody in this town. She's cool. *(She pulls the stapled sheaf of papers out of her pocket and offers it to MAGGIE.)* Hey! Look what my mom found on the Internet!

MAGGIE: *(Flips through pages)* What is it?

BRIANNA: A story about your grandmother: *(Shows cover page to MAGGIE)* "The Selfish Giant" by Oscar Wilde.

MAGGIE: *(Hands back story)* My grandmother's not a giant. She's a little old lady—all shriveled up.

BRIANNA: Like her heart, huh? *Squinched.*

MAGGIE: I guess.

BRIANNA: Well, it's not *really* a story about your grandmother, but it's *kind of* like her—this giant doesn't let children play in his garden. He has a sign, just like your grandmother's: TRESPASSERS WILL BE PROSECUTED.

MAGGIE: So?

BRIANNA: So look what happens—*(Reading, very dramatically—)* ". . . Spring came, and all over the country there were little blossoms and little birds. Only in the garden of the Selfish Giant it was still winter. The birds did not care to sing in it as there were no children, and the trees forgot to blossom . . . The only people who were pleased were the Snow and the Frost. *(As the characters in the story, with great bravado—)* "'Spring has forgotten this garden,' they cried, 'so we will live here all the year round.'" *(As herself, to MAGGIE)* You be the Snow and I'll be the Frost.

MAGGIE: What?

BRIANNA: Just do what the story says.

MAGGIE: No!

BRIANNA: Come on, it'll be fun! (*Reading*) "The Snow covered up the grass with her great white cloak, and the Frost painted all the trees silver." (*She drops the story and dashes around the yard, sweeping a pretend cape across the grass, calling to MAGGIE as she goes—*) Look! I'm the Snow! See my cape? Whoooosh! Whooosh! (*Stops and looks at MAGGIE expectantly*) Well?

MAGGIE: Well what?

BRIANNA: You be the Frost and paint all the trees silver! (*Continuing her "snow" swoops.*) Whooosh! Whoosh! (*MAGGIE still hesitates. BRIANNA stops "whooshing" and speaks as herself again—*) Just *try* it! (*No response*) Pretty please?

MAGGIE: Oh . . . okay. (*MAGGIE makes a feeble attempt at wielding an imaginary paintbrush.*) Whoosh. Whoosh. (*She stops short.*) I feel silly.

BRIANNA: (*Swooping circles around MAGGIE*) Nobody's watching. Come on! It's *really* fun! Whooosh! Whooosh! Go on! Whoooooooosh! (*MAGGIE tries again, with more success, dancing around the yard, waving a paintbrush.*) That's it! That's great! Whooosh!

MAGGIE and BRIANNA: Whooosh! Whooosh! Whooooosh! (*They swoop and dance, then join hands, whooshing and swinging each other until they collapse, laughing.*)

BRIANNA: Want to know what happens next?

MAGGIE: Okay.

BRIANNA: (*Scrambles for dropped story*) Then . . . then . . . (*Reads—*) "They invited the North Wind to stay with them." (*Jumps up again, a cross between Santa Claus and the hissing North Wind*) Ho! Ho! Ho! Ho! Ho! Swissshhhhhh! Swisssshhhhh! (*Blustering about, reads, in a deep voice—*) "This is a delightful spot! We must ask the Hail on a visit."

MAGGIE: What does the Hail do?

BRIANNA: (*Hands over the story*) You read it. I'm the North Wind now. (*Stalks the yard as her version of the North Wind*) Ho! Ho! Ho! Ho! Ho! Swissshhhhh! Swissshhhhh!

MAGGIE: (*Reads—*) "So the Hail came. Every day for three hours he rattled on the roof of the castle till he broke most of the slates, and then he ran round and round the garden as fast as he could go. He was dressed in grey, and his breath was like ice."

BRIANNA: (*Stops blustering and starts hopping about madly, one foot to the other, waving her arms, fingers curled and menacing)* Now I'm the Hail. *(In a shrill, creepy voice)* Rrrrrrr-rattle-rattle-rattle-rattle-rattle-rattle!

MAGGIE: *(Mimicking BRIANNA's movements)* I'm the Hail, too! Rrrrrr-rattle-rattle-rattle-rattle-rattle-rattle! *(They chase each other, still hopping from foot to foot and waving their arms while they compete at rattling noisily.)*

MAGGIE and BRIANNA: RRRRRR-RATTLE-RATTLE-RATTLE-RATTLE-RATTLE-RATTLE!

ALLISON: *(Appears on porch, waves to get their attention and calls softly)* Maggie? Brianna? *(The GIRLS shriek in surprise at the sight of her and fall to the ground, laughing.)* I'm sorry to interrupt your fun, girls, but the noise is disturbing Maggie's grandmother. If you could just keep it down a little?

MAGGIE and BRIANNA: Sorry.

ALLISON: That's all right, Rutabagas. Thank you! *(She smiles, disappears inside.)*

BRIANNA: *(Laughing)* *Rutabagas?*

MAGGIE: I told you.

BRIANNA: Rutabagas! That's good! *(Pulls MAGGIE into a huddle over the story on the ground)* Okay. Listen. This is my favorite part. *(Reading in her loud, dramatic voice)* "One morning, the Giant was—"

MAGGIE: *(A friendly reminder)* Shhhhhh!

BRIANNA: *(In hushed tones that only add to her sense of drama—)* ". . . the Giant was lying awake in bed when he heard some lovely music. It was only a linnet singing outside his window—"

MAGGIE: What's a linnet?

BRIANNA: My mom says it's a *bird*.

MAGGIE: *(Softly, but into the spirit of the game now)* Twee-twee-twee-twee-tweee!

BRIANNA: *(Giggling and reading)* ". . . but it was so long since he had heard a bird sing in his garden that it seemed to him the most beautiful music in the world."

MAGGIE: Twee-twee-twee-twee-tweee!

BRIANNA: *(Using a deep voice for the giant)* "'I believe Spring has come at last,' said the Giant, and he jumped out of bed—(She jumps up.)—and looked out." *(She pauses dramatically, "looking out.")* And guess what he saw?

MAGGIE: What?

BRIANNA: *(Tiptoes over to the fence and then back to the tree; reading—)* "Through a little hole in the wall the children had crept in, and they were sitting in the branches of the trees. And the trees were so glad that they had covered themselves with blossoms. Birds were flying about, and flowers were look-ing up through the green grass and laughing."

MAGGIE: My turn! (*She takes the story and reads as BRIANNA dances around the tree, twittering and tweeting. Together, they playact the rest of the scene as MAGGIE reads it, with herself as the giant and BRIANNA as the little boy.*) "Only in one corner, it was still winter. It was the farthest corner of the garden, and in it was standing a little boy. He was so small—" (*She pulls BRIANNA to the tree and with one hand on top of BRIANNA's head, pushes her down to her knees.*) "—that he could not reach up to the branches of the tree. The poor tree was still quite covered with Frost and Snow, and the North Wind was blowing and roaring about it." (*She stops reading to toss in a "Swissshhh-swisssshhhh," then continues in a gentle "tree voice," as BRIANNA hugs herself, shivering with cold.*) "'Climb up, little boy,' said the tree, but the boy was too tiny." (*She pushes BRIANNA down a little lower, then steps back and looks down at her lovingly. Then, using a deep voice for the giant—*) "And the Giant's heart melted as he looked out. 'How selfish I have been,' he said. 'Now I know why Spring would not come here. I will put that poor boy on the top of the tree—' (*She pretends to help as BRIANNA climbs up.*) '—and then I will knock down the wall—' (*Pushes open the gate and returns to tree*) '. . . and my garden shall be the children's playground for ever and ever.'" (*There's a beat while MAGGIE holds her pose and enjoys the moment, then BRIANNA reaches down and snatches away the story.*)

BRIANNA: The end.

MAGGIE: But there's more.

BRIANNA: No. That's it. Want to do it again?

MAGGIE: There are more pages! I can see them! What do they say?

BRIANNA: (*Shrugs*) Nothing important. I don't like that part.

MAGGIE: You can't just change the whole story because you don't like the way it ends.

BRIANNA: (*Slides out of tree*) Sure I can.

MAGGIE: But there's more! (*Reaches for the story; BRIANNA pulls it away*)

BRIANNA: (*As MAGGIE pursues her, attempting to get the story*) There isn't!

MAGGIE: There is, too, Brianna! (*She grabs story away from BRIANNA, quickly skims the last two pages.*) The little boy disappears. The giant never sees him again—until he dies. The little boy comes back to take him to Paradise. (*Reading—*) "And when the children ran in that afternoon, they found the Giant lying dead under the tree, all covered with white blossoms." (*Beat*) That's how it ends.

BRIANNA: That is a *terrible* ending.

MAGGIE: Why?

BRIANNA: It's *sad.*

MAGGIE: So what? Sometimes stories are sad.

BRIANNA: I *hate* sad endings! I like *my* ending *much* better.

MAGGIE: But *this is what happened!* Do you always go around changing what happened if you don't like it?

BRIANNA: Yes.

MAGGIE: Brianna, that's . . . kind of like *lying.* You can't just make things up.

BRIANNA: Sure I can! I do it all the time!

MAGGIE: Then how do you expect anyone to ever believe you?

BRIANNA: You believed me.

MAGGIE: No, I didn't. I saw there were more pages.

BRIANNA: Not about this.

MAGGIE: Then what?

BRIANNA: (*Realizing that MAGGIE is not amused*) Oh . . . stuff.

MAGGIE: What stuff?

BRIANNA: Just some old stuff. It doesn't matter anymore.

MAGGIE: Just *what* old stuff, Brianna?

BRIANNA: Just . . . what happened at the pool.

MAGGIE: To that kid who likes you — or hates you — or whatever?

BRIANNA: Ricky O'Malley.

MAGGIE: Yeah. The one who fell into the pool.

BRIANNA: He didn't.

MAGGIE: He didn't what?

BRIANNA: He didn't fall into the pool. (*Beat*) I did.

MAGGIE: What are you talking about?

BRIANNA: He's the one who stopped running when the lifeguard said. I'm the one who kept going and fell in.

MAGGIE: Then why did you tell it backward?

BRIANNA: *Because I like it better that way.* (*MAGGIE's mouth falls open, but she is speechless.*) It was still a good story, wasn't it? It made you laugh.

MAGGIE: But it was *a lie*, Brianna.

BRIANNA: No, it wasn't —

MAGGIE: Yes, it was! (*Hands BRIANNA back the story*) The lifeguard sent *you* home, didn't he? Not that Ricky O'Malley—*you*. (*BRIANNA backs away from her, edging toward the gate—and close to tears.*) And everyone laughed and laughed—at *you*! *That's* why you didn't want to go swimming today. Not because you wanted to play with me. Because you can't go back to that pool ever again! You *lied* to me, Brianna!

BRIANNA: No. I didn't! I *do* want to play with you—

MAGGIE: (*Backing her through gate*) Why? Because nobody else likes you? Because they already know you tell lies? Go home, liar.

BRIANNA: Meanie!

MAGGIE: (*Slamming gate*) Go on! I shouldn't have let you in here. I knew it! I should never have listened to my mom—or to you!

BRIANNA: (*From outside fence*) I don't see . . . what was so bad . . .

MAGGIE: *Go home!* (*MAGGIE is silent and stern as BRIANNA, in tears, runs off L. MAGGIE slumps down at base of tree. After a moment, ALLISON comes out onto porch.*)

ALLISON: Hey, Chimichanga!

MAGGIE: (*Glumly*) Hey.

ALLISON: Where's your friend?

MAGGIE: She had to go home.

ALLISON: Oh, I'm sorry, I didn't mean that you couldn't play out here at all—

MAGGIE: It wasn't that.

ALLISON: Oh. Want to talk about it?

MAGGIE: NO!

ALLISON: (*Unruffled, hands up in mock surrender*) Okey-doke, Artichoke! (*Beat; checking her watch anxiously*) But, listen, I'm afraid I have to leave, too. Your mom's not back yet?

MAGGIE: No. But you can go—(*Hesitating as what this means fully dawns on her*)—if you want.

ALLISON: That's very kind of you, Maggie. Really. But I'll stay until your mom gets back. Can't be much longer. (*She sits on porch step.*) Wow. Will you look at those roses! (*Attracted by ALLISON's humor and honesty, MAGGIE slowly gravitates closer and closer to her during the following conversation, until she's sitting beside her on the step.*)

MAGGIE: They belonged to my grandpa.

ALLISON: I know. I used to play in this garden, when I was a little kid.

MAGGIE: You knew my grandpa?

ALLISON: I grew up right around the corner. And he was my chemistry teacher in high school. He's one of the reasons I went into nursing.

MAGGIE: Did you know my mom, too, when she was little?

ALLISON: Sure. But I was just starting high school when she went off to college. (*Laughing*) When I was your age, she was one of those wild teenagers we all thought were *so cool*!

MAGGIE: My mom was *cool*?

ALLISON: Your mom is still cool, Calamari.

MAGGIE: Why do you call me all those food names?

ALLISON: 'Cause it's fun. Want me to stop?

MAGGIE: (*A beat, then—*) No.

ALLISON: If I were French, I'd call you "mon petit chou."

MAGGIE: What does that mean?

ALLISON: "My little cabbage."

MAGGIE: (*Laughing*) Cabbages are gross!

ALLISON: Apparently the French think they're quite nice!

MAGGIE: (*Suddenly serious*) Allison? What was my grandma like, before she got sick?

ALLISON: (*Laughs*) Oh, my goodness! She was a character, your grandmother. There are people in this town who are still afraid to go into her diner and ask for fries with their hot roast beef sandwich instead of mashed potatoes. "No substitutions!"

MAGGIE: She worked at a diner?

ALLISON: She owned it. She was a good cook, too. And *fast*. (*Demonstrating*) My boyfriend used to call her "The Octopus," because she could do eight things at once!

MAGGIE: Did he call her that to her face?

ALLISON: No, he did not! When I was in high school, there was a running bet—to see who'd be the first person in town to make your grandmother crack a smile.

MAGGIE: Who won?

ALLISON: (*A beat, then with sad realization—*) *Nobody*.

MAGGIE: (*Ruefully*) Nobody likes her, not even my mom.

ALLISON: Your mom loves her, Maggie. I know that for a fact.

MAGGIE: I don't think so.

ALLISON: Oh, yes, she does. You don't always have to *like* people to *love* them, you know. *Especially* not mothers!

MAGGIE: (*Grudgingly admits it*) I guess.

ALLISON: She's always been a tough cookie, your grandma, but I can't help feeling sorry for her.

MAGGIE: Because she's dying?

ALLISON: Well, that, of course—but mostly because she forgot to live.

MAGGIE: What do you mean? She lived—she's *old*.

ALLISON: But she never seemed to *enjoy* any of it. And now, it's too late.

MAGGIE: Is she going to die *soon*?

ALLISON: Yes, Maggie, she is.

MAGGIE: Very soon?

ALLISON: We can't be certain at this point—a few weeks, maybe. Or less.

MAGGIE: Are you ever afraid?

ALLISON: Of what?

MAGGIE: Of . . . people dying?

ALLISON: Yes. I am. But I'm a practical person, Maggie. Death is going to happen; there's no arguing with that. But there are things that can be done to make it easier—for the dying and their families and friends.

MAGGIE: Like what?

ALLISON: Oh, it depends. Getting people to talk. That helps. Getting them to say what needs to be said—before it's too late. People from Hospice did that for my family, when we lost my dad. So I try to do it, too. I focus on what *can* be done.

MAGGIE: It must be good to be a practical person.

ALLISON: Sure, most of the time. But it's also good to carry on once in a while, like you and your friend Brianna—dancing and rattling, or whatever you were doing down here.

MAGGIE: Brianna is *not* a practical person. (*Beat*) She's weird.

ALLISON: Brianna . . . is *unusual*, Maggie. (*A beat, as she takes a fallen weed and holds it to her face like a moustache*) I like unusual people, don't you?

MAGGIE: (*Smiles, thinks about that, shrugs*) I miss my friends at home.

ALLISON: I'm sure you do. But I can see why your mom wanted you here. It must be such a comfort to her, having you around.

MAGGIE: Why? I don't do anything.

ALLISON: You don't have to *do* anything. Sometimes I don't do anything either. Sometimes just being here is quite enough.

MAGGIE: I don't get it.

ALLISON: Yes, you do. Remember a couple of minutes ago—when I said I needed to go home and you said it would be all right if I left before your mom came back?

MAGGIE: Yeah. So?

ALLISON: Did you really mean that?

MAGGIE: Sure—

ALLISON: Really *really*?

MAGGIE: Well . . . kind of—

ALLISON: But you'd rather I stayed

MAGGIE: (*Admitting it*) Yes.

ALLISON: Was there anything in particular you wanted me to *do*?

MAGGIE: No.

ALLISON: See, then? Sometimes all we need is to know there's somebody in our corner, somebody cool on our side. (*She pats MAGGIE's arm and stands up.*) I'd better gather my things. Your mom should be back any minute now. (*She goes inside. MAGGIE is left to think as LIGHTS fade. MUSIC.*)

Scene 5

AT RISE: MUSIC. LIGHTS up. *Afternoon, several days later. Bright sunshine. The garden shows signs of more work. MAGGIE comes out on porch, carrying a book and a glass of lemonade and is settling on the step when BRIANNA enters L, wearing an old fedora and tiptoeing cautiously—like a spy. She makes a big show of frequently checking behind her to see if she's being followed, now and then flattening herself against the fence as if to avoid detection and hushing an imaginary someone behind her. Slowly but surely, she crosses to right, peers through knothole, and calls to MAGGIE in a stage whisper.*

BRIANNA: Hey? Maggie? Guess who? (*MAGGIE ignores her. She takes off hat, drops the spy routine and speaks in her regular voice.*) It's *me*. Brianna. (*No response; more cautiously—*) Are you still mad at me? (*Beat*) It's been three whole days! (*No response; she tries another tack—*) I'm not a liar, okay? I make things up, but I'm not a liar. There's a *difference*.

MAGGIE: Says who?

BRIANNA: My mom.

MAGGIE: Then go home and play with your mom.

BRIANNA: (*Earnestly*) I *have* been. (*MAGGIE rolls her eyes, but doesn't respond.*) But I can play with her any time, and you're only here for a little while . . . (*No response. BRIANNA takes a breath and summons up courage from down deep.*) Okay, look: My mom also said to *have* a friend, I need to *be* a friend. So, if you want the story to end the way it really ends, it's okay with me. (*Beat; she tries a better offer—*) I'll even be the giant and die, if you want. (*Nothing*) Or you could be the giant . . . ? (*Final offer*) The thing is, Maggie, I *was* afraid to go back to the pool. Because those kids make fun of me a lot, and this time was the worst. But that's not why I came over to play with you. I really *wanted* to come over and play with you. (*Beat*) I think you're cool. (*Beat*) Can't we make up and be friends? (*A pause; then MAGGIE gets up, crosses to knothole; peers through.*)

MAGGIE: You're not just saying that, are you?

BRIANNA: No.

MAGGIE: You're not just "telling a story"?

BRIANNA: *No.*

MAGGIE: Prove it.

BRIANNA: How?

MAGGIE: (*Opens the gate and confronts BRIANNA*) Go to the pool. And *then* come back and play with me.

BRIANNA: Oh, Maggie!

MAGGIE: See? You don't *want* to go the pool, because that's where all the kids are—except *me.* I'm *all that's left*, and *that's* why you want to make up and be friends.

BRIANNA: That's not true!

MAGGIE: A lot you know about what's true and what's not!

BRIANNA: (*A hurt pause, and then—*) I make up *stories,* Maggie. *Stories,* that's all. That's why they're called *stories*—because we make them up. We're *supposed* to. And if that Oscar Wilde guy can make up a story about a giant who *dies,* I can make up a story about a giant who *lives,* okay? And if I fell into the water instead of Ricky O'Malley, *who cares?* It was a *good story!*

MAGGIE: You should have *told* me it was just a story. You shouldn't have let me think it was true.

BRIANNA: (*Chagrined*) Okay.

MAGGIE: And you *do* care.

BRIANNA: What?

MAGGIE: You haven't been back to the pool since it happened, have you?

BRIANNA: No.

MAGGIE: So you care.

BRIANNA: I don't care if I was the one who fell in the pool. I care . . . that everyone laughed.

MAGGIE: I laughed at your story—

BRIANNA: That's different! I *wanted* you to laugh.

MAGGIE: Well, you can't hide out here forever. My grandmother's going to die—just like the giant. Death is going to happen—and then, we're going home.

BRIANNA: (*A beat, and then*—) Maybe your mom will decide to stay here and live in her old house, like when she was little—and you and I can go to school together and be best friends!

MAGGIE: (*Not cruelly; just explaining the facts*) We like the house where we already live, Brianna, and my dad wants us to come home, and my mom and dad have jobs, and I already have a best friend—*there*.

BRIANNA: (*Sadly, but also slyly*) Well—it would've made a good story.

MAGGIE: *Brianna*—!

BRIANNA: Okay, *okay*! Listen—I'll do it. I'll go back to the pool—my mom says I have to, anyway, I can't let the turkeys get me down—but you have to come with me.

MAGGIE: What?

BRIANNA: Please?

MAGGIE: (*Because she's already told SUSAN this*) I don't want to go to the pool.

BRIANNA: Why not? It's fun!

MAGGIE: If it's so much fun, why don't you just go?

BRIANNA: Because it'll be better if you're there.

MAGGIE: Why?

BRIANNA: It'll be *easier*.

MAGGIE: I'm not going to *do* anything.

BRIANNA: You don't have to *do* anything! Just come with me! Please? Pretty please? With chocolate fudge and sprinkles on top?

MAGGIE: (*Amused in spite of herself*) Ohhhhh. All right.

BRIANNA: Great! I'll get my stuff! See you back here in fifteen minutes! (*She plops the hat back on and dashes off L, arms stiffly out to her sides, roaring like a jet plane. MAGGIE throws up her arms in mock surrender, then makes a dash for the house. MUSIC. LIGHTS fade.)*

Scene 6

AT RISE: *MUSIC. LIGHTS up. Later that afternoon. SUSAN is in the garden, clearing away the weeds, when MAGGIE enters from alley and through gate, hair still damp from the pool. MUSIC fades. SUSAN continues working as they talk.*

SUSAN: Well, hello there.

MAGGIE: Hi.

SUSAN: Allison tells me you went swimming.

MAGGIE: Uh-huh.

SUSAN: With Brianna?

MAGGIE: Uh-huh.

SUSAN: And? How was it?

MAGGIE: It was okay.

SUSAN: Just "okay"? (*MAGGIE hesitates, then finally looks her mother in the eye and begrudges her a smile.*)

MAGGIE: It was fun. (*MAGGIE gets to work, pulling clipped vines into a pile. Another pause, while SUSAN nods, still working, and biting her lip to hold back the "I told you so" that MAGGIE is dreading, happy to see MAGGIE smile)*

SUSAN: (*Finally—*) I'm glad.

MAGGIE: Yeah. Me, too.

SUSAN: Good. (*Another awkward pause, then SUSAN faces MAGGIE fully—*) Maggie? I'm sorry I . . . *forced* you to come here. It was selfish of me, and I shouldn't have—

MAGGIE: It's okay.

SUSAN: It is? You're sure? Because Daddy could come and get you . . . we could arrange *something*, while he's at work—

MAGGIE: No. I'll stay.

SUSAN: I'm so glad! (*Beat*) Having a friend does help, doesn't it?

MAGGIE: It's not just that.

SUSAN: Then what?

MAGGIE: (*A pause, then—*) Allison . . . said . . . you *need* me.

SUSAN: (*A beat, as she realizes the depth of her need for the first time herself*) Oh, I *do*! I do, sweetheart!

MAGGIE: That's so weird. You're the *mother.* I'm supposed to need *you.*

SUSAN: (*Humbly*) Well, now we know: Mothers need daughters, too. (*She glances toward the house; chokes up.*) The Big Secret is out—

MAGGIE: Didn't you ever want to come back here—after Grandpa died?

SUSAN: (*Still facing the house, talking, in part, to her mother*) Every day.

MAGGIE: Then why didn't you?

SUSAN: (*Turning toward MAGGIE again—*) You cannot imagine what it was like, being her daughter . . . in a town like this . . . where everybody knew . . .

MAGGIE: But you still wanted to come back . . .

SUSAN: (*Shrugs*) She's my mother. (*Beat*) I told myself . . . she didn't want me back. I told myself . . . she didn't *deserve* to meet Daddy and you. But the truth is . . . I couldn't let her know . . . how much I wanted to—

MAGGIE: Like me not going swimming.

SUSAN: (*Another revelation—*) Yes! I was *punishing* her—but I was punishing myself, too. And she was doing the same thing. She never called. I never called . . .

MAGGIE: The kids at the pool couldn't believe I was her granddaughter. They said Brianna was just making that up. They couldn't believe Grandma had a family—like normal people. They said even their *parents* were afraid of her, back when *they* were kids.

SUSAN: Oh, yes! They cleared the yard the minute she got home.

MAGGIE: Brianna's mom thinks Grandma's like the selfish giant in the story— the giant who wouldn't let children play in his garden. It hurt my feelings at first.

SUSAN: (*Taking MAGGIE in her arms*) Oh, Maggie!

MAGGIE: But then I thought . . . it's kind of true—

SUSAN: All these years, I've been so determined the hurt would end with me—and now I've dragged you right into the middle of it! I am so sorry.

MAGGIE: I'm sorry, too, Mom. (*They hold each other for a moment, then ALLISON calls from offstage.*)

ALLISON: Susan? Susan!

SUSAN: (*Alarmed*) Allison! (*As ALLISON steps out on porch*) Is it time?

ALLISON: Time? (*A beat, until she realizes what SUSAN is referring to*) Oh! No! *No!* I didn't mean to alarm you. I just wanted you to know I was leaving. Call me if you need me.

SUSAN: I will. Thank you, Allison. (*Gestures toward MAGGIE*) For everything.

ALLISON: (*Smiling at them both*) You're welcome. So long, Sassafras!

MAGGIE: So long, Spumoni! (*ALL laugh as ALLISON gives them the "thumbs-up" sign and exits inside.*)

SUSAN: (*To MAGGIE*) Sweetheart, I think I'd like to go in and sit with your grandmother for a little while, okay?

MAGGIE: (*Gathering the pile of weeds and moving them out of sight*) I'll come with you.

SUSAN: Oh, Maggie, you don't need to do that! She doesn't even know who we are anymore—

MAGGIE: I want to.

SUSAN: There's nothing you can do—

MAGGIE: I know. I just want to be there with you. (*A beat, then—*) And Grandma.

(*A beat, then MUSIC begins as, deeply touched and inspired, SUSAN snips a rose and motions with it toward the house. MAGGIE nods enthusiastically and takes the rose. SUSAN snips another to carry in herself. As MAGGIE watches, SUSAN pauses for a moment, taking in the flower's significance—her father's work, his gift to her mother, their deaths. Then with their free arms around each other, she and MAGGIE go up the stairs and into the house to bring the roses to Grandma. LIGHTS fade.*)

Scene 7

AT RISE: *MUSIC. LIGHTS up. Several weeks later. The yard is aglow in morning light. The weeds are completely gone. The TRESPASSERS WILL BE PROSECUTED sign has been replaced by a realtor's FOR SALE sign. MAGGIE and BRIANNA are seated on branches of the tree.*

BRIANNA: (*Oddly ill at ease*) Sure is quiet around here.

MAGGIE: Yeah. Got pretty crazy for a while, though, huh?

BRIANNA: Yeah. I like your dad. He's nice.

MAGGIE: Thanks.

BRIANNA: (*A beat, then—*) I've never been to a funeral before.

MAGGIE: Me, neither.

BRIANNA: It wasn't as bad as I thought.

MAGGIE: It was okay.

BRIANNA: The coffin was closed. My mom says sometimes they're open. She warned me—

MAGGIE: Mom didn't want anyone ... *staring* at Grandma. People who didn't like her.

BRIANNA: Did you see her—before?

MAGGIE: Yes.

BRIANNA: Was it horrible?

MAGGIE: Yes. Well ... not really.

BRIANNA: You weren't scared?

MAGGIE: Sure I was scared. But she was dead, that's all. (*A beat, then*—) She was a lot scarier when she was alive.

BRIANNA: Yeah.

MAGGIE: (*Thinking it over*) Except ... Allison said that when Mom and I sat with her, Grandma seemed ... different.

BRIANNA: Different how?

MAGGIE: More peaceful. We couldn't tell. She was so *still*.

BRIANNA: So what did you *do*?

MAGGIE: We talked to her. I told her all about you and your stories.

BRIANNA: (*Wide-eyed*) "The Selfish Giant"?

MAGGIE: Uh-huh. But not what your mom said—about Grandma being the giant.

BRIANNA: (*Still uneasy*) Could she hear you?

MAGGIE: I don't know.

BRIANNA: (*A pause, then*—) You weren't talking about *me*—when it happened, were you?

MAGGIE: (*Laughs at this*) No. I was asleep when it "*happened*."

BRIANNA: (*Relieved of guilt*) Oh.

MAGGIE: My mom came and got me.

BRIANNA: (*A shade melodramatic, even in her sympathy*) Did you cry ... an awful lot?

MAGGIE: No. Just a little. Mostly because my mom was crying. I felt bad for her.

BRIANNA: Nobody cried at the funeral.

MAGGIE: No.

BRIANNA: I thought you were *supposed* to.

MAGGIE: (*Laughing again*) It's not a law, Brianna! (*Thinks about it; shrugs*) Anyway, that's the way it is—the sadness—it kind of comes and goes.

BRIANNA: (*Considers this, then—*) Your grandpa was my mom's chemistry teacher—isn't that funny?

MAGGIE: Yeah. My mom didn't realize she still had so many friends here in town.

BRIANNA: That means you'll have to come back . . . to visit.

MAGGIE: She said we might.

BRIANNA: And we'll go swimming again, every day, just like we have been—

MAGGIE: And you'll finally go off the high dive.

BRIANNA: That's how I want the story to end!

MAGGIE: Maybe this time it will. (*SUSAN comes out onto porch, shakes out a small rug and hangs it over railing. MAGGIE slides out of tree; goes to help her.*) Hey, Mom.

SUSAN: Hey, sweetheart. Have you packed everything? Your books? Your toothbrush?

MAGGIE: Yup.

SUSAN: Better double-check. We're leaving right after we eat.

BRIANNA: (*Slides out of tree, trying not to cry*) I think I better go now.

SUSAN: Brianna! Aren't you staying for lunch?

BRIANNA: I can't . . . I . . . need to get home.

MAGGIE: But it's our last time together—

BRIANNA: (*Already outside the gate, pulling it shut*) I *know* . . . I just *can't*. Bye! (*SUSAN and MAGGIE exchange a puzzled look. SUSAN nods toward gate meaningfully, then goes inside. Outside the gate, BRIANNA has started crying. She brushes the tears away impatiently, as MAGGIE runs to gate, opens it.*)

MAGGIE: Brianna?

BRIANNA: Don't come out! (*Slumps against fence, her back to MAGGIE, waving her away; plaintively—*) *I don't like this part* . . . where you leave.

MAGGIE: (*Gets it*) Oh. Okay. (*She backs into garden and closes gate, thinks for a moment, then goes to the knothole and peeks through.*) Brianna? Are you still there?

BRIANNA: Yes.

MAGGIE: There's something . . . I need to tell you.

BRIANNA: What?

MAGGIE: You know that kid—Ricky O'Malley—at the pool?

BRIANNA: Uh-huh. What about him?

MAGGIE: He likes you.

BRIANNA: (*Interested*) You said he hates me!

MAGGIE: I didn't even know him then. Now I do. He definitely likes you.

BRIANNA: All the other kids think I'm weird.

MAGGIE: You're not weird. You're *unusual*. I think that's why he likes you.

BRIANNA: Are you just making that up?

MAGGIE: *I'm* not the one who makes stuff up, Brianna. I'm a *practical* person.

BRIANNA: (*Smiling in spite of herself*) Okay.

MAGGIE: I just thought you'd like to know.

BRIANNA: Thanks.

MAGGIE: You're welcome. (*A beat, then, eye to knothole*—) Bye, Brianna.

BRIANNA: (*Eye to knothole, a mirror image of MAGGIE. A beat, then*—). Bye . . . Maggie. (*She turns away and starts slowly toward home. MUSIC begins to play softly as a smile grows on her face. She twirls once, twice, and then explodes*—) Whoooosh! Whooooooosh! Whooooooooosh! (*She swoops off L. MAGGIE listens to her go, her smile bittersweet, then raises her arms and also spins once or twice*—)

MAGGIE: Whoooosh! Whooooooosh! Whooooooooosh!

(*Laughing, she swoops across the yard and enters the house. LIGHTS fade. MUSIC fades.*)

CURTAIN

Production credits from the premiere of *In the Garden of the Selfish Giant* and details concerning performance rights are included in the acting edition of the play as published by Dramatic Publishing.

Future Societies

With Two Wings

With Two Wings

Anne Negri

Eleven-year-old Lyf has never ventured beyond the walls of his nestlike home deep in the forest; it's against the Five Rules his parents have set "to protect us, to keep us safe from harm." When a young girl named Meta happens to peek through the wall one day, a friendship forms. Meta's stories of learning to fly with the other "fledglings" at "flock" surprise Lyf, and she convinces him to break a Rule: he takes off his cloak to expose his wings. Lyf is surprised when his wings don't melt as his mother has warned, and Meta is surprised when her troublemaking brother Taur, an aspiring junior reporter for the newspaper, comes looking for her. Taur teases Lyf for being a dodo—someone flightless, and "the worst name you can call someone"—then snoops around in Lyf's father's workshop, hoping to write about a secret invention Lyf has mentioned. That the secret invention is actually a handmade wing is the latest in a series of revelations that lead Lyf to questions who his parents' Rules are really protecting. When it comes to light that each of Lyf's parents are indeed missing a wing, the family members must confront their fears and decide whether or not the Rules are helpful or harmful.

With Two Wings

Characters

LYF: (pronounced "life"): the boy, 11 years old.

META: (like "meta-theatrical"): Taur's twin sister, 12 years old.

TAUR: (pronounced "tore"): Meta's twin brother, 12 years old.

MOM: Lyf's mother, in her 30s or 40s.

DAD: Lyf's father, in his 30s or 40s.

AT RISE: Home. Small worknest. Yard. Wall. The wall and worknest are hand-crafted from fibrous, woven materials found in nature. It seems hodgepodge on first glance, but is purposefully and expertly constructed. The high, thick wall encircles the space. It is a protective, insular boundary. And yet there are spaces in the material where someone could see and reach through to the other side.

    LYF, MOM and DAD blend in with their environment with loose handmade clothing in muted colors. They all wear distinctive, long, earthy cloaks.

    Morning. DAD enters with a crate full of found materials. He reaches into the crate and delicately takes out a beautiful feather. He tucks the feather into his cloak. DAD enters the worknest.

    MOM enters and begins looking at the found materials in the crate. LYF enters. MOM pulls out a long band of elastic and begins stretching it.

LYF: What's that?

MOM: I don't know. Your dad found it. It's his job to go Out There.

(MOM and LYF each hold one end of the elastic band. LYF plucks the band, playing with the material.)

LYF: Boing!

MOM: Boing!

LYF: Whatever it is, it's got a lot of . . . BOING!

(MOM laughs and hands the elastic to LYF.)

MOM: (*Laughs*) All right, boingo, go put it on the wall.

(MOM ruffles his hair. LYF begins to weave the elastic into the wall. MOM rummages through the crate of materials. LYF peers through a space in the wall. LYF stops working, he peers more intently.)

MOM: Lyf? Lyf, did you forget Our Story?

LYF: (*Quickly pulls his head away from the wall*) I remember.

MOM: I think you forgot.

LYF: How could I forget? We say it everyday.

(MOM *reaches into her pocket and pulls out a beautiful stone, holds it in her hands and conjures the power of the stone.*)

MOM: Hello? Is there a story in there?

(MOM *pretends to put the stone into LYF's head. MOM makes a fun popping sound and with a flourish we see her slide the stone back into the pocket of her cloak.*)

MOM: That ought to do it. There once lived a mother . . .

LYF: And her boy!

MOM: Ah! It's working!

LYF: They lived on a tiny island . . .

MOM: And no one ever bothered them. The mother was very happy . . .

LYF: But the boy wanted to leave the island and explore the world. The boy begged his mother to teach him how to fly.

MOM: At first she refused . . .

LYF: But the boy wouldn't stop begging her.

MOM: Eventually the mother gave in, but it was a very foolish and dangerous decision.

LYF: After practicing for many days . . .

MOM: The mother decided that they would fly together.

LYF: Side by side.

MOM: Before they flew into the sky, the mother said to the boy, (*To LYF*) "This is a very important rule . . ."

LYF: "Don't fly too high in the sky, or the sun will burn your wings right up! Don't fly too low or the sea water will weigh your wings down and you will surely drown."

MOM and LYF: "You must fly a middle course."

MOM: They began to fly together in the sky . . .

LYF: And the sun was bright and warm that day and the sea sparkled like a shiny jewel . . .

MOM: But the boy could not control himself . . .

LYF: He flapped his wings and soared up, up, up in the air!

MOM: The mother tried to follow him . . .

LYF: But he was too fast . . .

MOM: She called to the boy . . .

LYF: But he ignored her.

MOM: Suddenly, high in the sky, his wings began to burn . . .

LYF: And he cried out in pain . . .

MOM: He faltered and swooped down towards the water to cool the burning . . .

LYF: But the sea spray clung to the boy's feathers and he was sucked down into the ocean.

MOM: The mother called out, "Where are you, where are you?" and she frantically searched the water, but she couldn't see her boy anywhere.

(*Beat.*)

LYF: Mom. Mom? I'm here. I'm right here.

(*MOM takes the stone out her pocket and brings it near LYF's head. She pantomimes popping the stone out with a sound and with a flourish we see her slide the stone back into the pocket of her cloak.*)

MOM: You hungry?

(*LYF growls playfully.*)

MOM: (*Laughs*) I guess I'd better get some food started!

(*DAD enters from the worknest.*)

DAD: Good morning!

(*DAD kisses MOM and LYF on the top of their heads.*)

MOM: What are your plans for today?

DAD: A little time in my worknest, dear.

MOM: (*Sighs*) Please, not too long.

DAD: I won't be long.

MOM: Lyf, you need to work on the wall. I'll give a whistle when the food's ready. (*Exits*)

DAD: (*Whispers*) Lyf!

(*LYF goes to DAD. DAD pulls a feather from his cloak.*)

LYF: A feather!

(*DAD and LYF stare at the feather inspecting it close up.*)

LYF: It's beautiful.

DAD: It's awesome!

LYF: Awesome!

(*DAD gives the feather to LYF. DAD goes into the worknest. LYF runs to the wall and puts the feather into a secret hidden spot. LYF pulls a folded paper flyer from the secret spot and begins playing with it.*

META, a girl, enters behind the wall. LYF does not see her. META is dressed in brightly colored clothing made from synthetic materials like plastic, nylon and polyester. She carries a messenger bag that clips in front of her. She has a pair of wings.

META pops her head up over the top of the wall. She watches LYF. LYF senses something and spins to look at the wall. META ducks down.

LYF returns to the paper flyer. Behind the wall, META finds an open space in the materials and she wriggles her hand through. She waves at LYF and signs: thumbs up, A-OK, peace, come here. Her other hand pops through the wall and her hands become mouth puppets.)

META: (*Left hand*) Hello, stranger! (*Right hand*) Who are you calling strange?

(LYF spins around and sees only the hands sticking through the wall's holes.)

LYF: (*Screams*) Ahhhh!

(LYF runs and hides on the side of the worknest.)

META: (*Right hand screams*) Ahhh! (*Left hand screams*) Ahhh!

(Both hands quickly turn towards LYF. META freezes her hand puppets, quickly pulls her arms back through the wall and pops her head through another hole.)

LYF: Ahhhh!

META: Oh, man, I hate it when that happens. Someone sneaks up behind you when you are super focused on something and they scare you. I didn't mean to . . .

LYF: Go away! (*Hides in his cloak, attempting to camouflage himself*)

META: Okayyyyy . . . that was a little rude, but I did scare you, so I bet that's just the fear talking. (*Beat*) You are forgiven. (*Starts to look around the yard*) Hey, dude! I can see you. Do you think you're invisible?

(LYF peeks just his eyes out from his cloak. META waves at him.)

META: That would be really cool if you were invisible . . . but you're not. (*Sees LYF's paper flyer in the yard. Pulls her head back out and jumps over the wall.*) Oh sweet, a paper flyer! We were making these at flock last week. We were learning about aerodynamics and we got to take them outside and see how far they would fly. Mine was the best! This is pretty good, but if you add a couple extra folds, I guarantee you are going to get 20 extra feet on each flight. Do you want me to fold this for you?

(LYF stares at META. Beat.)

META: I'll take that as a "yes."

(META begins refolding the paper flyer. During the following, LYF begins to emerge from his spot. Curious, he silently approaches META as she speaks and folds.)

META: Everyone else in my flock was like, "Whoa, Meta, how did you get yours to go so far?" They were impressed . . . well, most of them . . . some of them just don't get it. In order to make the perfect flyer you have to consider four major factors: lift, gravity, thrust and drag. If you don't understand the basic laws of aerodynamics, things will just crash and burn. The other kids at flock they don't care about any of that . . . but I do . . . and that. Is. Why. I. Always. WIN! (*Finishes her last fold on "WIN," lifts the paper flyer up in the air. Swiftly turns to show LYF.*) See?

(*LYF is directly behind her shoulder. META yelps in surprise and laughs.*)

LYF: Shhh!

(*LYF looks toward the house and worknest, grabs META by the arm and drags her to a hiding spot on the side of the worknest.*)

META: (*Still laughing*) You got me back! Well done.

LYF (*Whispers*) Who are you? Where did you come from? Why are you here?

META: I'm Meta. I'm supposed to be at flock right now, but I decided not to go this morning. This morning I decided to go off the beaten path. And this place is WAY off the beaten path. (*Beat*) What's your name?

LYF: (*Quickly steps away*) Rule number four: Don't talk to strangers.

(*Beat.*)

META: You already broke that rule.

(*Beat.*)

LYF: I'm Lyf.

META: Lyf?

LYF: What is a flock?

META: What do you mean?

LYF: What is it? I've never heard of a flock before.

META: It's where all fledglings go to learn new things. We study all kinds of subjects. Some of it's fun and some of it can be really boring! (*Beat*) Don't you go to a flock?

LYF: No. I don't go anywhere.

META: What do you mean?

LYF: Rule number three: Never go Out There.

META: You've never been outside of these walls?

LYF: Nope.

META: Never?

LYF: Nuh uh.

META: Never, ever?

LYF: No!

META: Really?

LYF: I don't lie. (*Beat.*)

META: I dare you to climb the wall and put one foot on the other side!

LYF: I'm not supposed to.

META: Just one, teeny, tiny little toe.

LYF: I shouldn't.

META: C'mon.

(*META starts to climb the wall. LYF goes to the wall and starts to climb with her, but stops himself and gets down.*)

LYF: I can't.

(*LYF pulls his cloak around himself and squats. META jumps off of the wall and goes and squats next to LYF. Beat.*)

META: Why are you wearing that?

LYF: (*Steps back, away from the wall*) What?

META: That cape.

LYF: (*Defensively*) It's a cloak.

META: OK…fine, cloak. But just so you know, (*Whispers*) capes are way cooler.

LYF: Why aren't you wearing yours?

META: My what?

LYF: Your cloak?

META: In the colony, nobody wears cloaks.

LYF: My mom says I have to wear mine at all times because our family is allergic to the sun.

META: I've never heard of that. My mom says I used to be allergic to nectar when I was a baby!

LYF: Rule number two: Always wear your cloak.

META: You have a lot of weird rules at your house. I don't think I would like wearing a cloak over my wings all the time. Besides, now that I'm becoming a fledgling, I'm going to start learning to fly and my wings needs to be free! (*Starts running around jumping up as high as she can. Chants, sings and dances.*) I'm going to fly so high, like a bird up in the sky! Oh, yeah! Uh huh! Oh, yeah! Uh huh!

LYF: Shhh! Not so loud. My mom might hear you. (*Beat*) Are you really going to fly?

META: Of course. We all learn to fly.

LYF: Rule number one: Never, ever try to fly.

META: But Lyf, you have to.

LYF: It's too dangerous.

META: No, seriously, Lyf, if you don't learn now, when you are young, you'll never be able to fly.

LYF: Really? (*Beat.*)

META: Do you want to learn?

LYF: Why would I?

(*Pause. META searches for a way to explain.*)

META: Lyf, have you heard about the ocean?

LYF: I've heard about it. My dad used to tell me a story about the ocean when I was really little! The sea spray, the wet sand, the breeze . . . he doesn't talk about the ocean anymore. (*Beat*) My mom does though.

(*META goes to her messenger bag, takes out a conch shell and holds it out to LYF.*)

LYF: (*Cont'd*) What is that?!

META: It's a shell. Listen to it!

(*LYF takes the shell and holds it up to his ear. He is amazed by what he hears.*)

META: (*Cont'd*) That's a little piece of the ocean! It's our first flying trip at flock. My mom says that when you fly over the ocean you can catch the breeze and just glide forever. (*Picks up the paper flyer*) Right now, this piece of paper can fly farther than we can. (*Zooms the paper flyer through the air*) If we could fly, we could go anywhere, we could zoom straight to the ocean, right now!

LYF: When do you start to learn?

META: We're supposed to learn the landing position this afternoon! I've got to go! I don't want to miss the first part. It was really nice meeting you, Lyf. (*Grabs her messenger bag and runs toward the wall with the paper flyer in her hand*)

LYF: META!

(*META turns.*)

LYF: Your shell?

META: You can keep it . . . until next time.

(*META holds out the paper flyer to LYF.*)

LYF: Keep it.

META: Thanks.

LYF: Will you come back?

META: Do you want me to?

LYF: Yes!

META: I'll be back right after flock!

(META *puts up her hand for a high-five. LYF mirrors her action. META slaps LYF's hand and he is mildly startled by this new activity. META jumps over the wall.*)

META: See you, dude. (*Whispers*) Don't break any rules without me!

(META *exits. LYF goes to the wall and puts the conch shell into the secret hidden spot in the wall. MOM enters and sees LYF near DAD's worknest.*)

MOM: Time to eat.

(LYF *jumps and moves away from the worknest.*)

MOM: Remind me, Lyf, what is rule number five?

LYF: Rule number five: Never go into Dad's worknest.

MOM: Thank you. (*Turns away*)

LYF: But I didn't even go in there.

MOM: Lyf? Are you questioning Our Rules?

LYF: No, but . . . why is Dad the only one who gets to go in there?

MOM: It's one of Our Rules. End of story.

LYF: I know, Mom, but what does he do in there?

MOM: He has some silly projects that he's working on.

LYF: Why can't I see them?

MOM: You know this. There are dangerous tools in there that could hurt you.

LYF: But I promise I'll be really careful . . .

MOM: It's on the rule list for a reason. Our Rules are made . . . (*Waits for LYF*)

LYF: Our Rules are made to protect us, to keep us safe from harm.

(DAD *enters from the worknest.*)

DAD: Food ready?

MOM: Lyf is forgetting some of Our Rules.

DAD: What happened?

MOM: Tell your dad.

LYF: (*Softly*) Rule number five.

DAD: (*Beat. To MOM*) Which one is number five again?

(LYF *giggles.*)

MOM: All of the rules are equally important.

DAD: He's just curious.

MOM: (*To LYF*) I'm not saying you can't be curious, but you need to channel your curiosity towards safe areas, like . . . like building the wall or cleaning up your roost.

LYF: There's nothing curious about cleaning my roost.

(*DAD smiles and chuckles. MOM gives DAD the death stare.*)

DAD: Something smells good.

LYF: Mom? Dad?

MOM: Yes, dear.

LYF: I have a question . . . about rule number one.

(*MOM and DAD exchange an uncomfortable glance.*)

DAD: Rule number one?

LYF: I've known that it's rule number one since I was a baby, but . . . why?

MOM: Enough of these silly questions. Go inside and eat!

(*LYF goes inside sulkily. MOM takes the stone out of her pocket and begins rubbing it in her hands nervously.*)

DAD: Calm down. Take a breath. (*Beat*) It's done. Our Project!

MOM: Your project.

DAD: No, it's Our Project. (*Grabs MOM's hands*) This is for both of us.

MOM: Stop being silly.

(*DAD is excited, bursting to share his news with MOM.*)

DAD: I used all new materials.

MOM: Do you remember what happened last time?

DAD: (*Overlapping MOM*) I think I created the perfect airfoil!

MOM: (*Overlapping DAD*) How long were you laid up in that bed?

DAD: (*Overlapping MOM*) The construction is such a precise process.

MOM: (*Overlapping DAD*) With me nursing you back to health?

DAD: (*Overlapping MOM*) But this time . . .

MOM: (*Overlapping DAD*) That was . . .

DAD: It's perfect!

MOM: Really hard!

(*Beat.*)

MOM: I can't do it again!

(*DAD goes to MOM and embraces her.*)

DAD: It's going to happen this time; I can feel it!

MOM: (*Beat*) Lyf's starting to ask questions.

DAD: That's what fledglings do.

MOM: I know . . . but I wish he wouldn't.

(*MOM exits. DAD stands in the yard. DAD quietly approaches one of the crates and tentatively steps on top of it. DAD closes his eyes and remembers the sensation of flying. LYF enters from the house.*)

LYF: Dad?

DAD: (*Quickly steps down from the crate*) Yes?

LYF: If I don't learn to fly when I'm a fledgling, I'll never be able to. Do you know that?

DAD: Where did you hear that?

LYF: (*Beat*) Is it true?

DAD: It is.

LYF: You used to tell me a story about flying. I can't really remember . . . it was a special day . . . your feet were in the wet sand and you thought you were stuck . . .

DAD: (*Laughs*) I did think I was stuck in that sand, but my dad was there next to me, wing to wing.

LYF: Side by side.

DAD: My dad said to me, "We practiced, and you're ready, but this is very important: you need to trust your wings and they will take you everywhere, anywhere you want to go."

LYF: (*Remembering*) And that's when you soared up, up, up in the air!

DAD: That's right! The sun was warm and bright that day.

LYF and DAD: And the sea sparkled like a shiny jewel.

DAD: With the sea spray in my face, we swooped, and dove, and zoomed, and raced . . . and then Dad and I, we found a spot in the sky and we just . . . floated. (*In his own world*) I felt so free, the happiest I'd ever felt in my life.

LYF: Teach me, Dad. Please! I know I can fly a middle course.

(*Beat.*)

DAD: I will make you a promise, right here, right now, that we will fly to the ocean together. How does that sound?

LYF: (*Loudly*) Awesome!

DAD: Shhh!

LYF: (*Whispers*) Awesome!

(*DAD and LYF perform a handshake that creates the image of two wings.*)

LYF: When can we start?

DAD: Very soon. (*Whispers*) Your mom thinks my work is silly, but little does she know . . . I have a top-secret invention that will change our world!

LYF: What is it? What did you make?

DAD: Sorry, Lyf, it's top secret. I wish I could tell you, but then I'd have to erase your memory!

(*DAD places his hands on LYF's head and makes a POOF! sound. LYF makes a no-memory-face and laughs.*

DAD exits into the house. LYF goes to the secret hidden spot and takes out the conch shell and feather. He holds the shell to his ear and begins to swoop the feather through the air.

META enters quietly on the other side of the wall. META pops her face through a wall hole.)

META: I'm back!

(*LYF yelps.*)

META: (*Giggles*) You're it!

(*LYF beckons META over the wall. She scrambles over.*)

LYF: How was it?!

META: We learned a few flight positions, and we are going to be soaring through the sky soon enough.

LYF: Can you teach me some?

META: What?

LYF: Flight positions.

META: What about rule number one? Are you going to get in trouble?

LYF: My dad promised to teach me. We're going to fly to the ocean together.

META: Excellent! Then we can start off with a few flight positions and your dad can teach you everything else.

LYF: How do we start?

META: My teacher says, "With two wings and a willingness to try!"

LYF: Is that the first rule?

META: No, Lyf. There are no rules in flying. You just need to follow your instincts. (*Beat*) You're gonna need to take your cloak off.

(*LYF looks at META uncomfortably.*)

META: What's wrong?

LYF: I've never taken my cloak off outside before. I only take it off when I sleep. After the sun goes down. Rule number two, remember?

META: Lyf, do you want to fly or not? You can't fly wearing that.

(*META looks to LYF. LYF signals to META to turn away.*)

LYF: Don't look! (*Winces*) If my wings start to burn, it could be pretty gross. (*Tightly closes his eyes and slowly removes his cloak. Rustles his wings.*) Alright.

(*META approaches LYF and inspects his wings.*)

META: Look like normal wings to me.

LYF: (*Opens his eyes in shock*) Really?

META: Yep. Just like everybody else's.

LYF: If my allergy starts acting up, I'll have to put it back on.

META: You'll be fine.

LYF: Let's fly! (*Runs, grabs a crate, jumps on top and strikes an enthusiastic flight pose*)

META: Whoa, whoa, whoa! Get down from there. You have to learn the landing position first.

LYF: Oh. How do I do that?

META: First we pick a starting point. How about here?

LYF: Got it.

META: And then when I say "Go," you run as fast as you can, leap into the air and try to land on both feet without falling over.

LYF: Sounds easy. (*Goes to the starting point*)

META: We'll see. Almost everyone in my flock fell down the first time they tried it. Of course, I didn't fall . . . but we'll see how you do. Are you ready, set, GO!

(*LYF runs, leaps and lands in a solid landing.*)

META: That was really good . . . for a beginner.

LYF: That was fun!

META: Are you sure you've never done this before?

LYF: I want to do it again!

META: OK. This time, you against me. Wing-to-wing combat. Let's see who gets the farthest. You ready?

(*META and LYF get into a starting position on the line.*)

META: I've got more experience, so you'd better watch out, dude.

LYF: You are going to taste my wing dust . . . dude!

META: (*Stops short*) I'm not a dude, dude!

LYF: Really? Oh . . . sorry.

META: You are forgiven. (*Beat*) Are you ready?!

LYF: (*Stops, gets into a silly starting pose*) I was born ready!

META: Bring it on. Ready, set, GO!

(*META and LYF run, leap into the air and they both land solidly. They stay in landing position and see how far they went. Their arms and wings are outspread.*)

META: I don't know . . .

LYF: It looks like . . .

META: My right foot is a smidgen farther than yours!

LYF: I don't think so. Look at my big toe! (*Beat*) And Meta . . . what in the world is a smidgen!?

META: Smidgen means a little bit.

LYF: I don't think that's a smidgen. (*Beat*) Look at us! Squatted down like small pigeons . . . small, pigeons, SMIDGENS!

(*LYF and META begin walking around pretending they are smidgens. Making smidgen noises at each other.*

TAUR, META's twin brother, enters behind the wall on the opposite side that META entered. TAUR is also dressed in brightly colored clothing made from synthetic materials. He has a pair of wings. He is carrying a voice recorder, camera and small notebook and pencil in his front shirt pocket.)

TAUR: (*Out of breath, speaking into his voice recorder*) Taur has been following Meta's tracks all over these woods and now Taur has no idea where he is! (*Scared*) TAUR MIGHT BE LOST!

(*META and LYF stop being smidgens.*)

META: OH, NO!

LYF: Who's that?!

(*TAUR pops his head over the top of the wall and pops back down.*)

TAUR: Taur found Meta at some strange house in the middle of the woods. Taur has never seen this place before . . . this requires further investigation.

(*TAUR begins to clumsily climb over the wall, grunting and struggling all the way. At the top of the wall, TAUR accidentally drops the camera case on the outside of the wall.*)

META: (*To TAUR*) Why are you here?

TAUR: (*To META*) What is this place? How did you find it?

META: (*To TAUR*) Did you follow me, AGAIN?

(*TAUR approaches LYF.*)

TAUR: Hi, I'm Taur. I'm Meta's twin brother. You'll have to excuse her surly behavior. She's never come to terms with the fact that I was born first.

META: Two minutes! Two measly, little minutes!

TAUR: Two minutes can equal a lifetime of wisdom and maturity.

META: (*Snort laughs, to LYF*) We're fraternal twins. We obviously didn't come from the same egg.

TAUR: (*To LYF*) What's your name?

(*TAUR takes his voice recorder out of his pocket and holds it out to LYF.*)

META: You don't have to tell him anything.

TAUR: Go ahead, say your name.

LYF: Uh . . . I'm Lyf.

(*TAUR plays back LYF's line "Uh . . . I'm Lyf" on his voice recorder. LYF smiles.*)

LYF: Awesome! What is that thing? Can I try it?

TAUR: Sure.

(*TAUR hands the voice recorder to LYF. LYF is fascinated by this new technology and he plays with the device.*)

META: Taur likes to pretend that he's a famous reporter.

TAUR: It's not pretend, Meta. (*To LYF*) And I prefer investigative journalist. I work for the *Winged Gazette*, the most popular newspaper in the colony.

META: He's an unofficial, junior reporter. Nobody listens to him because he's just a kid and they are never going to print anything he writes.

TAUR: They will notice me . . . as soon as I find the big story I've been looking for!

META: Good luck with that.

TAUR: I wasn't talking to you, Meta, I was talking to my new friend LYF!

META: He's not your friend!

TAUR (*To LYF*) Do you mind if I ask you a few questions?

(*TAUR pulls the voice recorder out of LYF's hands and presses the record button.*)

META: Just ignore him.

TAUR (*To META*) SHHHHHHH! (*To LYF*) Why do you live way out here, in the middle of nowhere?

LYF: I . . . don't know. This is where my house is. I've lived here my whole life.

TAUR: (*Into recorder*) Taur has always heard rumors that there are others living deep in the woods, but Taur thought it was a myth. Begin research on topic. (*Beat*) What do your parents do?

LYF: Well, we all take care of the house, but my dad is also an inventor.

TAUR: (*Impressed*) That's cool! What has he invented?

LYF: It's top secret. I actually shouldn't even be talking about it.

TAUR: My dad has invented stuff too.

META: No he hasn't!

TAUR: Yes he has, Meta, you act like you know everything, but you don't.

META: C'mon, Lyf! Let's practice the landing position! Hopefully Taur will get lost again.

TAUR: Only the landing position?

META: We can do other stuff too.

LYF: We can?

TAUR: Fine, let's see some mini-flights!

META: Fine. C'mon, Lyf.

LYF: I . . . can't.

TAUR: Why not? Are you some kind of dodo?

META: Taur! Don't say that word!

TAUR: Say what? Dodo? Dodo! (*Sing song*) Dodo, dodo, DODO! (*Laughs*)

META: Taur! Knock it off! Stop saying that. You show up uninvited, you interrupt our flying lesson and now you are shouting foul words!

LYF: (*Whispers*) Please! Keep it down!

TAUR: Go ahead and play your little flight games. I'm going to start a letter to the editor about the trials and tribulations of living with an evil twin. (*Takes out his notebook and pencil and begins scribbling down notes*)

LYF: (*Whispers to META*) What is that? A dodo?

META: Don't . . . don't say it.

LYF: Why?

META: It's the worst name you can call somebody.

LYF: Why? What does it mean?

META: It's someone who can't fly. They are stuck on land their whole life.

LYF: Why can't they fly?

META: (*Shrugs*) I don't know, lots of reasons. There are a few at flock . . . one of my friends . . . one wing is shorter than the other. Sometimes she tries to fly, but she only gets a little bit off of the ground.

LYF: Am I a dodo?

META: No, no way, your dad and I are teaching you how to fly, so you'll never become one. (*Beat*) You want to try a mini-flight?

LYF: How do you do those?

META: You just jump off of something and try to fly a little bit. Let's use this.

LYF: What if I fly right out of the yard?!

META: You can't. (*Looks around*) There's not enough room here. When you are really ready to fly, you'll have to go (*Points over the wall*) Out There to get a real takeoff.

LYF: (*Starts to breath heavily*) Out There? I've never been Out There.

META: Calm down. Take a breath. (*Beat*) Let's just start with mini-flights. They aren't that hard. (*Drags the crate over*) Just leap into the air and flap your wings as fast as you can.

LYF: That's it?

META: Pretty much.

(*LYF scrambles to the top of the crate. He stands apprehensively. He is scared, but he doesn't want to admit it to META.*)

LYF: What if I fall?

META: Just go with your instinct. We can do it! Ready, set, go!

(*TAUR gets up and starts wandering around the yard. LYF and META get ready and leap into the air flapping their wings. They land solidly with both feet on the ground. META rushes over to LYF.*)

META: That was awesome! An excellent takeoff and a solid landing. Yours wasn't as good as mine, but impressive.

(*LYF and META high-five, and LYF does a victory dance and repeatedly chants or sings the following.*)

LYF: I'm good, I'm good! I went so high, like a bird up in the sky! Oh, yeah! Uh huh! Oh, yeah! Uh huh!

TAUR (*Tries to peep inside the window of the worknest*) What's in here?

LYF: (*Turns and sees TAUR*) Rule number five!

TAUR: What's rule number five?

LYF: Rule number five: Never go into Dad's worknest.

TAUR: Why?

LYF: Because I'm not allowed.

TAUR: Who says?

LYF: My Mom. There's dangerous tools and stuff.

TAUR: Do you always listen to what your mommy says?

META: What does your dad do in there?

LYF: That's where he works on his top-secret invention.

TAUR: (*Runs over to LYF with his recorder*) Tell me more!

LYF: When I grow up I want to be an inventor just like my Dad.

TAUR: What has he invented?

LYF: I'm not sure.

TAUR: Aren't you curious? (*Beat.*)

LYF: A little. (*Beat.*)

TAUR: Well, rule number five is only for you, right? Not us.

META: I can go with him, Lyf, to make sure he doesn't mess anything up.

LYF: All right, we'll keep the door open and I'll be the guard. C'mon.

(*LYF, META and TAUR approach the door. Inside the worknest it is dark except for the light from the door.*)

TAUR: Where are the lights?

META: I don't know.

TAUR: (*Bumps into and trips on items in the worknest*) Whoa! (*Falls in the dark*)

LYF: Be careful! Don't mess anything up. Here, here! Found it.

(*LYF turns on the lights. LYF, META and TAUR look around in awe. The shed is full of hand tools for woodworking as well as fabrics, wire mesh, waxes and other adhesives. Hanging from the ceiling of the shed are intricately constructed tiny wings. They are experimental models and prototypes made from different materials. At the far end of the worknest, somewhat obscured, is a large wooden stand that is covered by a floor length sheet of fabric.*

META and TAUR begin walking around the shed looking at the things inside. TAUR takes out his notebook and begins to frantically take notes. He picks up a tool.)

TAUR: Look out, Lyf! It's one of those scary . . . dangerous . . . tools!

LYF: Please! Put that down!

(*META points to a tiny hanging wing. LYF approaches her.*)

META: These are amazing, look at how they are built! Each one is different. Your dad is an inventor and an artist.

TAUR: Is this his top-secret invention?

LYF: I don't know.

(*META gently picks up a small wing from a work table. LYF joins META and they are engrossed in the tiny wings.*)

META: (*To herself*) I wonder how air pressure would affect the lift on this one?

TAUR: His top-secret invention is just a bunch of little wings?!

LYF: I don't know!

TAUR: (*Gets an idea, scribbling in his notepad*) Maybe he's creating an army of tiny winged soldiers who will take over the world!

META: Maybe you can submit that story to the tabloids.

TAUR: Shut it, Meta!

META: Don't tell me what to do.

TAUR: What about that? (*Points to the large shrouded object at the back of the room. Approaches the shrouded stand.*)

LYF: Stay back. Don't touch it.

MOM: (*Offstage, from inside the house*) Lyf! Lyf!

LYF: Hurry! Get out, get out!

(*META and TAUR run for the door, exit quickly. LYF turns off the lights and shuts the door. META and TAUR both jump over opposite sides of the wall. LYF runs towards his cloak and puts it around himself quickly. LYF begins stuffing material into the wall haphazardly.*)

MOM: (*Offstage, shouts*) How's the wall?

LYF: (*Shouts to MOM*) Fine! Fine!

META: (*Whispers urgently through the wall*) Lyf!

LYF: (*Keeps looking back at the house, whispers*) What are you still doing here? My mom could catch us!

META: (*Whispers*) I really need to talk to you.

LYF: Hurry up!

META: Don't trust Taur. He'll do anything to get what he wants.

(*TAUR jumps back over the wall carrying his small, black camera bag.*)

TAUR: Is the coast clear?

META: Go away, Taur!

TAUR: I'm not interested in you, Meta.

META: Lyf, he's just trying to use you.

TAUR: (*To LYF*) Your life story would make a great front page, "A Life of Loneliness: The Young Forest Fledgling." I'm offering you a great opportunity to tell your story.

META: Lyf, he doesn't care about you. He just wants to get attention at the newspaper. (*To TAUR*) Leave him alone!

TAUR: Maybe Lyf wants me to stay.

(*TAUR puts his arm around LYF and pulls him aside.*)

TAUR: (*Whispers*) Have you ever noticed how Meta always wants to be the best at everything? She's just jealous of all of the attention you are getting right now.

(*META jumps back over the wall.*)

META: Are you talking about me? Lyf?! What's he saying about me?

TAUR: This is a closed, private interview. You need to flutter out of here.

META: But Lyf, you don't want to do this.

LYF: (*Hesitates*) Why not?

META: You don't understand!

TAUR: Fly away, Meta! Shoo!

META: Don't you "shoo" me!

LYF: Meta, I want to tell my story.

META: (*Angry*) Fine. Leave me out of it! (*Jumps over the wall and sits on the opposite side, sulking*)

LYF: What do I have to do?

TAUR: Great! Let me take a picture of you first. Hmm . . . cape or no cape?

LYF: Cloak.

TAUR: Whatever. We'll do one of each. Keep it on. (*Opens the camera bag and takes out a digital camera*) Stand right here, in front of the worknest. Ready?

(*TAUR takes the picture and LYF flinches with the flash.*)

LYF: What was that?

TAUR: Don't worry about it. Now one without the cloak.

(*LYF takes off the cloak and throws it on the ground. TAUR takes a picture.*)

TAUR: I need to get set up for the interview. (*Takes his voice recorder out of his pocket*) We need a table and we should each have an ice cold glass of nectar.

LYF: I . . . I don't know if that's a good idea.

TAUR: Why not?

LYF: It's just . . . my mom . . . she's home . . . and we have Our Rules.

TAUR: I'll be on my best behavior. Besides, I need to interview your mom for my story too.

LYF: No, you can't do that. She won't do it.

TAUR: I can be pretty convincing. I promise this won't take very long, just a few questions. Fetch the nectar!

(LYF goes inside. TAUR grabs a crate, sits down and begins preparing for the interview. LYF enters with a glass of nectar for TAUR. MOM follows quickly behind.)

MOM: Lyf! Who is this? Where did this fledgling come from? And why aren't you wearing your cloak?

LYF: He . . . he . . .

TAUR: Good afternoon! You must be Lyf's Mom. Lyf has told me so many wonderful things about you.

MOM: What is all this?

TAUR: My name is Taur. I'm Lyf's best friend and also an investigative journalist.

MOM: What?

TAUR: Lyf and I are working on a special project for the *Winged Gazette*.

(TAUR offers his hand to MOM for a handshake, but she doesn't shake it.)

MOM: I see . . . well . . . you are visiting at an unfortunate time. It's Lyf's work time.

LYF: I already finished!

MOM: (To LYF) I have new tasks for you. (To TAUR) You'll have to leave.

TAUR: Could I please finish my drink before I go?

MOM: If you must.

(TAUR begins to sip his glass of nectar very slowly. TAUR turns on the voice recorder.)

TAUR: (To MOM) So, are you some sort of top-secret inventor too? Or just your husband?

(MOM crosses her arms and does not answer.)

TAUR: I see you also wear one of those charming cloaks. Can I ask why you wear it?

LYF: We're allergic to the sun.

TAUR: What?!

LYF: The sun could melt our wings right off . . . (Looks at his own wings)

TAUR: (Laughs) That's the craziest thing I've ever heard. That can't happen. Who told you that?

LYF: (*Softly*) My Mom. It's true. Right, Mom? (*LYF looks to MOM for confirmation.*) Mom? (*Beat.*)

TAUR: (*Into voice recorder*) An awkward silence.

MOM: (*To TAUR*) You need to go now!

TAUR: (*Into the recorder*) Interview postponed until further notice. This is Taur signing off. (*Picks up his recorder, notebook and pencil*) We'll finish this later, dude! (*Exits*)

MOM: Who is that?!

LYF: He's my friend.

MOM: Rule number four. You shouldn't have friends if you followed rule number four.

LYF: What's wrong with having friends? And why do we live in the woods away from everybody?

MOM: Lyf! You will not question Our Rules!

LYF: Nobody else lives in the woods; they live in the colony.

MOM: Why aren't you wearing your cloak? Put. It. On.

LYF: I'm not going to wear that stupid cape anymore.

MOM: Rule number—

LYF: I know. I know! It's rule number two. Why did you tell me I'm allergic to the sun? I'm not allergic. I've been outside, without my cloak, practicing my flying and . . .

MOM: What was that? (*Beat*) Did you just say "practicing my flying!?"

LYF: Yes.

MOM: RULE NUMBER ONE!

LYF: I know, Mom. But I didn't go up high or down low and it's not dangerous for me!

MOM: Yes it is.

LYF: Not for me . . . I'm really good. My natural instincts just kick in, like all fledglings.

MOM: All fledglings?

LYF: Yeah, it's easy, you just jump, flap your wings and fly! C'mon, I'll show you. (*Goes towards a crate*)

MOM: (*Firmly*) It's not that simple.

LYF: I know.

MOM: Not all fledglings are the same.	LYF: I know.
Not all fledglings can just fly.	I can.
Sometimes they aren't strong enough.	But I am.
Sometimes their wings don't work.	I know, I know.
Sometimes they can't fly at all.	I know!
And when they jump . . .	I KNOW!

MOM: They plummet straight down to the ground!

LYF: MOM! I know, Mom. I know, I know all about them . . . the (*Whispers*) dodos.

(*MOM grabs LYF by the shoulders, gripping him tightly and getting in his face.*)

MOM: Don't you ever say that word. Where did you hear that word? Did he teach you that?!

(*LYF is frightened by MOM's intensity, pulls away from her and runs towards the crate.*)

LYF: MOM! I'm not! I'm not a dodo. Watch me, watch me! Look!

(*LYF leaps from the crate, flails frantically in the air. He is not ready for the landing position and he falls to the ground. LYF remains on the ground huddled in a mass. LYF's hands are balled up and he starts to cry in frustration. MOM goes to LYF and holds him in her arms.*

MOM pulls LYF towards her. MOM takes the stone from her pocket and pantomimes putting the stone into LYF's head.)

MOM: (*Trying to bring him back*) The boy could not control himself, he flapped his wings and soared up, up, up in the air. The mother tried to follow him, but he was too fast. She called to the boy, but he ignored her pleas. (*Beat*) You tell it. Your turn, Lyf.

(*LYF shakes his head "no."*)

MOM: What happened to the boy? What happened when he tried to fly?

LYF: I don't want to tell it.

MOM: Lyf, it's your story.

LYF: No.

(*LYF struggles out of MOM's embrace.*)

MOM: Yes, Lyf. Tell it. Tell it!

LYF: (*Looks back at her*) The boy was having a great time flying through the air. He flew up and up and up, closer to the sun. The sun felt nice and warm and the sea sparkled like a shiny jewel. (*Beat*) He swooped, dove, zoomed and raced and then he found a spot in the sky and just . . . floated.

MOM: And what else? What happened to him? Tell the rest.

LYF: The boy felt so free. The happiest he'd ever felt in his whole life. Then he flew away with his dad and lived happily ever after.

MOM: That's not the ending.	LYF:
High in the sky his wings began to burn . . .	No.
And he cried out in pain . . .	No.
He faltered and swooped down towards	No!
the water to cool the burning . . .	NO!
But the sea spray clung to the boy's feathers	NO!! NOOOO
and he was sucked down into the ocean.	NOOOOOOOOOO

MOM: The mother called out, "Where are you, where are you?"

(*Beat. MOM holds out her stone in her palms. LYF grabs the stone from MOM's hands and flings it to the ground. LYF exits.*)

MOM: I'm here. I'm right here.

(*MOM picks up the stone and begins rubbing it. It is not enough. She puts it back in her pocket. She goes to the wall, takes out a pair of scissors and begins anxiously snipping pieces of fabric.*

DAD enters quietly. MOM holds the scissors in her hands throughout the scene.)

DAD: (*Whispers*) Dear?

MOM: (*Jumps*) You scared me!

DAD: Didn't mean to.

MOM: Well, you did.

DAD: I'm sorry. I'm sorry. That's the answer to everything, I'm sorry.

MOM: There was a strange fledgling here. Apparently, he has been teaching Lyf how to fly. Lyf wasn't wearing his cloak and he told me that he doesn't want to become a . . . a . . .

DAD: No?!

(*MOM shakes her head "yes."*)

DAD: He used that word?

MOM: Yes . . . he shouted it, loud and clear, he doesn't want to become a . . . he's broken all of Our Rules . . . what can we do to stop him?

DAD: Nothing, unless we keep him here forever. It's time to let him try.

MOM: He did try. He fell!

DAD: Was he hurt? (*Beat, no reply*) Everybody falls.

MOM: Not everybody.

DAD: You're right. (*Beat*) But everybody gets hurt. And what really matters is if you stay down or get back up again. (*Beat.*)

MOM: There is one way to stop this.

DAD: What do you mean?

(*Long beat. MOM looks at the pair of scissors in her hands.*)

DAD: No. No—absolutely not!

MOM: (*Pleading*) It won't hurt him. We can do it while he sleeps. Just snip a few feathers here and there. He won't feel a thing.

DAD: If you clip his wings, he will never be able to fly. Ever!

MOM: Is that the worst thing you can imagine?

DAD: That's not what I said. Now put those away. NOW!!

MOM: (*Puts the scissors into the crate, breaking down*) I feel like everything is falling apart.

DAD: Then we'll have to build it back up again.

MOM: What if it can't be fixed?

(*DAD goes to MOM and embraces her.*)

DAD: We did it once. We can do it again. (*Gently*) I am going to talk to Lyf tomorrow . . . about Our Project.

MOM: Just leave me out of it.

(*MOM breaks out of his arms and goes into the house. LYF storms out of the house and into the yard. DAD follows MOM into the house.*

LYF opens the door to DAD's worknest and disappears inside. Inside the worknest. LYF turns on the light and he walks slowly towards the object shrouded in the sheet. He grabs the sheet and slowly uncovers a large, beautiful wing.

LYF takes it from the stand and comes out of the worknest. TAUR jumps over the wall with his digital camera.)

TAUR: Lyf, what is that?!

LYF: I think it's my dad's top-secret invention.

(*TAUR begins snapping pictures of the wing. META jumps over the wall from her side. META approaches the wing, crouching near LYF and she looks it over.*)

META: It's beautiful.

TAUR: (*Puts down his camera*) It looks like it attaches to your arm.

(*TAUR snatches the wing from LYF and begins to put it on.*)

LYF: Stop it . . .

META: Taur!

TAUR: I want to try it on!

META: You don't need another wing.

TAUR: I'm not going to break it. (*Tightens the wing and begins to jump around the yard with it. Superhero voice.*) I'm Three Wing Man! With my extra wing I have the speed and strength to out-fly any super villain! Whoo hoo! Hey, Meta, take a picture of me with my third wing.

META: No. And technically, if you had a third wing, you would just keep flying around in small circles.

TAUR: Nevermind. I'll take it myself. (*Attempts to take pictures of himself using various methods, stretching one arm out, setting a timer, etc.*)

META: (*To LYF*) Why would your dad make a fake wing?

TAUR: This is kind of like that wing from the old dodo story.

META: Taur, don't say that word!

LYF: What dodo story?

META: Lyf!

TAUR: Meta, you know that story. The one about the two dodos.

META: The father and the boy.

TAUR: Yeah, that one! They can't fly and they try to make fake wings.

LYF: You mean the mother and the boy?

META: The father was an inventor, just like yours.

TAUR: The father built two sets of wings.

TAUR: (*Mocking*) Before they flew into the sky, the father said to his boy, "I warn you . . . don't fly too high, or the sun will burn your wings right up! Don't fly too low or the sea water will weigh your wings down. You must —

LYF: Fly a middle course.

META: That's right!

TAUR: Fly a middle course.

LYF: My mom told me that story, but it was a boy with real wings. The sun melted his skin . . .

TAUR: The dodos in the story don't have real wings. They're fake. Like this one.

LYF: My mom told me that was why I shouldn't fly, because that might happen to me too.

META: That couldn't happen to you,

LYF: You are built to fly; your wings are real; you can't melt.

(*LYF looks at the wing, toward the worknest and finally towards the house.*)

LYF: (*Softly*) I've never seen my dad fly. (*Beat.*)

TAUR: News flash: That is crazy!

META: Never, ever?

LYF: Never.

TAUR: I've seen my dad fly a gazillion times!

META: Taur!

LYF: But my dad promised that we would fly to ocean together.

META: He did.

TAUR: YOU'VE NEVER BEEN TO THE OCEAN?!

LYF: No.

TAUR: But it's so close! Really close, a short flight!

META: You're not helping.

TAUR: No ocean? Ever? What kind of life is that?

(*LYF goes to TAUR.*)

LYF: Give me the wing.

(*LYF detaches it from TAUR's shoulder.*)

LYF: (*Looks toward the house*) DAD! DAD! DAD!!

META: Lyf, what are you doing?

LYF: DAAAAAAAAAD!!!

META: Taur! C'mon!

(*META and TAUR jump over the wall and watch through the holes together. LYF holds the wing behind his back. DAD enters.*)

DAD: What's all this shouting about?

LYF: Dad . . . it's time, I'm ready to fly with you! (*Beat*) I think you might need this. (*Takes the wing from behind his back*)

DAD: You took something that doesn't belong to you.

LYF: Tell me what this wing is for.

DAD: (*With difficulty*) Flying used to be my favorite thing in the whole world. (*Beat*) I had an accident. (*Points to the wing in LYF's hands*) And I've been trying to get my wing back ever since.

(*DAD slowly removes his cloak to reveal only one wing on his left side. He walks towards LYF.*)

LYF: (*Beat*) You're a (*Whispers*) dodo? (*Drops the wing and backs away*)

DAD: No, I'm your dad.

LYF: Why didn't you tell me about your accident?

DAD: I was waiting until you were old enough to understand . . . and I was afraid. I knew I couldn't teach you. Like a normal Dad. Like my dad taught me. (*Picks up the wing from the ground*) I've been in that worknest every day since the day you were born. Dreaming. And I think I've finally invented a way that we can still fly together.

LYF: Do you really think you can fly with that thing?

DAD: I don't know.

LYF: I don't know if I can fly.

DAD: I know you can.

LYF: We can.

(*DAD puts out his hand and offers a handshake. LYF helps DAD attach the wing to DAD's right shoulder. MOM enters. She runs towards DAD and LYF.*)

MOM: No, no! You are not going to do this again. Take that thing off right now!
(*Grabs at the fake wing*)

DAD: (*To MOM*) Stop it. He won't get hurt.

MOM: You can't promise that.

DAD: If I don't do this with him, we might lose him forever.

LYF: (*Reassuring*) Mom, we'll fly a middle course!

DAD: (*To MOM*) I made a promise. (*To LYF*) You ready, son?

LYF: Ready!

(*DAD and LYF exit together. MOM stares up at the sky.*

Two winged figures of DAD and LYF appear. They fly, tentatively at first, then with some confidence. The right wing on DAD's figure begins to move erratically. He starts to flap his wings wildly, but he falters and falls swiftly to the ground.)

LYF: Dad?! DAD!

(*LYF sees his father's fall and flies to the ground. DAD is in the yard. His right wing is smashed and hanging in pieces still attached to his shoulder. LYF is kneeling next to him.*)

LYF: (*Out of breath*) Dad?! Dad?!

(*DAD silently removes and flings the remainder of the fake wing to the side.*)

DAD: I'm sorry, Lyf.

LYF: It's OK. Everybody falls sometimes.

(*MOM rushes towards DAD.*)

MOM: I told you, I told you this would happen!

LYF: Mom. He's not hurt.

MOM: RULE NUMBER ONE.

LYF: No more rules! Why did you lie to me?

MOM: We were trying to protect you . . .

LYF: From what? The truth?

(*Pause.*)

MOM: (*Tapping into wounds from her past*) Here's the truth, Lyf. When I was at flock, they used to hurt me, taunt me . . . it was terrible. I couldn't fly away.

(*MOM slowly removes her cloak. She turns around to face Lyf. She only has one wing on her right side.*)

MOM: (*Cont'd*) I built this shelter for you, so nothing and no one could hurt my Lyf. (*Beat*) It was meant to protect you.

DAD: And it did, for a long time.

LYF: But now, I want to go. Out There.

(*TAUR storms back into the yard to get a picture.*)

TAUR: (*To LYF*) Both of your parents are dodos?!

META: Leave them alone, Taur!

TAUR: Shut up, Meta!

META: Taur, don't be mean.

TAUR: Me? I'm being mean?! (*Flipping quickly through his notebook*) These crazy dodos trapped him here in this house his whole life, they lied to him, made him follow their crazy rules and they kept him from seeing the world . . . seeing the ocean . . . and you think I'm the mean one?!

LYF: Fly away, Taur.

META: You heard him. Shoo!

TAUR: But Lyf, I can see the headline now: "Two Dodos and Their Normal Son!"

LYF: Fly away, Taur.

TAUR: Fine. I've got everything I need. I've got a camera full of photos and I've already written half of the story.

META: You can't!

TAUR: You can't stop me!

LYF: FLY AWAY, TAUR!

TAUR: Your parents are dodo freaks.

LYF: No! That's not the true story, Taur.

(*LYF turns to MOM and holds out his hand. MOM gives LYF the stone.*)

LYF: Here's my story. There once was a boy who lived with his Mom and his
   Dad. The boy was sheltered in the warmth of their love, until one day, a
   new friend went off the beaten path. (*Looks to META*) The boy begged her to
   teach him how to fly. But before he could find his own course, he had to
   make his own rules. (*Beat*) Rule number one: Whether I fly sky high or
   to the ocean below, I must always remember who cares for me most.

(*LYF embraces MOM and DAD.*)

TAUR: Boring! The *Winged Gazette* would never print that version of the
   story. (*Gathers his things together. To META*) Are you coming? Or are you
   gonna stay here with these freaks?

META: I happen to like freaks.

(*TAUR exits.*)

LYF: Mom, Dad, this is Meta!

MOM: You are . . . ?

LYF: Taur's sister.

META: Twin, actually. He's the bad egg. I'm not like him at all, so please don't
   even put us in the same category. I have a few questions. First of all, (*To DAD*)
   can you teach me how to make wings like that? Can I be your apprentice or
   something? (*To MOM*) Also, can I keep giving Lyf flying lessons?

MOM: (*Reflexively, but trails off*) Rule number . . .

(*DAD touches MOM's arm or holds her hand.*)

DAD: We may need to rethink some of Our Rules.

LYF: Can we show you the landing position?

MOM: (*Beat*) I guess you have to.

LYF: We just pick a spot . . .

META: Right here.

LYF: And leap as far as we can . . .

META: And try to land solidly on both feet!

(*META and LYF approach the starting line.*)

LYF: Ready . . .

META: Set . . .

META and LYF: GO!

(They run together, stop at the jump point and leap as far as they can. LYF challenges META with a smidgen noise. META smidgens back.)

META: What do you want to do next?

(LYF and META simultaneously turn to each other. They grin and nod together.)

LYF: I want to fly to the ocean!

DAD: Do you think you're ready?

LYF: Yes.

(LYF goes to MOM.)

LYF: May I?

(MOM turns away, still struggling. LYF runs over to the crate near the wall. He takes out the conch shell and hands it to MOM.)

LYF: Listen.

(MOM listens. MOM passes the shell to DAD. DAD listens to the shell. LYF takes MOM's hand and holds it to his heart.)

LYF: You're here. You are always here.

MOM: *(Nods her consent, softly)* Go.

(LYF and META scramble over the wall. They fly high up in the sky. We hear the ocean. MOM and DAD stand linked together looking up to the sky. Standing together their two wings become a pair. They watch LYF and META soar.)

CURTAIN

Production credits from the premiere of *With Two Wings* and details concerning performance rights are included in the acting edition of the play as published by Dramatic Publishing.

Appendices

Twelve More Plays with Mature Themes for
Consideration / Deliberation

Better Angels or *Lincoln's Log*
Barry Kornhauser
Dramatic Publishing
A tender coming of age story featuring the life of Tad Lincoln told through puppets, narrative, music, and projections set against the presidency of his famous father, his troubled mother, and the Civil War.

Doors
Suzan L. Zeder
Dramatic Publishing
A story of separation, divorce, and ultimately healing that emphasizes the importance of talking and listening as Jeff, through the help of his friend Sandy, faces the impending change resulting from the break-up of his parents' marriage.

Dragonwings
Lawrence Yep
Dramatists Play Service
An epic Chinese-inspired parable about family, fear, freedom, and flight as a love for kite making and flying helps an immigrant father and son bond and embrace the spirit of diversity.

The Ice Wolf
Joanna Halpert Kraus
Dramatic Publishing
Featuring the theme of peoples' fear, discrimination, and hatred of those who are different, *The Ice Wolf* is the moving story of Anatou, the blonde Inuit, who is feared and hated by her tribe. She is transformed by the Wood God into a wolf and seeks revenge on those who persecuted her as a human, but in the end, forgiveness prevails.

Bless Cricket, Crest Toothpaste and Tommy Tune
Linday Daugherty
Dramatic Publishing

Cricket is a teenage girl embarrassed by Tom, her older brother who has Down syndrome. With the help of Reese, a boy from her new school, she learns to embrace the gifts Tom has to offer, even though they are different from others. And in doing so, she discovers the power of acceptance and inclusion.

Number the Stars
Sean Hartley
Based on the book by Lois Lowry
Dramatic Publishing
A gripping dramatization of the Newberry Award–winning novel authentically captures and chronicles the experiences of ten-year-old Annemarie Johansen and her Jewish friend Ellen Rosen during the Nazi occupation of Denmark during World War II. It is a story of friendship, loyalty, and courage set against one of the most dangerous and difficult periods in human history.

Tale of a West Texas Marsupial Girl
Lisa D'Amour
Plays for Young Audiences
Small-town West Texas is not sure what to make of Marsupial Girl (MG) and her wonderful magical pouch. Ninety-five percent girl and five percent marsupial, MG initially uses her pouch to right wrongs, but when everyone expects the worst of her, she begins stealing whatever she can, until there's nothing left but her and her really huge pouch. With the help of her best friend, Sue, order is restored, and MG's difference is celebrated as a wonderful thing.

The Yellow Boat
David Saar
Dramatic Publishing
Through story, word, metaphor, drawings, and colored ribbons that move the action of the play seamlessly from reality to fantasy, and present to past, we sail across time and place and enter the world of eight-year-old Benjamin, a child who contracts AIDS from a tainted blood transfusion. This compelling story continues to teach important lessons of love, loss, fear, sadness, and death.

Bocón!
Lisa Loomer
Dramatic Publishing
An imaginative play skillfully combines Central American political turmoil and folklore with the story of a boy who leaves his war-torn village for freedom and peace in Los Angeles. Using both Spanish and English dialogue, we follow Miguel's journey and the acquisition of his bocón (big mouth) to speak bravely against the injustices he has witnessed and his hopes to remain in America.

The Witch of Blackbird Pond
Y York
Dramatic Publishing
Adapted from the novel by Elizabeth George Speare
In this compelling, historically-rooted dramatization of the award-winning novel, sixteen-year-old Kit challenges the ignorance, bigotry, and fear that abound in her Puritan surroundings. Living during the witch hunts prevalent in Colonial America, Kit is forced to make important life choices.

A Thousand Cranes
Kathryn Schultz Miller
Dramatic Publishing
Performed as stylized Japanese theatre, a small ensemble of actors, mixing mime, mask, movement, and sound, retell the story of Sadako, and her heroic fight against post atomic bomb leukemia. Inspired by the ancient belief that an ill person will be restored to health if they fold a thousand origami cranes, Sadako's efforts launch a national movement to honor the memory of all of the children who died in the attack on Hiroshima.

Ezigbo the Spirit Child
Max Bush
From an Igbo folktale as told by Adaora Nzelibe Schmiedl
Dramatic Publishing
Nigerian culture, language, dancing, song, game, and ritual take center stage in this dramatic retelling of the legend of Ezigbo, a spiritual "forever-child" who, with the help of Medicine Woman and River Spirit, teaches her mother the important lesson of appreciating one's blessings or they may be lost forever.

Another Twelve Plays with Mature Themes for Reading / Study

Baba Yaga and the Black Sunflower
Carol Korty
Dramatic Publishing
A fascinating adaptation from the original folktale that weaves traditional Russian motifs, story, and song to tell the story of Baba Yaga, her magical black sunflower, and Maryushka's struggle to find her place in the world as she overcomes one obstacle after another in order to save her brother.

The Butterfly
Bijan Mofid from *Shaparak Khanum* by Farideh Fardjamt, translated from Persian by Don Laffoon
Dramatic Publishing
The Butterfly is a tender interpretation of the age-old theme "think of others before yourself." A butterfly is caught in a web within a dark barn and is spared from being eaten, first by her determination to trick another insect into exchanging fates with her, and finally, by her beauty and honesty.

Don't Tell Me I Can't Fly
Y York
Inspired by the life and art of Della Wells
Dramatic Publishing
The compelling story of nine-year-old Tonia Bridge, set in Milwaukee, 1964, the play follows Tonia's endearing attempts to please her mentally ill mother and garner praise and attention from her discouraged father. In the end it is Tonia's spirited imagination that allows her to reveal her authentic, beautiful self to her family.

Getting Near to Baby
Y York
Adapted from the Newberry Honor Book by Audrey Couloumbis
Dramatic Publishing
A heart-warming story of survival and hope that illustrates how the support of family and the power of love can combine to bring us all nearer to and comfortable with truth, and that what we think we see in people and what we think we want from them are not always the same.

King Chemo
Brian Guehrig
Dramatic Publishing
Kevin and Melissa are both undergoing chemotherapy. Kevin hides his fear of his illness by preferring to become the star of his own "super hero" fantasy. With the

help of Melissa, he discovers that facing reality with courage and humor is the most super hero power of all.

Braille: The Early Life of Louis Braille
Lola H. and Coleman A. Jennings
Dramatic Publishing
The life of Louis Braille and his fight for literacy and education for the blind is at the core of this drama, which emphasizes the universal bonds that unite us all—sighted and blind alike.

Steal Away Home
Aurand Harris from the novel by Jane Kristof
Dramatic Publishing
In 1854, two young slaves, Obie and Amos, leave their mother to escape to Philadelphia on the Underground Railroad. Along the way they encounter supportive, courageous people from many walks of life, as well as despicable ones who try to prevent their escape. The boys arrive at their destination and are reunited with their waiting father.

The Crane Wife
Barbara Carlisle from Japanese folklore, based on a production idea by Randy Ward
Dramatic Publishing
A riveting story told through Japanese theatre-inspired visual and aural effects that shares the story of love, respect, greed, and ultimately, loss. A chorus of villagers narrates the plot, takes minor roles, comments on the situation in song and chants, and creates sounds to accompany the dancers as their movements augment the dramatic action and suggest the time, place, and world of the play.

Home on the Mornin' Train
Kim Hines
Dramatic Publishing
Two groups of children from two historical eras and countries, African American slaves on the Underground Railroad in 1839 and Jews in Nazi Germany in 1939 are trying to escape their oppressors. As the scenes alternate between the two groups, each shares important reflections on the circumstances of their respective historical time period as well as their personal fears, homesickness, uncertainty for the future, and the desire for freedom.

The Rememberer
Steven Dietz
Based on the memoir *As My Sun Now Sets* by Joyce Simmons Cheeka, as told to Werdna Phillips Finley
Dramatic Publishing

In 1911 Joyce Simmons Cheeka, a member of the Squaxin Indian tribe of Puget Sound, is forcibly taken from her family and sent to a government boarding school. When her grandfather, the tribe's "Rememberer" of his people's oral history dies, she learns that she is now the new "Rememberer" for her tribe. As Joyce realizes her worth and usefulness to both her tribal and school worlds, she discovers the important role she plays in both of them, and the value of preserving cultural heritage through memory.

A Village Fable
James Still
Adapted from *In the Suicide Mountains* by John Gardner
Dramatic Publishing
The dramatic retelling through story and song about three souls who are shunned for their differences and their journey against conformity.

The Odyssey
Greg A. Falls and Kurt Beattie
From Homer's *The Odyssey*
Dramatic Publishing
A retelling of Homer's epic poem brought to dramatic life through text, movement, mask, song, and instrumentation.

Quotation from the Foreword by Jed H. Davis to the first edition of *Theatre For Youth: Twelve Plays With Mature Themes*, 1986

What is a "mature theme?"

A theme, of course, is a statement of universal truth derived through the action of a play. It is the rule of life and living that one carries away after the play is over. It goes beyond the play's subject matter, but is, of course, tied to it. It is the distillate that remains after the nonessentials have been stripped away. A mature theme is one that requires of the interpreter a rather advanced reasoning power, one that allows a universal truth to emerge from apparently unhappy, disastrous, or immoral occurrences. The simple reasoning of younger children must eventually give way to awareness of complexities, to precise associations of cause and effect, to connections between premises and outcomes. The good-bad morality concepts so prevalent in children need to be augmented by consciousness of degrees of goodness and badness found in real people, so that the "greater good" or the "lesser evil" can be admitted in judging the events. An ability to project the play's happenings into future time comes with increasing age and experience; so perceptions of themes as they related to the ultimate, rather than immediate, ends can afford greater pleasure and meaning to the youthful psyche. It takes mature judgment for one to see that Hamlet's personal tragedy and death ultimately result in straightening out the rotting state of Denmark. The rightness of causes—even those that result in death for the protagonist—determine how poetic justice is served in the long run.

Such reasoning is possible as young people reach what Jean Piaget identified as the cognitive stage of "formal operations." At that point, one seeks out the kinds of activities and stimuli that challenge the intellectual capacities being developed. Young adolescents reject subjects that seem childish; they have gone beyond that. A play that reminds them of that stage through which they have successfully passed will be met with marginal tolerance if not open derision. But one such as those in this volume, which require challenging intellectual activity as well as emotional involvement through their subject matter, will be a delight.